Which Way Social Justice in Mathematics Education?

Which Way Social Justice in Mathematics Education?

Edited by Leone Burton

INTERNATIONAL PERSPECTIVES
ON MATHEMATICS EDUCATION
Leone Burton, *Series Editor*

PRAEGER

Westport, Connecticut
London

Library of Congress Cataloging-in-Publication Data

Which way social justice in mathematics education? / edited by Leone Burton.
    p. cm.—(International perspectives on mathematics education, ISSN 1530–3993)
    Includes bibliographical references and index.
    ISBN 1–56750–680–1 (alk. paper)
    1. Mathematics—Study and teaching—Social aspects. I. Burton, Leone, 1936– II.
Series.
    QA11.2.W45   2003
    510'.71—dc21   2002030739

British Library Cataloguing in Publication Data is available.

Library of Congress Catalog Card Number: 2002030739
ISBN: 1–56750–680–1
ISSN: 1530–3993

First published in 2003

Praeger Publishers, 88 Post Road West, Westport, CT 06881
An imprint of Greenwood Publishing Group, Inc.
www.praeger.com

Printed in the United States of America

The paper used in this book complies with the
Permanent Paper Standard issued by the National
Information Standards Organization (Z39.48–1984).

10 9 8 7 6 5 4 3 2 1

Which way social justice in
mathematics education?

In the hope, but not the expectation, that the issues dealt with in this book will no longer be a concern for Samuel Jonathan, and other new arrivals, developing and facing the pleasures and demands of learning mathematics.

Contents

Figures and Tables

FIGURE

TABLE

Series Editor's Preface

International Perspectives on Mathematics Education is a series of books that provides entry to practitioners and researchers into the many and varied issues of Mathematics Education and looks forward to new challenges and developments in the field. This present volume, which focuses on issues within the broad theme of social justice, is the third to be published within this now well-established series. An underpinning rationale for the series, which has persisted from conception through to the present, is that volumes provide an introduction for new researchers as well as stimulation for those seeking to develop their thinking in new or unfamiliar directions. As Series Editor, I am confident that this purpose is being fulfilled, both by the books already in print and those that will follow.

I have enjoyed the role of Series Editor in the preparation of earlier volumes in the series, as this has provided the opportunity to collaborate with the editors of those books to assure the quality of the work published. This book is different because I have also taken on the editorial role, and thus it has been something of a lone enterprise. It is my earnest hope that this book matches the high standards set by the previous volumes despite the absence of the productive dialogue between editors.

The genesis of this book is explained in the introduction; however, it is appropriate here to draw attention to its roots in the activities of the International Organization of Women in Mathematics Education (IOWME) at the quadrennial meetings of the International Congress of Mathematics Education (ICME). This is the fourth publication of IOWME, and it reflects the development of the group's interests that have evolved over 16 years from a sharp focus on gender issues to its present wider interest in social justice. Although there are a number of chapters specifically dealing with gender, most authors have adopted one of the following strategies: Their gender-specific questions are set in a wider sociocultural and/or pedagogical context; they challenge what have threatened to become (false) orthodoxies; or they raise other important considerations that have implications for social justice but have, until recently, remained unresearched. Such issues include the meaning of democratic citizenship for mathematics classrooms (Chapter 3), the links between parents and children learning mathematics (Chapter 4), the crisis of poverty, as evidenced in parts of Peru that are multilingual (Chapter 5) and in the beliefs of some teachers of underprivileged children in Australia (Chapter 6). Other authors explore different forms of classroom organization (Chapter 7), participation and assessment (Chapters 8, 9, and 11), the relationship with mathematical thinking (Chapter 10), and computers and their impact on mathematics learning (Chapters 12 and 13). The broad review of the field is provided in the opening two chapters.

The other tradition of the series that I hold very dear has been maintained in this volume. The international authorship of chapters, although still dominated by the Western world, includes those from Africa and South America. I continue to hope that those colleagues in countries where publication is difficult will, in the future, see the potential for publishing in books in this series and that those in the so-called developed world will continue to offer help and guidance to their less-favored colleagues. In the meantime, the breadth of representation in this book bodes well for the international collegiality of our field.

Leone Burton

Introduction

Leone Burton

This book was conceived in the sessions run by the International Organization of Women and Mathematics Education at the Ninth International Congress of Mathematics Education (ICME9) in Tokyo, Japan, in 2000. At the same time, the International Perspectives on Mathematics Education series was launched with the first book, *Multiple Perspectives on Teaching and Learning Mathematics*, edited by Jo Boaler. Papers that were given in those sessions were invited for submission to the book, but a call was also sent out much more widely. All submitted papers went through a thorough review process, and I am deeply indebted to all those whose names are listed at the end of this introduction, who acted as referees. They were rigorous, without being hurtful, and productive in their suggestions; the quality of the chapters is testament to their hard work, together of course with that of the authors. In addition, chapter authors were paired, trying to put together authors with similar interests, and were invited to exchange critiques of each other's chapters. It was hoped that this strategy would encourage dialogue within the book by providing author(s) of each chapter with another critical-reflective-supportive voice but also, possibly, with cross-referencing possibilities or at least awarenesses.

The title of the present book—*Which Way Social Justice in Mathematics Education?*—was chosen to reflect a number of developments in the field since earlier publications on gender and mathematics education and the choices these offer to practitioners and researchers. There has been a shift in focus from equity to a more inclusive perspective that embraces social justice as a contested area of investigation in mathematics education. This is in line with Elizabeth Fennema's position outlined in Fennema (1995). She said:

It appears logical to me that as I try to interpret the problem [of gender and mathematics] from a feminist standpoint, it is different from what I focused on earlier. Instead of interpreting the challenges related to gender and mathematics as involving problems associated with females and mathematics, I begin to look at how a male view of mathematics has been destructive to both males and females. I begin to articulate a problem that lies in our view of mathematics and its teaching. I am coming to believe that females have recognized that mathematics, as currently taught and learned, restricts their lives rather than enriches them. . . . We should be open to the possibility that we have been so enculturated by the masculine dominated society we live in that our belief about the neutrality of mathematics as a discipline may be wrong, or at the very least, incomplete. (pp. 33–34)

In Chapter 1, Helga Jungwirth makes the point that there has been approximately 30 years of work in the area of gender bias and its impact on the learning and teaching of mathematics. The focus of this work has, in the main, been gender sensitivities in the classroom and their outcomes in terms of attainment and subsequent career development. In 1995, Carey et al. pointed out that, in the United States,

two decades of intensive work have resulted in comprehensive knowledge about the major inequities that exist in mathematics outcomes for females, certain ethnic groups, speakers of English as a second language (ESL), and those from lower socioeconomic groups. Among the most notable of these inequities is the fact that people from these groups tend not to participate in mathematics-related occupations. (p. 93)

One shift in the sites of research has been from the Anglo-Saxon–developed axis (particularly Australia, Canada, New Zealand, the United Kingdom, and the United States) to other countries where inequities, for differing reasons, have been identified, and many of the same outcomes have been observed. Some of this work is represented in chapters in this volume (see Chapters 1, 5, 7, and 10). A major shift, however, has been to recognize the lack of utility in single variable or simple causal relational explanations that hide the multiple voices used by individuals and the complexity of the social situations within which they move (see in particular Chapters 1, 3, 4, 5, 6, 8, and 9). Helga's helpful typology gives us a way of looking at, and classifying, the interpretations found in the contributions to this volume. But is there a relationship between gender sensitivities, equity, and social justice? And if there is, what might it look like?

A concern with gender sensitivity already presupposes, in my mind, some concern with justice and, consequently, with equity. As Helga makes clear, that can be quite limited; but, nonetheless, even if all that a teacher wants to do is give equal amounts of attention to girls and boys, that indicates a recognition of some need. What we cannot say is what the subsequent effects of this strategy might be. From this perspective, equal treatment might, or might not, result in equity where equity is understood as equal opportunities to learn. In 1990, Elizabeth Fennema discussed different approaches to equity, as then understood (pp. 1–9). Some regarded equity as equal opportunity to learn mathematics, but she pointed out that even though this legalistic approach might be enshrined in the law, examination of actual practices showed that it was not yet implemented. Another approach to equity was as equal educational treatment both in the classroom and in terms of outcomes. She said: "[I]f justice is equity in outcomes of mathematics education, justice for the sexes has not yet been achieved" (p. 4). Laurie Hart, in Chapter 2, gives an overview of developments in equity research in the United States.

There does seem to me to be a difficulty with the concept of equity, as with the previous concept of equal opportunities, in that it can mean very different things and be used in very different ways. Of course, this is most usually the case with words—their benefit as well as disadvantage. However, the concept of social justice seems to me to include equity and not to need it as an addition. Apart from taking a highly legalistic stance, how could one consider something that was inequitable as socially just?

Researchers in the field of gender would now, I believe, see gender not as a single variable within equity but situated within a complex of variables so that identifying single causes for inequities or relationships that are simply connected would be seen to be narrow and less helpful. Also, more and more researchers would, I think, see gender studies as being exemplary of wider issues that were about social justice, rather than seeing gender as a unique area of study. Hence, the breadth of interpretation that is to be found in the chapters of this volume.

In a book of the new millennium, *Just Schooling: Explorations in the Cultural Politics of Teaching*, Trevor Gale and Kathleen Densmore address the distributive, retributive, and recognitive perspectives on what is meant by social justice. They say:

First when it comes to the distribution of society's resources, education systems lay claim to a large share of the financial cake. . . . On its own, this is reason enough for us to examine how this large sum of money is distributed and to consider what it might mean to face the fact that this distribution is socially unjust, given that it disproportionably favours the upper levels of education systems in which there are fewer numbers of students and when it seems to favour those distinguishable by particular social indicators, such as their gender, race and social class. . . . Second, education has a significant and growing influence within society. It is often positioned as central to a nation's economic viability, providing societies with a particular kind of skilled workforce and informed citizenry and, more recently, has been positioned as a financial enterprise in itself. . . . Third . . . it constitutes more than a simple algorithm of resources plus curriculum plus pedagogy. . . . [T]he various ways in which systems and teachers deal with students can be just as much an affront to the socially just provision of education. Not all students are alike and their differences may well be the cause for different treatment, not only in the distribution of educational products but also in the institutional processes involved in educating students. (2000, pp. 8–9)

I have quoted these authors at length, as they seem to me to offer an approach to social justice that is appropriate to the contents of this volume, helpful in its structure, and cognizant of the kinds of issues with which the authors in this book are dealing.

Theorizing about gender and its relationship with equity and social justice is recognized as being more and more necessary to the underpinning of whatever research is being undertaken. Part I of this volume, "Setting the Scene," engages with the dynamic of theory and practice. I have departed from the approach of earlier volumes in which an opening chapter surveyed the field and looked forward to potential areas of development. In this book, both Chapters 1 and 2 provide such a survey. In Chapter 1, Helga Jungwirth gives a strong theoretical overview, but based in classroom behaviors, to the chapters that follow. In Chapter 2, by Laurie Hart, the origins of gender studies in the United States within the field broadly classified as equity are recognized and acknowledged as she reviews developments and offers outlines of two American studies as examples of ways of moving forward to a more integrated perspective. Although not yet widely utilized in mathematics education, postmodernist and poststructuralist approaches are nonetheless evident, I believe, in the thinking of many of the authors present in this volume. I would point to where issues of complexity are acknowledged and the disadvantages of simplistic reasoning challenged. Once complexity is recognized, multivoicing is inevitable, and in many of these chapters, we find an avoidance of overgeneralization and/or an introduction of different and competing voices into the argument being offered. As Helga points out: "Gender no longer has its classifying and unifying power. Sensitivity means that all may develop 'their' relation to mathematics . . . and moreover go their own ways, beyond gender. Stating justice by applying one overall measure becomes problematic." This provides us, I believe, with a more layered way of looking at the previously puzzling phenomenon of who does, and who does not, become a learner of mathematics. (I speak as a female who successfully studied mathematics at university level.)

Hilary Povey, in Chapter 3, raises the important issue of the links between democratic citizenship and the learning of mathematics. Just what do politicians mean when they invoke "citizenship" and particularly when, as in the United Kingdom, it is introduced as a subject in school? Is citizenship a right, or only a responsibility? Can it, does it, address plurality and diversity? If it can, or does, what are the implications for the learning and teaching of mathematics? Hilary draws on data from an initial teacher education course to demonstrate the potential and the dangers, and she makes clear why democratic citizenship and mathematics education should not be seen as discrete entities when constructing and implementing a school curriculum and pedagogy.

Laurie Hart, in Chapter 2, points out how little research has been done on the relationship between parents and their children's learning of mathematics. Christine Brew redresses this in Chapter 4, where she reports on an interview-based study done with mothers returning to study and their children. She points to the "changing dialogue in the home" through which mothers and children enquired together, sharing and challenging their respective learning and growing in confidence in the process. She refers to this as an "underexplored dynamic in the relationship between mothers and children as peers in learning."

Part II of the book focuses on learning in classrooms. It begins with the chapter from Peru by Walter Secada, Santiago Cueto, and Fernando Andrade (Chapter 5) that amply demonstrates the point made above about the complexity and interrelatedness of variables. Problems of resources, living and social conditions, communal demands, and needs such as language are shown in sharp relief under the kinds of circumstances explored by these authors. In this setting, what does access to schooling—never mind to mathematics schooling—mean, and how is its cultural capital both accorded and understood? Social justice here is not specifically about gender, although it features in the analysis, but much more widely about inequalities in opportunities to learn, including social, structural, resource, curriculum, and instructional questions. Using a very broad set of data, Walter and his colleagues offer a depressing picture of teachers, and students, doing their best with odds persistently stacked against them. They ask the crucial question: "Is it the case that there is no way of adapting professional development for teachers who teach in the distressed areas of the world so that efforts to improve the material resources that are made available can proceed apace with efforts to improve the professional lives of teachers and the quality of the instruction that their children receive?"

In Chapter 6, Robyn Zevenbergen explores the beliefs held by some teachers she interviewed about the socially and economically disadvantaged students to whom they taught mathematics in Queensland, Australia. The teacher beliefs literature has demonstrated the links between such beliefs and outcomes for their pupils. In the case of this study, most of the teachers pathologized their pupils and their families—in Helga Jungwirth's terms, probably operating as Type I teachers. But Robyn draws hope from one teacher who presented a very different perspective asking important questions about the relationship between success in the schooling of mathematics and the culture of the community in which the school is sited. Far from seeing her students as deficient, this teacher read them as coming from legitimately different cultures with needs, expectations, and demands that were not consistent with the conventions of Western schools. She would probably be a Type III teacher, using Helga's classification. This poses poignant social justice questions for the reading of mathematics learning, for its meaning for different communities, and for its implications not only with respect to teacher education but much more broadly. Just how far is a government like that in the United Kingdom, for example, willing to go in interrogating its own policies when it sets up a Social Exclusion Unit?

Chapter 7, by Panji Chamdimba, takes us to Malawi where some of the social conditions are reminiscent of those in Peru, described in Chapter 5. Panji queries the relationship between the equal access policies of the government and the poor performance in mathematics of girls in school, drawing attention to achievement and dropout as factors that have socially just relevance. Her study of cooperative learning in three Malawian mathematics classrooms asks, therefore, about the interactions experienced by students in these classrooms and their impact on the behavior of girls and boys and, consequently, on their learning. As with studies done in other countries, this one found that, at best, teachers were Type I and were constraining learning in part by socially stereotyping pupils but that when offered the opportunity to collaborate, positive effects were noticeable in the attitudes of the girls.

Heather Mendick, in Chapter 8, moves us to a poststructuralist account of interview data focusing on three boys taking mathematics at the advanced level in the United Kingdom. The data come from a wider study of students who chose to take mathematics after postcompulsory schooling and their reasons for so doing. Heather points out that media comments asking what has happened to boys' performance in school apply only to the compulsory years and the examination results at the end of these. In the case of mathematics, she says: "[T]he male dominance of advanced maths courses persisted despite all attempts to shift it. . . . [T]he proportion of the total number of 17- and 18-year-olds entered for A level mathematics in England who are male showed very little change, dropping only slightly from 65% to 63%." By focusing on structure and agency and the discourses through which mathematics, femininity and masculinity, and schooling are constituted by her interviewees, Heather writes a narrative of explanation as to how these interconnect and are made to work for and by them. Her narrative has relevance to the different ways in which teachers of Types I, II, and III construct and make meaning for themselves, and their students, about mathematics, its power and influence, mathematical pedagogy, and the access to meaning-making and gender. This not only writes the story about choosing maths *and* doing gender but draws attention to a much broader way in which we write, and are written into, our worlds.

Assessment is one crucial way in which students are written. In Chapter 9, Dylan Wiliam offers supporting evidence for confronting two "orthodoxies." The first is that, contrary to the commonly accepted view, effect sizes showing gender differences in mathematics in the studies he reviewed are extremely small and "much smaller than the variation within males and within females." However, as he points out, despite being small, the differences "are nonetheless widespread, and so females are systematically disadvantaged where particular levels of performance or competence are required." Hence, his second challenge is to the location of explanations for differences; since biological explanations do not stand up to examination, he evokes the construction of difference through "the social processes that have shaped what we choose to call mathematics." In this way, the values that we use to help us to make choices and judgments are recognized as contributing to the outcomes. "The struggles over what is to count as mathematics (in other words, its value implications) are important because assessments send messages about what is and is not important in mathematics education. The result is that teachers and students change what they do." He concludes by asking what the implications of these arguments are for recruitment and selection.

In Chapter 10, Rita Borromeo Ferri and Gabriele Kaiser take us back into the classroom, this time in Germany. They were particularly interested in looking for mathematical thinking style differences in 15- to 16-year-old students, and using a case study approach, they interviewed 12 students, observed them solving problems, used stimulated recall with them, and interviewed their teachers. Although their analysis, not yet completed, did not show a relationship between thinking style and problem-solving strategies, they did demonstrate the close connection between the thinking style of the teacher and the fluency, or difficulty, of learning of the student whose thinking style is similar or different. They point to the implications of these findings for the education of teachers, and their behavior. They conclude, "Diversity—not only in connection with mathematical thinking styles but in general—is needed in mathematics teaching." I would add that a recognition of diversity and the development of means of embracing it are both fundamental to socially just classrooms.

Helen Forgasz, Gilah Leder, and Jan Thomas bring us up to date, in Chapter 11, with participation rates and achievement levels, and current beliefs about gender stereotyping, of grade 12 students in Victoria, Australia. As do many of the authors of previous chapters, they emphasize the oversimplistic nature of the argument that males are now the educationally disadvantaged group and invoke social and political contexts as evidence. Like Heather Mendick, they demonstrate male dominance in mathematics past compulsory schooling as a function both of how mathematics is written and how mathematical careers are socially described; and like Dylan Wiliam, they draw attention to the ways in which, socially, mathematics *and* women are defined and interact to produce the kinds of data on which they report.

Part III of the book contains two chapters that focus on computers and mathematics learning. In recent years, computers have become a widespread resource to both mathematics research and teaching. However, there is still too little research that has been done on whether their introduction into the mathematics classroom is supportive of, or detrimental to, the learning of all students. In Chapter 12, Leigh Wood, Dubravka Viskic, and Peter Petocz produce their research evidence suggesting that the introduction of computers into pretertiary and tertiary mathematics courses is not affected by gender concerns. They offer caveats to reading their results, however. They live in a wealthy country where such resources are widely available; the reactions of their students might be less to the technology than to the epistemological climate in the classroom. They say that "all three of our courses actively encouraged students to work together in groups, and this fact may have been enough to engender more positive female attitudes toward technology." Nonetheless, their results are encouraging.

In Chapter 13, Colleen Vale reports on two junior secondary mathematics classrooms where computers featured in the teaching and learning of mathematics. Her results confirm the caveats offered in the previous chapter. She concludes: "Unless the teacher adopts deliberate strategies in computer-based mathematics learning environments to enhance mathematics learning and gender equity, the classroom tends to become a masculinized domain that threatens the principle of achieving social justice." Again, we have the picture that it is less the resources than the sociocultural contexts within which those resources are used, together with the human expectations, that dictate who becomes a learner of mathematics and how.

So which way for social justice in mathematics education? Will we be able to respond to the challenge set out by Carrie Paechter (2000): "[I]f we want a future significantly different from our present, we will need to educate our future citizens differently" (p. 3). She points out that "networks of power, gender and knowledge intersect to determine how school knowledge is constructed, what knowledge is made available to which students, who is permitted to supply that knowledge and how they are allowed to do so" (p. 4). Out of the chapters of this book, I think the picture that emerges is of many different possible routes, choices that are available to suit different conditions, different needs, different demands. However, on one thing every author agrees: Social justice in mathematics education is still not attained, and as Carrie Paechter indicates, attempts to move in that direction are necessary to and inherent not only in good educational practice but also in building and maintaining stable, caring societies. It is my hope that this volume will support those wishing to work on this agenda.

In conclusion, a book of this kind cannot be compiled without the help of a lot of people. In particular, I wish to express my warm thanks to all of the following colleagues who acted as reviewers of chapters:

Barbara Allen, United Kingdom

Dave Baker, United Kingdom

Bill Barton, New Zealand

Margaret Bernard, Trinidad

Tamara Bibby, United Kingdom

Liz Bills, United Kingdom

Ezra Blondel, United Kingdom

Jo Boaler, United States

Chris Breen, South Africa

Megan Clark, New Zealand

Diana Coben, United Kingdom

Tony Cotton, United Kingdom

Pat Drake, United Kingdom

Mairead Dunne, United Kingdom

Simon Goodchild, United Kingdom

John Izard, Australia

Barbara Jaworski, United Kingdom

Sue Johnston-Wilder, United Kingdom

Lesley Jones, United Kingdom

Cyril Julie, South Africa

Daphne Kerslake, United Kingdom

Christine Knipping, Germany

Gilah Leder, Australia

Steve Lerman, United Kingdom

Thomas Lingford, Sweden

Anthony Mitchell, United Kingdom

Candia Morgan, United Kingdom

Melissa Rodd, United Kingdom

Tim Rowland, United Kingdom

Nathalie Sinclair, Canada

Gunnar Sjoberg, Sweden

Andrew Tee, United Kingdom

Paola Valero, Denmark

Anne Watson, United Kingdom

Anne Woodman, United Kingdom

REFERENCES

Carey, Deborah A., Fennema, Elizabeth, Carpenter, Thomas P., and Franke, Megan L. (1995). Equity and Mathematics Education. In W.G. Secada, E. Fennema, and L.B. Adajian (Eds.), *New Directions for Equity in Mathematics Education* (pp. 93–125). Cambridge: Cambridge University Press.

Fennema, Elizabeth. (1990). Justice, Equity, and Mathematics Education. In Elizabeth Fennema and Gilah C. Leder (Eds.), *Mathematics and Gender* (pp. 1–9). New York: Teachers College Press.

Fennema, Elizabeth. (1995). Mathematics, Gender and Research. In Barbara Grevholm and Gila Hanna (Eds.), *Gender and Mathematics Education* (pp. 21–38). Lund, Sweden: Lund University Press.

Gale, Trevor, and Densmore, Kathleen. (2000). *Just Schooling: Explorations in the Cultural Politics of Teaching*. Buckingham, UK: Open University Press.

Paechter, Carrie. (2000). *Changing School Subjects: Power, Gender and Curriculum*. Buckingham, UK: Open University Press.

Part I

Setting the Scene

Chapter 1

What Is a Gender-Sensitive Mathematics Classroom?

Helga Jungwirth

INTRODUCTION

Feminist movements in the early 1970s criticized male-dominated society and claimed women's equality with men. As a consequence, the education system was also questioned with respect to gender bias. Girls, it was demanded, should be educated as extensively as boys and should become as well qualified for reputable jobs and leading positions. This has been quite a general demand, on the one hand, but on the other hand it refers to mathematics and science education in particular because of the social relevance of these fields and the influence of mathematics and science on occupational options. Educational efforts in these disciplines have become an important issue in feminist pedagogical discussion in many countries and resulted at least in some awareness of the concern in pedagogical practice. Nevertheless, gender differences favoring males, in particular in mathematics and science course-taking in upper secondary and tertiary education or in career ambitions, have not disappeared (see Armstrong 1985; Flitner 1992; Hanna 1996 for detailed country reports). Where it was not yet institutionalized, often it was coeducational schooling that was demanded as a solution at the beginning of the debate. But findings on the role of the formal organization of schooling are inconsistent (Baumert 1992; Giesen et al. 1992; Leder and Forgasz 1998; Marsh 1989), and there are even studies giving evidence of an increase of these gender differences within the coeducational setting (Kauermann-Walter, Kreienbaum, and Metz-Göckel 1988; Lee and Bryk 1989). The organizational framework is only one of the school-related factors that may contribute to gender imbalances in participation rates and so on. The actual teaching and learning that take place in a classroom are supposed to have much impact, too (Becker 1998; Hanna 1996; Higgins 1995; Niederdrenk-Felgner 1998). Models for a "better" coeducational schooling, which are, for example, developed under the slogan "reflective coeducation" (Faulstich-Wieland 1991), start out just from this aspect. Classroom processes are considered to be an important element in endeavors toward conditions that are "sensitive" to girls as well as to boys and, as a consequence, might help to close the gender gap in the relationship toward mathematics and science.

This chapter is about gender sensitivity in the mathematics classroom. Though the talk about it may be in different terms and though the importance of the issue varies nationally, it is undoubtedly a point of interest today: It is a concern of mathematics educators who, for instance, develop concepts for gender-balanced teaching, investigate teaching processes, or evaluate intervention programs in this respect. It is a concern of teachers who try to adjust their teaching to girls as well as to boys, and there is preservice and in-service teacher education on it supporting these efforts. And it is also a matter of official politics of education if governmental programs on equity mention the issue.

In order to give a general idea of how things stand, I set up a typology of gender-sensitive mathematics teaching. It is not the outcome of a systematic analysis of scientific literature or of material for teachers. Yet the types are empirical in the sense that they rest on my general experience with the issue. Many talks with teachers inside and outside teacher education, with colleagues at conferences, my involvement in projects on mathematics and science education, and of course my knowledge of the literature and former reflections on it (Jungwirth 1993, 1994) are the basis of my treatise. My typology might be culture biased, as I am involved, first of all, in the Austrian or, a bit more generally, in the German-speaking "scene" with its particularities, which have surely affected my experience. But every classification is a certain view of things based upon explicit and "tacit" knowledge and is therefore subjective in the end.

I put a certain order on things that reduces complexity. The purpose is to support a profound discussion about gender sensitivity of the mathematics classroom whether it may be carried out in practice or whether it may be just outlined in papers, programs, teacher material, and so on. Using the type as a lens could help to weigh the pros and cons of the various approaches and to clarify one's own position because attention is not distracted by their respective details. It is easier then to identify differences from other positions and to make out potential alliances.

My way to put an order on things is to look at gender-related activities and concepts of gender and gender difference within the mathematics teaching context. Within this context, general concepts of equity and justice get a specific meaning, too, and the classroom-bound gender concepts also reflect more general perspectives. What is, or should be, done in practice in order to enhance sensitivity is related to a basic understanding of the two genders and their relationship. Feminists have classified its modes variously (Kenway and Modra 1992; Mura 1995; Offen 1988; Prengel 1986). From my point of view, the historical stages worked out by Prengel offer a particularly clear structure that is mirrored in classroom-bound concepts.

I produced my typology by application of the "method of documentary interpretation," which is used in everyday life as well as in scientific work within the "interpretative paradigm" (Wilson 1981). This method means "that a pattern is identified which is at the root of a number of phenomena. Thereby each phenomenon is considered as related to the underlying pattern—as an expression, as a 'document' of this pattern. This, on the other hand, is identified by the various concrete phenomena so that the phenomena and the pattern itself determine each other" [Daß ein Muster identifiziert wird, das einer Reihe von Erscheinungen zugrunde liegt; dabei wird jede einzelne Erscheinung als auf dieses zugrunde liegende Muster bezogen angesehen,—als ein Ausdruck, als ein 'Dokument' des zugrunde liegenden Musters. Dieses wiederum wird identifiziert durch seine konkreten individuellen Erscheinungen, so daß die das Muster wiedergebenden Erscheinungen und das Muster selbst einander wechselseitig determinieren.] (Wilson 1981, p. 60).[1]

In my case, the pattern is located at the level of the gender concepts intertwined with the practical activities in the classrooms, and I could identify three principles of thinking and acting. I start the presentation of each type by addressing the way in which girls and boys are perceived and the tasks of the teacher in order that s/he is sensitive toward them; then I ask by which methods one can find out whether this aim has been achieved and turn to the notion of equity, which figures in these. In a second step, I then unfold the general concepts of gender and justice, which build the framework for the classroom-related ones. Of course, the general positions I see from my point of view may remain unnoticed or may even be denied by teachers or scientists who approve of the classroom described in the respective paragraph. But this is nothing unusual. There is a "surplus of meaning" (Ricoeur 1976) in (self) descriptions of reality; that is, interpretations may go far beyond what the acting people themselves are realizing.

As my topic addresses the equity issue, an application of categories stemming from pedagogical equity discussion could be considered as reasonable. Different notions of equity have been worked out, and one could ask which one is represented when mathematics teaching is done or conceptualized in one or the other way. For instance, equity could refer to educational opportunities, on the one hand, or to the outcome of the educational processes on the part of the students, on the other hand. Flitner (1985) in his classification of the notion distinguishes between within-school equity, referring to processes as well as to results, and beyond-school equity, induced by education and referring to improvement in social status. Starting out from my experience, all these analytical separations do not provide distinctive marks really appropriate to grouping mathematics classrooms. Being sensitive to girls and boys is related to opportunities to learn as well as to students' outcomes, for instance, and the latter is often understood in a broad sense including achievements as well as future career options.

As a second alternative to my way of grouping, one might suggest classifying along philosophical currents and positions referring to society. Concepts of gender sensitivity in mathematics teaching involve ideas of justice in general and of the structure of society. For that reason, such an approach would make sense in principle. But as far as I can see, it would be difficult to group mathematics classrooms under philosophical terms because there are no really clear conditions. In talk on pedagogical questions in a narrower sense, persons may indicate another philosophical position than in their talk on more contextual societal issues linked with these questions. For example, Inhetveen (1979) argues that females have the same ability to learn mathematics and would participate in mathematics as males if they were equally encouraged and supported. This may be interpreted as a "liberal" position (Kauermann-Walter, Kreienbaum, and Metz-Göckel 1988). But when she addresses more general social reasons for male dominance in mathematics, she is far from a liberal stance; she looks at the issue explicitly from a Marxist point of view.

GENDER-SENSITIVE CLASSROOM TYPE I: "TO BOTH GROUPS THE SAME"

Classroom-Related Thinking and Acting I

In this classroom, being sensitive to girls and boys means that the teacher attempts to treat them equally in all respects that relate to the learning of mathematics. First, this concerns the subject matter: Approaches to mathematical topics, problems, and tasks are whatever the teacher considers the most appropriate to meet the curriculum demands, but they are kept uniform for the whole class, girls and boys. Second, sensitivity is also a matter of social interaction. The teacher has to give both genders the same amount of attention and to provide the same opportunities to take part in the classroom processes. The genders are assumed to be equal in principle with respect to their internal conditions to learn mathematics so that it is assumed that interacting with them equally leads to an equal outcome in terms of achievements, interests, and so on. At the least, an evenly balanced interaction is regarded as necessary since, conversely, existing differences, mainly seen as represented in girls "lagging behind," are considered the result of differential classroom treatment disadvantaging girls or of general differential socialization. This basic view does not deny that there might be differences between the students to which a teacher has to react. Students with specific learning problems could need specific encouragement and support for some time, but according to the assumed necessity of equal treatment to get equal gender results, in Type I this is not linked with gender; it is not taken into account when the gender sensitivity of a mathematics classroom is discussed.

The teacher, in this type of classroom, does what a mathematics teacher "normally" does, in that s/he has to think about how best to achieve the goals for the class—through which subject matter representations, tasks, and social forms of learning, such as teacher-students-discussions and group working. S/he does this to the best of her/his knowledge and beliefs. Gender, however, is not taken into account in all these considerations. The question whether this approach would better suit girls or boys does not present itself. In this view, the teaching and learning of the subject matter itself are not gendered, and therefore they cannot be sensitive or insensitive. Sensitivity refers to the treatment of girls and boys only, independently of what is taught. In this respect, the teacher has to be very accurate. S/he is expected to ask both genders the same number of the same kinds of questions, feedback (praising, criticizing, etc.) has to be evenly balanced, as do the responses of girls and boys. Girls must not be disadvantaged. Actual equal treatment is difficult to achieve because real teacher-student exchange develops through turn-by-turn interaction. In any case, in Type I, which treatment satisfies the needs of the girls and boys is predetermined before the teacher comes into contact with the students. The teacher has to be aware of and able to apply this knowledge within the teaching process. It is important to notice that attention is paid to the gender groups as a whole. Being sensitive to gender means equal treatment of the girls as a group and the boys as a group; the individual girl or boy does not count.

Quantitative interaction analysis gives evidence of whether or not the classroom practice is sensitive. With respect to the intended result of classroom efforts, analysis of the mathematics-related behaviors of girls and boys regarding, for example, their achievements or attitudes will be informative. As sensitivity refers to the gender groups as a whole, it is always group characteristics that are compared. For example, a researcher might consider the frequency of teacher questions addressed respectively to girls and to boys, or a researcher might consider girls' means and boys' means in achievement tests. By disregarding the specific measures, the underlying notion of equity becomes clear: It means equal "access" to the same learning opportunities in the classroom for both gender groups as well as equal group outcomes afterward without any problematization of these.

Within the pedagogical equality discussion, gender-balanced interaction was one of the first demands to be made, as this imbalance was considered an important cause of mathematics-related gender differences. Many studies were carried out and gave evidence for this reasoning. Joanne Becker (1981) wrote:

Why do so many women elect not to study mathematics when given the choice? . . . The study reported here attempted to determine whether differential treatment of the sexes occurs in high school mathematics classes, and, more generally, to identify what, if anything, is occurring in such classes that may negatively affect the continued study of mathematics by young women. (p. 40)

In the quantitative part of her study she observed 10 geometry classes of ninth-
and tenth-graders and found that

57% of the contacts (direct questions, open questions and immediate reactions on call-
outs) were with male students, even though there was 50% male distribution in the 100
classes. In addition, teachers initiated 63% of their individual academic contacts with
males. Students' answers to teacher questions varied only slightly in quality between
females and males. . . . Although males and females received an equal percentage of
praise following correct answers, males were more likely to get feedback from the teacher
that sustained the interaction when they gave a partially correct, incorrect, or no response
answer. (p. 45)

And she concluded: "The differential treatment found in this study occurred
most often in directions that may indirectly benefit male students, both in their
learning of mathematics and their future course choices" (p. 47).

Within teacher research the question of imbalance in teacher-student interaction became a major topic, too. For example, Andrea Leitgeb (1991), an Austrian mathematics teacher, carried out a project on gender-specific behavior at
school and, among other issues, asked some colleagues about teacher-student
interaction in their classrooms: "With a few exceptions in particular male teachers think that they pay as much attention to girls as to boys and devote as much
time to the one as to the other group, even to favour girls" [Mit wenigen Aus-
nahmen schätzen vor allem Lehrer sich selbst so ein, daß sie Mädchen und
Buben gleich viel Aufmerksamkeit und Zeit widmen bzw. die Mädchen sogar
bevorzugen.] (p. 61). She put this to the test in one class with a male mathematics teacher (counting direct and open questions) and came to the conclusion
that the teacher interacted more with boys than with girls, although in fact she
observed an intensive interaction with one boy only. Taking this as evidence of
insensitive favoring of males is not surprising nor an isolated case, as in this
type of classroom, equity is understood as equality of gender group characteristics (whether the interaction rate increases due to one boy or all boys does not
matter to the result).

Background Thinking I

Thus far the topic has been the equal treatment of the genders and their equal
behavior resulting from it, but I put to one side the question of the norms to
which this equity refers. For example, should saying nothing to the questions
of a teacher be a participation practice used equally frequently by both girls and
boys? Presumably the answer will be no; and this little example already indicates
that there are certain implicit beliefs regarding "good" mathematics-related behaviors on the part of students (inside and outside of school) and "good" teaching practices as well. The former are particularly relevant, as they express which
kind of relationship toward mathematics is thought desirable. Becker's study,

for example, gives evidence of the underlying norm. Her question, "Mathematics courses in high school continue to attract fewer women than men. . . . Why do so many women elect not to study mathematics when given the choice?" (1981, p. 40) indicates that women's behavior is the problem—they ought to do as men do. This means, however, that the norms are set by boys' behavior. What they do and how are the unquestioned reference points expected that girls can and should reach. Remarks such as "Girls can do math just as boys do" are therefore quite common in the context of classroom Type I.

Kaiser and Rogers (1995, pp. 4ff) discuss this understanding of gender equity in their description of the development of the mathematics and gender issue. Applying McIntosh's general model of curriculum development from a male to a gender-inclusive state, they distinguish five phases:

1. In Phase One, "Womenless Mathematics," mathematics appears as a strictly male business.

2. In Phase Two, "Women in Mathematics," mathematics is still a male domain, despite some token women.

3. In Phase Three, "Women as a Problem in Mathematics," there is an awareness of females' aptitude for mathematics provoked, and followed, by programs like the EQUALS project in North America aiming at a higher participation of women in the field of mathematics.

4. In Phase Four, "Women as Central to Mathematics," females' experiences and pursuits are considered as an essential source of the development of mathematics.

5. In Phase Five, "Mathematics Reconstructed," mathematics is a gender-balanced undertaking.

Classroom Type I reflects a Phase Three position. The relative importance of Phase Three as a whole varies from country to country in today's mathematics education; and there are different opinions as to its overall relevance. According to Kaiser and Rogers, "we are in a transitional stage, between Phase Three (seeing women as victims or as problems in mathematics) and Phase Four (seeing women as central to the development of mathematics)" (p. 2). As for Type I, judgments presumably will be more uniform. Those to whom gender sensitivity is a real concern do not exclusively practice or suggest this type. The concept of equity as females catching up with males, such as in the gender-sensitive classroom Type I, is still widespread in society. It is a stage in the understanding of gender difference and gender relationship called the "discourse of equality" ("Gleichheitsdiskurs"; Prengel 1986). As females have been domesticated and disciplined by society and situated as socially inferior, this appears as an historically consistent reaction. They should become emancipated citizens on an equal footing with men by "education and qualification, civil rights and sufficient own means, high-level employment and self-determination in love-affairs" [Bildung und Qualifikation, Bürgerrechte und ausreichende eigene finanzielle Ressourcen, qualifizierte Erwerbsarbeit und Selbstbestimmung in der Liebe.] (Prengel 1986, p. 32).

This discourse was historically important and undoubtedly successful, but it did not fundamentally change gender relationships. Its problem is that gender difference is understood as an hierarchical difference with the male on the top and the female on the bottom. Attitudes, behaviors, lifestyle, and so forth, of men are at least implicitly much more appreciated than those of women. The male is the norm, and applying it, all female-specific behavior looks deficient. Equity of the genders, in this discourse, means an approximation of females to the norm set by males.

The Type I classroom also has a parallel in society with respect to the general understanding of justice in which "statistical understanding" (Schlöglmann 1997) dominates, considering a social sphere to have a fair structure if all relevant groups in society are represented proportionally to their strengths. This is, for instance, the case if in higher education the body of students consists of "enough" members of all social classes, or if in technical fields women and men are represented by 50% each. These examples are quite analogous to the equal-treatment concept of classroom Type I. It is interesting to ask, for instance, whether the statistical interpretation is consistent with the notion of justice as an individual right. A further discussion of this understanding and of the question of what justice in society might be otherwise goes beyond the scope of this chapter. I just want to quote Mura's (1995) critical question: "How would we react to the idea of the percentage of women in mathematics climbing to 70 or 90 per cent? And, would we then be happy to see women fill positions that men no longer wanted?" (p. 160).

GENDER-SENSITIVE CLASSROOM TYPE II: "TO EACH GROUP ITS OWN"

Classroom-Related Thinking and Acting II

In a classroom of this type, being sensitive to girls and boys means meeting with gender-specific learning prerequisites and preferences in both social and subject matter respects; the emphasis is on girls' needs again. By social respects, I refer to the kind of setting (if there are teacher-student conversations, students working individually, group working, etc.) and how it is implemented. For example, teacher-student conversations may strictly follow the elicitation-response-evaluation scheme guiding students more or less directly toward the correct answer, or may have the features of a more "realistic" discussion where all participants deal seriously with the arguments of the others. Or there may be a difference with regard to the (implicit) values emphasized in the social life in classrooms, such features as competitiveness versus supportiveness, academic correctness versus openness to failure. Yet gender sensitivity also relates to how the mathematical subject matter is presented. For instance, fundamental mathematical ideas, procedures, or applications may be stressed, and within the application approach, there may also be different orientations, such as toward science and technology or toward the everyday life of the students.

The basic assumption of Type II is that girls and boys differ in their internal conditions for learning mathematics, and these include social as well as subject matter aspects. Both genders' conditions, however, are considered of equal value—girls are not inferior. Partly, at least, this also refers to the outcome. Girls and boys should develop mathematics-related behaviors governed by their respective prerequisites and preferences. With regard to interests in specific topics, approaches, or work settings, there may be differences in the end. With respect to achievement or attitude in general, there are different points of view within Type II. Girls should not be less qualified, or stay away from mathematics, although striving for typical male careers in the field of science and technology is not regarded, necessarily, as worthwhile.

Teaching in Type II has to be adjusted to the needs of both genders. Again, the focus is on the gender groups; that is, the talk is about "girl-specific" and "boy-specific" needs without asking about differences within the genders. The groups are assumed to be homogeneous. The teacher implementing a classroom of this kind needs to be aware of the basic gender differences existing in this philosophy; that is, that girls and boys have developed different specific beliefs, ways of living, and so on, that affect their relation to mathematics in particular. Many studies have been carried out aiming at an extensive knowledge of the nature of these differences in detail (e.g., see Beerman, Heller, and Menacher 1992, for an overview). The teacher needs to be aware of them and to be able to put results into practice: by gendered subject matter approaches (e.g., taking up girls' specific life experiences) and social settings (e.g., providing cooperative learning according to girls' strengths and preferences in this respect).

Within Type II, two differing positions toward coeducational schooling can be identified. The one position (I want to call it "moderate") holds to the principle of coeducation. This does not exclude separation of girls and boys for a certain purpose, but these are actions limited by time and extent. By contrast, the other position (the "fundamental" one) speaks to the abolition of the coeducational system and pleads for a strictly separated education of girls and boys. Its concern is the education of girls. There is no belief in gender sensitivity within the given system; for example, the founder of the feminist girls' school in Vienna (the "Virginia Woolf School") states:

In spite of several intensive efforts of dynamic and feminist female teachers the structural sexism in the education system as a whole and in school (with regard to its subjects and organisation) cannot really be eliminated: the educational system, too, reproduces that hierarchy of values which considers all male higher-ranking in principle than all female, and therefore lays one of the foundations of the hierarchical relationship of the two genders. (Devime and Rollett 1994: 17)

[Trotz so mancher intensiver Bemühungen von engagierten und feministischen Lehrerinnen läßt sich am strukturellen Sexismus im Bildungswesen und in der Schule (auf
inhaltlicher und organisatorischer Ebene) nur sehr schwer etwas verändern: Auch die
Institution Schule reproduziert jene Bewertungshierarchie, die Männliches grundsätzlich
höher bewertet als Weibliches, und legt damit einen der Grundsteine für hierarchische
Geschlechterverhältnisse.]

To find out whether a Type II classroom is sensitive or not is more complex
than in the Type I arrangement. One way is to observe in the classroom if both
genders' needs (well known from the literature), particularly those of girls, are
sufficiently taken into account. An evaluation could try to find out, for example,
whether teaching materials include tasks referring to girls' and women's everyday life. Another way is to examine the final result of classroom efforts by the
students with the expectation that both genders should perform comparably
within their different settings and arrangements (e.g., in single-sex schools). That
is, in tests or examinations provided by the educational system, boys and girls
should achieve equally. Yet the methods for assessment themselves are no longer
considered to be ungendered. Several analyses indicate that in mathematics they
might be biased to girls' disadvantage (Forbes 1996). There is a claim for a fair
assessment. It could be reached by broadening out procedures (Forbes 1995),
or as Clarke (1996) stated quite generally without explicit reference to the gender
issue: "Our obligation to minimize disadvantage can be met by employing a
range of task types, offering students the opportunity to demonstrate their learning through a range of communicative modes, and employing a range of different contextual settings" (p. 34).

Again, the concept of equity underlying Type II includes two aspects. On the
one hand, equity refers to access; in this classroom type, however, this means
access to differentiated, gender-specific teaching and learning arrangements. On
the other hand, equity refers to equality of gender group results, although this
is not uniformly accepted, as a skeptical view of "typical" male behaviors may
be taken.

In its moderate version, classroom Type II seems to be the most common
way in which gender-sensitive education is practiced today. There are some
countries in which this perspective on gender teaching is the basis of official
programs and materials for teachers edited by Ministers of Education or public
institutions for teacher education (Bundesministerium für Unterricht und kulturelle Angelegenheiten 1996; Landesregierung Nordrhein-Westfalen 1991; Ministerium für Familie, Frauen, Weiterbildung und Kunst und Ministerium für
Kultus und Sport 1995). However, with respect to teacher-student interaction in
particular, the equal treatment idea has also survived. Hence, in practice, there
is some mix of types. But notwithstanding, a lot of research and development
work in science and schools is oriented to Type II.

Background Thinking II

The general perspective on gender and mathematics education related to classroom Type II is the transitional state from Phase Three ("Women as a Problem in Mathematics") to Phase Four ("Women as Central to Mathematics"), or Phase Four itself in the model of Kaiser and Rogers (1995). In this transitional state, on the one hand, women should change their mathematics-related behavior; on the other, mathematics education is seen as male centered, making it understandable that females and males do not have the same relation to mathematics, and education should be changed according to the specific needs of females. Phase Four itself is characterized by a substantial change of mathematics and mathematics education by females according to their values and perspectives on life: "[W]omen's experience and women's pursuits are made central to the development of mathematics. Work in this phase seeks to uncover privilege and to redistribute power. It emphasizes cooperation over winning and losing, difference and multiplicity over 'one right way' " (p. 8). In Phase Four, pedagogy as well as the discipline mathematics is thoroughly questioned. Mathematics is understood as a sociocultural phenomenon and reflects the life experience and self-understanding of its "producer," the white male. To be more inclusive—meaning, in particular, to create a more female-oriented mathematics—would be quite another undertaking. The knowing in mathematics itself would be much more comprehensive: "Knowing mathematics would, under this definition, be a function of who is claiming to know, related to which community, how that knowing is presented, what explanations are given for how that knowing was achieved, and the connections demonstrated between it and other knowings (applications)" (Burton 1995, p. 221).

Type II adheres to the "difference perspective" upon gender held in feminist pedagogy. This asserts, briefly, that there are two different yet equally important and esteemed genders. However, it is not quite clear what the range of application is. On one side, it is considered appropriate only for dealing with childhood phenomena. In this phase, a substantial difference that has to be taken into account within education is assumed. In the world of adults, however, the "discourse of equality" holds true. The moderate version of Type II described above tends toward this divided view when it pleads for a classroom that meets girls' needs as well as those of boys and simultaneously aims at males' relation to mathematics for all. The question as by what "switch" the substantial difference in childhood can vanish in adulthood is not tackled. The fundamental version is not so ambiguous. It emphasizes, as does the "radical feminist discourse" (Prengel 1986) or the "feminism of difference" (Mura 1995), that there is a female way of being that has developed in the course of history and is at least of equal value to the male. Feminist movements have tried to work out the specific female capacities and attainments and their value for society. Gilligan's (1982) description of the "different voice" of women and Belenky et al.'s (1986) categorization of the stages of women's knowing are well-known contributions to this discourse. It is undoubtedly an important and consequent reaction to the "discourse of equality" disparaging all females. Yet there is the risk of a simple reversal of the gender relationship to considering all-female good and all-male evil, as the following example shows:

Man has said that women cannot think logically; however, I do not want to think "logically" in this sense at all if logically means as the patriarchal practice shows to ruin the earth and to drive everything to death in the end. Instead of this I plead for: *thinking consistently*, that means we consider the consequences, we do not float somewhere through the world of thought, we do not think straight on in abstract chains of reasoning, into space. For us it is not the process itself which is in the focus . . . for us the content, *what* we must consider, is central. (Wisselinck 1984: 49; emphases in original)

[Mann hat gesagt, Frauen können nicht logisch denken—ich will auch nicht in diesem Sinne "logisch" denken, wenn logisch denken, wie die patriarchale Praxis zeigt, in letzter Konsequenz heißt, die Erde in ihren Unteragng zu treiben und alles tödlich enden zu lassen. Ich setze dagegen: *folgerichtig denken*—das heißt: wir bedenken die Folgen, wir machen keine Denkoperationen im luftleeren Raum, wir denken nicht in abstrakten Gedankenabfolgen darauf los, ins Leere. Für uns steht nicht der Gedankengang als solcher im Mittelpunkt . . . für uns steht im Mittelpunkt, *was* wir zu bedenken haben.]

Justice, in the sense of the "radical feminist discourse," means openness in society to both the female and male way of life. What the measure of this could be is not defined in this context. The idea of measurement as a whole seems to be questioned, as it might indicate a typical male approach to justice.

Although the difference perspective may appear a reasonable basis for society as a whole, criticism by feminists is increasing. On the one hand, the neglect of within-gender differences has been pointed out. Within mathematics education, Burton's (1998) work on female and male mathematicians' perceptions of mathematics does away with the idea of a "typical female" stance. Her investigation brought to light a great variety of positions with respect to the main features of mathematics, the way of understanding mathematics, the way of thinking about mathematics, and the way of working in mathematics. Research on female scientists and engineers has revealed large differences also between these women making it obsolete to hold on to a unifying concept of female:

They resemble neither men nor each other, are neither marked by certain female features nor beyond any identification with female stereotypes. In any case, however, they are involved in quite specific subject matter and occupational contexts. They have developed their respective competencies and abilities, gained insights, and adopted behaviours and social manners to cope with the situations they are confronted with and to stand the social interactions. (Roloff and Metz-Göckel 1995, p. 265)

[Sie sind weder mit Männern, noch unter sich gleich, weder durch weibliche Besonderheiten gekennzeichnet, noch unabhängig von der Identifizierung mit Stereotypen ihres

Geschlechts. Immer aber müssen sie sich mit einer ganz bestimmten Fach- und Beruf-skultur auseinandersetzen. Sie haben je spezifische Kompetenzen und Fähigkeiten ent-wickelt, Einsichten gewonnen und sich Verhaltens- und Umgangsweisen angeeignet, um mit den Situationen, mit denen sie konfrontiert sind, zurechtzukommen und in den so-zialen Interaktionen zu bestehen.]

On the other hand, gender differentiation as such is considered a problem. The chance of overcoming existing gender hierarchy and ever attaining a fair, balanced gender relationship by holding on to the concept of a basic difference is questioned (Walkerdine et al. 1989). In particular, research on labor and pro-fessions has pointed out:

By defining genders as different and their becoming socially "real" as different ones, they are already in a hierarchical relationship. . . . The social ascription of gender to occupations is in any case the social construction of a hierarchical relation between men's jobs and women's jobs, men's working places and women's working places. (Wetterer 1995a, p. 228)

[Bereits indem die Geschlechter als verschiedene bestimmt und als verschiedene sozial "wirklich" werden, befinden sie sich immer schon in einem hierarchischen Verhältnis. . . . Die soziale Konstruktion der Geschlechtszugehörigkeit von Berufen ist immer auch die soziale Konstruktion einer hierarchischen Beziehung zwischen Männerberufen und Frauenberufen, Männerarbeitsplätzen und Frauenarbeitsplätzen.]

GENDER-SENSITIVE CLASSROOM TYPE III: "TO ALL THEIR OWN PREFERENCES"

Classroom-Related Thinking and Acting III

In this type of classroom, gender sensitivity means that the teacher is sensitive to the individual, girl or boy. Students are basically ascribed to the gender groups, as we do in our "natural attitude" (Schütz 1971); that is, girls are per-ceived as girls, boys are perceived as boys, but this does not influence classroom choices. Attention is paid to the learning prerequisites and preferences of each individual, and these dictate classroom practices. The goal is an optimal mathematics-related development of all students without emphasizing sex nor taking this attribution as a criterion of teaching decisions. It may turn out that, in a given case, similarities in attitudes, for example, within both sexes are closer than similarities between one sex and the other and that therefore there are gender differences, too; but this is a finding in this case only and not a phe-nomenon to be expected. Classroom Type III focuses on the differences within both genders, whereas Type I and Type II, both in their specific way, focus on the two genders and the differences between them. The question may arise what this Type III concept has to do with gender sensitivity when it is so individually oriented. The answer is that it does because the students are initially classified as male or female and because of this, gender (or better, sex) is introduced as a category. Being sensitive, from this point of view, is best done without further looking upon students as members of one sex, because this, like every other classification, abstracts from individual features and imposes stereotypic expectations.

To meet with individual needs has, again, two dimensions, the subject matter and the social. Students may differ with respect to their preferred approach to mathematics, to their ways of tackling a mathematical problem, and to their participation in classroom interaction and the task-solving setting they like best. The teacher has to cope with the manifoldness in each dimension, and therefore teaching varies more or less, depending on the students and their features. In addition to the subject and pedagogical knowledge the teacher possesses, in classroom Type III, her or his "analytical view" on the classroom situation is particularly important. In a sense, this is a basic requirement for all teaching and necessary to all teachers in each of the types; "reflection in action" (Schön 1991) is the common mode of these analyses, but "reflection on action," that is, analyses based on data gathered for that purpose (Stenhouse 1975), could be necessary, too. With respect to gender sensitivity, however, in Types I and II, the teacher merely has to apply general knowledge stemming from outside. S/he has to put into practice the results about, for instance, the dimensions of correct equal treatment or a gender's learning styles. In contrast, in Type III the students' needs have yet to be uncovered. The appropriate ways of teaching the students in one class may be wrong for the students in another one. Thus, more than in Types I and II, the teacher is a teacher-researcher in the full meaning of this notion.

The first way to find out whether the classroom is gender sensitive is to do such research, for example, by asking students if, individually, their needs are being met. The second way is to analyze students' mathematics-related behavior. Whatever the relevant dimensions of this might be (to solve certain application tasks, to have a well-balanced attitude toward mathematics as a whole, etc.) and whatever methods of evaluation are used corresponding to these, there are two aspects to it. Primarily, each student should reach her/his best; that is, the measure is individual progress. But, on the other hand, Type III is embedded in the educational system and therefore has to consider the standards demanded. Thus sensitivity is also a question of meeting these; the more students do, the better it is. Equity in the previous sense no longer applies in this context. There is no gender group comparison in the dimensions of access nor results, as there is no gender grouping. Equity here refers to the individual, with respect to learning arrangements and, somewhat qualified, to outcomes.

Type III is quite a new approach to sensitivity within a coeducational setting, although the underlying perspective on gender and gender difference has been well established outside of pedagogy for several years. There is some common ground with the idea of "hidden potentials" of both genders such as is found in the field of technical education; this also pays attention to the differences within the genders (Kahlert and Müller-Balhorn 1994; Roloff and Metz-Göckel 1995). In the ongoing Austrian project IMST[2] ("Innovations in Mathematics, Science and Technology Teaching") (Krainer 2001), the Type III concept was developed as a basis for an improvement in the quality of teaching done by teachers themselves. One goal of this project is to develop teachers' competencies in reflecting on teaching and learning processes in their classrooms and innovating according to the needs of the students there (Jungwirth 2001; Stadler 2001).

Background Thinking III

In the model of development of gender and mathematics worked out by Kaiser and Rogers (1995), Phase Five ("Mathematics Reconstructed") seems to share some qualities with this classroom type. In this phase, mathematics "will be what people do" (p. 9). This sounds similar to the concern of Type III to meet with the individual needs of the students, yet there remains some uncertainty due to the prospective nature of Phase Five, making its precise description difficult.

As far as perspectives on gender and gender relationships are concerned, affinities are much more distinct. As I have already said, Type III classrooms emphasize diversity within genders; they are not considered as homogeneous groups; even this grouping itself is questioned. It is no longer legitimate to take gender as a criterion in mathematics education. Empirical research supports this point of view quite strongly. Research on youth life, for instance, indicates that the category of gender loses its relevance, as "according to the latest findings attitudes of girls and boys as well as their living, at least before founding a family, become more and more similar" [daß sich nach den neuen Erkenntnissen der Jugendforschung sowohl die Einstellungen von Mädchen und Jungen als auch ihre Lebensrealitäten, zumindest vor einer Phase der Familiengründung, angleichen] (Meyer 1999, pp. 18ff). Differences that occur in the ways of living are individual. Mathematics-related research, too, indicates a closing of the gender gap: Metaanalyses state small effect sizes (e.g., Hyde, Fennema, and Lamon 1990; Hyde et al. 1990) indicating small gender differences in such important fields as performance and overall attitude. In any case, empirically there are always spectra of results within the genders that partly overlap, even if gender means and such measures are clearly distinct. It requires decision making, and that is a matter of background philosophy as to whether differences between genders, or differences within them which make the gender groups disappear, are put in focus.

On a theoretical level, the "discourse of openness" (Prengel 1986) provides a concept of gender and gender relationship in which the heterogeneity of both genders is the crucial point, just as in the Type III classroom. According to this discourse, we realize through, or in spite of, talking about gender difference that we cannot really define what the essence of being a woman or being a man might be. Instead of this, manifold and changeable female and male ways of living and of maintaining social relations become imaginable without any need to compare them and to look down or up to them. (p. 35)

[daß wir nicht wirklich sagen können, was Frausein und Mannsein dem Wesen nach wäre. Statt dessen werden vielfältige, auch sehr unterschiedliche und veränderliche, weibliche und männliche Lebensentwürfe und Beziehungsformen denkbar, ohne daß diese vergleichend ab- bzw. aufgewertet werden müßten.]

Relinquishing gender as a unifying category is a feature of "postmodern" thinking, just a special case of its general critique of "foundationalism" and of universals (like "nature," "man," etc.). Postmodern thinking, on the contrary, emphasizes the constructivity and contextuality of these, often by referring to them by the ambiguous term *discourse*. Feminism therefore took a skeptical stance on postmodern approaches to gender, arguing that without its defining category "female" neither feminist theory nor politics would make sense. In the last few years, however, the position has changed. Postmodern ideas have proved fruitful for feminist work, for instance, by clarifying the social constitution of (female) identity (Mohanty 1991; Nicholson 1995). For feminist politics, new perspectives arose. They emphasize the importance of alliances, as "woman" as a general reference point no longer exists (see Dingler et al. 2000 for an overview). Prengel in her discussion of the discourse of openness considers the diversity within the genders as important to pedagogy in particular, as it suggests letting students find their own ways of being female or male.

Research on mathematics education has also adopted postmodernity for discussions on the gender issue. Walkerdine et al. (1989) focus on girls' putative lack of genuine mathematical understanding starting out from the discursive construction of the "truths" about gender, child, and mathematics working together in mathematics education. Their analyses show that these constitute quite a different framework for girls' and boys' learning of mathematics. Girls are faced with contradictory demands: The ideal child—and in the higher grades, the ideal "mastery" of mathematics—and the ideal girl are irreconcilable antagonisms. Girls are placed in a double-bind (Isaacson 1989) from which they try to escape in one way or another. In any case, female success at mathematics threatens underlying truths. One way of coping with this threat is to develop the story of female "lacking." Evans (1995) takes the view that activities are based in discourses. Therefore, in a given situation, certain (discursive) practices are at play or may be called up. His study indicates that mathematical performance is also affected by this "positioning in practices" and in particular raises the question whether gender differences could be traced back to differences in positioning. In his case study of Ellen, the anxiety of this woman, which at first sight appeared to be related to academic mathematics, is evoked by the everyday situation in which the task is embedded. Walshaw (2001) refers more specifically to Foucault and his idea of the constitution of the subject in knowledge/power relations (discourses and practices) by processes of subjection as well as active participation and resistance. She is interested in the way that girls become gendered within school mathematics. Her case study of a female student Donna shows that femininity is constructed within the discursive production of an autonomous and capable mathematics learner. That is done in situations somewhat upsetting to Donna or that question her mathematical capability. Yet this happens in a way that indicates clearly her personal distance from the cultural definition of femininity.

The idea of social construction of gender expressed in postmodern thinking illustrated by the studies above is a necessary condition for a Type III classroom; otherwise, it would not make any sense to suggest an abstraction from gender. But this idea is not quite sufficient as a basis because it does not really show a route for the practical functioning of this type. This is provided by the recent work of ethnomethodologists, thereby rooting this classroom perspective on gender in ethnomethodology. Although this is a particular school within sociology, the teacher in classroom III is not assumed to be a researcher in this area. The ethnomethodological perspective on gender is adopted in the same way as in other cases in pedagogical practice; or in everyday life in general, perspectives stemming from other scientific disciplines (primarily from social psychology) are applied. A teacher, for example, who holds a Piagetian model of cognitive development is not a psychologist in the Piagetian tradition.

Ethnomethodologists study social acting more intensely than is done in general talk on discourses within the framework of postmodern thinking. They are always interested in the methods by which members of society make their social world happen. Accordingly, gender is interactively established in a mutual process of representing and ascribing (Garfinkel 1967; Goffman 1979; Hirschauer 1994; Kessler and McKenna 1985; West and Zimmerman 1991). Gendered society is the result of "doing gender" on many levels simultaneously, or, in other words, the category of gender becomes the category of universal social relevance that it is today as a result of all these processes (see Chapter 8, this volume). In order that the crux within my argument will become distinctive, I briefly sketch the methods of doing gender altogether.

First, grouping people into women and men at first sight as it is done is not simply applying a given difference, although there are good reasons why that happens (see, e.g., the symbolization of generativity [Landweer 1993]). All people have learned to "see" women and men in bodily representations, that is, to focus on certain physical features and to overlook others. Sex itself is a social construction; or, in other words, gender includes sex. Our common explanation, in which we refer to biology and its classification into female and male, is also a social decision. A second method of doing gender is ascribing femininity or masculinity to human behaviors, objects, entire social fields. However, as Hirschauer (1994) pointed out in contrast to former ethnomethodological work, this is no completely continuous process. There are situations in which, for instance, persons are sexually classified, but this distinction does not figure in interaction (as in certain emergency situations where neither the sex of the victims nor of the rescuers matters). A third kind of gender construction is done through "institutional genderism" represented by all social arrangements that point out gender difference, from separate store departments for women and men to single-sex education. Additionally, science contributes to doing gender through its working out differences between females and males in cognitive, affective, behavioral, and so on, aspects and presenting them as ontological entities.

From this point of view, endeavors to overcome gendered society within the framework of the "discourse of equality" as well as the "radical feminist discourse" can never succeed because they do not question the construction of gender difference itself; within the latter the historically grown difference is just the point. Classrooms of Type I and II are never sensitive under an ethnomethodological perspective; single-sex schooling, which is optional under Type II, makes it all the worse, as it emphasizes the gender difference. These classrooms do not contribute to social justice. The solution is "undoing gender"; that is, acting in a way that this category loses its importance, although this is, with respect to practice, an arduous venture, nor, since its beginning, has it been seen as promising in ethnomethodology. But there are, nevertheless, prospects. The crux is not to actualize the differences. Gender can become a "seen but unnoticed feature" (Hirschauer 1994); it can sink into oblivion within social processes when it is not called up. For example, not ascribing certain "abilities" to a person classified as female and not treating her "as a female" would be a step in this direction. Classroom III, by emphasizing the individuality of the students, tries to put this into effect. To utilize the potential that arises from the first way of doing gender, that is, not doing sex, is utopian in today's world. But at least ethnomethodologists have shown that the common distinction between "females" and "males" by physical appearance is not a simply given basis for further social gender construction. Besides, there might be quite different structuring elements, but "to use the length of the ears or the colour of the hair as a criterion of social differentiation" [die Länge der Ohren oder die Farbe der Haare zum strukturbildenden Moment sozialer Differenzierung zu machen] (Wetterer 1995b, p. 42) is beyond the horizon.

Another way to begin undoing gender is to reveal the constructivity of gender by making the procedures of its construction obvious. Thus it cannot be regarded as a given property any longer. This is the aim and feat of all deconstructivist "reading" of the world, as is done in postmodern work. With respect to the topic here, this means, as I said above, to reveal how, by which ascriptions, references, allusions, and so on, mathematics today is made a male sphere (see Jungwirth 1996 for a step in this direction based on ethnomethodology). Although this can be practiced everywhere in principle, and in classrooms, too, it is not the attitude of everyday life with its orientation toward making things happen rather than questioning them. In first line, deconstruction will be a task for scientists replacing their search for "gender-specific" phenomena.

A society where gender has completely sunk into oblivion would no longer have a criterion for justice with respect to gender, as the category itself would have faded away. In particular, the popular statistical argument would not apply anymore. For example, what sense would it make to state that there are as many women in mathematics as men when the property being female or male no longer exists? And when the sex of persons is seen but unnoticed in the ongoing social interaction, as the Type III classroom demands, reference to gender groups is unreasonable.

CONCLUSION

A definite answer to the question of which of the three types of classroom I have described is the most sensitive with respect to gender cannot be given. Every decision depends on background philosophy, the understanding of gender difference, and the ideal of gender relationship and of social justice. And there are rivaling philosophies, as the concepts related to each type of classroom show. Historically, there is a certain order, and one might grapple with the question as to whether there was a development toward a "higher" quality of gender sensitivity. But my concluding remark will be confined to a brief formal comparison.

There is a development from limitation and regulation to complexity and openness from the first to the last type. With respect to relations between mathematics, gender, and the measure of justice, the simplest approach is found in the classroom of Type I where there is only one "correct" mathematics-related behavior, or reasonable way of life, and by measuring interaction rates or the quantities of females and males doing mathematics, it can be seen whether the sensitive state has been reached. A Type II classroom is more complex because there are two different ways of dealing with and behaving toward mathematics, and proportionality is no longer the absolutely decisive factor. Besides, the context and the way of measuring have to be taken into account when judging the sensitivity of a situation. Classroom Type III is the most complex. There are not just two kinds of mathematics-related behaviors but as many as the people contained therein. Gender no longer has its classifying and unifying power. Sensitivity means that all may develop "their" relation to mathematics (although meeting given expectations at school and in society) and moreover go their own ways, beyond gender. Stating justice by applying one overall measure becomes problematic, as personal development plays a crucial role in judgment.

NOTE

1. The translations of all German quotations are mine.

REFERENCES

Armstrong, Jane M. (1985). A National Assessment of Participation and Achievement on Women in Mathematics. In Susan F. Chipman, Lorelei R. Brush, and Donna M. Wilson (Eds.), *Women and Mathematics: Balancing the Equation* (pp. 59–95). Hillsdale, NJ: Lawrence Erlbaum.

Baumert, Jürgen. (1992). Koedukation oder Geschlechtertrennung. *Zeitschrift für Pädagogik*, 1, 83–110.

Becker, Joanne R. (1981). Differential Treatment of Females and Males in Mathematics Classes. *Journal for Research in Mathematics Education*, 1, 40–53.

Becker, Joanne R. (1998). Research on Gender and Mathematics in the USA: Accomplishments and Future Challenges. In Christine Keitel (Ed.), *Social Justice and Mathematics Education: Gender, Class, Ethnicity, and the Politics of Schooling* (pp. 251–257). Berlin: Freie Universität.

Beerman, Lilly, Heller, Kurt, and Menacher, Pauline. (1992). *Mathe: Nichts für Mädchen? Begabung und Geschlecht am Beispiel von Mathematik, Naturwissenschaft und Technik.* Bern: Verlag Hans Huber.

Belenky, Mary F., Clinchy, Blythe McVicker, Goldberger, Nancy Rule, and Tarule, Jill Mattuck. (1986). *Women's Ways of Knowing: The Development of Self, Voice, and Mind.* New York: Basic Books.

Bundesministerium für Unterricht und kulturelle Angelegenheiten. (1996). *Unterrichtsprinzip "Erziehung zur Gleichstellung von FRAUEN und MÄNNERN." Informationen und Anregungen zur Umsetzung.* Wien: Eigenverlag.

Burton, Leone. (1995). Moving Towards a Feminist Epistemology of Mathematics. In Pat Rogers and Gabriele Kaiser (Eds.), *Equity in Mathematics Education: Influences of Feminism and Culture* (pp. 209–225). London: Falmer Press.

Burton, Leone. (1998). Thinking about Mathematical Thinking—Heterogeneity and Its Social Justice Implications. Plenary Address to the Mathematics Education and Society Conference (MEAS 1), Nottingham, UK, September.

Clarke, David. (1996). Assessment. In Alan J. Bishop, Ken Clements, Christine Keitel, Jeremy Kilpatrick, and Colette Laborde (Eds.), *International Handbook of Mathematics Education. Part 1* (pp. 327–370). Dordrecht: Kluwer Academic Publishers.

Devime, Ruth, and Rollett, Ilse. (1994). Die Virginia Woolf-Schule. Gelebte feministische Praxis von Mädchen und Frauen. In Ruth Devime and Ilse Rollett (Eds.), *Mädchen bevorzugt. Feministische Beiträge zur Mädchenbildung und Mädchenpolitik* (pp. 16–38). Wien: Verband Wiener Volksbildung.

Dingler, Johannes, Frey, Regina, Frietsch, Ute, Jungwirth, Ingrid, Kerner, Ina, and Spottka, Frauke. (2000). Dimensionen postmoderner Feminismen. *Feministische Studien*, 1, 129–144.

Evans, Jeff. (1995). Gender and Mathematical Thinking: Myths, Discourse and Context in Practices. In Barbro Grevholm and Gila Hanna (Eds.), *Gender and Mathematics Education* (pp. 149–157). Lund: Lund University Press.

Faulstich-Wieland, Hannelore. (1991). *Koedukation—Enttäuschte Hoffnungen?* Darmstadt: Wissenschaftliche Buchgesellschaft.

Flitner, Andreas. (1985). Gerechtigkeit als Problem der Schule und als Thema der Bildungsreform. *Zeitschrift für Pädagogik*, 1, 1–27.

Flitner, Elisabeth. (1992). Wirkungen von Geschlecht und sozialer Herkunft auf Schullaufbahn und Berufswahl. Neue französische Untersuchungen. *Zeitschrift für Pädagogik*, 1, 47–63.

Forbes, Sharleen, D. (1995). Are Assessment Procedures in Mathematics Gender-Biased? In Barbro Grevholm and Gila Hanna (Eds.), *Gender and Mathematics Education* (pp. 159–165). Lund: Lund University Press.

Forbes, Sharleen D. (1996). Curriculum and Assessment: Hitting Girls Twice? In Gila Hanna (Ed.), *Towards Gender Equity in Mathematics Education* (pp. 71–91). Dordrecht: Kluwer Academic Publishers.

Garfinkel, Harold. (1967). *Studies in Ethnomethodology*. Englewood Cliffs, NJ: Prentice-Hall.

Giesen, Heinz, Gold, Andreas, Hummer, Annelie, and Weck, Michael. (1992). Die Bedeutung der Koeduaktion für die Genese der Studienfachwahl. *Zeitschrift für Pädagogik*, 1, 65–82.

Gilligan, Carol. (1982). *In a Different Voice*. Cambridge, MA: Harvard University Press.

Goffman, Ervin. (1979). *Gender Advertisement*. Cambridge, MA: Harvard University Press.

Hanna, Gila. (1996). Introduction. In Gila Hanna (Ed.), *Towards Gender Equity in Mathematics Education* (pp. 1–7). Dordrecht: Kluwer Academic Publishers.

Higgins, Joanna. (1995). We Don't Even Want to Play: Classroom Strategies and Curriculum Which Benefit Girls. In Pat Rogers and Gabriele Kaiser (Eds.), *Equity in Mathematics Education: Influences of Feminism and Culture* (pp. 200–208). London: Falmer Press.

Hirschauer, Stefan. (1994). Die soziale Fortpflanzung der Zweigeschlechtlichkeit. *Kölner Zeitschrift für Soziologie und Sozialpsychologie*, 46, 668–692.

Hyde, Janet S., Fennema, Elizabeth, and Lamon, Susan J. (1990). Gender Differences in Mathematics Performance: A Meta-Analysis. *Psychological Bulletin*, 2, 139–155.

Hyde, Janet S., Fennema, Elizabeth, Ryan, Marilyn, Frost, Laurie A., and Hopp, Carolyn. (1990). Gender Comparisons of Mathematics Attitudes and Affect: A Meta-Analysis. *Psychology of Women Quarterly*, 14, 299–324.

Inhetveen, Heide. (1979). Frau und Mathematik. In Dieter Volk (Ed.), *Kritische Stichwörter zum Mathematikunterricht* (pp. 67–85). München: Wilhelm Fink Verlag.

Isaacson, Zelda. (1989). Of Course You *Could* Be an Engineer, Dear, but Wouldn't You *Rather* Be a Nurse or Teacher or Secretary? In Paul Ernest (Ed.), *Mathematics Teaching: The State of the Art* (pp. 188–194). London: Falmer Press.

Jungwirth, Helga. (1993). Reflections on the Foundations of Research on Women and Mathematics. In Sal Restivo, Jean Paul Van Bendegem, and Roland Fischer (Eds.), *Math Worlds: Philosophical and Social Studies of Mathematics and Mathematics Education* (pp. 134–149). New York: State University of New York Press.

Jungwirth, Helga. (1994). Die Forschung zu Frauen und Mathematik: Versuch einer Paradigmenklärung. *Journal für Mathematikdidaktik*, 3–4, 253–276.

Jungwirth, Helga. (1996). Symbolic Interactionism and Ethnomethodology as a Theoretical Framework for the Research on Gender and Mathematics. In Gila Hanna (Ed.), *Towards Gender Equity in Mathematics Education* (pp. 49–70). Dordrecht: Kluwer Academic Publishers.

Jungwirth, Helga. (2001). Geschlechtssensibel statt geschlechtsspezifisch. In Gabriele Kaiser (Ed.), *Beiträge zum Mathematikunterricht. Vorträge auf der 35. Tagung für Didaktik der Mathematik* (pp. 324–327). Hildesheim-Berlin: Franzbecker.

Kahlert, Heike, and Müller-Balhorn, Sigrid. (1994). Mädchenförderung (nicht nur) in Naturwissenschaften und Technik. In Edith Glumpler (Ed.), *Koedukation. Entwicklungen und Perspektiven* (pp. 31–48). Bad Heilbrunn: Klinkhardt.

Kaiser, Gabriele, and Rogers, Pat. (1995). Introduction. In Pat Rogers and Gabriele Kaiser (Eds.), *Equity in Mathematics Education: Influences of Feminism and Culture* (pp. 1–10). London: Falmer Press.

Kauermann-Walter, Jaqueline, Kreienbaum, Maria Anna, and Metz-Göckel, Sigrid. (1988). Formale Gleichheit und diskrete Diskriminierung: Forschungsergebnisse zur Koedukation. In Hans-Georg Rolff et al. (Eds.), *Jahrbuch der Schulentwicklung. Daten. Beispiele. Perspektiven*, Band 5 (pp. 157–188). Weinheim: Beltz.

Kenway, Jane, and Modra, Helen. (1992). Feminist Pedagogy and Emancipatory Possibilities. In Carmen Luke and Jennifer Gore (Eds.), *Feminisms and Critical Pedagogy* (pp. 138–166). New York: Routledge.

Kessler, Suzanne J., and McKenna, Wendy. (1985). *Gender: An Ethnomethodological Approach.* Chicago: University of Chicago Press.

Krainer, Konrad. (2001). Ausgangspunkt und Grundidee von IMST². In Interuniversitäres Institut für Forschung und Fortbildung (Ed.), *Endbericht zum Projekt IMST²— Innovations in Mathematics, Science and Technology Teaching. Pilotjahr 2000/ 01* (pp. 8–47). Im Auftrag des BMBWK. Klagenfurt: Interdisziplinäres Institut für Forschung und Fortbildung.

Landesregierung Nordrhein-Westfalen—Ministerin für die Gleichstellung von Frau und Mann. (1991). *Mädchen, Macht (und) Mathe.* Düsseldorf: Eigenverlag.

Landweer, Hilge. (1993). Kritik und Verteidigung der Kategorie Geschlecht. *Feministische Studien*, 2, 34–43.

Leder, Gilah, and Forgasz, Helen J. (1998). Single-Sex Groupings for Mathematics? An Equitable Solution? In Christine Keitel (Ed.), *Social Justice and Mathematics Education: Gender, Class, Ethnicity, and the Politics of Schooling* (pp. 162–179). Berlin: Freie Universität.

Lee, Valerie E., and Bryk, Anthony S. (1989). Effects of Single-Sex Secondary Schools on Student Achievement and Attitudes. *Journal of Educational Psychology*, 5, 381–395.

Leitgeb, Andrea. (1991). Geschlechtsspezifisches Rollenverhalten in der Schule. Bericht über ein Aktionsforschungsprojekt. In Elisabeth Birmily, Daniela Dablander, Ursula Rosenbichler, and Manuela Vollmann (Eds.), *Die Schule ist männlich. Zur Situation von Schülerinnen und Lehrerinnen* (pp. 59–69). Wien: Verlag für Gesellschaftskritik.

Marsh, Herbert W. (1989). Effects of Attending Single-Sex and Coeducational High Schools on Achievement, Attitudes, Behaviors, and Sex Differences. *Journal of Educational Psychology*, 1, 70–85.

Meyer, Dorit. (1999). Die Dimension des Geschlechts im Kontext des Strukturwandels der Jugend und Jugendphase. In Sozialpädagogisches Institut Berlin (Ed.), *Geschlechtersequenzen. Dokumentation des Diskussionsforums zur geschlechtsspezifischen Jugendforschung* (pp. 13–23). Berlin: Eigenverlag.

Ministerium für Familie, Frauen, Weiterbildung und Kunst und Ministerium für Kultur und Sport. (1995). *Schule der Gleichberechtigung. Eine Handreichung für Lehrerinnen und Lehrer in Baden-Württemberg zum Thema "Koedukation."* Stuttgart: Eigenverlag.

Mohanty, Chandra T. (1991). Under Western Eyes: Feminist Scholarship and Colonial

Discourses. In Chandra T. Mohanty, Ann Russo, and Lourdes Torres (Eds.), *Third World Women and the Politics of Feminism* (pp. 51–80). Bloomington: Indiana University Press.

Mura, Roberta. (1995). Feminism and Strategies for Redressing Gender Imbalance in Mathematics. In Pat Rogers and Gabriele Kaiser (Eds.), *Equity in Mathematics Education: Influences of Feminism and Culture* (pp. 155–162). London: Falmer Press.

Nicholson, Linda. (1995). Interpreting Gender. In Linda Nicholson and Steven Seidman (Eds.), *Social Postmodernism. Beyond Identity Politics* (pp. 39–67). Cambridge: Cambridge University Press.

Niederdrenk-Felgner, Cornelia. (1998). *Entdeckendes Lernen und Problemlösen im Mathematikunterricht. Studienbrief des Projekts Mädchen und Computer*. Tübingen: Deutsches Institut für Fernstudienforschung.

Offen, Karen. (1988). Defining Feminism: A Comparative Historical Approach. *Signs: Journal of Women in Culture and Society*, 1, 138–166.

Prengel, Annedore. (1986). *Konzept zum Vorhaben. Verwirklichung der Gleichstellung von Schülerinnen und Lehrerinnen an hessischen Schulen*. Sonderreihe Heft 21. Wiesbaden: Hessisches Institut für Bildungsplanung und Schulentwicklung.

Ricoeur, Paul. (1976). *Interpretation Theory: Discourse and the Surplus of Meaning*. Fort Worth: Texas Christian University Press.

Roloff, Christine, and Metz-Göckel, Sigrid. (1995). Unbeschadet des Geschlechts . . . Das Potentiale Konzept und Debatten der Frauenforschung. In Angelika Wetterer (Ed.), *Die soziale Konstruktion von Geschlecht in Professionalisierungprozessen* (pp. 263–286). Frankfurt: Campus.

Schlöglmann, Wolfgang. (1997). Der Abschied von der Technologischen Steuerung der Gesellschaft über die statistische Gerechtigkeit? Unpublished paper, Johannes Kepler University of Linz.

Schön, Donald A. (1991). *The Reflective Practitioner: How Professionals Think in Action*. Aldershot, UK: Ashgate.

Schütz, Alfred. (1971). *Gesammelte Aufsätze*. The Hague: Nijhoff.

Stadler, Helga. (2001). Geschlechtssensibler Unterricht—Individualisierung des Lehrens und Lernens unter der "Gender"-Perspektive. Der Schwerpunkt 3 des Projekts IMST[2]. In H. Niedderer (Ed.), Vorträge Frühjahrstagung des Fachverbands Didaktik der Physik in der Deutschen Physikalischen Gesellschaft Bremen 2001. Bad Honeff, Germany: Deutsche Physikalishe Gesellschaft (CD-ROM).

Stenhouse, Lawrence. (1975). *An Introduction to Curriculum Research and Development*. London: Heinemann.

Walkerdine, Valerie, and The Girls and Mathematics Unit. (1989). *Counting Girls Out*. London: Virago Press.

Walshaw, Margaret. (2001). A Foucauldian Gaze on Gender Research: What Do You Do When Confronted with the Tunnel at the End of the Light? *Journal for Research in Mathematics Education*, 32(5), 471–492.

West, Candace, and Zimmerman, Don. (1991). Doing Gender. In Judith Lorber and Susan Farell (Eds.), *The Social Construction of Gender* (pp. 13–37). Newbury Park, CA: Sage Publications.

Wetterer, Angelika. (1995a). Dekonstruktion und Alltagshandeln. Die (möglichen) Grenzen der Vergeschlechtlichung von Berufsarbeit. In Angelika Wetterer (Ed.), *Die soziale Konstruktion von Geschlecht in Professionalisierungprozessen* (pp. 223–246). Frankfurt: Campus.

Wetterer, Angelika. (1995b). Enthierarchisierung oder Dekonstruktion der Differenz. Kritische Überlegungen zur Struktur von Frauenförderung. *Zeitschrift für Hochschuldidaktik*, 2, 38–50.

Wilson, Thomas. (1981). Theorien der Interaktion und Modelle soziologischer Erklärung. In Arbeitsgruppe Bielefelder Soziologen (Eds.), *Alltagswissen, Interaktion und gesellschaftliche Wirklichkeit* (5th ed., pp. 54–80). Opladen: Westdeutscher Verlag.

Wisselinck, Erika. (1984). *Frauen denken anders*. Straßlach: Sophia-Verlag.

Chapter 2

Some Directions for Research on Equity and Justice in Mathematics Education

Laurie E. Hart

Scholarship about equity and justice in mathematics education has grown tremendously over the past 25 years and comprises many different perspectives both within countries and internationally. Much of this scholarship represents what Secada, Fennema, and Adajian (1995) call "classical" notions of equity, including issues such as differential student achievement, patterns of course taking and entrance into careers, student attitudes, and teacher-student interactions. Recently, scholarship on equity and justice in mathematics education has asked new questions and used new perspectives. For example, previously accepted notions about the place of mathematics in society have been questioned; gender, race, and social class have been problematized; and postmodern, poststructural, and postcolonial analyses have been conducted. This chapter focuses on some examples of recent research and directions for future work on equity and justice in mathematics education.

IMPORTANCE OF EQUITY AND JUSTICE IN MATHEMATICS EDUCATION

There are many reasons why issues of equity and justice are important in mathematics education. Mathematics has been used as a filter that influences who may study particular fields and who may advance to higher levels of education and career success (D'Ambrosio 1990; Popkewitz 2002; Sells 1973). However, D'Ambrosio (1990) argues that

it is misleading to see mathematics education primarily as something that prepares for a job. Instead it should be looked upon as something that prepares for full citizenship, for the exercise of all the rights and the performance of all the duties associated with citizenship in a critical and conscious way. Mathematics education ought to prepare citizens so that they will not be manipulated and cheated ... so that they will be allowed to change and to accept jobs which fulfill and appeal to their personal creativity; that is, so that individuals will be allowed the satisfaction of their own creativity and will be free to pursue personal and social fulfillment thus being able to achieve happiness. In the modern world mathematics surely interferes with this. (p. 21)

Robert Moses (Moses and Cobb 2001) posits that knowledge of algebra is the next civil rights issue for African Americans, Hispanics, and poor people in the United States. He argues that the essential issue for African Americans during the 1960s was voting rights but that now, at the beginning of the twenty-first century, knowledge of algebra is as important a gateway to freedom and opportunity as voting was 40 years ago.

In related work, Skovsmose and Valero (2001) analyzed the relationship between mathematics and democracy. They described curriculum reform documents from South Africa, Colombia, the United States, and Denmark that "seem to agree on the fact that mathematics education can contribute to the achievement of the democratic ideals of society" (p. 37). However, there is also evidence that mathematics has contributed to warfare, insecurity, disease, and the decay of the environment. In addition, mathematics has "served as a gatekeeper to participation in the decision-making processes of society" (Volmink as cited in Skovsmose and Valero 2001, p. 41). "Instead of opening opportunities for all, mathematics education generates selection, exclusion, and segregation. A demarcation is established between those who have access to the power and prestige given by mathematics and those who do not" (Skovsmose and Valero 2001, p. 41).

In countries around the world, members of certain groups identified by characteristics including gender, race, ethnicity, social class, and language have been limited in their opportunities to participate and achieve in mathematics. Members of these groups have also been limited in their freedom to pursue personal and social fulfillment, and mathematics is a part of the system that constrains them. Mathematics education plays important roles in the political, social, and economic fabric of society and is essential in addressing issues of equity and justice both within and outside of schools.

MEANINGS OF EQUITY AND JUSTICE

What do we mean by equity and justice in general and in the context of mathematics education? Because the terms *equity*, *equality*, and *justice* have been used in different ways in the literature, it is important to briefly consider some of the meanings of these terms. According to Apple (1995),

[W]ords such as equity are sliding signifiers. They do not have an essential meaning, but—as Wittgenstein (1953) reminded us—are defined by their use in real social situations with real relations of power. What equity actually means is struggled over, in the same way that concepts such as democracy are subject to different senses by differing groups with sometimes radically different ideological and educational agendas. (p. 335)

Kreinberg (1989) used equity to mean socially just outcomes in mathematics education. Grant (1989) defined equity as "fairness and justice." In the context of gender and mathematics education, Fennema (1990) discussed three definitions of equity: equity as equal educational opportunity, equity as equal educational treatment, and equity as equal education outcome. Her purpose was to explore these definitions in relationship to achieving justice for female and male students but is helpful for other equity considerations, too. Equal educational opportunity for students often means having equal opportunity to take mathematics courses and not being overtly tracked into different mathematics courses or classrooms. Although equal opportunity is important, Fennema did not see it as sufficient for a just mathematics education. Even when female and male students study mathematics in the same courses and classrooms, their experiences can be quite different, leading to different and unjust outcomes.

With respect to equity as equal educational treatment, Fennema (1990) cited many studies that document unequal treatment of female and male students in mathematics classes. (And there are examples of unequal treatment of students in mathematics classes by ethnicity and language [e.g., Moody 2001; Zevenbergen 2001].) If differential treatment were eliminated in mathematics classrooms, we would not necessarily have achieved justice. Students come to school with different backgrounds and different needs. Even though some kinds of differential treatment (e.g., teachers paying less attention to some students; teachers holding inappropriately low expectations for students based on their gender, ethnicity, or class) are certainly detrimental to students, treating all students the same will not necessarily meet their needs nor provide justice.

According to Fennema (1990),

At the end of schooling, there should be no differences in what females and males have learned, nor should there be any gender differences in how students feel about themselves as learners of mathematics. Males and females should be equally willing to pursue mathematics-related careers and should be equally able to learn new mathematics as it is required. The definition of equity as the achievement of equal outcomes offers the greatest promise for achieving true justice. (p. 5)

In several chapters of Secada's (1989b) edited book about equity in education, the authors explore conceptualizations of equity, equality, and justice. Secada (1989a) views equity as "our judgments about whether or not a given state of affairs is just" (p. 68). He traces this connection between equity and justice back to Aristotle's writings about justice and law:

There are two kinds of right and wrong conduct towards others, one provided for by written ordinances, the other by unwritten. . . . The other kind (i.e., the unwritten kind) has itself two varieties . . . (of which the second variety) makes up for the defects in a community's written code of law. This is what we call equity; people regard it as just; it is, in fact, *the sort of justice which goes beyond the written law.* (Aristotle as cited in Secada 1989a, p. 68; emphasis added)

Based on this notion, Secada argues that equity is more than following a set of rules, even if those rules were established to achieve justice. "Equity gauges the results of actions directly against standards of justice, and it is used to decide whether or not what is being done is just. Educational equity, therefore, should be construed as a check on the justice of specific actions that are carried out within the educational arena and the arrangements that result from those actions" (Secada 1989a, pp. 68-69).

In this chapter, I will use *equity,* as Secada (1989a) did, to mean justice. Secada's book provides important insights into equity. However, I think it is important for mathematics educators to further explore what we mean by equity, equality, and justice. Too often equity is defined as the absence of inequality. Many times *equity* and *justice* are used without a discussion of what they mean. A recent book from an international group concerned with equity policies and education across 13 industrialized nations was edited by Hutmacher, Cochrane, and Bottani (2001). It provides extensive discussions of equity, equality, and justice and how these concepts are related. One of the foundations for the analysis in the book is Bourdieu's work on cultural capital, economic capital, and social capital (Benadusi, 2001). A chapter by Meuret (2001) provides an extensive and provocative explanation of both old and new theories of justice along with implications of these theories for educational policy and practice. Mathematics educators may find these discussions helpful in advancing our analyses of equity, equality, and justice.

Another approach to extending our notions of equity was suggested recently by Martin (2002). He argues that in mathematics education our definitions of equity have tended to take too narrow a view and have, therefore, led to approaches to achieving equity that did not draw sufficiently on theoretical and empirical work from areas such as educational anthropology, urban education, sociology of education, and critical theory. Martin also argues that equity within mathematics education has often been viewed as an "external, top-down construct." In its place he recommends a view of

equity as it is lived and experienced (or not) by students and members of the communities to which students belong. This . . . conception of equity is likely to be related as much to students' day to day experiences in the out-of-school contexts that define their lives, their experiences with mathematics in these larger contexts, and their overall senses of self with regard to opportunities in mathematics as it is to their school-based experiences. (n.p.)

Martin's more emic view of equity could be used as a basis for research in schools and their surrounding communities so that students' and families' own conceptions of equity in mathematics education would serve as a foundation of the research rather than basing research only on conceptions of equity developed outside the particular school and community. I recommend that we consider Martin's suggestion in our research as we come to understand what equity and justice mean in particular school and community contexts.

RESOURCES NEEDED TO ACHIEVE EQUITY

Recent policy documents (e.g., Campbell and Silver 1999; National Council of Teachers of Mathematics [NCTM] 2000) acknowledge that resources are needed if equity is going to be achieved for students of mathematics. However, insufficient theory, research, and policy have focused on the details of what resources are needed and how resources can be distributed to areas where the greatest need exists. For example, an extensive infrastructure already exists in the United States to support improvements in mathematics education. The National Council of Teachers of Mathematics (1989, 1991, 1995, 2000) has developed and disseminated a series of standards documents that provide detailed descriptions of reforms that are needed in mathematics curriculum, teaching, and assessment at the elementary and secondary school levels. In addition, schools and school districts provide extensive support to teachers and administrators to guide their efforts to improve mathematics education. These policy documents and school support systems acknowledge the need to provide equitable education for diverse students but do not offer sufficiently detailed ideas about how to actually achieve equity. There is a deep need for an infrastructure to help teachers and administrators that focuses specifically on how to achieve equity in mathematics learning in specific community contexts (Weissglass 2000).

An equity infrastructure might include resources to support high levels of mathematics learning for all students (Allexsaht-Snider and Hart 2001). Financial, human, leadership, curricular, and evaluative resources are critical to equitable outcomes in mathematics. Responsibility for ensuring that these resources are available is shared by communities and the levels of government that fund, organize, and evaluate schools. Institutions of higher education also can play an important role in identifying needs and supporting efforts to improve school practice for equity.

The following financial components are examples of important resources if educators are to accomplish equitable instruction for diverse students: (1) funds for building construction and repair, (2) competitive salaries for teachers, teacher leaders, and administrators, (3) funds for implementing and maintaining smaller class sizes and collaborative planning time for teachers, (4) financial support for leadership and professional development for administrators, teachers, and families, (5) funds to provide technology for teachers and students, and (6) resources to develop and implement academic support systems for students and families.

Recruiting and retaining teachers with strong backgrounds in mathematics is an ongoing concern in many communities but particularly in poor communities. Part of the challenge of striving for equity in mathematics education is to ensure that a stable teaching staff is sustained over time. Recruiting and retaining administrators with a commitment to both equity and ongoing improvements in mathematics education is also an essential human resource.

Knowledgeable and committed educational leaders who have developed their own understanding of the ways in which racism, classism, and sexism affect mathematics teaching and learning are important features of an equity infrastructure for schools. Educational leaders need to develop capacity to improve both mathematics education and skills for providing leadership in equity in order to support teachers and diverse students and their families in mathematics learning. Administrators and teacher leaders require professional development support in the areas of: (1) identifying needed improvements in mathematics education, (2) mathematics content, (3) mathematics pedagogy, (4) inequities and strategies for equity in mathematics education, and (5) building partnerships with families and communities.

Administrators and teacher leaders need to be prepared to select and implement new curriculums and fund high-quality curricular resources that are essential to programs for improving mathematics learning for all students. Mathematics curriculum materials that are articulated and coordinated across elementary and secondary levels of schooling are needed for every teacher and student. In many communities, multiple sets of standards and assessments are used to structure programs to improve schools. This can lead to confusion on the part of administrators, teachers, parents, and students about the focus of efforts to improve mathematics education. Such confusion and lack of consensus can create formidable barriers to achieving equity in mathematics classrooms.

Administrators, researchers, teachers, and community members need structures and financing in place to support ongoing evaluation of a school's progress toward achieving equity in mathematics education. Educators can use specific data about the mathematics participation and performance of students from underrepresented groups, such as students of color, poor students, and women, as well as information about availability and distribution of resources, to assess needs. Evaluation regarding factors related to equity in mathematics education can serve as a catalyst for examining beliefs and seeking strategies to modify classroom processes and teaching practices to promote mathematics learning for all students.

Little research in mathematics education has examined the examples of resource issues discussed here. Apple (1992), Campbell and Silver (1999), Mac Iver and Balfanz (1999), and Tate (1997) have written about mathematics education policy in the United States and its relationship to equity and justice in schools and classrooms. From South Africa, Adler's (2001) examination of resource and equity issues is a good example of the type of research that is needed. More research attention needs to be focused on resources for equity. Beyond resource issues, there is a need for research that provides an integrated view of equity and social justice in mathematics education within schools and communities, focusing on students, teachers, and administrators within schools and their connections with social, cultural, and historical issues in the larger community.

MULTILEVEL FRAMEWORK FOR ANALYZING MATHEMATICS SOCIALIZATION AND IDENTITY

Martin's (2000) work is an important example of mathematics education research that integrates perspectives from a particular school, parents from the community in which the school is located, and mathematics students and teachers within the school. He examined factors that contribute to the success and failure of African American students in mathematics through a study that focused on a middle school in Oakland, California, and its surrounding community. The school, called Hillside Junior High School, served a student population with serious academic problems that was 95% African American. From this study, Martin developed a multilevel, context-based framework of sociohistorical, community, school, and intrapersonal themes to use in analyzing mathematics socialization and identity formation among African Americans. See Figure 2.1 for Martin's framework.

Sociohistorical and Community Factors

Martin studied the sociohistorical and community influences on students' mathematics socialization and identity through extensive interviews with 10 parents and community members who lived near Hillside Junior High. The adults Martin interviewed were African American and from a range of socioeconomic levels—lower socioeconomic level, working-class, or middle-class. Although these adults were from the community near Hillside, none of them were parents of the seventh-grade students Martin studied.

In the interviews with community members, Martin found that opportunities and rewards denied to African Americans in the past and present had an impact on their daily lives. For example, Harold, a 55-year-old African American man, described the social climate in the United States during the 1950s and 1960s in which he and other African Americans responded with rage to the inequities they faced. Harold has been deeply affected by the differential treatment he had experienced "for no reason other than his race" (p. 41). This treatment communicated to Harold that "his opportunities in life would be limited" (p. 41), and there were some areas of life where there was no sense even trying.

Harold said the racism and differential treatment he experienced affected his motivation in school. He did not see opportunities for employment that required extensive education in mathematics. Harold decided that multiplication and division of fractions and decimals was the most advanced mathematics he would need for the kinds of jobs that would be open to him. So he did not learn any mathematics beyond that. Even more important, Harold did not put any pressure

Figure 2.1
Multilevel Framework for Analyzing Mathematics Socialization and Identity among African Americans: Key Themes

---

Sociohistorical

- Differential treatment in mathematics-related contexts

Community

- Beliefs about African American status and differential treatment in educational and socioeconomic contexts
- Beliefs about mathematics abilities and motivation to learn mathematics
- Beliefs about the instrumental importance of mathematics knowledge
- Relationships with school officials and teachers
- Math-dependent socioeconomic and educational goals
- Expectations for children and educational strategies

School

- Institutional agency and school-based support systems
- Teachers' curricular goals and content decisions
- Teachers' beliefs about student abilities and motivation to learn
- Teachers' beliefs about African American parents and communities
- Student culture and achievement norms
- Classroom negotiation of mathematical and social norms

Agency and Mathematics Success among African American Students

- Personal identities and goals
- Perceptions of school climate, peers, and teachers
- Beliefs about mathematics abilities and motivation to learn
- Beliefs about the instrumental importance of mathematics knowledge
- Beliefs about differential treatment from peers

Source: Martin 2000, p. 30.

on his 17-year-old son to excel in mathematics or to continue his education beyond high school. Harold's expectations for his son in mathematics were "just to pass" (p. 46) and to achieve at about the same level Harold had.

In the four case studies of parents presented in his book, Martin (2000) describes adults with school-age children. Each of the parents had negative experiences in school and with mathematics. Two of the four parents had set limited goals for themselves and their children based on their negative experiences early in life. These children were not achieving beyond the goals set for them by their parents. The other two parents developed new educational and socioeconomic goals for themselves and their children even though these parents had negative experiences with mathematics and in school. In both cases where the parents had developed new views of mathematics and more positive mathematics identities, their children were doing well in school and in mathematics.

In his interviews, Martin found that the majority of the parents in the study had negative views of teachers. Several held the belief that their children's teachers were prejudiced against black children and did not insist on learning by black students. These findings along with the negative experiences with mathematics of many of the community members contribute to an understanding of the importance of school-community relationships. It is important for research in mathematics education to examine not only the sociocultural contexts within classrooms and schools but also the sociocultural contexts in the communities that are served by schools. Martin's work also leads mathematics educators to pay closer attention to the mathematics socialization and identity held by community members and parents in the past.

School Factors

One reason Martin selected Hillside as the site for his study was the Algebra Project curriculum the mathematics teachers were implementing. The Algebra Project is compatible with the recommendations in the NCTM *Standards* (1989, 1991, 1995) and was developed by Robert Moses and colleagues (Moses and Cobb 2001). It is designed to develop students' understanding of mathematics so that students are ready to study algebra in grades 8 and 9 and proceed to high-track, college preparatory mathematics during high school. This approach to mathematics curriculum and teaching was created specifically for African American students and has been used with students from many groups in several different areas of the United States. The Algebra Project stresses experiential learning, communication of mathematical ideas, cooperative learning, emphasis on multiple representations, and problem solving.

Martin spent many months observing in seventh-grade mathematics classrooms at Hillside and participating as an extra helper for students in the mathematics classes of three teachers. He also interviewed the teachers individually. Martin identified

five general goals that appeared to guide [teachers'] in-class behaviors and interactions with their students . . . : (a) raising the achievement and motivation levels of students, (b) changing student beliefs about the nature of mathematical practice, (c) changing student beliefs about the instrumental importance of mathematics, (d) adhering to standards and beginning to implement reform-oriented activities, and (e) increasing parental involvement and awareness of students' in-class activities. (p. 97)

Based on the data collected in mathematics classrooms, Martin found resistance to the reform curriculum by many students. Even though the teachers consistently worked to connect the mathematics curriculum to everyday aspects of students' lives, some students did not believe they were really doing mathematics when they were engaged in activities that were not textbook or worksheet assignments. Many students paid little attention to classroom activities and assignments in mathematics, and the majority of students did not view mathematical knowledge and learning as important. Further, these negative attitudes toward school and mathematics on the part of some students made it difficult for others to allow their peers to see that they liked mathematics and were capable of doing well in it. In addition, the teachers felt that lack of support from parents affected students' attitudes and their learning of mathematics.

Martin's examination of the school context was important in understanding the experiences of the African American students in his study. Many studies about equity in mathematics education have focused on the mathematics curriculum and teachers' practices and interactions with students without studying the school context. To understand what is happening in an individual mathematics classroom it is important to examine the experiences of teachers both inside and outside the classroom and the culture of the school as a whole.

Successful African American Students

The final level of Martin's framework focuses on agency and mathematics success among African American students. The primary data for this level of the framework were gathered from extensive observations inside and outside of classrooms and from interviews conducted with seven students he identified as successful in mathematics. The seven students were selected from a larger group of 35 successful mathematics students Martin observed. He presents extensive narratives from these seven successful students.

Martin used the term "mathematics identity" to describe students' beliefs about their ability to learn mathematics, their motivation to learn mathematics, and their beliefs about the instrumental importance of mathematics. Most of the successful students expressed strong beliefs in their ability to learn mathematics and high levels of motivation to be successful mathematics students. Most were not satisfied with any grade other than an A in mathematics and would be very concerned with lower grades. Further, most of these students indicated that mathematics was their favorite subject, but even the students for whom mathematics was not their favorite subject saw the importance of doing well in it. In addition, each of the seven students highlighted by Martin made strong statements about the value of mathematics for their future life, describing the benefits of mathematics knowledge for getting into college or getting a good job.

Among the successful students, there was a consistent perception that a majority of their peers were underachievers and did not take full advantage of the opportunities available to them in school. These students often commented on the negative aspects of their school atmosphere and pointed out how these factors disrupted their studies. . . . They readily identified groups of students whom they considered "the bad kids" and those whom [they] considered "the nerds" or "good kids." They consistently placed themselves in the "good kids" group and did not care about negative labels that their peers tried to assign them. (pp. 165–166)

Martin's successful students described how they were treated by their peers because they were good students. This ranged from "good-natured teasing and being called 'nerd' to accusations of trying to 'act White.' Despite this teasing, most maintained a strong resolve to continue in the pursuit of their goals and not let the actions of others deter them" (p. 167). The successful students held on to their long-term goals and the notion that their hard work would pay off later in life.

Though the successful students were critical of some teachers and some aspects of the school's administration, they were mainly positive about the school faculty. Most of the successful students were respectful of their teachers and appreciative of the instruction teachers offered. This was not the case with many of the less successful students Martin observed. Many of them were openly disrespectful of teachers and engaged in disruptive behavior during class.

The student narratives were powerful in communicating that a number of African American students at Hillside were successful in mathematics even though they faced many forces in the school and the community that could easily have blocked that success. This focus on students' agency and identity in the face of severe obstacles is an important finding from Martin's research. He acknowledges the importance of the school setting, the curriculum and pedagogy used by the teachers, the influence of parents, and the attitudes of members of the community outside of school. And he does not hide the complexity of the forces that contribute to students' success and failure in mathematics. Within the framework developed by Martin, student agency is a powerful element in students' success in school and mathematics. It will be important for additional research to examine the role of individual student agency in the attainment of success in mathematics and school.

One reason Martin's study is important is that it highlights students who are successful in the face of numerous barriers to success. He studied an individual school in a particular cultural context. His integration of perspectives from teachers, curriculum, students, parents, and the surrounding community is valuable as a model for future research. Martin's work is an example of how a qualitative study can move beyond earlier research about students' attitudes, teachers' perspectives of students, and teacher-student interactions. Rather than only understanding attitudes or teacher-student interactions, his study helps us gain a much more complex view of students and teachers in the context of a particular school and community.

PEDAGOGIES FOR EQUITY AND SOCIAL JUSTICE

Many researchers in mathematics education are now working to develop pedagogies for creating a more just society. This scholarship builds on a number of theoretical foundations and acknowledges structural patterns in society that systematically sustain privilege based on race, gender, wealth, and language. These pedagogies are situated within many different literatures, including critical mathematics education (e.g., Skovsmose 1994; Skovsmose and Nielsen 1996), ethnomathematics (e.g., Barton 1996; Borba 1990; D'Ambrosio 1997; Frankenstein 1995; Freire, D'Ambrosio, and Mendonca 1997; Gerdes 1996; Stillman and Balatti 2001), feminist pedagogy (e.g., Goodell and Parker 2001; Jacobs 1994; Solar 1995), culturally relevant pedagogy (e.g., Gutstein 2002; Gutstein et al. 1997; Ladson-Billings 1995, 1997; Tate 1995), socially just pedagogy (e.g., Burton 1996), politics of mathematics education (e.g., Kitchen 2001; Mellin-Olsen 1987), and sociocultural aspects of mathematics education (e.g., Wong, Taha, and Veloo 2001). In this section, I will highlight a few of the threads that run through this work on pedagogy for equity and social justice.

Culturally Relevant Pedagogy

Ladson-Billings's (1995) research on culturally relevant pedagogy has implications for mathematics teaching even though it was not conducted exclusively with mathematics teachers (Ladson-Billings 1997). She spent three years studying the pedagogical practices of eight teachers who were recognized as exemplary elementary school teachers who were successful with African American students in a particular low-income school district in northern California. In brief, the teachers Ladson-Billings studied "(a) believed that all the students were capable of academic success, (b) saw their pedagogy as art—unpredictable, always in the process of becoming, (c) saw themselves as members of the community, (d) saw teaching as a way to give back to the community, and (e) believed in a Freirean notion of 'teaching as mining' or pulling knowledge out" (1995, pp. 478–479). Further, the teachers "(a) maintain[ed] fluid student-teacher relationships, (b) demonstrate[d] a connectedness with all of the students, (c) develope[d] a community of learners, and (d) encourage[d] students to learn collaboratively and be responsible for [one] another" (p. 480). The teachers had particular conceptions of the curriculum and how to assess student knowledge: "(a) Knowledge is not static; it is shared, recycled, and constructed. (b) Knowledge must be viewed critically. (c) Teachers must be passionate about knowledge and learning. (d) Teachers must *scaffold*, or build bridges, to facilitate learning. (e) Assessment must be multifaceted, incorporating multiple forms of excellence" (p. 481).

Ladson-Billings (1997) wrote about the explicit connections between her model of culturally relevant pedagogy and mathematics education. For example, she described a teacher who taught algebra to her regular sixth-grade students using an approach that ensured high levels of involvement among her low-income African American students:

Mathematics in Margaret's class was a nonstop affair. . . . Although her students were engaged in problem solving using algebraic functions, no worksheets were handed out, no problem sets were assigned. The students, as well as Margaret, posed problems. . . . By asking a series of probing questions, Margaret was able to help students organize their thinking about a problem and develop their problem-solving strategies. (p. 703)

Margaret's high expectations and insistence that each and every child in her classroom could and would learn algebra are examples of her pedagogy for equity in mathematics education.

Belongingness and Engagement in Culturally Relevant Pedagogy

In a review of literature on equity in mathematics education, Allexsaht-Snider and Hart (2001) identified the concepts of *belongingness* and *engagement* as essential in supporting equity in mathematics classrooms. Belongingness focuses on the extent to which each student *senses* that she or he belongs "as an important and active participant in all aspects of the learning process" (Ames, 1992, p. 263) in mathematics. This sense of belongingness can be fostered by many different aspects of classroom processes and becomes evident in students' sense of confidence about learning mathematics and their attitudes about participating in the community of mathematics learners.

The concept of engagement is drawn partly from the *Principles and Standards for School Mathematics* of NCTM (2000) and partly from anthropological work in schools with Native Hawaiian students by D'Amato (1993). NCTM's vision includes the notion that "students will confidently engage in complex mathematical tasks . . . work productively and reflectively . . . communicate their ideas and results effectively . . . [and] value mathematics" (2000, p. 3). Contrary to this vision, the *Principles and Standards* assert that "too many students disengage from school mathematics" (p. 371). A number of reasons for student disengagement related to motivation and confidence in learning mathematics are outlined in the *Principles and Standards*. Students may find parts of the content difficult and abstract, or they may not find it interesting or relevant. Based on beliefs communicated by parents, teachers, peers, and the media that high achievement in mathematics is only necessary and valuable for certain groups, students may have developed low expectations for themselves.

D'Amato (1993) offers insight that expands educators' understanding of why students might disengage from school mathematics. His research with Native Hawaiian students indicated that students who neither found value in the direct experience of schooling nor saw how school could lead to long-term life goals were likely to disengage. D'Amato's perspective urges educators to go beyond the *Principles and Standards'* recommendation for interesting and relevant curriculum and suggests that culturally relevant classroom processes are necessary to foster diverse students' engagement and sense of belongingness in the mathematics classroom.

Allexsaht-Snider and Hart (2001) argue that the extent to which students feel they belong as members of the community in the mathematics classroom is related to how deeply and completely they engage in efforts to learn mathematics and the degree to which they find the cultural patterns embedded in classroom processes accessible. Reference to a student's sense of belongingness highlights the relationship between students' confidence and motivation in mathematics and their active participation in mathematics classroom processes. When students have a limited sense that they belong, it is important for teachers to use appropriate strategies to help students connect mathematics and their goals in and out of the classroom.

The work of Tate (1995) provides an example of how a teacher's strategies for engagement fostered a sense of belongingness in the mathematics community for students. He used culturally relevant pedagogy in his collaboration with a teacher in a predominantly African American middle school in Texas who developed a program for students that focused on community problem solving. One class was concerned about the 13 liquor stores located near their school and decided to communicate their concerns to key government agencies. They were assisted by a newspaper editor who helped them develop mathematically based arguments that caused students to raise questions such as: "Will percentages, decimals, fractions, or whole numbers make a more striking impression? How can we minimize the appearance of data or variables that may weaken the public perception of our position?" (p. 170). Eventually the students' work resulted in the removal of two of the liquor stores and a city council resolution prohibiting the consumption of alcohol within 600 feet of the school.

Engagement and a sense of belongingness are missing for many students of mathematics in a variety of social contexts in countries around the world. An important goal for mathematics educators is to develop approaches to teaching that engage the specific students in mathematics classrooms and develop a sense that they belong in the community of the classroom and the larger community of people who know and use mathematics.

Social Justice and Culturally Relevant Pedagogy

The goal of research by Gutstein (2002; Gutstein et al. 1997) in the United States was to create social justice through a culturally relevant pedagogy to educate students for empowerment. He taught mathematics in an elementary/middle school in a Mexican American neighborhood in a large midwestern city. When Gutstein (2002) conducted his most recent study, he had full responsibility for teaching a seventh-grade mathematics class in this school and continued to teach the same group of students during the eighth grade. For Gutstein, an important principle of culturally relevant pedagogy is that students are empowered to critique society and act on that critique to change society. He helped students understand the sociopolitical dynamics in their world and helped them pose questions about the forces and institutions at work. For example, he asked questions such as: "Why is the complexion of your neighborhood changing, and what's behind those changes?" (p. 4). To remedy unjust situations, Gutstein argues that students need a sense of agency, that is, "a belief in themselves as people who can make a difference in the world. . . . Educators working towards an equitable and just society cannot only help students develop a sophisticated understanding of power relations in society, but as well, the belief in themselves as conscious actors in the world" (p. 4). Gutstein also helped students "develop positive social and cultural identities by validating their language and culture and helping them uncover and understand their history" (p. 5).

Gutstein accomplished the goals of developing a sociopolitical consciousness, agency, and positive social and cultural identities by assigning his students "several real-world mathematics projects in which students investigated various forms of discrimination and inequity using mathematics as a key analytical tool" (p. 3). In one of Gutstein's projects the students "simulated the distribution of wealth in the world by continent, using cookies as the 'wealth' and people as the 'continents.' [Gutstein and his students] randomly distributed the students . . . to each continent based on the continent's percentage of the world population, then distributed the cookies in like manner. When the four people in Africa received one cookie [among them], the inequality was clear" (p. 10). Gutstein and his students then conducted a similar analysis of inequalities in wealth within the United States. Gutstein's students gained a sense of the unfairness of wealth distribution in the United States and around the world; they also saw an example of using mathematics as a tool to conduct social analysis.

Socially Just Pedagogy

Burton (1996) examined socially just pedagogy and feminism in mathematics. She argues that the pervasive myth of mathematics as an objective discipline distorts how mathematics is taught and learned. The way that mathematics is often taught, as a set of rules and algorithms to be memorized, leaves students with a fragmented view of mathematics that limits their conceptions of mathematics and how to learn it. Burton believes that a socially just pedagogy would shift the authority from a fixed, objective mathematics to the learners themselves, drawing on and validating the knowledge and skills they bring to the classroom.

Instead of allowing pupils to be "grossly underestimated," we need to accord them respect for what they know and can do and place them in a context where they generate, compare and negotiate meanings amongst themselves. In this way not only would we be working on the educative function of the classroom, but we would also be nearer to the potential multiple meanings present in the mathematics. (p. 141)

Ethnomathematics and Pedagogy

There is a huge literature within mathematics education on ethnomathematics. Ubiratan D'Ambrosio, a mathematician and mathematics educator from Brazil, has been instrumental in the development of ethnomathematics. In an extensive review of international work on ethnomathematics, Gerdes (1996, p. 909) defined ethnomathematics as the "cultural anthropology of mathematics and mathematical education . . . [lying] at the confluence of mathematics and cultural anthropology." The views of pedagogy within the literature on ethnomathematics are compatible with work on culturally relevant pedagogy. However, pedagogy is only one piece of the large body of work on ethnomathematics. Ethnomathematics argues that mathematics is a cultural product and that every culture and subculture has developed its own forms of mathematics. Further,

ethnomathematicians emphasise and analyse the influences of sociocultural factors on the teaching, learning and development of mathematics. . . . Ethnomathematicians try to contribute to and affirm the knowledge of the mathematical realisations of . . . formerly colonised peoples. They look for cultural elements which have survived colonialism and which reveal mathematical and other scientific thinking. [In addition,] ethnomathematicians also look for . . . *cultural elements and activities* that may serve as a *starting point* for doing and elaborating mathematics in the classroom. (pp. 917–918)

Mellin-Olsen's (1987) work on the politics of mathematics education can be placed within ethnomathematics. Mellin-Olsen did extensive work to develop pedagogy that helps students apply mathematics to real problems in their world. Other typical approaches to pedagogy within ethnomathematics emphasize learning activities in which students critique power relations within society and use mathematics to make changes in their community (e.g., Frankenstein 1995).

Feminist Pedagogy

Feminist pedagogies provide additional approaches to teaching for equity and social justice. The writings of Jacobs (1994), Solar (1995), and Goodell and Parker (2001) discuss pedagogy designed with feminist theories as a foundation. Solar developed a detailed model of inclusive mathematics education that combines "elements of feminist pedagogy, non-discriminatory classroom practices, and guidelines for an inclusive pedagogy in mathematics education" (1995, p. 325). Her model encourages teachers to use strategies that will involve all students actively in the learning processes of mathematics. Inclusive pedagogy also encourages the use of cooperative learning and other pedagogical approaches that make it easier for students to speak in class. The contributions of women in mathematics are highlighted as are applications of mathematics using situations related to women's lives. Solar's inclusive pedagogy is compatible with both ethnomathematics and culturally relevant pedagogy. Jacobs (1994) describes a feminist pedagogy for mathematics based on *Women's Ways of Knowing* (Belenky et al. 1986). *Women's Ways of Knowing* explores how women know and how their ways of knowing differ from men's. Jacobs uses women's ways of knowing to design a mathematics pedagogy that is more hospitable to female students, being careful to avoid language that may be alienating to females such as problems that are *tackled* and content that is *mastered*. She also explores ways to use experiential and intuitive knowing to prove a mathematical theorem as opposed to using the typical deductive argument. Jacobs's feminist pedagogy also emphasizes an egalitarian classroom environment in which students learn from each other (in addition to learning from the teacher) and share their ideas with one another individually, in small groups, and with the entire class. She also emphasizes learning activities that make extensive use of writing as a means of learning mathematics. The approaches to feminist pedagogy described by Solar, Goodell and Parker, and Jacobs "capitalize on females' strengths and interests in order to facilitate their success in mathematics" (Jacobs 1994, p. 16).

Synthesis of Research on Pedagogies for Equity and Social Justice

There are a number of themes that run through these examples of pedagogies for equity and social justice. Teachers' and students' traditional conceptions of the nature of mathematics are questioned. Mathematics is viewed as a social and cultural construction. Ways are explored to involve students more actively in the exploration of mathematics through student-centered activities and group activities. And real problems in the world of the students are examined and solved. In many cases the teachers and students identify examples of injustice in their community and work to make changes in that community. Some important themes in these pedagogies focus on teachers' expectations that all students are able to learn mathematics and will need to use mathematics in their work and personal lives. Equity pedagogy involves an insistence on the part of teachers that all students develop a sense of belongingness and engagement in the mathematics classroom community.

DIRECTIONS FOR RESEARCH

As we consider directions for future research, it would be beneficial if issues of equity and social justice played a bigger role in mathematics education research. Too often equity is at the margins of mathematics education efforts to improve theory and practice (Meyer 1989; Secada 1992, 1995). Leder (2001) reported an analysis of how often papers about gender issues were included in the proceedings of the conferences organized by the International Group for the Psychology of Mathematics Education (PME) over the past 25 years. She found that a large percentage of the participants in PME conferences were female, but she raised questions about the research on gender and mathematics that was represented in the conference proceedings.

Where are the reports of research studies . . . in which more radical feminist perspectives are being adopted, females are less frequently considered as a homogeneous group, and fine grained rather than collective data are presented? Where are the reports of scholarly evaluations of large scale interventions? Or detailed case studies which focus on individual rather than group differences? Or reflective accounts of the impact of the personal beliefs and theoretical orientation of the researchers undertaking the research on design of the study, data gathering decisions, choice of instrumentation? (p. 53)

As we continue our efforts to achieve equity in mathematics education, we still need to conduct classical studies of equity that explore differential student achievement, patterns of course taking and entrance into careers, student attitudes, and teacher-student interactions. These studies are needed within individual schools and school districts, for individual states and countries, and across countries. It is also important for us to go beyond such studies. We need to explore further what we mean by equity and social justice, and what students and families in particular sociocultural contexts mean by equity and social justice in mathematics education. We also need research that examines the roles that differential resource availability plays in gaps between groups in mathematics achievement and participation in optional mathematics courses.

More research like that conducted by Martin (2000) is needed in which the perspectives about teachers, curriculum, students, parents, and the surrounding community are integrated. Further, more research is needed that examines the historical relationship of marginalized groups to mathematics and how these groups' relationship with mathematics facilitates or hinders their opportunities for success within society.

Scholarship on pedagogies for equity and social justice has expanded greatly during the past 10 years, but more is needed. Research is needed that examines the existing models of equity pedagogy and how well they work for different kinds of students in different social and cultural contexts. The question of how well these pedagogies work is complex. It is not clear what criteria should be used to determine if a pedagogy is working. Certainly it is important to understand how well students learn mathematics as well as how motivated and interested they are. How do we measure student learning? The pressure to use standardized achievement tests as the main criterion of student learning in mathematics is extreme in the United States. This limited criterion puts undue pressure on teachers and students to limit the curriculum and activities to a focus on objective mathematics tasks similar to the ones on standardized tests. More research is needed that explores how assessment of students' mathematics learning can contribute positively to their learning as well as research that examines the potential negative effects of high-stakes testing on diverse students.

It would be helpful for individual teachers or groups of teachers to study their own practice to achieve equity. Wilson and Hart (2001) recently described strategies and questions mathematics teachers can use to examine gender issues through teacher research. Teacher research that focuses on equity pedagogy would be especially helpful in building both theory and practice. Collaborations between researchers and classroom teachers would also be valuable in extending the existing models of pedagogy for equity in mathematics education.

There is also a need for more research that explores constructs such as student motivation, socialization, identity, and agency with respect to mathematics. Traditional measures of attitudes toward mathematics as developed by Fennema and Sherman (1976) and others have been important in research on equity in mathematics education. Mathematics education research needs to extend the traditional measures of attitudes and to explore new theoretical foundations from sociology, cultural psychology, and anthropology. Research is also needed that deconstructs traditional attitudinal variables such as confidence and usefulness to provide a more complex view of students' conceptions of mathematics and themselves as learners of mathematics. Qualitative research that examines students' attitudes and motivation in the context of mathematics curriculum, pedagogy, and assessment as well as the school and community context will be important.

In this chapter I have presented a few ideas from recent scholarship on equity and justice in mathematics education that hold promise for future research and practice. There is no question that there is a need for more research on equity in mathematics education. Student characteristics such as gender, race, ethnicity, language proficiency, and socioeconomic status often make a difference in the quality of education students receive and the achievement level they attain in mathematics and in school more generally. As long as this continues to be true, equity issues will be an important concern for mathematics education researchers, practitioners, and policymakers.

REFERENCES

Adler, Jill. (2001). Resourcing Practice and Equity: A Dual Challenge for Mathematics Education. In Bill Atweh, Helen Forgasz, and Ben Nebres (Eds.), *Sociocultural Research on Mathematics Education: An International Perspective* (pp. 185–200). Mahwah, NJ: Lawrence Erlbaum.

Allexsaht-Snider, Martha, and Hart, Laurie E. (2001). "Mathematics for All": How Do We Get There? *Theory into Practice*, 40(2), 93–101.

Ames, Carol. (1992). Classrooms: Goals, Structures, and Student Motivation. *Journal of Educational Psychology*, 84, 261–271.

Apple, Michael W. (1992). Do the Standards Go Far Enough? Power, Policy, and Practice in Mathematics Education. *Journal for Research in Mathematics Education*, 23, 412–431.

Apple, Michael W. (1995). Taking Power Seriously: New Directions in Equity in Mathematics Education and Beyond. In Walter G. Secada, Elizabeth Fennema, and Lisa Byrd Adajian (Eds.), *New Directions for Equity in Mathematics Education* (pp. 329–348). Cambridge: Cambridge University Press.

Barton, Bill. (1996). Anthropological Perspectives on Mathematics and Mathematics Education. In Alan J. Bishop, Ken Clements, Christine Keitel, Jeremy Kilpatrick, and Colette Laborde (Eds.), *International Handbook of Mathematics Education* (pp. 1035–1053). Dordrecht, The Netherlands: Kluwer.

Belenky, Mary F., Clinchy, Blythe M., Goldberger, Nancy R., and Tarule, Jill M. (1986). *Women's Ways of Knowing: The Development of Self, Voice, and Mind*. New York: Basic Books.

Benadusi, Luciano. (2001). Equity and Education: A Critical Review of Sociological Research and Thought. In Walo Hutmacher, Douglas Cochrane, and Norberto Bottani (Eds.), *In Pursuit of Equity in Education: Using International Indicators to Compare Equity Policies* (pp. 25–64). Dordrecht: Kluwer Academic Publishers.

Borba, Marcelo C. (1990). Ethnomathematics and Education. *For the Learning of Mathematics*, 10(1), 39–43.

Burton, Leone. (1996). A Socially Just Pedagogy for the Teaching of Mathematics. In Patricia F. Murphy and Caroline V. Gipps (Eds.), *Equity in the Classroom: Towards Effective Pedagogy for Girls and Boys* (pp. 136–145). London: Falmer.

Campbell, Patricia F., and Silver, Edward A. (1999). *Teaching and Learning Mathematics in Poor Communities: A Report to the Board of Directors of the National Council of Teachers of Mathematics*. Reston, VA: National Council of Teachers of Mathematics.

D'Amato, John. (1993). Resistance and Compliance in Minority Classrooms. In Evelyn Jacob and Cathie Jordan (Eds.), *Minority Education: Anthropological Perspectives* (pp. 181–207). Norwood, NJ: Ablex.

D'Ambrosio, Ubiratan. (1990). The Role of Mathematics Education in Building a Democratic and Just Society. *For the Learning of Mathematics*, 10(3), 20–23.

D'Ambrosio, Ubiratan. (1997). Where Does Ethnomathematics Stand Nowadays? *For the Learning of Mathematics*, 17(2), 13–17.

Fennema, Elizabeth. (1990). Justice, Equity, and Mathematics Education. In Elizabeth Fennema and Gilah C. Leder (Eds.), *Mathematics and Gender* (pp. 1–9). New York: Teachers College Press.

Fennema, Elizabeth, and Sherman, Julia. (1976). Fennema-Sherman Mathematics Attitude Scales. *JSAS: Catalog of Selected Documents in Psychology*, 6(1), 31. (Ms. No. 1225)

Frankenstein, Marilyn. (1995). Equity in Mathematics Education: Class in the World Outside the Class. In Walter G. Secada, Elizabeth Fennema, and Lisa Byrd Adajian (Eds.), *New Directions for Equity in Mathematics Education* (pp. 165–190). Cambridge: Cambridge University Press.

Freire, Paulo, D'Ambrosio, Ubiratan, and Mendonca, Maria do Carmo. (1997). A Conversation with Paulo Freire. *For the Learning of Mathematics*, 17(3), 7–10.

Gerdes, Paulus. (1996). Ethnomathematics and Mathematics Education. In Alan J. Bishop, Ken Clements, Christine Keitel, Jeremy Kilpatrick, and Colette Laborde

(Eds.), *International Handbook of Mathematics Education* (pp. 909–943). Dordrecht: Kluwer Academic Publishers.

Goodell, Joanne E., and Parker, Lesley H. (2001). Creating a Connected, Equitable Mathematics Classroom: Facilitating Gender Equity. In Bill Atweh, Helen Forgasz, and Ben Nebres (Eds.), *Sociocultural Research on Mathematics Education: An International Perspective* (pp. 411–431). Mahwah, NJ: Lawrence Erlbaum.

Grant, Carl A. (1989). Equity, Equality, Teachers, and Classroom Life. In Walter G. Secada (Ed.), *Equity in Education* (pp. 89–102). Philadelphia, PA: Falmer.

Gutstein, Eric. (2002). *Roads towards Equity in Mathematics Education: Helping Students Develop a Sense of Agency.* Paper presented at the meeting of the American Educational Research Association, New Orleans, LA, April.

Gutstein, Eric, Lipman, Pauline, Hernandez, Patricia, and de los Reyes, Rebeca. (1997). Culturally Relevant Mathematics Teaching in a Mexican American Context. *Journal for Research in Mathematics Education, 28*(6), 709–737.

Hutmacher, Walo, Cochrane, Douglas, and Bottani, Norberto (Eds.). (2001). *In Pursuit of Equity in Education: Using International Indicators to Compare Equity Policies.* Dordrecht: Kluwer Academic Publishers.

Jacobs, Judith E. (1994). Feminist Pedagogy and Mathematics. *ZDM Zentralblatt fur Didaktik der Mathematik, 26*(1), 12–17.

Kitchen, Richard S. (2001). The Sociopolitical Context of Mathematics Education in Guatemala Through the Words and Practices of Two Teachers. In Bill Atweh, Helen Forgasz, and Ben Nebres (Eds.), *Sociocultural Research on Mathematics Education: An International Perspective* (pp. 151–162). Mahwah, NJ: Lawrence Erlbaum.

Kreinberg, Nancy. (1989). The Practice of Equity. *Peabody Journal of Education, 66*(2), 127–146.

Ladson-Billings, Gloria. (1995). Toward a Theory of Culturally Relevant Pedagogy. *American Educational Research Journal, 32*(3), 465–491.

Ladson-Billings, Gloria. (1997). It Doesn't Add Up: African American Students' Mathematics Achievement. *Journal for Research in Mathematics Education, 28*(6), 697–708.

Leder, Gilah C. (2001). Pathways in Mathematics towards Equity: A 25 Year Journey. In Marja van den Heuvel-Panhuizen (Ed.), *Proceedings of the 25th Conference of the International Group for the Psychology of Mathematics Education* (Vol. 1, pp. 41–54). Utrecht, The Netherlands: Freudenthal Institute, Utrecht University.

Mac Iver, Douglas, and Balfanz, Robert. (1999). *The School District's Role in Helping Poverty Schools Become High Performing.* Paper presented at the Mid-Continent Research for Education and Learning (McREL) Diversity Roundtable, Aurora, CO, November.

Martin, Danny Bernard. (2000). *Mathematics Success and Failure among African-American Youth: The Roles of Sociohistorical Context, Community Forces, School Influence, and Individual Agency.* Mahwah, NJ: Lawrence Erlbaum.

Martin, Danny Bernard. (2002). *Is There a There There? Avoiding Equity Traps in Mathematics Education and Some Additional Considerations in Mathematics Achievement and Persistence among Underrepresented Students.* Paper presented at the meeting of the American Educational Research Association, New Orleans, LA, April.

Mellin-Olsen, Stieg. (1987). *The Politics of Mathematics Education*. Dordrecht: Kluwer Academic Publishers.

Meuret, Denis. (2001). School Equity as a Matter of Justice. In Walo Hutmacher, Douglas Cochrane, and Norberto Bottani (Eds.), *In Pursuit of Equity in Education: Using International Indicators to Compare Equity Policies* (pp. 93–111). Dordrecht: Kluwer Academic Publishers.

Meyer, Margaret R. (1989). Equity: The Missing Element in Recent Agendas for Mathematics Education. *Peabody Journal of Education*, 66(2), 6–21.

Moody, Vivian R. (2001). The Social Constructs of the Mathematical Experiences of African-American Students. In Bill Atweh, Helen Forgasz, and Ben Nebres (Eds.), *Sociocultural Research on Mathematics Education: An International Perspective* (pp. 255–276). Mahwah, NJ: Lawrence Erlbaum.

Moses, Robert P., and Cobb, Charles E., Jr. (2001). *Radical Equations: Math Literacy and Civil Rights*. Boston: Beacon.

National Council of Teachers of Mathematics (NCTM). (1989). *Curriculum and Evaluation Standards for School Mathematics*. Reston, VA: Author.

National Council of Teachers of Mathematics (NCTM). (1991). *Professional Standards for Teaching Mathematics*. Reston, VA: Author.

National Council of Teachers of Mathematics (NCTM). (1995). *Assessment Standards for School Mathematics*. Reston, VA: Author.

National Council of Teachers of Mathematics (NCTM). (2000). *Principles and Standards for School Mathematics*. Reston, VA: Author.

Popkewitz, Thomas S. (2002). Whose Heaven and Whose Redemption? The Alchemy of the Mathematics Curriculum to Save (Please Check One or All of the Following: (a) The Economy, (b) Democracy, (c) the Nation, (d) Human Rights, (e) the Welfare State, (f) the Individual). In Paola Valero and Ole Skovsmose (Eds.), *Proceedings of the Third International MES Conference* (pp. 1–26). Copenhagen: Centre for Research in Learning Mathematics.

Secada, Walter, G. (1989a). Educational Equity versus Equality of Education: An Alternative Conception. In Walter G. Secada (Ed.), *Equity in Education* (pp. 68–88). Philadelphia, PA: Falmer.

Secada, Walter, G. (Ed.). (1989b). *Equity in Education*. Philadelphia, PA: Falmer.

Secada, Walter, G. (1992). Race, Ethnicity, Social Class, Language, and Achievement in Mathematics. In Douglas Grouws (Ed.), *Handbook of Research on Mathematics Teaching and Learning* (pp. 623–660). New York: Macmillan.

Secada, Walter G. (1995). Social and Critical Dimensions for Equity in Mathematics Education. In Walter G. Secada, Elizabeth Fennema, and Lisa Byrd Adajian (Eds.), *New Directions for Equity in Mathematics Education* (pp. 146–164). Cambridge: Cambridge University Press.

Secada, Walter G., Fennema, Elizabeth, and Adajian, Lisa Byrd (Eds.). (1995). *New Directions for Equity in Mathematics Education*. Cambridge: Cambridge University Press.

Sells, Lucy. (1973). *High School Mathematics as the Critical Filter in the Job Market*. Berkeley: University of California Press. (ERIC Document Reproduction Service No. ED 080 351)

Skovsmose, Ole. (1994). *Towards a Philosophy of Critical Mathematics Education*. Dordrecht: Kluwer Academic Publishers.

Skovsmose, Ole, and Nielsen, Lene. (1996). Critical Mathematics Education. In Alan J. Bishop, Ken Clements, Christine Keitel, Jeremy Kilpatrick, and Colette Laborde (Eds.), *International Handbook of Mathematics Education* (pp. 1257–1288). Dordrecht: Kluwer Academic Publishers.

Skovsmose, Ole, and Valero, Paola. (2001). Breaking Political Neutrality: The Critical Engagement of Mathematics Education with Democracy. In Bill Atweh, Helen Forgasz, and Ben Nebres (Eds.), *Sociocultural Research on Mathematics Education: An International Perspective* (pp. 37–55). Mahwah, NJ: Lawrence Erlbaum.

Solar, Claudie. (1995). An Inclusive Pedagogy in Mathematics Education. *Educational Studies in Mathematics*, 28, 311–333.

Stillman, Gloria, and Balatti, Jo. (2001). Contribution of Ethnomathematics to Mainstream Mathematics Classroom Practice. In Bill Atweh, Helen Forgasz, and Ben Nebres (Eds.), *Sociocultural Research on Mathematics Education: An International Perspective* (pp. 313–328). Mahwah, NJ: Lawrence Erlbaum.

Tate, William F. (1995). Returning to the Root: A Culturally Relevant Approach to Mathematics Pedagogy. *Theory into Practice*, 34, 166–173.

Tate, William F. (1997). Race-Ethnicity, SES, Gender, and Language Proficiency Trends in Mathematics Achievement: An Update. *Journal for Research in Mathematics Education*, 28(6), 652–679.

Weissglass, Julian. (2000). No Compromise on Equity in Mathematics Education: Developing an Infrastructure. In Walter G. Secada (Ed.), *Changing the Faces of Mathematics: Perspectives on Multiculturalism and Gender Equity* (pp. 5–24). Reston, VA: National Council of Teachers of Mathematics.

Wilson, Patricia, and Hart, Laurie E. (2001). Linking Gender Issues in Mathematics Education and Action Research. In Judith Jacobs (Ed.), *Changing the Faces of Mathematics: Perspectives on Gender* (pp. 43–57). Reston, VA: National Council of Teachers of Mathematics.

Wittgenstein, Ludwig. (1953). *Philosophical Investigations*. New York: Macmillan.

Wong, Khoon Yoong, Taha, Zaitun Binti Hj Mohd, and Veloo, Palanisamy. (2001). Situated Sociocultural Mathematics Education: Vignettes from Southeast Asian Practices. In Bill Atweh, Helen Forgasz, and Ben Nebres (Eds.), *Sociocultural Research on Mathematics Education: An International Perspective* (pp. 113–134). Mahwah, NJ: Lawrence Erlbaum.

Zevenbergen, Robyn. (2001). Mathematics, Social Class, and Linguistic Capital: An Analysis of Mathematics Classroom Interactions. In Bill Atweh, Helen Forgasz, and Ben Nebres (Eds.), *Sociocultural Research on Mathematics Education: An International Perspective* (pp. 201–215). Mahwah, NJ: Lawrence Erlbaum.

Chapter 3

Teaching and Learning Mathematics: Can the Concept of Citizenship Be Reclaimed for Social Justice?

Hilary Povey

INTRODUCTION

Citizenship is a complex and elusive concept that is employed in shifting and competing discourses about civil society and the social good. It has often been used in the recent past in England to support a conservative perspective: the good citizen as conforming, individual, and law-abiding rather than critical, socially engaged, and able to challenge the law. In this chapter, the ideas about citizenship currently prevailing in England are reviewed, critiqued, and related to the context of education. Citizenship education and the new National Curriculum for citizenship are described. The intention is to explore what opportunities this context allows for a definition of citizenship that is progressive for and applicable to a more just mathematics education. Thus the next section reviews the literature on democratic mathematics and mathematics education with a view to framing the question, Can the concept of citizenship be reclaimed for social justice in the context of teaching and learning mathematics? Some work with a group of initial teacher education secondary mathematics students is described and their views on mathematics and citizenship reported. In conclusion, it is suggested that the contested concept of citizenship may be exploitable in some contexts in support of a more democratic mathematics and mathematics education.

A commitment to avoiding overgeneralization means that the chapter is located firmly in its local context. However, it is hoped that the contest being played out between the neoliberal agenda prevalent in Anglophone countries and the rhetoric of social inclusion emanating from Europe will make this local case of wider interest.

CITIZENSHIP

Citizenship can be conceptualized as existing along three dimensions—political, legal, and social (Marshall 1963). Political citizenship deals with the rights and duties that obtain through the equal suffrage of the citizen of a state. Legal citizenship refers to equality before the law and to the requirement of citizens to enact and conform to the laws of the state. These two aspects of the concept of citizenship have been very much to the fore in England in recent times when a discourse of neoliberalism has been dominant in discussions of social and political life. Much neglected over the last quarter of a century has been the need to understand what is meant by social citizenship, particularly as it relates to the need for the state to compensate for inequalities—material and nonmaterial—among its citizens. Also neglected has been what this might have to do with the (mathematics) education of future citizens.

Recently, however, a renewed role for discussions about civil society and social citizenship has emerged. The British prime minister has published his concern about the fact that "so many of our fellow citizens are missing out" (Blair 2001). The engine driving this policy rhetoric has been the negative implications this state of affairs has for the social fabric: "Our society is less cohesive and everyone pays the bills for social failure." Consequently, the "social" is back on the agenda, albeit arising out of a concern for civil peace rather than a concern for social justice. (In this context, it is difficult not to recall the oft-quoted comment from Margaret Thatcher that there is "no such thing as society".) There is even room to recognize that society may be seen as "erecting obstacles" in the paths to progress of certain individuals and groups and "even to citizenship itself" (Evans 2000, p. 117).

The current British government has indicated its commitment to social inclusion for all through the concept of "active citizenship" (Williamson 2000, p. 175). What is meant by this? All are to become *able* and *willing* to participate in civic, economic, and community life. Citizenship is extended not just to cover formal rights and obligations but to be experienced by all as "a reality of their lives" (Giddens 1998, p. 103). So, on the one hand, society's exclusionary practices, debarring some from full citizenship, are to be erased. It was recognized, for example, that the United Kingdom was distinguished from its neighbors in the European Union by high levels of social exclusion, government policies over the previous two decades having failed to tackle increasing child poverty, exclusions from school, unemployment, and poor access to basic services (Social Exclusion Unit 2001). On the other hand, the ability of all to participate effectively through active citizenship is to be inculcated, partly through the exercise of civic engagement in the local community but also, and importantly, through education.

The claim is that a deficit of "social capability" (Sen 1999) prevents some people from participating, that inequalities are not just about access to material and nonmaterial social goods but also about having the capability to engage with them effectively. Guido Walraven notes, "People [are] being excluded from participation in all kinds of institutional, social, cultural and political associations. They lack the resources that people commonly use to participate in society; in other words, theirs is a 'deficient citizenship' " (2000, p. 13). Civic engagement is to be achieved by a (highly problematic) "rights and responsibilities" approach that makes government help available but requires a contribution: For example, new funding for neighborhoods is conditional on community involvement (Social Exclusion Unit 2001). But what of (mathematics) education?

Education is to provide a two-pronged attack on this "deficient citizenship"— the raising of attainment (especially in "literacy" and "numeracy") through the Standards agenda and the engagement of young people with the citizenship curriculum. It seems to me, and to many engaged professionals, that there are powerful, destructive tensions and contradictions between these two aspects of government policy that are intrinsic to the way they are to be implemented. The stated motive for the Standards agenda is to raise the achievement of young people, but it is inextricably linked up with the market approach to education (Ball 1994) introduced by the Conservative administration and maintained by New Labor. There is no evidence that a political agenda to "raise standards" does, in fact, improve the quality of the educational experience of schoolchildren in mathematics classrooms, nor is it agreed what the implications for such a policy might be on social justice issues. The link between equality, poverty, and justice is obscured in the face of such technocratic solutions to including people (Parsons 2000). The market has reproduced and augmented differences between schools and the educational opportunities of the young people who attend them. Institutionalizing differences, statutory testing, particularly in English, mathematics, and science, is now omnipresent in schools in England. There is some evidence for the view that the narrow and instrumental curriculum that results from such testing and the accompanying league tables of results are reducing the likelihood that disadvantaged young people will engage with school education positively (Povey, Stevenson, and Radice 2001): Education for "social capability" seems distant indeed.

Yet alongside this there is a view that some government initiatives are genuinely focused on reducing the exclusion from social goods of some citizens. Responding to one such initiative, the creation of Education Action Zones, Peter Evans points out the factors contributing to low achievement that it is intended to combat—"inertia and restricted experiences, parochiality, hopelessness about the future, low educational aspirations, disaffection and community anger" (2000, p. 126). The key components of a new culture of education are to include "learning for capability and active membership of society" (p. 126). He writes: "The challenge is to reconceive the purposes of education as being a preparation for living and becoming active citizens of the communities in which [the young people] are to live and work" (p. 126). It is far from clear that forging such a reconception is a political reality, or that such an interpretation of the government's agenda is sustainable. However, it provokes the questions, Does the new discourse of citizenship provide a space in which to work for social justice and progressive social change? And how might this apply to mathematics education in particular?

One key issue that has to be considered is that of plurality. This is particularly pertinent at the time of writing when the Home Secretary is questioning whether there should be "citizenship tests" assessing both command of English and civic knowledge of England before new citizenship is granted. The expectation in Western industrial societies has been that educational institutions will produce citizens schooled in the language, history, and culture of the nation–state. In such a context the concept of citizenship can maintain the culturally dominant, keeping some citizens marginalized or indeed not recognizing their citizenship at all. Contemporary usage seeks to extend the notion of citizenship beyond that simply of the nation–state both to the local level, through participation in local decision making and community action (see, e.g., Social Exclusion Unit 2001), and also to the European and indeed global level. This has an impact on the extent to which citizenship implies conformity to a single cultural form or allows for difference and heterogeneity. We can ask, along with Tuula Gordon and her colleagues: "Does 'citizenship' as a concept have any potential for encompassing pluralism and diversity? Or does it inherently imply notions of sameness resulting in marginalisation of different others? Does it have potential to enable claims to be made about social justice? Or is citizenship a myth that in its neutrality necessarily hides and maintains inequalities?" (Gordon, Holland, and Lahelma 2000, p. 21).

It seems to me that we can answer yes, in part, to all of these. Thus, citizenship remains a contested concept. It is often gendered (Yural-Davis 1997) or raced or Eurocentric (Weiner 2002) or all three. But there have been historical opportunities to enlist it in support of democracy and against racism (see, e.g., James 1980). Nevertheless, only inasmuch as these exclusionary features are challenged will the idea of active citizenship contribute to the reduction of social exclusion and the increase of social justice.

Thus we see that the concept of citizenship has often been used to emphasize individualism and conformity to hegemonic ideals rather than to underline the need for social inclusion to promote equal engagement by an active citizenry. However, my intention is to explore whether or not, within the context of mathematics education, we can "reclaim the concept of citizenship as a radical, rather than as a conservative, concept" (Gordon, Holland, and Lahelma 2000, p. 9). It appears that the current context and its associated rhetoric may provide a (contested) space in which to do so. It was interest in exploiting such a potential space for action that led to this look for connections between the new citizenship curriculum and secondary mathematics classrooms.

This is, of course, a dangerous game. It may be that, as with the introduction by the previous administration of the National Curriculum itself, the potentially progressive aspects of the citizenship curriculum "are unlikely to offer much precisely because they are prescribed by governmental edit" (Dowling and Noss 1990, p. 5), that working with the citizenship curriculum involves too much "readiness on the part of educators precisely to suspend their powers of criticism" (p. 8). However, with other educators working for social change, I hold the view that "because some aspects of the social environment resist transformation, and others are in flux, activists must be ingenious and adaptive" (Casey 1993, p. 73). Thus is this contribution to the debate intended.

CITIZENSHIP EDUCATION

There is no recent tradition of education for citizenship in English schools. Writing as recently as 1996, Madeline Arnot stated that, in the United Kingdom, "citizenship as a concept is not often used in common everyday speech" and that "the status of the citizen is unclear to most people" (Arnot 1996b, p. 1). Education for Citizenship was one of the five cross-curricular themes that were intended to form part of the National Curriculum for schools (National Curriculum Council 1989), but none of these themes was high on schools' agendas, and education for citizenship was the least favored of all (Whitty, Rowe, and Aggleton 1993). There was concern among teachers committed to equity issues that courses developed in the context of Education for Citizenship would "do little to ensure that young people develop a critical awareness with respect to citizenship issues. Such courses are often pro-establishment with an emphasis on knowledge rather than the development of skills" (Wilkinson 1992, p. 123).

These concerns must remain about the new citizenship curriculum. From September 2002, citizenship has become a compulsory curriculum subject for all young people in English schools up to the age of 16. For younger children, "preparing to play an active role as citizens" is part of their personal, health, and social education curriculum (PSHE), but for 11-year-olds upward, it is to be taught as an independent curriculum subject by specially trained citizenship teachers. In addition, it is the intention that the citizenship curriculum be addressed and supported in other curricular areas. Students are to acquire knowledge and understanding about becoming informed citizens and to develop skills of enquiry and communication and of participation and responsible action (National Curriculum 2000). As I draw out more fully and argue for in the next section of the chapter, mathematics learning for social justice is also concerned with the development of such skills and knowledge: for example, knowledge of mathematical models and how they shape what it is possible to think and to say about social issues; understanding connectedness and co-construction of meaning in the mathematics classroom; and engagement and participation in joint problem solving of difficult problems with personal epistemic authority. However, there is a concentration in the new English citizenship curriculum on the acquisition of civic knowledge about the nation–state (although there are nods in the direction of a more pluralist perspective). The view of citizenship offered is characterized by

- "knowing about" being a citizen;
- "becoming" a citizen, or preparation for being a citizen;
- the focus on civic knowledge and understanding of the principles of civic society (McGettrick 2001, p. 3).

As Bart McGettrick points out, there is no sense of an encouragement for teachers and schools to participate in a debate about what sort of teaching and learning will effectively inculcate the learning for capability and active membership of society demanded by the social inclusion agenda. Nor is there a commitment to reinspecting the ways that schools are organized and managed with a view to making them more democratic and participatory. Pupils are to negotiate, decide, and take part responsibly in school-based activities, but the institution itself remains unchanged. To harness mathematics learning for social justice involves rethinking and reframing mathematics classrooms so that both the relationship between participants and the relationship of the participants to mathematics (as well as the mathematics itself) is changed (Angier and Povey 1999; Povey and Burton 1999).

McGettrick contrasts the English citizenship curriculum with the Scottish advice on citizenship in education, which is characterized by "acting or behaving as a citizen; recognising that learners in schools are citizens; encouraging participation in democratic communities and practices" (2001, p. 3): It is this understanding of education as being already engaged and participatory rather than being for some future engagement and participation that is needed for mathematics classrooms for social justice. Despite the shortcomings, I want to offer some small indication that it may be possible to mobilize the concept of citizenship to make mathematics classrooms more democratic spaces. But the concept will have to be more plural, more active, and more concerned with participation in the here and now.

DEMOCRATIC MATHEMATICS

There have been various conceptions of what a more democratic mathematics clsssroom might look like. There is not space for a thoroughgoing review and critique of these, but I point briefly to what seem to be some of the key ideas.

First, the question of what "counts" as mathematics is not unproblematic (Ernest 1991; Fasheh 1991; Harris 1991; Restivo 1992; Verhage 1990), and it is sometimes viewed wholly with suspicion. It has been suggested, for example, that mathematics is the epitome of a suspect reason: The "path to rationality, displayed best in mathematics, is a path to omnipotent mastery over a calculable universe" (Walkerdine 1990, p. 23), and "this kind of thinking, to put it starkly, is destroying our planet and perpetuating domination and oppression" (Walkerdine 1994, p. 74). However, it is *reason separated from emotion* rather than reason itself that has been the servant of patterns of domination: We need to be suspicious of the fruits of reason but to argue instead for a caring, responsible rationality (Rose 1994, ch. 2). A mathematics and a way of knowing mathematics that supports the development of concern, connectivity, personal accountability, and respect for the experience of the knower (Collins 1990) alongside the development of reason is more appropriate to the aims of the citizenship agenda.

Claims are made that mathematics has a democratic pedigree (Hannaford 1999). However, it is more often experienced as authoritarian with its pedagogy deeply implicated in the "banking" metaphor of education where learning is seen as "receiving, filing and storing deposits . . . bestowed by those who consider themselves knowledgeable upon those whom they consider know nothing" (Freire 1972, p. 46). The kind of mathematics valued currently in educational institutions is formalist, abstract, and bleached of context. Other ways of thinking, knowing, and learning exist (e.g., see Belenky et al. 1986; Turkle and Papert 1990). An inclusive approach to mathematics needs to acknowledge and respect such person relatedness and the nurturing of intuition and insight it implies (Burton 1999).

Understanding the subjective meaning of mathematics and how it contributes to the meaning-making of learners is of central significance in devising a mathematics curriculum that is democratic. Traditionally, mathematical knowledge is constructed as impersonal and external; it is presented as being stratified into hierarchies and also as appropriately "delivered" through an educational system itself stratified. Students are encouraged not to rely on their own experience but to deny it and to accept in its place the knowledge and experience of experts, through a hierarchical and competitive epistemology that denies the validity of their own knowledge (Freire 1972; Gerdes 1985; Giroux 1983).

Mathematics classroom practices that take social justice issues seriously include: promoting a willingness to share ideas; making space for the ideas of others; supportive listening; and less valorizing of the individual and of individual success. This needs to be accompanied by a new epistemic strategy for mathematics that is "intimately related to the continuing struggles for social, political, and economic freedoms, and the freedom of individuals from the *authority* of one or a few parts of their selves and from external *authorities*" (Restivo 1983, p. 141; emphasis in original).

Paul Ernest attempted a typology of what he considered to be "the five educational ideologies" in mathematics education occurring in (at least) the Anglophone Western countries. He described the industrial trainer, the technological pragmatist, the old humanist, the progressive educator, and the public educator. Empirical research suggests, unsurprisingly, that individual educators are not located wholly, exclusively, or unproblematically within one of these ideologies (Povey 1995). Specifically, those who might be styled and style themselves as democratic socialists might want to include in their moral values, their view of mathematics, their mathematical aims, and so on, much that he labels liberal. For example, Ernest claims for his public educator the moral values of social justice, liberty, equality, fraternity (*sic*), social awareness, engagement, and citizenship. But many democratic socialists would also want to claim the person-centeredness, empathy, human values, and so on, of the progressive educator. This has been particularly true of those influenced by feminist thinking and is now clearly apparent in the speeches and writings of many of those engaged in the antiglobalization movements. These latter are striving for a deep ecological democracy that stresses interconnectedness—and not just between people but with the planet, too.

A further element in linking mathematics teaching and learning with democratic participation is provided by Ole Skovsmose. He writes that "mathematics is formatting our society . . . perhaps God did not organise the world according to mathematics but . . . [it seems] humanity has now embarked on just such a project" (1994, p. 43). It is important for all students, inasmuch as they are to participate in democratic citizenship, to have sufficient mathematical literacy to be able to understand the mathematical models being presented, to be aware of the preconditions of the modeling process that become hidden when mathematics gives it a neutral tone, and to address the way that the existence of mathematical models affects fundamentally the context of social problem solving.

Drawing together some of these ideas, some key characteristics of a mathematics classroom predicated on such an epistemology will be that the learners make the mathematics; mathematics involves thinking about difficult, not trivial, problems; and difference and individuality are respected in the context of the social group (Povey 1996). Students work together to produce as well as critique meanings (Giroux 1983), with the mathematics being coconstructed by a community of validators (Cobb et al. 1992, p. 594). A problem-centered curriculum involves the need to take risks, which is a precondition for imagining a different and more just world (Giroux 1992, p. 78); posing and reposing problems help uncover the linguistic assumptions hidden in their original formulation (Brown 1986). There needs to be room for students to move and breathe rather than to experience the current and increasing demands of performativity and patterns of surveillance (Angier and Povey 1999). And respect for difference and the individual presents a fundamental challenge to the "feudal" (Tahta 1994, p. 25) construction of ability, a keystone of the current discourse of schooling in mathematics and underpinning all its practices.

CAN "CITIZENSHIP" BE RECLAIMED?

So, can "citizenship" be reclaimed for social justice? I offer a small piece of evidence that, at this juncture, a discourse of citizenship may be mobilized progressively. I work in initial teacher education, and with a colleague, I set out to explore, with a small cohort of students, how the idea of citizenship might be deployed in their mathematics teaching. The activity was voluntary, but the whole group of eight agreed to participate. I sent them copies of a few ideas from a published resource (Wright 1999) that focused on areas of topic content for citizenship in mathematics rather than issues of pedagogy. The intention was to find out how, if at all, their school teaching placement had led them to encounter the incoming citizenship curriculum and then to see if it had impacted on their understanding of their own teaching of mathematics. However, my colleague and I began by asking them to reflect on themselves and their own mathematical learning, and it is on that I report here.

The students were following two-year routes into teaching. Their first year had been spent very largely in learning mathematics. They had worked with a range of tutors, but for about half of their modules they had been taught by tutors with a commitment to a pedagogy based on authoritative knowing (Povey 1995) and to teaching for progressive social change. At the point at which they met together to discuss ideas about citizenship, they were halfway through their second year between their two major block placements in school.

I knew that as recently as 1996 citizenship had not figured in initial teacher education students' conceptual maps. I had taken as a starting point for considering the perspectives of initial teacher education students the work of Madeline Arnot and colleagues (Arnot and Miles 1996). They found a great deal of confusion among the student teachers they interviewed about what the concept of citizenship was; and the student teachers saw it as having little relationship to everyday life.

The male student who commented, "I have no idea what a citizen is," spoke for many of the student teachers . . . the concept of citizenship was largely irrelevant to their personal identity:

Interviewer: Does it mean anything to you to say I am a citizen?

Student X: No.

Student Y: Nothing at all. (Arnot 1996a, p. 5f)

Would our teacher education students be similar? During the first group meeting, they were asked to consider what education in citizenship they had themselves received during their own schooling; what their views had been before coming on the course; and whether they believed any of their learning on the course had addressed citizenship issues either explicitly or implicitly. Unsurprisingly, as pupils, the students had had little experience of citizenship education; that which they could recall had been when specific relevant content formed part of the standard academic curriculum, for example, issues connected with suffrage arising in the history syllabus. They did not report this as having connected with their own life worlds. (The group knew each other well. The sample comments recorded during the discussion and reported here are those about which there was an expressed consensus.)

At the time we didn't think about it. It was just, erm, it was just a lesson. . . . [O]utside the lesson you didn't think about what it was or what it revolved around.

None of the students had brought with them to their initial teacher education a strong sense of the importance of citizenship from their own previous educational experience. They had not explicitly met the idea of citizenship on their course, nor had tutors linked it for them to the mathematics curriculum and mathematics teaching. They did not report having any input about citizenship education in their teaching placement. It therefore appears to be the case that, again unsurprisingly, wider changes in political discourse and its framing of educational issues had brought this concept "in from the cold."

What is perhaps less expected, however, is how the students were conceptualizing citizenship in their reflections on their mathematics learning on the course. Their responses could be grouped into two categories, the first of which was anticipated and related to particular content. This was perhaps most clearly experienced in the context of their history of mathematics unit where topics tackled had included Eurocentrism, gender, and the epistemological status of mathematics. They also remembered particular instances where the mathematics they were learning had been explicitly linked to social or political issues. One example was the use of the Peters projection map of the world; another was work on statistics showing emigration from the United Kingdom exceeding immigration.

However, the other aspect about which the students had by far the most to say related instead to the style and structure of their mathematics learning.

First student: The only thing I thought is just how we were taught last year generally. It was quite difficult to start with. I was having to think. . . . I wasn't just told the answers. I had to go into myself, my own resources and actually struggle with it, work things out. So it created a skill to be able to go away and find things out for yourself and work things out for yourself . . .

Second student: It's vital, isn't it. Because you can't really contribute as a citizen unless you're able to make your own decisions. You are not going to contribute.

They raised as relevant to a citizenship agenda their experience that they had been forced to be creative, to think hard, to struggle with their mathematics. They also linked citizenship to their learning as having been very much a mutual endeavor and connected this with developing recognition of diversity and respect for others as knowers.

It [learning at the university] is also more about working with each other as well. That was something else that was encouraged. Group work.

It helped identify different ways of working things out where you look at problems, but if everyone's . . . initially got their own angle sort of how they are going to approach the problem, by discussing it and everything you can merge the ideas together. Like if some have got a good idea, but are like tackling it slightly wrong, someone might point that out.

> I thought one of the overriding things I went away with last year was how smart the people were on the course—but all in different ways. Just the variety of people. I thought it was astonishing.

All of the students thought that a pedagogy of citizenship would seek to inculcate this sense of learners as authoritative knowers, and they linked this with their feelings about mistake making. One described overcoming his initial experience of "feeling scared about giving ideas and getting them wrong," and another talked about the significance of "being allowed to make mistakes"; this then permitted all kinds of ways of working that had previously been prevented in their mathematics learning by a fear of "getting it wrong" and "looking an idiot."

A sense emerged of more democratic and participative experiences in their own mathematics learning being significantly and legitimately relevant to citizenship education in schools.

> [We need to be] giving pupils situations where they have to come to a decision of their own, basically. That's encouraging them. That sort of critical thinking.

The students made direct links between the social relations within the classroom and the wider aims of citizenship education. The changes the students identified in themselves (an increased sense of themselves as authoritative knowers, appreciation of other people's talents and contributions, a positive response to challenge) and their valuing of a mathematics classroom where the responsibility for learning is shared, where students are given opportunities to reflect upon their learning, to feed back their ideas, and to make decisions, were all cited by them in the discussion: The model is of active and inclusive citizenship.

CONCLUSION

In this chapter, I have outlined how the concept of citizenship is operating in contemporary social and political discourse in England. It is clear that the meaning of "citizenship" remains contested and that it cannot simply be linked with a will to promote social justice. I have briefly described some of the characteristics that more democratic mathematics classrooms might have, and I have asked if the concept can be mobilized in pursuit of such classrooms. The answer to the question depends on such issues as how liberal democracy is being conceived and defined and whether citizenship is only understood in terms of formal political rights and equality before (often unjust) laws.

My conclusion is that it *may* give some space in some present circumstances to influence mathematics education in the direction of a deep democracy in which equality and person centeredness, engagement, and creativity are recognized as key to effective participation. Whether or not it does seems to me to be a pragmatic question as well as a theoretical one, and each must test the idea out in the local space for action.

ACKNOWLEDGMENT

I am very grateful to Corinne Angier, who initially worked with me on this project, and to the anonymous reviewers for their helpful comments.

REFERENCES

Angier, Corinne, and Povey, Hilary. (1999). One Teacher and a Class of School Students: Their Perceptions of the Culture of Their Mathematics Classroom and Its Construction. *Educational Review*, 51(2), 147–160.

Arnot, Madeline. (1996a). Gender and Education for Citizenship in the UK. In Madeline Arnot and Sheila Miles (Eds.), *Promoting Equality Awareness: Women as Citizens* (pp. 5–13). A pedagogic handbook from the European Commission project of the same name, unpublished.

Arnot, Madeline. (1996b). Introduction. In Madeline Arnot and Sheila Miles (Eds.), *Promoting Equality Awareness: Women as Citizens* (pp. 1–3). A pedagogic handbook from the European Commission project of the same name, unpublished.

Arnot, Madeline, and Miles, Sheila (Eds.). (1996). *Promoting Equality Awareness: Women as Citizens*. A pedagogic handbook from the European Commission project of the same name, unpublished.

Ball, Stephen. (1994). Better Read: Theorising the Teacher. In J. Dillon and M. Maguire (Eds.), *Becoming a Teacher: Issues in Secondary Teaching* (pp. 239–250). Milton Keynes: Open University Press.

Belenky, Mary, Clinchy, Blythe, Goldberger, Nancy, and Tarule, Jill. (1986). *Women's Ways of Knowing: The Development of Self, Voice and Mind*. New York: Basic Books.

Blair, Tony. (2001). Government on Track in Tackling Social Inclusion. Cabinet press release, March 23.

Brown, Stephen. (1986). The Logic of Problem Generation: From Morality and Solving to De-posing and Rebellion. In L. Burton (Ed.), *Girls into Maths Can Go* (pp. 196–222). Eastbourne: Holt, Rinehart and Winston.

Burton, Leone. (1999). Why Is Intuition So Important to Mathematicians But Missing from Mathematics Education? *For the Learning of Mathematics*, 19(3), 27–32.

Casey, Kathleen. (1993). *I Answer with My Life: Life Histories of Women Working for Social Change*. New York: Routledge.

Cobb, Paul, Wood, Terry, Yackel, Erna, and McNeal, Betsy. (1992). Characteristics of Classroom Mathematics Traditions: An Interactional Analysis. *American Educational Research Journal*, 29(3), 573–604.

Collins, Patricia H. (1990). *Black Feminist Thought: Knowledge, Consciousness and the Politics of Empowerment*. London: Routledge.

Dowling, Paul, and Noss, Richard (Eds.). (1990). *Mathematics versus the National Curriculum*. Basingstoke: Falmer Press.

Ernest, Paul. (1991). *The Philosophy of Mathematics Education*. London: Falmer Press.

Evans, Peter. (2000). Social Exclusions and Children—Creating Identity Capital: Some

Conceptual Issues and Practical Solutions. In G. Walraven, C. Parsons, D. Van Veen, and C. Day (Eds.), *Combating Social Exclusion through Education* (pp. 117–138). Leuven-Apeldoorn: Garant.

Fasheh, Munir. (1991). Mathematics in a Social Context: Math within Education as Praxis versus Math within Education as Hegemony. In M. Harris (Ed.), *Schools, Mathematics and Work* (pp. 57–61). Basingstoke: Falmer Press.

Freire, Paolo. (1972). *The Pedagogy of the Oppressed.* Harmondsworth: Penguin.

Gerdes, Paulus. (1985). Conditions and Strategies for Emancipatory Mathematics Education. *For the Learning of Mathematics,* 5(1), 15–20.

Giddens, Anthony. (1998). *The Third Way: The Renewal of Social Democracy.* Cambridge: Polity Press.

Giroux, Henry. (1983). *Theory and Resistance in Education: A Pedagogy for the Opposition.* London: Heinemann.

Giroux, Henry. (1992). *Border Crossings.* London: Routledge.

Gordon, Tuula, Holland, Janet, and Lahelma, Elnia. (2000). *Making Spaces: Citizenship and Difference in Schools.* Basingstoke: Macmillan.

Hannaford, Colin. (1999). The Garden of Democracy. May Newsletter. Available online at http://www.gardenofdemocracy.org/news.html.

Harris, Mary (Ed.). (1991). *Schools, Mathematics and Work.* Basingstoke: Falmer Press.

James, C.L.R. (1980). *The Black Jacobins: Toussaint l'ouverture and the San Domingo Revolution.* London: Allison and Busby.

Marshall, T.H. (1963). *Sociology at the Crossroads.* London: Heinemann.

McGettrick, Bart. (2001). *Citizenship in Initial Teacher Education.* Available online at http://www.escalate.ac.uk/initiatives/thematic/BartMcGettrick.php3.

Miller, Dave. (1990). *Activity Math.* Ormskirk: Causeway Press.

National Curriculum. (2000). *Citizenship Education for Key Stage 3.* Available online at www.nc.uk.net.

National Curriculum Council. (1989). *Curriculum Guidance 8: Education for Citizenship.* London: Her Majesty's Stationery Office.

Parsons, Carl. (2000). The Third Way to Educational and Social Exclusion. In G. Walraven, C. Parsons, D. Van Veen, and C. Day (Eds.), *Combating Social Exclusion through Education* (pp. 83–97). Leuven-Apeldoorn: Garant.

Povey, Hilary. (1995). *Ways of Knowing of Student and Beginning Mathematics Teachers and Their Relevance to Becoming a Teacher Working for Change.* Ph.D. thesis, University of Birmingham.

Povey, Hilary. (1996). Constructing a Liberatory Discourse for Mathematics Classrooms. *Mathematics Education Review,* (8), 41–54.

Povey, Hilary, and Burton, Leone (with Angier, Corinne, and Boylan, Mark). (1999). Learners as Authors in the Mathematics Classroom. In L. Burton (Ed.), *Learning Mathematics, from Hierarchies to Networks* (pp. 232–245). London: Falmer Press.

Povey, Hilary, Stevenson, Kathy, and Radice, Martha. (2001). Four Teachers Talking: Social Inclusion, Professional Development and (Un)Contested Meanings. *Journal of Inservice Education,* 27(30), 377–404.

Restivo, Sal. (1983). *The Social Relations of Physics, Mysticism and Mathematics.* Dordrecht: D. Reidel.

Restivo, Sal. (1992). *Mathematics in Society and History.* Dordrecht: Kluwer Academic Publishers.

Rose, Hilary. (1994). *Love, Power and Knowledge: Towards a Feminist Transformation of the Sciences.* Cambridge: Polity Press.

Sen, Amartya. (1999). *Development as Freedom.* Oxford: Oxford University Press.

Skovsmose, Ole. (1994). *Towards a Philosophy of Critical Mathematics Education.* Dordrecht: Kluwer Academic Publishers.

Social Exclusion Unit. (2001). *Preventing Social Exclusion.* Available online at www.cabinet-office.gov.uk/seu.

Tahta, Dick. (1994). Coming Up to Russian Expectations. *Mathematics Teaching* (146), 25–26.

Turkle, Sherry, and Papert, Seymour. (1990). Epistemological Pluralism: Styles and Voices within the Computer Culture. *Signs: Journal of Women in Culture and Society,* 16(1), 128–157.

Verhage, Helen. (1990). Curriculum Development and Gender. In L. Burton (Ed.), *Gender and Mathematics: An International Perspective* (pp. 60–71). London: Cassell.

Walkerdine, Valerie. (1990). *Schoolgirl Fictions.* London: Verso.

Walkerdine, Valerie. (1994). Reasoning in a Post-Modern Age. In P. Ernest (Ed.), *Mathematics, Education and Philosophy: An International Perspective* (pp. 61–75). London: Falmer Press.

Walraven, Guido. (2000). General Introduction: Discourses in Politics and Research on Social Exclusion. In G. Walraven, C. Parsons, D. Van Veen, and C. Day (Eds.), *Combating Social Exclusion through Education* (pp. 1–15). Leuven-Apeldoorn: Garant.

Weiner, Gaby. (2002). Europe, Feminism and Teacher Education: Mapping the Debates. *Review Journal of Philosophy and the Social Sciences,* 27, 298–317.

Whitty, Geoff, Rowe, Gabrielle, and Aggleton, Peter. (1993). Subjects and Themes in the Secondary School Curriculum. *Research Papers in Education,* 9(2), 159–181.

Wilkinson, Sarah. (1992). Education for Citizenship. In Kate Myers (Ed.), *Genderwatch!* (pp. 117–132). Cambridge: Cambridge University Press.

Williamson, Howard. (2000). Status Zero: From Research to Policy and Practice in the United Kingdom. In G. Walraven, C. Parsons, D. Van Veen, and C. Day (Eds.), *Combating Social Exclusion through Education* (pp. 175–188). Leuven-Apeldoorn: Garant.

Wright, Peter. (1999). *The Maths and Human Rights Resource Book.* London: Amnesty International.

Yural-Davis, Nira. (1997). *Gender and Nation.* London: Sage.

Chapter 4

Mothers Returning to Study Mathematics: The Development of Mathematical Authority through Evolving Relationships with Their Children

Christine Brew

Samantha: I realized that they are requiring different things of me. They are not requiring to have their nappy changed, or mashed food on the table; they are requiring a more intelligent person to be around them, and someone who has got the life experience to listen to them. So I decided I had the life experience; probably I needed to brush up on the academic aspect and I think that has probably encouraged me more than anything. To not follow them and not be ahead of them, but to be walking with them. And realizing that whatever I do now will be applicable later. And I think maths is definitely an area where I need to be knowing what they are doing. Like I have interesting conversations with my oldest son now. Where I can't understand something he'll say, "Have you seen this or have you done that?" or "This changes that." And yet there will be times when I say, "Can you help me with this?" . . . And he will say, "What is that?" And I can teach him where I am up to, but I can't go the next step. We've shared. That is important to me. I want the kids to know they are not on their own. (three school-age children)

INTRODUCTION

The further education sector in Australia plays a crucial role in ongoing learning for adults, particularly for women. For those people the schooling system has failed, it generally provides a safe, friendly, and noncoercive learning environment. This chapter draws on case study data of mothers who had returned to study mathematics in this sector. The majority of these women were early school leavers who expressed varying levels of mathematics anxiety. Apart from financial considerations, personal fulfillment, and wanting to develop a career, many of these women also reported wanting to return to study in the hope that it would enable them to assist their school-aged children with their studies.

It is well documented that children of middle-class parents generally do better at school than their working-class peers. Social reproduction theories are often used to describe this phenomenon in which it is assumed that a family's class position is generally fixed by early adulthood, based on the occupation, education, and associated values and attitudes acquired by the parents-to-be. When social class becomes more fluid, and parents markedly raise their educational status after their children are born, a question arises as to whether or not their children inherit their parents' old level of cultural capital. If instead they inherit the new level of cultural capital, then what are the processes through which this occurs?

Empirical studies focused on children's successes in mathematics education demonstrate a strong relationship between the home environment and mathematical achievement. Previous studies of mothers returning to study have noted educational benefits for their children. In this chapter, I explore this process further and identify hitherto unrecognized aspects of the home environment that can affect both the child and adult learners' attitudes toward and successes in mathematics. Data are drawn from two interviews and classroom observations of 16 studying mothers over a 12-month period. For the first time, interviews with these studying mothers' children contribute empirically to this underexplored phenomenon.

In this chapter, I describe the benefits that can occur for both women and their children when the women return to study, with a particular focus on the learning of mathematics. Through the changing dialogue in the home, these women and children began to engage in a dialogue of inquiry and experienced increased confidence as they applied and integrated new learning together.

The data reported in this chapter evolved out of a research study that aimed to integrate the epistemological frameworks of Belenky et al. (1986) and Baxter Magolda (1992) in the context of women returning to study high school mathematics in the further education sector in Australia (Brew 2001b, 2001c). The research focus is consistent with the call for strategies to counter traditional mathematics pedagogy and epistemology that, it is argued, alienate many girls and women by not appreciating or validating their ways of coming to know (Becker 1995, 1996; Burton 1995, 1996). Becker (1996) suggested that the epistemological frameworks of both Belenky et al. (1986) and Baxter Magolda (1992) might be fruitful for this endeavor.

The study by Belenky et al. (1986) was, in part, a reexamination of the major work of William Perry on adult intellectual and ethical development. Perry (1970) proposed a hierarchical epistemological schema of nine positions that are frequently collapsed into four categories: dualism, multiplicity, relativism, and commitment. Perry's longitudinal study was based on the experiences of mainly male undergraduates during their college years in the 1950–1960s period. In contrast, the study by Belenky et al. (1986) included 135 women from diverse backgrounds, in which they were asked them to reflect upon their lives, focusing on catalysts for change and impediments to growth. A comparable but also distinctly different epistemological framework was proposed by Perry (1970) of how women draw conclusions about truth, knowledge, and authority. They derived five epistemological perspectives that they related to the metaphorical notion of "voice." Baxter Magolda (1992) chose to replicate Perry's longitudinal study in a similar university context but included near-equal numbers of men and women. Her derived epistemological framework identifies four broad hierarchical epistemological perspectives that include many of the features of Perry's (1970) and Belenky et al.'s (1986) schemas. Viewed together, both Belenky et al. and Baxter Magolda describe two related processes, the development of a genuine voice and a shift toward viewing knowledge as inherently uncertain. Belenky et al., however, emphasize the former, while Baxter Magolda emphasizes the latter. Both frameworks are discussed again later in the chapter.

The extant literature on women returning to study is largely based within the higher education context. Reported in three substantial studies is that women gain new confidence, wider interests, and better conversation skills and that the women report a beneficial flow-on effect to their children (Burns and Scott 1997; Burns, Scott, and Cooney 1993; Edwards 1993, Kelly 1987). These authors describe this flow-on effect in terms of the women providing specific tutoring support for their children as well as their influence as a role model for learning good study habits, their increased ability to understand their children's thinking, and the more intellectual climate in the household. "The women spoke of how they felt their children had become better informed because of the discussions, and mentioned that it might also have some effects upon their children's current and/or future education" (Edwards 1993, p. 120). What now appears to be lacking in the relevant literature is an explicit acknowledgment or any thorough exploration of the equally powerful effects that these factors could have had on the mothers' intellectual and emotional development. Furthermore, both Kelly (1987) and Burns and Scott (1997) noted that a limitation of their studies was a reliance on the women's impressions concerning the impact of their return to study on their children. An apparent current gap in the literature was the absence of children's voices—their perspectives and experiences—when their mothers return to study.

In Australia, for those people the schooling system has failed, the further education sector generally provides a safe, friendly, and noncoercive learning environment, particularly for women (Teese et al. 1999). Historically, adult education has had a problematic status, viewed as the "poor cousin" of the school system (Newman 1979) where women have been viewed as the "invisible owners" but not directors of the sector (Tennant 1991). Pathways from the further education sector into the higher education system remain problematic in Australia as the extent to which adult education courses are recognized by universities varies widely (Teese et al. 1999). This is currently being addressed at the policy level with the aim of continuing to recognize the unique value of the sector in terms of its social transformational potential (Bradshaw 1999). The four key principles in this policy document are multiplicity, connectedness, critical intelligence, and transformation, which resonate with the epistemological schemas of Baxter Magolda (1992), Belenky et al. (1986), and Burton (1995).

In the context of children's mathematical learning, Crane (1996) noted that the effect of the home environment is not well documented. Crane examined the impact of the home environment, socioeconomic status, ethnicity, and maternal cognitive skills on students' mathematical achievement and found that the home environment had a notable effect, particularly when the children were younger. Reynolds and Walberg (1992) also found that for grade 8 students the home environment had the largest indirect effect on their mathematical skill level. Crane (1996) concluded that ways are needed to influence the home environment because the implications for children's mathematical learning are potentially quite large. Research on parent-child interactions with respect to the learning of mathematics is in its infancy and has focused on early mathematics learning (Anderson 1997). When parents are asked what they do to support the early mathematics learning of their children, they cite playing games (Young Loveridge 1989), having their children help in the kitchen (Leder 1992), and general conversations (Walkerdine 1988). Anderson (1997) points out that while these events seem highly social, we know little about the nature of the parent-child interactions during these shared experiences. She goes on to state that "further research into parent-child interactions during everyday activities is needed to document the characteristics of these supportive environments so that teachers, parents and researchers can put the appropriate value on such activities and gain insights into their contribution to children's mathematical development" (p. 510). As Anderson's earlier work (1995) has documented, parents from different sociocultural groups mediate literacy differently, so research "with diverse groups is similarly warranted."

"Social reproduction" theory is used to explain the lower school achievements of the children of parents from lower socioeconomic backgrounds (Burns and Scott 1997). Within this frame of reference there are two deficit models: Working-class parents are proposed to value education less highly and to have lower aspirations for their children, and parents from lower socioeconomic backgrounds lack knowledge and confidence to be involved in their children's education due to limited or poor school experiences (Coleman 1988; Hunt 1969; Marjoribanks 1995). The descriptions the women in this study provided of their family of origin contexts were consistent with these theories. Due to their educationally impoverished childhoods, these women had been put at risk and according to the theory would be more than likely to transmit the same risk factors through to their children. However, cognitive deficit theories are insufficient in their ability to characterize fully the people who are responding to "the unique demands of their distinctive environments" (Ginsburg 1997, p. 132).

Burns and Scott (1997, p. 210), who state that "social reproduction theory assumes that a family's class position is generally fixed by early adulthood, based on occupation/education and the associated values acquired by the parents-to-be," also challenge the deficit models in terms of their inflexibility. They ask,

"[I]f parents raise their own educational status" while still raising a family, "do the children inherit their old level of cultural capital or the new level? And if it is the new level, what are the processes through which this is transmitted?" I suggest it is far more complex and interesting than merely a matter of transmission and that it is likely to involve a range of interacting processes that are involved in making the transition from one level of cultural capital to another.

Ginsburg (1997, p. 149) proposes that withdrawing from the cognitive deficit model requires persistent focus on understanding learning potential, motivation, cognitive style, and the role of sociopolitical factors through supplementing "our cognitive notions with genuinely psychological and ecological considerations." In this chapter I address these two considerations by exploring motivation in relation to sociopolitical context and propose the utility of an epistemological lens. The epistemological frame of reference helped to reveal the way these mothers and their children made meaning together and drew conclusions about truth, knowledge, and authority in the context of learning mathematics.

THE EPISTEMOLOGICAL FRAMEWORKS

In a study by Belenky et al. (1986), women who were mothers were explicitly included as the researchers were "particularly interested in how maternal practice might shape women's thinking about human development and the teaching relationship" (p. 13). The five epistemological perspectives that they related to the metaphorical notion of "voice" include *silence* (no voice), *received* knowledge (emphasis on listening to the voice of others), *subjective* knowledge (emphasis on listening to the inner voice), *procedural* knowledge (the voices of reason—connected and separate knowing), and *constructed* knowledge (integration of connected and separate ways of coming to know).

While they do not consider their notion of *silence* to be parallel to the other four epistemological perspectives, the authors position it as an important anchoring point in their overall schema. Many of the women in their study often spoke retrospectively about feeling "deaf and dumb." "They felt deaf because they assumed they could not learn from the words of others and dumb because they felt so voiceless." In essence, this perspective represents "an extreme in denial of self and in dependence on external authority for direction" (Belenky et al. 1986, p. 24). A link between mathematics anxiety in adults and the *silence* perspective was developed in the integrated epistemological framework proposed by Brew (2001c) with respect to someone who experiences major cognitive blocks when asked to engage in mathematics due to the surfacing of emotions associated with feeling dumb and stupid. These emotional messages are generally associated with past traumatic school experiences of mathematics and the struggle to obtain a mathematical voice.

The *receiver* perspective is associated with learning by listening where there is an emphasis on authorities as sources of truth. In the context of learning mathematics, it was associated with someone who perceives they can learn math-

ematics but who only acknowledges mathematical knowledge derived explicitly
from an external authority (namely, textbooks and the teacher). The *receiver*
perspective can also be likened to an emphasis on rule following in mathematics
without deliberate attention to understanding process (Brew 2001c). This perspective is consistent with an absolute epistemological orientation in terms of a
belief that one is either right or wrong in the actual outcome of doing mathematics.

The *subjective* knower was a more difficult perspective to link theoretically
with the mathematical context, as it represented a very diverse perspective within
Belenky et al.'s epistemological framework. It is associated with an emphasis
on listening to the private voice—a more intuitive response to learning situations—and yet absolutist in the sense that there is still one right answer. A form
of *subjective* knowing in the doing of mathematics by adult participants was
identified by Brew (2001c, p. 24): "Unless something makes complete total
sense to me I refuse to acknowledge it. My brain discards it." In essence, "the
mathematical knowledge has to be personally owned or will be rejected." It was
also associated with those who had rejected the study of mathematics because
it was perceived to be an uncreative pursuit.

The abandoning of absolutism and subjectivism in favor of "reasoned reflection" (Belenky et al. 1986, p. 88) was described as the emergence of the voice
of reason. This procedural perspective is associated with a belief in the need to
be able to justify one's point of view with evidence. The term *procedural* is an
unfortunate use of terminology in the context of learning mathematics, as this
could be associated with blind rule following. Instead, the emphasis is to reason
and understand how mathematical knowledge is constructed. With respect to the
two procedural voices, connected and separate knowing, the former is proposed
to be an orientation within which alternative solutions or methods of mathematical reasoning are appreciated by trying to understand the other person's way
of thinking—how does it make sense to them? The latter, separate knowing, is
proposed to be an orientation within which alternative solutions or methods of
mathematical reasoning are examined for inconsistencies and hence it is an ad-
versarial or doubting approach. Both modalities, however, are aimed at developing a strategy to understand one's own method of analysis and to locate it
within a constellation of other approaches.

Through her longitudinal study of 101 students, Baxter Magolda (1992) identified four broad epistemological perspectives and gender-related reasoning
patterns within the first three: the *absolute* knower; the *transitional*; the *independent*; and the *contextual* knower. The *absolute* knower is very comparable
to the *receiver* in Belenky et al., and there are elements of the *independent*
knower in the *procedural* voice. The two models converge in *contextual* and
constructed knowing, as they both represent the development of an authentic
voice and a perception that knowledge is socially constructed within given contexts. (For further details see Brew [2001c].) Central to Baxter Magolda's framework is that there is a direct relationship between one's epistemological

perspective toward knowledge and the role that significant others (identified as teacher and peers) play in learning. For students who view knowledge as absolute, the role of the teacher is limited to imparting the knowledge that is required, and the role of peers is limited to a social one, or at best, to share knowledge gained from the teacher and text. As students gain an appreciation and understanding of how knowledge is constructed, that it is inherently uncertain (*independent* knowing), the views of peers gain greater validity and play an increasingly more significant role in learning. While similar ideas are also evident in Belenky et al. (1986), Baxter Magolda more clearly identifies the changing role of significant others as students' views develop on the nature of knowledge, truth, and authority.

Unlike the present study, the role of children as significant others was not an identified theme in the process of shifting epistemological perspectives in Baxter Magolda's 1992 study. Belenky et al. (1986) discussed family of origin as a factor in influencing women's epistemological perspectives in a general way, and Belenky (1996) discussed how the positive benefits of parenting programs for marginalized women could be traced to changes in their ways of knowing.

These women influenced their children's behaviour by engaging them in reflective dialogue, drawing out their problem solving abilities. By contrast, the women who did not see themselves as thinkers seemed much less aware of their children's thinking processes. They relied almost exclusively on authoritarian, power-oriented child rearing techniques. ... These programs might well lead to more democratic families and the ripple effect will be felt down through the generations. (pp. 396–397)

The research reported on here is particularly significant in its exploration of shifts in the epistemological perspectives of mothers within the context of learning traditional mathematics.

THE PARTICIPANTS

In 1999, 19 women were interviewed who were enrolled at one of the two further education centers included in this study. Of these, 18 were mothers, 10 had school-aged children, 4 had only infants, and 4 others either still had adult children at home or their children no longer lived with them. The centers where these women had enrolled to return to study are located in two of the most economically depressed areas of Melbourne, Australia. One site was a Community Learning Center, often the first step for women returning to study. The other site was a Technical and Further Education (TAFE) college where courses are better articulated for entry into higher education. In the first year of the study (1999), two classes at the Community Learning Center participated in the research. One class covered essential numeracy skills as a component of a full-time Information Technology course designed to provide the women with computer skills for immediate employment. The other class studied grade 11 mathematics, with the aim of providing them with a mathematics prerequisite to enter the higher education sector. In the year of the study only women were enrolled in these classes, though men were not excluded.

The TAFE college course was developed for women who were early school leavers to provide them with a pathway to areas of further study that are non-traditional for women (e.g., engineering, medical technology). This was a full-time course with a significant component devoted to mathematics up to year 10 content with a particular focus on algebra. According to the teacher, the women-only class composition was meant to encourage women to take more risks than they might normally have done if men were present. There was also a commitment to group work, as it was believed there was immense value for learners to verbalize their own understanding and hear others clarify and justify their mathematical reasoning. The 19 women interviewed ranged in age from 22 to 50 years. Thirteen were early school leavers, and all but a very few expressed differing levels of anxiety with mathematics, which, as can be expected, they brought with them into the classroom.

DATA COLLECTION

Following three weeks of class observations, the students were each interviewed over a period of two months. Regular observations of classes continued to the end of the course, and the second interview occurred by telephone in all but three cases. The interviews were semistructured, covering issues with respect to the five domains of learning of Baxter Magolda (1992)—their perception of mathematics, the roles of the learner, teacher, and peers, and assessment. In the first interview, students were also asked about their reasons for returning to study, their previous school experiences, particularly in mathematics, and the influence of their parents on their schooling. The follow-up interview explored similar issues with a focus on any apparent shifts in the students' perspectives on the role of the teacher and peers in the mathematics classroom.

Prior to the first interviews I had been informed by staff at the Community Center that one of the reasons that some women gave for returning to study was to provide their children with more homework support. At that time I did not envisage that this issue was related to the central aim of the study, and so it was not a focus question in the first interviews. As many of the women spoke in the first interview about the role of their children as a motivating factor in their return to study and the impact their studies were having on their relationship with them, this issue became a featured focus in the second interview.

During this second interview, I also requested the opportunity to interview the women's children. Six women initially agreed, but one subsequently declined when her children conveyed they did not wish to participate, and contact was lost with another woman. Ten children (four girls and six boys), from four families, whose school levels ranged from grade 1 to 12 (see Figure 4.1), were interviewed.

Figure 4.1
Number and Grade Level of the 10 Children Interviewed from Four Families

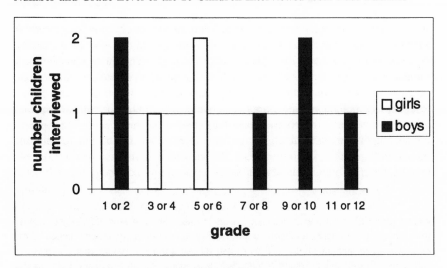

Interviews with the children were delayed after the second interviews for several months, with the aim of also collecting a third round of data from the women. In retrospect the delay might have been a mistake, as some of the women were no longer studying and hence some of their children found it difficult to answer questions that related to a time that was long passed for them. With one exception, where the children were interviewed at their father's work, the children were interviewed in their family home with their mother present. The children in each family were also interviewed together. Sample questions for the children included:

• Thinking back to when your mother first told you she was going back to study, can you remember what you first thought about that?

• Has your mother been able to help you more with your homework? Mathematics home-work?

• Have you been able to help your mother with her mathematics homework?

• What has changed in your life since your mother returned to study?

To ensure a high level of anonymity, pseudonyms are used throughout this chapter, the site at which the students were enrolled has been omitted, and some family details have been altered.

CHILDREN AS A MOTIVATING FACTOR FOR RETURNING TO STUDY

Apart from personal development, ambition, and financial motivation, 7 of the 10 women with school-aged children conveyed that one of their reasons for returning to study was to be able to assist their children more academically. Support with their mathematical learning specifically featured in their comments. Their experiences resonated with the findings of Burns and Scott (1997), Edwards (1993), and Kelly (1987) with respect to providing not only direct tutoring support but also the wish to be good role models in terms of academic study. In the opening quote to this chapter, Samantha's comments suggest both of these themes. Furthermore, 5 of these 7 women, including Samantha, implicitly recognized the threat of the transmission factor in "social reproduction" theory. They spoke about wanting to break the cycle of learning difficulties, and they wished to do this by attempting to improve their children's educational opportunities through enhancing their own. Two examples follow to illustrate this theme.

Jane: I wanted my son to have an education and I could see that I couldn't help him. And I wanted to. . . . I could add, subtract, multiply and probably divide. That's basically what I could do. . . . I didn't want him to go through life and struggle at school like I had done. When he went to school he got bullied . . . so the same thing happened in any case. The abuse happened in a different way. When there is abuse, whether it is physical or emotional, spiritual, sexual, when abuse happens to a person they don't learn. So that is what I have suffered from nearly all my life. (first interview)

Samantha: I remember sitting in the maths room and quaking in fear of all this big maths that we were going to learn in year 7. I just remember walking to class from assembly and thinking, "Oh, I don't know if I can do this." That's funny, because I hear my kids saying it now and I say, "Yes, you can, yes, you can." (first interview)

Two of the three women with school-aged children who did not indicate that part of their motivation to return to study was to assist their children spoke instead about the difficulties of balancing the responsibilities of child rearing and their studies. Several other women also spoke about this issue.

Apart from the women with school-age children, one of the four women with only infants also stated that her major motivation to return to study was ultimately to be a good role model for her young daughter.

Nancy: I remember when I was younger I had friends with mums who were housewives and they worked at supermarkets. I was so proud to say my mum works at the hospital. I want my daughter to be proud of me. That's why I am doing it.

Another woman with only preschool children spoke initially about feeling guilty about leaving her two young children in crèche while she attended classes. Over time, however, she said she had come to believe that they were now benefiting from the peer interaction they were experiencing. Two of the four women who no longer had children at school described how this was now their time to pursue delayed personal opportunities. As they put it, "There must be more to life than children."

In terms of intended outcomes with respect to assisting their children academically, all but one of the seven women reported that through their return to study they had been able to provide more academic support for their children. Five of these women also stated directly that they had obtained assistance with their mathematical learning from their older children. Peta revealed in her first interview that she did not have the mathematical ability to determine basic percentages at the time she returned to study. This is an important consideration with respect to the following discussion she describes with her son.

Peta: When it comes to percentages he is like, "What are they talking about?" But I help him out, and he helps me out.

Interviewer: Can you give me some examples of some conversations that you have had?

Peta: He came up to me at the start of this year and said I don't understand a thing about this, mum. And I have gone, "Easy son." And I have taken his book and read it and gone, "Oh my God, don't worry about that book. Here, use my book." I said, "Read it through and then come back to me." And he has read it through and gone, "Your book is easier than mine." Now why put out a year 11 book that is simpler than a year 10 book? That is high as pie for me. I don't understand why they can't bring out a simpler book for a younger year. Why bring out something so damn complicated? (Peta, three school-age children, second interview)

An examination of Peta's experience through an epistemological lens identifies the textbook to represent the authority in this context. In Perry's (1970) epistemological schema, dualism, an absolute orientation toward knowledge and truth, is associated with a belief in one "authority" while a more pluralist perspective recognizes that there are many valid experts or authorities who can assist us in constructing meaning from our experiences in context. Typically in school mathematics classrooms, only one textbook is used, which implicitly reinforces inadvertently a single view of what mathematical knowledge is and how it should be presented. When Peta refers to "what are they talking about," authority and authorship are invested in the mathematician(s) who wrote the book. Through the opportunity to compare and assess together this text with another that is more accessible, both Peta and her son have engaged in comparing two mathematical authorities. The more powerful notion of authorship versus ownership, first described by Hilary Povey (1995) within the context of learning mathematics—"authoring as the means through which a learner acquires facility in using community-validated mathematical knowledge and skills" (Povey and Burton 1999, p. 232)—becomes apparent. Through their dialogue, Peta and her son might also be considered to be involved in the process of becoming mathematical authorities themselves by assessing the relative usefulness of either text and through making an active choice about which resource best meets their needs in context. What is also important is that Peta chose to send her son away to read her text, but with the invitation to return to dialogue. This approach provides insight into how she prefers to learn mathematically;

that is, she is recommending to her son that mathematical learning involves both individual study and reflective dialogue with others. In this shared experience with her son that began with a simple request for support with his homework, one gets a sense that both have had their mathematical confidence and skills enhanced through a process of connecting and validation.

Peta also had a daughter who, she said, had assisted in her mathematical learning. Initially Peta did not think she had had an impact on her daughter's mathematical learning, as she was doing extremely well and had done so for some time. As the conversation unfolds, however, subtle shifts emerge suggesting that she has indeed had an effect on her daughter.

Peta: My daughter is doing year 9, but she is doing year 10 maths.

Interviewer: Do you think that she would be in that class if you had not gone back to study maths?

Peta: I think she would have been there this way or that way.

Interviewer: Because?

Peta: She is very bright. She is a straight A student.

Interviewer: So what impact do you think you have had on her going back to study?

Peta: Um, with her I don't think I have had much. In fact, she has helped me! . . . Like, she helps me in respect that if I don't understand something, she is more like the way my father used to do it. Sometimes she works from the back forward. She gets the question, she looks at it, if she doesn't understand it, she will go and look at the answer. And we think, "Okay, how do we get that answer from this?" And she will then figure it out.

Interviewer: So do you think her confidence has grown because she has been able to help you?

Peta: Yeah, I think it has.

Interviewer: Are there any conversations that you can remember that would indicate that?

Peta: Um, yeah. She has actually gotten a slightly higher mark being so confident.

Interviewer: Than she normally would have?

Peta: Yeah. It is not a significant higher mark because she is already getting A's, like 93, or 87. Now she is getting nearer to the 100s. Which really, if you think about it, it might not be significant to everybody else, but one or two points might be significant to her.

Interviewer: So you going back may have kept her interest, do you think?

Peta: Oh yeah. I think it has given her that little extra push. And the fact that I have started to do further study she has thought, "Well, if mum can do this, why can't I?"

Interviewer: Has she actually said that?

Peta: Sometimes, but in her riddly way. [*Laugh*]

Interviewer: Can you tell me how she talks in riddles?

Peta: Well, the pass mark in a test was 50%, the teacher's competency rate was 80%, and I got 81. Which I was thrilled about, because when I go into a test I normally come out babbling I don't know what I have done. But this time I went in mildly confidently and thought I don't know what the hell I wrote afterwards. [Laugh] The next week I have gone, "Look what I got, 81!" And she goes, "Really good, mum, but I got a 94 in my maths test!" (second interview)

Applying an epistemological lens to this discussion, there is, first, clear evidence of a focus on process and understanding the mathematics, rather than the minimalist outcome approach to obtain just a right answer. While both are having to work with the traditional approach to the learning of mathematics with standard problems and one right answer in the back of the text, Peta's daughter would appear to be teaching Peta how to use all the available information effectively for understanding. Further evidence of this occurring is the shift in pronoun use from *she* to *we* by Peta when she states, "She gets the question, she looks at it, if she doesn't understand it, she will go and look at the answer" and "And we think, okay, how do we get that answer from this?' " This is suggestive of the emergence of a connecting dialogue about mathematical understanding. The joining in partnership implied by her shift to the pronoun *we* suggests that Peta has located her own emerging mathematical authority within their shared membership in the larger rubric of mathematical knowledge processes. That Peta then defers to her daughter when she states, "And she will then figure it out" speaks to the fledgling nature of her newfound mathematical authority and a continuing tendency to defer to her learning partner's expertise. The sense of mother and daughter being learning partners with respect to their academic pursuits is further evident in the playful competition about their respective test scores.

In the next example from Dianne, while brief, there is further evidence of a meaningful sharing in action between mother and child with respect to mathematical learning.

Dianne: Now when I go to the supermarket I always do estimations. I just floored my daughter the other day, and you know, anything in your trolley, you sort of just go, one dollar, two dollars, la de da de da, and I said this will be about $47–$48, which it was. She went, "Wow, how did you do that?" She did! [*Laugh*] She said, "I must try that." So, it is just confidence to make sure you have enough money and also so they don't make a mistake! (second interview, daughter 16)

Dianne was one of the three women with school-aged children who did not indicate that wanting to assist her children academically was part of her motivation to return to study. All the same, this excerpt does have some resonance with the experiences of the other women who did, in terms of the connecting dialogue about mathematics eventuating with her daughter. In this case, you can sense the new confidence that Dianne has gained with arithmetic estimation through her ability to apply it usefully in a practical context and the way her daughter is both impressed and eager to learn about the process she has employed. Dianne makes it clear that the ability to estimate is a useful application of her new mathematical learning. First, she finds it useful for keeping within budget and avoiding the embarrassment of lack of funds at the checkout. Additionally, she is empowered by her new mathematical prowess as surveying the checkout clerk, which locates her in a position of mathematical authority.

In the quote at the beginning of the chapter, Samantha reveals a very strong connection between her motivation to return to study and her desire to assist her children in their intellectual development. As the first set of interviews had borne out this theme to varying degrees among the women, during subsequent observational visits to the classes I asked the participants to let me know of any conversations about mathematics they were having with their children. During one of these visits Samantha told me that her daughter, who was in year 8, had come home that week and announced that she had excelled in an algebra test. Samantha revealed that her daughter normally failed mathematics tests. This outcome was followed up in the second interview by asking Samantha the extent to which she thought this event had been influenced by her return to study. In response, Samantha thought that her daughter would be unlikely herself to say that she had been influential. However, Samantha perceived that she had been a good role model.

Samantha: I think it would be a refusal comment to say that mother helped. [*Laugh*] Mothers don't get much credit when they are this age. But . . . she has become more open to realizing that maths can be fun even if it is tough. . . . To the point where she has gone from not understanding the concept of maths at all to doing a lot of maths that was at my level. Her maths teacher said, "I want her in my advanced maths class next year." . . . But I don't know if the credit would directly come back to me. I think the environment of seeing maths as being a regular thing in my house, my books over the table, my determination, the late nights, and the successes in the end have inadvertently led to an openness for the subject.

What is apparently different in this case is the lack of evidence of any actual dialogue about mathematics between Samantha and her daughter apart from the announcement of having done well in her test and the likelihood that this success had continued, given the further information that her mathematics teacher wanted her to be in his advanced mathematics class. As Samantha stated she was now enjoying holding discussions about mathematics with her son of similar age, I was left wondering why the likely opportunity for similar conversations had apparently not been taken advantage of by her daughter. The opportunity to talk with Samantha's children was unfortunately not possible, as her children declined to be interviewed. I now focus on the case studies from the four families where the children did agree to be interviewed.

CASE STUDIES

Clare and Her Children

Clare was in her early thirties, had left school at the end of year 10, and was married with three children ranging in age from 6 to 15 years. Clare described her family of origin as "typical—mum at home, that sort of thing." Her reflections on her life pathway in her first interview suggest an emergent sense of indignation about the way she had been failed both by the school system and by the educational values held by her family of origin. Clare's description of herself doing mathematics at school resonates with Belenky et al.'s (1986) notion of the silent student—voiceless, unable to learn.

Clare: Maths and reading were always a chore for me. . . . Maybe because I was so quiet and I never asked for help. . . . I just seemed to have a mental block with maths. Maybe it was the way I was being taught. . . . If somebody shows me how to do something, I find that much easier to pick up than reading instructions. So I am a hands-on person. . . . I think women are streamed one way and men are streamed another. . . . If their parents didn't think they could cope with university, they would stream them one way.

Interviewer: Is that what happened to you?

Clare: Yes . . . I have always wanted to go back and do something myself, but whether I will get the chance or not. [*Laugh*]

In this first interview Clare revealed that being able to assist her children was an important anchoring point in her efforts to remain focused on her studies.

Clare: I am plodding. I am not sinking yet. [*Laugh*] I am actually amazed at what I am doing. I suppose I look at it differently, and I am not going to let it beat me. Like even if I don't sit tests or anything like that, I feel that I can help my kids and look at things differently too.

In the second interview, when asked to talk about any shifts she had experienced with respect to the learning of mathematics, Clare spontaneously used recent interactions with her children to respond.

Clare: I know what my kids are talking about when they are doing their maths. I have some idea. [*Laugh*] Whereas before I had NO idea. So in that respect it is GREAT! . . . Even with the eldest, when he is talking about different aspects of maths, I know what he is talking about. Not necessarily maybe helping him, but I know where he is coming from.

Clare also reflected on her school experiences again, and in the excerpt below, one can hear Clare's growing awareness and concern of how her children are at risk of replicating her own experience at school.

Clare: At school I wouldn't even ask questions, ask for help, whereas now I ask. I am there to learn. I don't have the same attitude as I did when I was younger. And I look at my kids and they are probably a bit that way too. They don't necessarily ask when they need help. Leon is a very sensitive kid, and I was too, I never wanted to look as though I was an idiot by asking a question.

What appears to have been instrumental in this shift for Clare was the influence of a collaborative classroom environment.

Clare: What I used to find frustrating was that you would get to a point and then I just couldn't go any further, especially with algebra. You would get to a certain point, and you would think, "Does this go down there, or what do I do with that?" Eleanor would say, "Well, do you remember when we did this?" You know. And I would say, "Oh yeah."

Interviewer: She wouldn't necessarily tell you what to do?

Clare: No. It was good. So I found that great. You couldn't do that in a classroom environment with the teacher up the front. Especially when they have 30 in a classroom.

While we might want to query whether this is not possible in a large class, the important point here is that Clare is challenging the typical pedagogy of the mathematics classroom that she recalls is focused on students learning alone. In the context of describing how his mother now helped him with his homework, Clare's son Leon described a near-matching style of interchange with his mother that she had experienced with her classroom peer.

Leon: She didn't give us the answers for them; she just helped us.

Interviewer: Okay. And how did she do that?

Leon: What do you mean?

Interviewer: Well, you made a distinction between not giving you the answers and something else.

Leon: She reminded us of things, and if I had forgotten something she might say, um, like, "Do you remember when you did that?"

Leon's comments suggest that the type of peer interaction Clare had come to appreciate in her mathematics classroom, the invitation to dialogue, was now being applied in the home. Leon also conveyed that he felt more able to talk with his mother generally, and she in turn confirmed this perception.

Leon: I don't know if this is with us getting older or something, but we have been able to talk with mum a bit more as in "Mum's not really strict." She is still strict, as in we have laughs with her; it has just changed in that way.

Clare: They are probably changing just as much as I am. But I think that my listening skills are better. I am definitely more articulate, and I can express how I feel, and I am more observant of how they feel too. Makes a difference.

These two comments resonate with the findings of Belenky (1996), as discussed earlier, with respect to an apparent shift away from an authoritarian approach to parenting when the women in her study began to see themselves as thinkers. In turn they became aware of their children's thinking processes. While Belenky (1996) emphasized the "thinking" domain, Clare emphasizes the "feeling" domain with respect to her own and her children's learning.

What is a key finding in this case study is that Clare's epistemological perspective on mathematical knowledge itself, not just the process of coming to know mathematics, shifted during this time, too. In the first interview, Clare had an absolutist orientation toward mathematical knowledge: "Maths is a set of rules" and "There is a right or wrong answer." Clare went on to say, "You can't sort of manipulate it to suit yourself." This suggested she felt a distance between her preferred way of making meaning and what the rubric of mathematical knowledge entails. When a subjective way of coming to know is powerfully formative in the knowledge and meaning making of an individual, the seeming certainty of mathematical knowledge becomes alienating, and this is the point that Becker, Burton, and others have alluded to in their critique of traditional mathematical learning contexts. During Clare's second interview, some 12 months later, this way of meaning making in mathematical learning seems to have been accommodated to some extent.

Interviewer: In the first interview you said you "viewed maths as a set of rules," that "there is a right or wrong answer. You can't sort of manipulate it to suit yourself."

Clare: Well, I suppose that is the classical, what I enjoy and what I don't. Because with statistics you can. There is no right or wrong answer. Are you with me?

Interviewer: Please keep going. It is interesting.

Clare: Yeah, I suppose financial. You are working it out to be, what would some statistics be, you are finding what your median and mean to be. Whereas it is not BLACK and WHITE.

Interviewer: Why is it not black and white?

Clare: [*Pause*] Well, it depends on the information you are actually using. That's a hard question. . . . I found it easier, so I perceive it as being different. I don't know. [*Laugh*]

One interpretation of Clare's reflections is that she has recognized how the different measures of central tendency—in this case, the mean and the median—provide the opportunity to interpret data in different ways. It is perhaps intellectually "easier" for her because it suits her way of coming to know. For the first time she perceives there is some flexibility in the interpretation of mathematical knowledge, that there is room for dialogue in making sense of the mathematics.

Turning back now to the home environment, apparent in the comments from Clare's oldest son Daryl (15) was evidence of some adjustments in the family dynamics in response to her return to study, and this was within the theme of greater responsibility.

Interviewer: What did you first think when your mother returned to study, Daryl?

Daryl: That I would have to look after the kids more. I thought, "That is going to be great!"

Clare: But you didn't have to! [*Challenge*]

Daryl: I did! . . . Wasn't that bad. Didn't really worry me that much.

While Daryl initially conveyed he had experienced some hesitancy about taking on more of a caregiving role with his younger siblings, the experience had not been as scary or inconveniencing as he had anticipated. Perhaps, in the light of being a 15-year-old boy, in his cryptic understated way, he might well be implying that it was actually quite an enjoyable experience for him. Together with the following comment the theme of shifting roles emerges.

Clare: Daryl showed me a thing or two with the maths! [*Laugh*]

Daryl: I did a little bit. Not much. She was doing year 11 and I was only doing year 9, so [*laugh*], it was a bit hard, but I helped her with a few things.

What seems to be happening between Clare and her oldest son is a kind of blurring at times of their roles as parent and child if you position that the one caring is the parent and the one cared for is the child (Noddings 1984). In assisting his mother with her mathematics and assisting his younger siblings, Daryl is acting as the one caring, and his mother is the "cared for." Friendly, though pointed, jibing continued throughout the interview between Clare and her son.

Clare: Leon has always been conscientious with his homework, whereas . . . [*Turning to Daryl*]

Daryl: [*Laugh*]

Clare: [*As if to quote a typical comment from Daryl*] "just because I get A's doesn't mean I am going to get A's."

Interviewer: What does that mean, Daryl?

Daryl: Just to rack her up. "Oh, you get high distinctions, you're square." Stuff like that.

At the end of the interview when asked, "Was there anything else you would like to say?" Daryl volunteered that he thought his mother was "probably happier" (and I confirm this observation), having been able "to get her own time away." In Clare's home there is a strong sense of caring for each other, and while Daryl seemed a little reluctant to reveal fully his commitment to others, this is likely to reflect his age. His awareness of his mother's greater happiness since returning to study is very much a sign that he actually is engaged in the new style of dialogue in the home. He has taken on further responsibilities that for his age are likely to be appropriate in assisting him to develop both emotionally and intellectually.

Linda and Her Children

Linda was in her early forties and married, with three children ranging in age from 6 to 15 years. Linda described a secondary school experience similar to Clare's and comparable family of origin values. Like Clare, her parents seemed to have had low educational aspirations for her and also lacked the knowledge and confidence to be involved in her education.

Interviewer: How did your parents influence you in your studies?

Linda: They didn't sort of worry. School was supposed to take care of that. It wasn't to be brought home. Occasionally my homework wasn't done on time, and Dad would sit down and try and help. But Mum, well, wouldn't be able to. You were a girl and you were going to finish in fourth form anyway and go on and do office studies. Dad would say, "You are not doing any good, so as soon as fourth form comes up, you are out of there." Not to say sort of, "Why aren't you doing well in maths?"

Linda gave many reasons for returning to study, but wanting to be able to support her children with their education clearly featured. Evident again is the implicit desire to circumvent the repeat of learning difficulties across the generation.

Linda: The business went broke, so obviously I had to get out there and just move myself. A bit of reality sets in, and the old pay packet gets a bit thinner. [*Laugh*] And that was really financially motivated, and I just needed my brains to get working. . . . The kids were coming home and talking and some days I was just switched off. And I thought, "This is hopeless . . . I am just stagnating." . . . With my son, he is 14 now and I have noticed his work is becoming a bit daunting, and I felt the need to sort of help him, whereas my parents didn't do that.

In the second interview, I continued to gauge the level of importance of her children in her decision to return to study.

Interviewer: In the first interview you said that the kids were coming home some days and talking and you were just switched off and you thought, "This is hopeless." It sounded like the kids kind of triggered you in some ways?

Linda: Yeah, you do things for your family. I mean, I really, possibly. . . . Oh well, I did it for myself, I suppose ideally. But in the back of your mind . . . like I had this mundane job . . . but I had to get out there and do something and improve myself. FOR the kids.

What Linda seems to be saying is that she feels she is breaking a rule when she emphasizes that her return to study was very much connected with her family needs. The source of this perceived rule is not clear, though it might be positioned as coming from Western feminist discourse that posits the preferability for women to define themselves separately from their role as mothers. The recognition of an "ideal" that is associated with separateness is resolved by

Linda into a connectedness in her self-affirmation that her motivation to improve herself is for her children.

In the second interview, Linda's comments resonated with Belenky et al.'s (1986) notion of the development of one's own voice. There is a sense of her moving away from silence that is epitomized by a sense of feeling dumb and stupid.

Linda: I do feel more self-assured. And I do speak out a bit more. Whereas I tended to hang back and think, "I better not say that because that might be stupid."

Interviewer: Does that also relate to the kids' schooling?

Linda: Oh yeah. Speaking to my son, I speak out more about schooling now than I did before I did the course. In the way that he should think about school.

In the context of learning mathematics there also came a greater opportunity for relationship with her son.

Interviewer: In the first interview you said his work was becoming daunting. Are you able to help him now?

Linda: Yes. I am now because he is doing similar things to what we did last year. [*Laugh*] Working out the areas, perimeters. Actually we were only doing that yesterday, and I thought, "Wow, I did this! I can do this with you." [*Laughing*]

Interviewer: And what does he think about that?

Linda: He just smiles. He is actually asking ME questions. [*Laughing*] Sometimes I have to sit down and think, "Hang on. What did we do here?" And then it comes back, and we go ahead with it, so that is good.

Interviewer: So that wouldn't have happened before?

Linda: I probably would have looked at it and gone, "Ask your father." Whereas now, I haven't had to say, "Wait till your father comes home" or "Don't show me that."

Interviewer: Did you say that, "Don't show me that?"

Linda: Oh yeah! A couple of times I said, "I haven't got time for that," only because [*voice dropped*] I didn't know what he was talking about. But now I can read it, say, "All right, let's have a look."

Previously, being silent (feeling dumb and stupid) and her shame with being mathematically incompetent led her to be inauthentic in her relationship with her son. Linda now invites dialogue about mathematics with her son. Linda's comments on the peer support that she experienced in the classroom reveal how crucial this environment was for her new confidence to engage in mathematical dialogue.

Interviewer: How important were peer interactions in your own learning?

Linda: I think it was very important. I really do. So much so that it gave you a bit of confidence because you felt you are not the only one not understanding, but you are all in the same boat. Whereas before you were in a classroom, you weren't allowed to talk, you were not allowed to interact with anybody, so you thought your problem was the only problem or you were the only one with that problem in the classroom. You didn't know how everyone else was feeling.

In the interview with Linda's son, I followed up her comments about how she now felt able to assist him with his mathematics. This was the only time in the data that the child did not corroborate the mother's experience.

Interviewer: Did your mum help you with your maths?

Anton: No [*laugh*], not really. [*Laugh*] Sort of had to do that by myself. Maybe small things, but not that much really. Not much I remember.

Interviewer: Something about measuring areas and perimeters came up with your mum. She thought she was able to help you with some of that. Can you remember?

Anton: No, not really, no. . . . Most questions, like harder questions, I used to ask dad to help me with them rather than mum because dad knew more about the maths questions than mum did.

It is difficult to know the extent to which Linda did assist her son with his mathematics, though she clearly recalls trying to do so. In discussing this case with colleagues, it was suggested to me that the way his father assists him with mathematics may be quite different from the way his mother does. It was suggested that perhaps his father is more directive, while his mother encourages him to engage in a dialogue about his work. Another interpretation from colleagues was that her son may not be as willing to admit he has received assistance from his mother academically, and there may be certain loyalties he maintains with his father. Yet Anton did go on to explain enthusiastically that his mother had been of major support at least in another academic context: "When mum first went to school she didn't know much about computers. Then once mum started learning about computers, she was really helpful."

Having interviewed Linda and seen the delight on her face in telling me her rendition of the experience, one interpretation is that being able to attempt to assist her son with his mathematics may have been of far greater significance to her than it was for him. Clearly this experience had come to reflect for her a measure of her new mathematical confidence, her ability to tackle now what had once been daunting academic tasks.

Linda had two younger daughters who she said were also influenced in a positive way by her return to study: "They like it because they can simulate me. Like I would have my homework out and like, 'Mum's doing her homework. We have to do ours.' " [*Laugh*] Linda went on to say that her youngest daughter actually did not have homework as such because she was only in grade 1, but she would still go and get paper and do a drawing next to her as she studied. The women in Edwards's (1993, p. 120) study reported similar experiences of their children copying them. "If I pick up a book, they'll want to pick up a book, which is quite good. . . . Every time I get paper to write, they want paper to write as well, you know!" Linda's oldest daughter Janie, aged 10, corroborated Linda's experience. The vibrancy of the changing home environment was conveyed with a touch of humor.

Interviewer: When your mum told you that she was going back to study, what did you first think about that?

Janie: I thought it was good for Mum that she was going back to school. I didn't think of it at first, but then when she started, I started to really get it, because Mum used to come out and do all her work and sometimes I used to get my homework and sit right next to her.

Interviewer: What was that like?

Janie: Quiet! [*Giggle*]

Interviewer: Quiet was it? What used to happen before?

Janie: We were all loud! [*Laugh*]

The comment by Janie "I started to really get it" suggests she has made a link between her mother's study endeavors and the implications for herself. The child conveys enjoying learning in a focused way. This resonates with Samantha's story whose older daughter finally chose to apply herself to her mathematical studies after "seeing maths as being a regular thing in my house, my books over the table, my determination, the late nights, and the successes in the end."

Linda's children also spoke about having to assume greater responsibility for household chores since their mother returned to study. This was not conveyed to be problematic for them. Rather, it was conveyed as a matter of fact, just part of the new home environment. "We clean our own rooms now" (Janie) and "we also do the bathroom once a week" (Anton). This perspective resonated with some findings from the study by Edwards (1993, p. 119): "They've got the feeling that they're contributing to the household. We're more of a team."

With respect to a further impact on the children, Linda's youngest daughter, Vicki, aged six, had a sad story to tell: "I was embarrassed that I was happy that mum was going back to school." At this point in the interview I inadvertently did not follow this point up. This occurred because Vicki spoke so softly, and it was only picked up on the tape later. At this time her mother was out of the room, but fortunately when she returned, she asked whether Vicki had spoken about her embarrassing experience. The tape was turned back on and Vicki then told her story.

Vicki: After Mummy started, I said it at Show and Tell and I had my questions and everyone started laughing and they were talking to each other. And I got upset.

Interviewer: When you said you had your questions ready, what were they?

Linda: The children ask questions at Show and Tell. They will tell and the teacher then asks the children, "Have you got any questions about that?" And I don't think they had questions.

Linda went on to describe further how her returning to study had been discussed within her own family very positively in terms of it being an important opportunity for her to finish her schooling. The explanation given by Linda for the humiliating response by peers at school was explained in this way.

Linda: I can remember Vicki saying that she thought that the kids thought that mum wasn't very clever. Because you are an adult, you don't need to go to school. So she was embarrassed because they thought . . . [*Janie interrupted*]

Janie: Well, Mum is smarter than any other Mum now. The smartest Mum in the world!

Linda: I don't think so. Maybe more confident now, perhaps.

The powerful peer response fed back to both Vicki and Janie was that their mother must be dumb to have had to return to study. Instead of Vicki being able to enjoy her pride in her mother's success, she was robbed in the moment by the normative dissonance between learning and adulthood. Edwards (1993, p. 119) also found that some of the older children "took some pride in their mother's unconventionality" as they "told people that their mother was a student." If Linda had been going to university rather than a further education center to complete her schooling, Vicki's experience would likely have been quite different. The resultant shame that Vicki felt is a poignant concrete example of the marginalized nature of this sector.

Lynette and Her Children

Lynette was in her late thirties and was married with 4 children aged 10 to 18 years at the time of the interview with them. She also left school early in year 10 to care for her younger siblings. Like Clare and Linda, for Lynette there was little support to continue her academic studies from her parents despite doing well in her studies, particularly in mathematics.

Lynette: I dropped out at the end of year 10. I was always very good at maths, but in year 10 I had this teacher who you could say was pretty bloody hopeless [*laugh*] and I found that really frustrating. A lot of the time I was actually showing her how to do some of the work. . . . I just went downhill and lost interest then. . . . My parents didn't encourage me to stay at school. I just said I am not going back next year and it was all hunky dory, "fine, go and get a job." They were quite happy for me to go out and bring some money in.

Compared to Clare and Linda, Lynette did not convey as strongly in the first interview that her reason to return to study was motivated by wanting to assist her children. Rather, this was a time to focus on her life. Yet when we discussed the impact of returning to study mathematics on her everyday life, her children came immediately into focus, and later a sense of needing to remain relevant in her children's lives as they got older was perhaps a factor motivating her, too.

Lynette: I have been able to use it a bit with my kids because they are in high school. Measuring triangles and all that sort of stuff came in handy. I finally know how to do it now. [*Laugh*] So, yeah, I have been able to help them out, so it has been good.

Interviewer: That is one thing that has come up in other interviews is the extent to which people come back also for their children.

Lynette: That was part of it. But basically I needed something to do with myself. I was I suppose in a midlife crisis. [*Laugh*] I sort of needed to do something. I was getting frustrated with myself, and I didn't have enough to keep me going. Like my kids are getting older, so I thought, "Well, I've just got to do it. I've got to go back to school and learn something."

Lynette said the response of her children to her returning to study had been very positive, and this was with respect to an enhanced attitude toward their own studies. Similar experiences as told by Linda with her younger daughters emerged.

Lynette: They think it is terrific. It has given them actually a bit of a buzz, because they are more keen now to actually get down and study themselves. I say, "Look, I dropped out at 16, and here I am. I have gone back now. Because you know I have missed out on a lot." That has given them a boost. They are really getting stuck into it. And Susie thought it was fantastic because she has been doing decimal work and I would come home with a decimal sheet and we would sit there and do it together. And she is only in grade 5. She thought it was so funny. She says, "I can't believe I am doing the same work as you Mum." [*Laugh*] It was good, though. We work on her sheet and then we work on mine.

The comments from both Lynette's daughter and son (16) confirmed this greater sense of shared academic experiences, including the emphasis that Lynette gave to her interactions with her daughter.

Susie: She helped me with my maths. Because my teacher last year didn't exactly explain everything to me. And that made it a bit harder. So everyday I went back home and asked her to explain it properly to me.

Interviewer: And did your Mum explain it better than the teacher?

Susie: Yep.

Interviewer: Any examples, like, "One day I had this problem and . . ."

Susie: [*Laugh*] Well, one day when we were at school and doing decimal numbers the teacher just, like she likes to talk a lot. And she was just talking about stuff that we don't need to talk about. So I went back home and my Mum explained everything to me, not like the teacher.

Rob: She would help us with our homework a bit better.

Interviewer: Can you give me some examples of that?

Rob: Just practically my maths. . . . When I couldn't do stuff, she just explained it to me.

Interviewer: Did she used to help you before?

Rob: Oh, a little bit.

Interviewer: But more when she went back?

Rob: Yeah. She knew more about the maths.

Lynette's experiences of her adult mathematics classroom conveyed that she was enjoying a shift away from rule following toward understanding the mathematical knowledge. As Lynette had been successful in mathematics at school this would suggest that perhaps she had experienced this success through being a good rule follower.

Lynette: The teacher is great because she can explain things in a way you can understand it. [*Laugh*] A lot of hands on, cutting and pasting, you can see the reasoning. Probably better off in a logical sense than learning all the old rules and stuff, because that is not study really. . . . If you don't know the reasoning behind why you have got this rule, you are buggered, you are not going to remember it. (first interview)

According to Baxter Magolda's (1992, p. 105) framework, for those with an absolutist orientation toward knowledge, the role of peers is mainly social, as knowledge is acquired from the teacher. When teaching methods are "aimed at understanding, many of which included applying knowledge within class and to life in general . . . peers took on more active roles, perhaps because understanding was described as necessitating more exploration than that required for the acquisition of knowledge."

Lynette's initial perception of the role of peers in her adult classroom was consistent with an absolutist perspective on the learning of mathematics, too, as they had only played a social role: "Everyone is there to encourage each other. If you have got that back up, it makes it so much easier." However, by the second interview her conception of the role of her peers had broadened, suggesting an epistemological shift here, too, and this is consistent with Baxter Magolda's schema on adult intellectual development where the different perspectives that peers convey become important in one's own conceptual understanding.

Lynette: It just broadens your mind, because you do learn from other people, ideas of how they look at things. . . . You can look at things from different angles, rather than just the normal way you would look at them, and think, like that's it, that's the way it is, when it doesn't have to be like, that is the way it is, there are different avenues into a problem.

The following extract from Lynette's daughter strongly suggests that with her children Lynette was applying as well as sharing her new approach to the learning of mathematics.

Susie: She would come home when she had learned her maths experiment or something at school and show me it.

Interviewer: Can you give me an example?

Susie: Well, [*pause*] she was doing this thing out of a piece of paper and had to get it like that without cutting it. And so she taught. I tried to do it, and then I finally got it [*laugh*] . . . then . . . we got everyone else to do it.

Interviewer: So do you think your attitude towards maths changed at all because your Mum was doing it at school?

Susie: Yeah. Mine did.

Interviewer: Can you tell me a bit more about that?

Susie: Well, how my teacher never explained anything, I was able to do more of the work than I used to, and it was easier for me.

While her son Rob was more circumspect, he also volunteered that his mathematical skills had also improved.

Interviewer: What about you, Rob?

Rob: I felt more confident, and I could get the work in on time.

Paula and Her Children

Paula was in her late thirties and was married with four children aged 2 to 10 years. Paula's description of her background was comparable to the other three women.

Paula: My father had died, and Mum never pushed education, really. She was of the old generation when women were going to get married anyway. So you really didn't need an education. You just needed to work until you got married. So, no, she never suggested I stay at school. The teachers wrote on my report that it seems a shame that I was leaving, that I could cope with the work. But that was all. There was no extra influence or great incentive to stay on.

Paula's reason for returning to study was to complete her secondary school education, as dropping out had been something she had always regretted. She also had a dream to go to university. With respect to the role of children in her studies, Paula only spoke about the difficulties she was having balancing study with her family commitments. Due to several absences from class during the year, I asked Paula whether there were times during the year when she felt like dropping out: "Oh, several. After half time really, it seemed just a long year. I was simply too busy. The kids weren't sick or anything. I just couldn't find any time away from the kids." We also talked about whether she had found she had been able to help her school-age children more with their mathematics.

Paula: Sally struggles with maths concepts.

Interviewer: Can you help her with that?

Paula: I try to, but I can't see why she doesn't grasp it. I do try to help her with it, and we don't fight, fortunately. She will listen. But I have trouble getting back down to that level. Things seem so obvious to me, and she can't grasp it. I guess that's why you need a primary school teacher.

Interviewer: I think part of it is to get them to talk about it, to see how they see it.

Paula: Yeah, that's right. I have realized that because I have said the same thing three times and then I think, "What am I doing? There is no point saying this thing three times, is there?" If they can't grasp it the first time, then you've got to find a different way of saying it that is not how they are learning it.

These reflections suggest Paula perceived a need to shift in how she viewed the process of learning mathematics. Her approach to working with her child Sally suggests that she tends to utilize a teaching style that is based on attempting to transfer her acquired knowledge through telling, rather than encouraging a dialogue to explore her child's mathematical understanding. Paula's epistemological perspective on the learning of mathematics, below, gives some insight into why she struggles with engaging in this way. For while she agrees with me that it may be important to find out what her child is thinking, she is still focused on *saying* it rather than having a conversation. Like Clare, Paula conveyed in her first interview an absolute orientation toward mathematical knowledge. Unlike Clare, though, this was the reason that she liked mathematics: "There is one answer with maths. It is either right or wrong. Very clear-cut. That's what I like." The initial role of peers for Paula was consistent with the absolutist orientation. Additionally, however, she rejected even the social role of her peers, preferring to work alone: "I prefer minimal interaction. . . . I am not really looking for the social side of it. That is not really why I am here. I am really here to do the maths." As with the other women in the study, however, Paula did make some shifts in her perspective on the learning of mathematics in relation to the role of peers in her learning.

Interviewer: In the first interview you said you liked minimal interaction in the classroom. And yet I thought there was more interaction in the classroom later on?

Paula: Yes, there was, and I initiated a lot of it too. [*Laugh*] . . . Although Clare helped me, too, I felt it was more me supporting her. With Samantha, she had a different perspective on it, I think. She saw things very differently to me, and when I got stuck, I could rely on her to, what do you say, look outside the square you live in. . . . And I think it would help 100% if the teenagers could do that with each other. I know that would be really hard, because a lot of the kids would carry on and muck around or whatever. But if they were able to feel more comfortable in speaking up, then the other kids might be able to think, "Oh, is that what it means?" Because you tend to think in your own language, don't you?

Paula's comments on the changing role of peers in her adult mathematics classroom resonate with those made by Lynette. She has come to value dialogue in the learning of mathematics, that her learning can be enhanced through making meaning with others. Her recognition of the value of differentness through learning from the perspectives of others indicates an epistemological shift. Furthermore, her comments also resonate with the comments made by both Lynette and Clare, with respect to reconsidering the optimal conditions for mathematical learning in schools. Given that Paula—and Lynette probably, too—had formerly enjoyed the nonnegotiable certainty of the traditional school mathematics classroom, these epistemological shifts are very significant.

When Paula was asked to talk about the impact her returning to study was having on her children, like the other mothers, she also positioned the impact to be beneficial. However, rather than a focus on how she has been able directly to support her children academically, Paula positions the benefits for her children in terms of encouraging them to view her as someone other than their mother and to be more independent.

Paula: It has forced them to be more independent. It has forced me to be, I don't know if you call it selfish—I think more about myself. When I went back to school I couldn't do some things for the kids, I didn't have the time. . . . So when I went back to school, it was actually, "I have to do this homework right now. I will have to do that when that fits in." And I think that is good. I don't think that is a bad thing. They realize that you are a person outside of just being mum, so I think it was good that they saw me go back to school. They couldn't believe it. Why would you go back to school when you don't have to! And do maths! [*Laugh*]

Again, the child reflected and corroborated the mother's experience.

Interviewer: Do you remember the time when your Mum first told you she was going back to study?

Sally: I think I was 8 or something, but I think I said, "Why are you going back to school?"

Interviewer: What do you remember thinking about that?

Sally: Um, that she is too old to go to school.

Interviewer: In terms of doing homework, did you sit up and do your homework together?

Sally: Sometimes. Sometimes mum would be doing her work and, "Mum, I need your help." And she goes, "Hang on. I gotta do this first, this page."

Interviewer: So can you think of any way that your life changed because mum went back to study?

Sally: I think I had to do a little bit more work, but I was always a helpful person. I always used to get up on the chair and wash the dishes. Mum had to do them again, though.

Like Vicki (Linda's daughter), Paula's daughter reflects the normative dissonance between learning and adulthood when she states that she thought her mother was too old to go back to school. She now experiences her mother as not always available, as she sees her mother placing a priority on her own learning, and she responds positively by assisting with chores as much as she can. Paula added during the interview that her daughter regularly cleaned her bedroom while she was studying. This practice immediately stopped, however, when her mother decided to have a year off from studying, evidence of her child's responsiveness to her mother's special needs while she was a student.

While Paula's original motive for returning to study was less about her children, still she positions her experience as having had beneficial impacts on them. What she is providing for her children, or at least for her daughter, is a model of reconciliation of the apparent dichotomy between child centeredness and learning centeredness. In other words, she can still care about her children and yet from time to time be so focused on her own learning that they will have to wait patiently for her help. Sally's experiences reflect the emphasis conveyed by her mother, that her return to study has led to a greater focus on encouraging her children to be more independent and interdependent within the home environment.

CONCLUSION

In this chapter, I have explored the changing home environment when mothers with school-aged children return to study in the further education sector, a sector known for its transformational potential in adults' lives (Bradshaw 1999), particularly for women in the thirty to forties age group (Teese et al. 1999). While the number of women in the study was relatively small, there were at least five factors that suggest they represent a relatively homogeneous group. First, their family of origin experiences were similar with respect to being thwarted or unsupported in their educational opportunities. Second, they had spent several years raising their children and had come to a point in their lives where they had recognized a need to make a radical change to enhance both their employment prospects and their sense of personal fulfillment. Third, 7 of the 10 women with school-age children were partly motivated to return to study to improve their children's educational opportunities, to break the cycle of learning difficulties that they had experienced in their childhood, and to remain relevant in their children's lives as their needs were changing, too. Fourth, they were all studying mathematics, and finally, they had come into their respective courses with a rule-based notion of learning mathematics or that in learning mathematics one is only right or wrong; there is no room for interpretation. This notion, in association with their initial perceived role of classroom peers to be mainly social, is consistent with an absolutist perspective on mathematical knowledge and learning (Baxter Magolda 1992).

The ways in which adults made shifts in their epistemological perspectives in the study by Baxter Magolda were also evident in this study. First, there was evidence of an epistemological shift away from an absolutist perspective toward a focus on making meaning through dialogue and interpretation. This was initiated by the formal learning context where peer interaction was encouraged, which then led to the women's deepening appreciation for the value of peers' different perspectives as they assisted in the women's developing understanding. Through the women applying their new knowledge through dialogue in the home with their children, they were affirmed and further stimulated in this learning mode. While previous research of women's experiences on returning to study has documented beneficial flow-on effects to their children generally, what has been largely ignored is the pivotal role that children can play, in turn, in providing not only a consistent motivating factor but also enhancing their mother's intellectual development. This occurred through a synergistic effect in their explorations together into new ways of making mathematical meaning. Through the changing dialogue in the home, evidence emerged of a growing sense of mathematical authority, a sense of ownership, and perhaps the early signs of authorship (Povey 1995) of the mathematics. Further evidence suggests that through the greater validity placed on peers' knowledge in the women's learning came a growing awareness of the impoverished pedagogy of the traditional mathematics classroom with its focus on individual learning. Three of the case study women made remarks to convey this challenge. Paula did so when she spoke about how she could rely on Samantha to assist her in looking "outside the square you live in . . . and I think it would help 100% if the teenagers could do that with each other." Clare did so when in relation to the critical peer support she received she added, "You couldn't do that in a classroom environment with the teacher up the front." And it is also possible to infer this perspective from two of Lynette's comments: "It broadens your mind, because you do learn from other people . . . how they look at things . . . from different angles, rather than just the normal way" and "The teacher is great because she can explain things in a way you can understand it. [*Laugh*] A lot of hands on, cutting and pasting, you can see the reasoning. Probably better off in a logical sense than learning all the old rules . . . that is not study really." Through challenging her child's school textbook, Peta also implicitly challenged the notion of a single mathematical authority. The implications of this finding for the children from low socioeconomic backgrounds needs to be viewed in the context of the broad response of the children to their mother's sharing of mathematical knowledge with them and the subsequent dialogue that takes place. There is considerable evidence that the children's attitudes toward studying mathematics is enhanced, and there is some further evidence that greater success has occurred, too. That this occurs within a context where there is also a challenge to the status quo of traditional mathematics teaching provides the children with a greater opportunity to avoid suffering in silence, as their mothers did, when they struggle to make meaning during their school experiences. As the women say, they are now more keenly aware of the risk of repeating learning difficulties in their children because of their family of origin experiences.

In Edwards's typological account of education and family in women's lives, she identified an apparent tension between two ideological constructs, "that of separated private and public worlds and a connecting feminine psyche" (1993, p. 128). She identified how some women returning to study strove for "connection and integration" of these two worlds, while others strove for "separation." Other women sought "a mix whereby they separated some aspects of education and family, but in other areas they felt and wanted connection." Edwards positioned these ideological constructs as not necessarily existing in reality, nor being static, but rather as positions from which the women begin to move toward or away over time. Edwards went on to interpret that while retrospectively "one might discern certain particular connecting or separating strategies and their outcomes . . . for the women themselves . . . they continued to be unintended outcomes rather than goals they worked towards. Their only aim was to move between the two—a process rather than an end" (pp. 138–139). I wish to problematize this interpretation. At one level the women's experiences in my study resonated more with the women in Edwards's (1993) study who sought connection between their public and private worlds. Edwards (p. 129) positioned these "connecting" women as wanting to talk with their families about their academic knowledge, that they felt this, in turn, had affected the way they brought up their children, and also viewed their family experience and knowledge "feeding into their academic learning." Not discussed by Edwards, however, was the notion that this sense of connection might well be a sustaining motivating factor for their academic studies. This was explicit in the current study. In addition, Edwards did not discuss the issue that the women may have grown intellectually and emotionally from the new dialogue they were stimulating in the home (which is strongly implied in the current study). Upon reviewing some of the participants' accounts in the study by Edwards (pp. 119–120), I find evidence of this phenomenon in her study as well: "[W]e sort of encourage each other" and "We sit around the box . . . I use programmes to discuss things" and "doing the degree makes you more aware about how important parent involvement is . . . it makes you more aware." Very early in her book Edwards (p. 56) did report that 8 of the 23 women with school-aged children "stressed how their children provided an added impetus to study." Apparently this was only positioned by the women in terms of needing to provide materially for their families.

I also wish to reconsider the dichotomizing retrospective stance that Edwards takes with respect to positioning the connecting of the private and public world as process oriented rather than goal focused. In this present study the children played a key role in meeting the current needs of their mothers. To illustrate, Clare knew she needed to overcome her mathematics anxiety to enable her to pursue higher education. Through being able to assist her children, or at least understand what they were talking about, this was a type of measure for her that she had begun to deal with her fear of the subject and the distance and embarrassment this was causing.

Similarly, Linda knew she had to overcome her lack of mathematical competence if she was going to get a better-paying job. Being daunted by her son's mathematics homework was a very concrete reminder. That she was subsequently able at least to grapple with his mathematics homework after completing the course was for her a measure of her success in her goal.

Lynette, who was experiencing a midlife crisis, felt she was stagnating and needed to experience the sense of learning again. While her children were not positioned strongly as part of her motivation to return to study, the fact that she was able to assist her children more academically might well be positioned as feedback to her of success in learning.

Paula's experience on first reading does seem different from the other three women. Her motivation to return to study seems less about her children, and her daughter's comments were not about mathematics. However, a closer examination of Paula's comments does reveal a more subtle similarity with the experiences of the other women. Paula wanted to complete her schooling and eventually enter higher education. With four young children it had been a very difficult year to balance family and study commitments. When she commented, "They realize that you are a person outside of just being mum," this is indicative that her children are providing a kind of mirror to her endeavor. Similarly, when she states, "I think it was good that they saw me go back to school. They couldn't believe it," Paula gets the feedback from her children that she is succeeding in constructing a new identity.

This latter point is consistent with the three other case studies. The children of all four women provided feedback to their mothers that they were experiencing her in new ways. To me, these data convey that these formerly marginalized women literally constructed the context within which they could reinvent themselves, not in spite of or to the detriment of or simply because of or only for their children—but more. By remaining connected to their children and utilizing the home environment, they were able to discover and experiment with new strengths and exciting dimensions of themselves in an integrated way. This was of critical importance as they were able to apply their preference for collaborative processes. By so doing, they had enhanced their emerging authority in connection with mathematics, increased their confidence in themselves, and developed new partnerships with their children.

Noddings (1984) calls it the joy of the one caring. What the women seem to have tapped into is a natural synergistic potential between mothers and their children. Perhaps both Paula and Lynette, the two women whose motivation to return to study was positioned as being less about their children, just fell into this synergy potential as their descriptions of experiencing the new learning were expressed in the context of their relationships with their children. In contrast to the notion that returning to study ought to affirm ideally women's separateness from their children, a perspective of which Linda was aware, for these women the ideal was actually in the connectedness, both from the learning point of view and from their personal commitment to their children. Crucial to this line of argument is that the mother-child relationship, viewed as a teacher-student relationship, became more fluid through the children being able to support their mothers with either their academic work and/or through taking more responsibility for chores. In making contributions of one kind or another, the children enter into the transformational process of moving from being exclusively the one "cared for" to participating as the "one caring" (Noddings 1984). This is why it is synergistic, not just in terms of intellectual exchange. It is further synergistic within the rubric of care. "One must meet the other in caring. From this requirement there is no escape for one who would be moral" (Noddings 1984, p. 201).

The implications for practice is that rather than just the public world (the formal learning setting), being the source of new knowledge and ways of how to engage effectively with students about mathematical meaning, the private world of the parent-child relationship deserves greater attention for its potential contribution to constructing new mathematical knowledge. For those practitioners, both of adults and children who wish to encourage mathematical dialogue and find ways to create a mathematics curriculum that builds in the possibility for interpretation, the type of dialogue that occurs at home may be fertile ground for informing practice. Utilizing the parent-child relationship to assist students' mathematical learning is not new, and strategies for how to assist schoolteachers to do this effectively through an inquiry approach have recently been detailed by Brahier (2000). The obverse, to utilize the parent-child relationship to assist adults' mathematical learning, does not appear to have been considered. In the adult classroom, encouraging women to verbalize their mathematical thinking can be quite challenging for adult practitioners. Encouraging adults to talk about the conversations they have with their children about mathematics is clearly a fruitful avenue to explore. Legitimizing and validating the changing conversations that occur at home about mathematics with their children is likely to initiate the valuing of different perspectives and approaches earlier than might be expected. Adult practitioners who may be focused on wanting their adult students to come to focus on their own learning, to make a shift to seeing their own learning as distinct from their children's, might be better off encouraging and supporting this connectedness, rather than insisting on separateness. It is through this connectedness that I believe the potential for challenging the hitherto non-negotiable mathematics curriculum and addressing the nature of knowing mathematics may grow.

The reason this synergistic potential has been largely overlooked in the literature on early school leavers who are mothers returning to study is, I suggest, because we have been focused elsewhere. In the early stages of this research project, before I had developed some of the ideas presented in this chapter, I would have conversations with my academic colleagues about the role of children in the women's motivation to return to study and that through working with their children it seemed to be assisting the women's intellectual develop-ment. Quite often, the nonverbal response would be to roll their eyes. The verbal response was to suggest that the women were merely rationalizing their self-interest by hiding behind their dedication to their children. One adult educator said she would like to see the proof of how it helps women as when adult students finally make the shift to focusing on their own learning and away from their children's, that is when the adult practitioner often quietly celebrates a sense of personal achievement. Perhaps there is some truth in this interpretation, but I see clearly now that it comes from a deficit model. It is based on women being seen as deficient for not feeling fully entitled to pursue further education for themselves and that children are equally seen in terms of only being able to deplete their mother, that they are incapable of giving something back. The other truth I believe is more inclusive and celebratory. We have accepted the nor-mative ideology that the private world of mothering is less valuable academi-cally than the teaching that occurs in the public domain and that learning at school is other to mothering. Apparently this is simply not so. The women's stories discussed here are ones of transformation, of growing mathematical con-fidence and shifting epistemological perspectives, with both their classroom peers and their children playing a central role in this process. It is my hope that these ideas will resonate with and encourage others to look at this underexplored dynamic in the relationship between mothers and children as peers in learning.

ACKNOWLEDGMENTS

This study was supported by a La Trobe University postdoctoral fellowship research grant, Melbourne, Australia. I first wish warmly to thank the women who participated in the research, including the students and their teachers. I wish them well on their life journey and appreciate that they provided a space for me to enter their lives at this time. I would also like to thank Gilah Leder for her continuous professional and personal guidance over the past five years and for supporting the initial idea for the research. I would also like to acknowledge the invaluable input of Brenda Beatty for reading and editing several earlier drafts of the manuscript and for discussing with me enthusiastically the ideas that I have integrated in this chapter that flowed from our numerous discussions in the winter of 2002, San Marcos, Texas. Finally, I would like to thank my official reviewers for the excellent feedback that I received from them; their critical and en-couraging comments motivated me to think more deeply about the issues that I raise in this chapter.

REFERENCES

Anderson, A. (1995). *Parents' Perspectives of Literacy Acquisition: A Cross Cultural Perspective*. Paper presented at the American Education Research Association, Atlanta, GA.
Anderson, A. (1997). Family and Mathematics: A Study of Parent-Child Interactions. *Journal for Research in Mathematics Education*, 28(4), 484–511.

Baxter Magolda, M. (1992). *Knowing and Reasoning in College: Gender-Related Patterns in Students' Intellectual Development*. San Francisco: Jossey-Bass.

Becker, J.R. (1995). Women's Ways of Knowing in Mathematics. In P. Rogers and G. Kaiser (Eds.), *Equity in Mathematics Education: Influences of Feminism and Culture* (pp. 163–174). London: Falmer Press.

Becker, J.R. (1996). Research on Gender and Mathematics: One Feminist Perspective. *Focus on Learning Problems in Mathematics*, 18(1–3), 19–25.

Belenky, M. (1996). Public Homeplaces: Nurturing the Development of People, Families, and Communities. In N. Goldberger, J. Tarule, B. Clinchy, and M. Belenky (Eds.), *Knowledge, Difference, and Power: Essays Inspired by Women's Ways of Knowing* (pp. 393–430). New York: Basic Books.

Belenky, M.F., Clinchy, B.M., Goldberger, N.R., and Tarule, J.M. (1986). *Women's Ways of Knowing: The Development of Self, Voice, and Mind*. New York: Basic Books.

Bradshaw, D. (1999). *Transforming Lives, Transforming Communities: A Conceptual Framework* (2nd ed.). Victoria: Adult Community and Further Education Board.

Brahier, D.J. (2000). *Teaching Secondary and Middle School Mathematics*. Boston: Allyn and Bacon.

Brew, C. (2001a). Implications for Women and Children When Mothers Return to Tackle Mathematics. In M.J. Schmitt and K. Stafford-Ramus (Eds.), *Proceedings of the Seventh Annual Adults Learning Mathematics Conference ALM-7* (pp. 167–172). Boston: National Center for the Study of Adult Learning and Literacy, Harvard Graduate School of Education, in association with ALM.

Brew, C. (2001b). Tracking Ways of Coming to Know with the Role of Teachers and Peers: An Adult Mathematics Classroom. In M.J. Schmitt and K. Stafford-Ramus (Eds.), *Proceedings of the Seventh Annual Adults Learning Mathematics Conference ALM-7* (pp. 97–103). Boston: National Center for the Study of Adult Learning and Literacy, Harvard Graduate School of Education, in association with ALM.

Brew, C. (2001c). Women, Mathematics and Epistemology: An Integrated Framework. *International Journal of Inclusive Education*, 5(1), 15–32.

Burns, A., and Scott, C. (1997). Two-Generation Effects of Maternal Tertiary Study. *Journal of Family Studies*, 3(2), 209–225.

Burns, A., Scott, C., and Cooney, G. (1993). Higher Education of Single and Married Mothers. *Higher Education Research and Development*, 12(2), 189–206.

Burton, L. (1995). Moving Towards a Feminist Epistemology of Mathematics. *Educational Studies in Mathematics*, 28, 275–291.

Burton, L. (1996). Mathematics, and Its Learning, as Narrative—A Literacy for the Twenty-first Century. In D. Baker, J. Clay, and C. Fox (Eds.), *Challenging Ways of Knowing: English, Maths and Science* (pp. 29–40). London: Falmer Press.

Coleman, J. (1988). Social Capital in the Creation of Human Capital. *American Journal of Sociology*, 94 (Suppl. 95), S94–S120.

Crane, J. (1996). Effects of Home Environment, SES, and Maternal Test Scores on Mathematics Achievement. *Journal of Educational Research*, 89(5), 305–314.

Edwards, R. (1993). *Mature Women Students: Separating or Connecting Family and Home*. London: Taylor.

Ginsburg, H. (1997). The Myth of the Deprived Child: New Thoughts on Poor Children. In A.B. Powell and M. Frankenstein (Eds.), *Ethnomathematics: Challenging Eu-*

rocentrism in Mathematics Education (pp. 29–154). Albany: State University of New York Press.

Hunt, J. (1969). *The Challenge of Incompetence and Poverty.* Urbana: University of Illinois Press.

Kelly, S. (1987). *The Prize and the Price: The Changing World of Women Who Return to Study.* North Ryde: Methuen Haynes.

Leder, G. (1992). Mathematics before Formal Schooling. *Educational Studies in Mathematics,* 23, 386–396.

Marjoribanks, K. (1995). Families, Schools and Children's Learning: A Study of Children's Learning Environments. *International Journal of Educational Research,* 21, 439–555.

Newman, M. (1979). *The Poor Cousin: A Study of Adult Education.* London: Allen and Unwin.

Noddings, N. (1984). *Caring: A Feminine Approach to Moral Education.* Berkeley: University of California Press.

Perry, W. (1970). *Forms of Intellectual and Ethical Development in the College Years: A Scheme.* New York: Holt, Rinehart and Winston.

Povey, H. (1995). *Ways of Knowing of Student and Beginning Mathematics Teachers.* Ph.D. dissertation, University of Birmingham.

Povey, H., and Burton, L. (with Angier, C., and Boylon, M.). (1999). Learners as Authors in the Mathematics Classroom. In L. Burton (Ed.), *Learning Mathematics: From Hierarchies to Networks* (pp. 232–245). London: Falmer Press.

Reynolds, A.J., and Walberg, H.J. (1992). A Process Model of Mathematics Achievement and Attitude. *Journal for Research in Mathematics Education,* 23(4), 306–328.

Teese, R., Davies, M., Polesel, J., and O'Brien, K. (1999). *Accreditation in the Victorian Adult and Community Education Sector.* Educational Outcomes Research Unit, Department of Educational Policy and Management, The University of Melbourne.

Tennant, M. (Ed.). (1991). *Adult and Continuing Education in Australia: Issues and Practices.* London: Routledge.

Walkerdine, V. (1988). *The Mastery of Reason.* London: Routledge.

Young Loveridge, J. (1989). The Relationship between Children's Home Experiences and Their Mathematical Skills on Entry to School. *Early Child Development and Care,* 43, 43–59.

Part II

What Does Social Justice Mean in Classrooms?

Chapter 5

Opportunity to Learn Mathematics among Aymara-, Quechua-, and Spanish-Speaking Rural and Urban Fourth- and Fifth-Graders in Puno, Peru

Walter G. Secada, Santiago Cueto, and Fernando Andrade

INTRODUCTION

The promulgation of a new mathematics curriculum in Peru, the dearth of information on Peruvian student achievement and its distribution throughout the country, poorly documented yet obvious rural-urban inequalities, beliefs among policymakers that workshops provide adequate training for curriculum implementation, economic instability, the end of terrorist activity a few years prior to our study, and the political instability that led to then-President Fujimori's resignation while the data were being gathered all provided context for the study reported, in part, in this chapter. Of particular interest was the availability of mathematics education to people who were not necessarily Spanish speaking and whose living conditions are often affected by a confluence of circumstances.

Peru is a developing nation on South America's Pacific coast. Bounded by Ecuador, Colombia, Brazil, Bolivia, and Chile, Peru's geography incorporates the Amazonian rainforest to the northwest, a relatively narrow coastal plain, the Andes, their associated highland plateaus, and the world's highest freshwater lake, Titicaca. Spanish is the nation's most common and politically dominant language; Quechua, Aymara, and other languages, spoken by the nation's indigenous peoples, have received official constitutional and/or legal recognition during the past 30 years.

During the early 1990s, Peru was submerged in deep economic instability, with inflation over a million percent per year and a decades-old internal war between the government and several terrorist groups that had resulted in over 25,000 deaths. With the capture and imprisonment of the uprising's leaders, some semblance of political stability has been restored to the nation. Inflation has been controlled, and terrorist groups have almost disappeared from public awareness.

Political scandals that came to light after we had started our study resulted in President Alberto Fujimori—under whose regime the terrorist leadership had been captured—resigning while on a state trip to Japan and his subsequent self-imposed exile to that nation. Fujimori's chief of secret police was himself arrested and detained in the same military installation that was created for housing the terrorists he had helped to apprehend. Peru's newly elected President Alejandr Toledo took office under the promise of fostering economic and human development and increasing social justice among the nation's peoples.

A large percentage of Peru's population continues to live in poverty (around 54% for 2000; Banco Central de Reserva 2001). Poverty is more likely in rural areas (66% of the rural population lives in poverty). In 1997, 36% of the population in Latin America lived in poverty; other countries, like Peru, show this difference in poverty, favoring urban over rural areas (CEPAL 2001).

OVERVIEW OF THE PERUVIAN EDUCATIONAL CONTEXT

Historically, it has been very difficult to obtain nationally, or even regionally, representative data about levels of Peruvian achievement. In 2001, the Ministry of Education (Ministerio de Educación 2001) began to release results from Peru's most recent national assessments in language arts and mathematics. Yet data from prior assessments remain unavailable to policymakers and other interested stakeholders.

In spite of the country's political turmoil and its economic problems, Peruvian literacy rates have been increasing steadily over the past decade. In 1993, 87.2% of the population reported having basic literacy skills; in 1997, the rate rose to 91.1% (Cuanto 2000). As in other Latin American countries, most illiterates are elderly women living in rural areas.

Currently, there is almost universal primary school enrollment (World Bank 1999). On the other hand, there is ample evidence that the quality of education that is provided to Peruvian students needs improvement and that there are large inequalities across different locales and demographic groups (for instance, urban and rural students). An international study that included 12 Latin American countries showed that third- and fourth-grade Peruvian students are the lowest or among the lowest in achievement in mathematics and language tests (Unidad de la Medición de la Calidad Educativa [UMC] and GRADE, 2001). The same study showed that Peruvian rural students performed worse than did their urban counterparts. Another study showed a strong negative correlation between several indicators of poverty and achievement in language and mathematics at the national level (UMC and GRADE 2000). It is hard to pinpoint reasons for and/or solutions to this state of affairs, but among those that have been proposed is the relatively low investment in education by the Peruvian government: The

Peruvian budget in education is 2.4% of the gross domestic product, well below the regional average of around 5% (Saavedra 2001).

Mathematics Curriculum Reform

Peru's national curriculum is passed by an act of its Congress. A new K–6 curriculum was issued under Peru's previous administration (Ministerio de Educación, 2000b). The mathematics section of this curriculum sought a more balanced treatment of content among the four areas of arithmetic (number sense and computation, geometry, data analysis, and algebra) than was the case for earlier curricula. This balance was created by reducing what had been an almost exclusive treatment of arithmetic (i.e., number sense and computation) to include the other areas. Additionally, the new curriculum emphasized connections among mathematical topics and on student understanding of those topics; and it renamed mathematics as logic-mathematics in order to emphasize the analysis that should take place in classrooms. The Peruvian Ministry of Education issued new workbooks and provided wide-scale teacher training (primarily in the form of full-day workshops) on the use of the new materials in order to support the implementation of Peru's new curriculum. There is a widespread assumption that teachers have been adequately trained to implement the new curriculum. No formal evaluations of these programs have yet been published.

The Legal and Educational Status of Peru's Indigenous Languages

More than 40 indigenous languages currently are spoken in Peru. Many languages are spoken by just a few hundred people in the Amazon. The most widely spoken languages are Quechua and Aymara. In Peru, over 3 million people speak Quechua, which is found in several departments, especially in the Andes (Ministerio de Educación 2000a). Almost all of Aymara's 300,000 speakers are clustered in one department, Puno (Ministerio de Educación 2000a). Peru's Ministry of Education also administers an intercultural-bilingual education program (EBI) that is intended to support the use of indigenous languages.

Peru's constitution recognizes Spanish and all indigenous languages as official. This recognition does not mean that all speakers of Peru's indigenous languages attend an EBI school. There is an insufficient supply of indigenous-language materials, and teachers are not adequately prepared to accommodate all of Peru's indigenous-language-speaking students. Thus many of them attend Spanish-speaking-only schools (exact figures are not available). Over the past few years, workbooks and textbooks have begun to be published in several indigenous languages. Moreover, Peru's current government has expressed the desire to make rural education and specifically EBI a priority.

CONSTRUCTING A POLICY-RELEVANT STUDY

The above context defined our study: first, a new mathematics curriculum; second, the lack of information on student achievement and its distribution throughout the country; third, obvious rural-urban inequalities that were not well documented; fourth, policymakers' beliefs about the adequacy of curriculum implementation training for teachers. These were all set within economic instability, the recent end of terrorist activity, and eventual political instability. We focused on the quality of instruction found in Peru's altiplano with a particular interest in the problems of bilingual education for mathematics learning. We chose this geographic area because of our concerns for the educational attainments of Peru's indigenous peoples, many not Spanish speaking, and our personal and professional commitments to social justice.

Our particular research methodology was designed to address the dearth of large-scale studies that might provide an overview of the educational landscape. While some ethnographies involving bilingual education in Peru's altiplano (e.g., Hornberger 1987) provide insights into the processes that give rise to important educational problems and to the meanings that some individuals attach to their experiences, Peruvian policymakers and other stakeholders are concerned about how typical such findings might be. As a result, they ask how much they can rely on those findings when making decisions on how to invest resources that are scarce in the nation's educational infrastructure resources.

Under previous Peruvian governments, many new schools had been built throughout the nation's rural zones. These schools were equipped with chalkboards and other, relatively inexpensive supplies. Many policymakers also believe that workshops, curriculum materials based on the nation's newly enacted curriculum laws, and the assignment of teachers provide an adequate investment in the nation's educational infrastructure. Through our study, we hoped to test those assumptions and to help sharpen the debate on what to do next.

We also confronted the challenge of how to incorporate concerns for social justice within a policy-relevant study. Conceptions of equity and social justice vary among school personnel, professional educators, and interested stakeholders in education (Secada 2001); Norway, a developed country, commissioned a series of large-scale studies to evaluate how well its educational reforms of the late 1990s promoted equity where different studies are grounded, at least implicitly, in multiple conceptions (Secada, 2002). Yet in the context of a developing nation that is emerging from years of political and economic turmoil linked to terrorist activity, many conceptions of equity that are accepted in developed nations or within academic circles would be dismissed out of hand not just by policymakers but also by many everyday people. Our challenge was to find ways of incorporating concerns for equity that would fit within the nation's prevailing political discourses. We settled on two ways of framing concerns for equity: as an issue of distributive social justice and as an issue of socially enlightened self-interest.

Inequality in the Opportunity to Learn Mathematics and Social Justice

Societies construct—or at least, support the construction of—mechanisms and other social arrangements for the distribution of economic, material, and other goods. Societies also establish and support arrangements for the distribution of the costs of social living, such costs as taxation, military and other forms of compulsory service, and even more draconian personal sacrifices that people are asked to shoulder, depending on the conditions of their societies at particular historical moments. In our view, education is a social good (as opposed to a social cost); hence, we do not discuss the distribution of social costs. We focus on education—mathematics education, in particular—as the good that gets distributed through a particular set of social arrangements, to wit, public schools.

Schools distribute many different social desiderata, some by design and others through the active coconstruction of the students and school personnel. For example, though schools were not specifically designed for the creation of social networks among students, they are places where children interact with each other and create friendship-based networks that extend beyond their immediate families. By design, Peru's schools often provide meals to students who would otherwise go hungry, athletics to interested students, and other nonacademic opportunities for students to experience. Also by design, schools distribute mathematics learning (and achievement) indirectly. What schools are designed to do is to distribute the *opportunity* for students to learn mathematics. Schools provide students with the opportunity to learn mathematics through the mathematics curriculum and through the pedagogical methods of teachers whose job it is to teach mathematics. Students are expected to avail themselves of these opportunities since if they do not, neither learning nor achievement can take place.

Recognizing that the relationships between teacher and student and among students are all quite complex and further recognizing that the relationships themselves interact complexly to create student learning, we framed *opportunity to learn mathematics* as something that can be analyzed and manipulated in terms of social justice. Opportunity to learn mathematics is an important social good precisely because it undergirds student learning and achievement in mathematics. Peruvian students who do not learn mathematics—whether or not they have had adequate opportunities—often repeat their earlier grades and experience a very limited mathematics curriculum that is focused on basic skills remediation to the virtual exclusion of all else—what one of our (the authors') children once called "boring math." The later-life consequences of these limited experiences range from school dropout, through limited postsecondary educational opportunities and attainments, to constrained career paths and salaries.

Some philosophers, such as Rawls (1971), might argue that a just society should distribute educational opportunity to learn aggressively in order to counter the impact of an unequal playing field on children of poverty or, more generally, to ensure that children who through an accident of birth have been positioned at a disadvantage relative to other children, have a fair chance to learn mathematics. The argument is very simple: Given the consequences of the failure to learn mathematics, a just society must take affirmative steps to ensure that everyone has a fair chance to succeed at learning mathematics so that the consequences of failure are, in some sense, that individual's own fault. We would question the "fairness" of visiting the consequences of someone's childhood actions on that individual throughout her/his life in as rigid a manner as this formulation seems to imply. Moreover, it is very possible for people who do not succeed at mathematics to be quite successful in later life and to be fully contributing members of society; hence, the consequences of underachievement in mathematics are not that rigid. What is more, we would endorse steps to help children who did not learn mathematics the first time to achieve either immediately or through lifelong learning opportunities.

The viewing of group-based inequality as an issue of equity has a long tradition within policy-relevant social science research in general (e.g., Bowles 2000; Moen, Dempster-McClain, and Walker 1999; Tilly 1998) and in different forms of educational research in particular (Coleman 1968; Fennema and Leder 1990; Howe 1997). This study builds on those well-established lines of inquiry.

Inequality and Socially Enlightened Self-Interest

Many social scientists, economists, and educators (e.g., Reimers 2000) argue that group-based inequalities in the distribution of social goods—in our case, opportunity to learn mathematics—is bad social policy from a position of socially enlightened self-interest. Unless society actively includes its least-advantaged members in the distribution of its opportunity to learn mathematics, the cumulative costs—in terms of lost earnings and the other negative consequences of people's not knowing mathematics—will be socially disastrous. This position was taken in the original manuscripts involving the reform of school mathematics in the United States (Secada 1989–1991). It is a position that can be traced back at least to the time of the economist Adam Smith (1904), if not before.

These converging formulations of equity (as an issue of distributive social justice and as an issue of socially enlightened self-interest) suggest a standard—to wit, that the distribution of opportunity to learn mathematics be unrelated to the accidents of an individual's birth. Specifically in this study, we looked at the relationship between opportunity to learn mathematics and the kinds of schools that fourth- and fifth-grade students attended. Our study illuminates the functioning of the educational system. Insofar as we find any consistent pattern of differences in student opportunity to learn mathematics, we identify areas where the educational system is differentially advantaging (or disadvantaging) students as a function of location and language. Second, our study helps to identify areas of needed improvement based on views of socially enlightened self-interest.

Quality and Socially Enlightened Self-Interest

Moreover, equity perspectives derived from socially enlightened self-interest also support a higher standard for the achievement of equity. One way of creating equality is to lower the bar, that is, to provide equally low levels of a social good across particular social groups. In the case of Peru, equality of this sort would be meaningless since that country's investment in education is low relative to that of other South American nations. What is more, the Peruvian congress certainly hoped for a more efficient use of its resources than would be implied by equality derived from the provision of low levels of educational opportunity. Our standard for equity, hence, approaches that of Secada, Gamoran, and Weinnstein (1996) who argued that equity must contain both high quality and equality.

THE STUDY

We focused our work on Puno, located in the south of Peru in the altiplano, on the borders of Lake Titicaca, which forms part of the border between Peru and Bolivia. Puno is at around 4,000 meters (13,123 feet) above sea level. Puno was chosen for this study because of the status of Quechua and Aymara among Peru's indigenous languages and because some prior research had found that the mathematics achievement of rural Aymara students was above that of Quechua students and near the achievement of Spanish-speaking students, after controlling for several covariates (World Bank 1999). We were interested in replicating these results and, if so, trying to understand the processes by which mathematics learning was superior in Puno's Aymara over its Quechua schools. Very few studies have documented educational processes within the classroom. This study was set up to do so in different environments (urban and rural) and with students with different maternal languages (Spanish, Quechua, and Aymara).

In the 1993 national census, Puno's population was over 1.1 million (INEI 2001). The six provinces included in the study are considered very poor, poor, or medium according to several socioeconomic indicators so that, in general, Puno is considered as a poor department in Peru, with none of its provinces reaching an "acceptable" level of life (FONCODES, 2000). For instance, 68% of Puneños lack electricity at home; 81% have no sewage; and 56% have no running water. As in other departments in Peru, the situation is much worse for the rural population, as compared to the urban.

In some of Puno's provinces, Quechua is the dominant language; in one province, for example, 84% of the population declared Quechua their mother tongue in the 1993 national census. In other provinces, Aymara is dominant; for example, 80% of the population in one province declared Aymara as their mother tongue. Finally, in other provinces, Spanish predominates—for example, for up to 45% of that province's population. Most Puneños speak an indigenous language (or at least understand it) and also speak Spanish. However, Quechua and Aymara are mostly oral languages in that few people know how to read or write in them. In contrast, Spanish is the only language used in official documents, newspapers, and advertisements on the streets. Thus, Spanish is the more prestigious language in Puno.

Hornberger's (1987) study of educational processes in Puno described vividly the loss of pedagogical time occurring in several rural Puno schools. The 1998 national tests in language arts (Spanish only) and mathematics in four grades showed that Puno's urban students were at least half a standard deviation below the national average (UMC and GRADE 2000).

Sample Selection

We selected 29 elementary schools for this study. Nine urban schools were located in a provincial or district capital. In Peru's 1993 census, the populations of their respective towns ranged from 520 to 38,536, with a median size of 4,041 people. The largest group of students at 4 of the 9 urban schools were ethnic Aymara; ethnic Quechua students predominated at 4 other schools; and the last school enrolled an ethnically mixed population of students. Most of the urban students spoke Spanish as their dominant language; none of the schools offered instruction via either Aymara or Quechua. Ten rural schools were drawn from areas where Aymara is the language of everyday culture and commerce and where, as a result, almost all the students speak Aymara as their native language. Teachers at 5 of the schools received training from the national government and mathematics materials written in Aymara to run an EBI program. Ten rural schools were drawn from areas where Quechua is the language used for home and within the larger community. As a result, again, almost all students at these schools speak Quechua as their native language. Six schools from this sample run an EBI program.

Within each school, we selected a fourth- and a fifth-grade classroom to participate in the study. We focused on fourth and fifth grades because Peru's national mathematics curriculum shows a sharp break in the content that is to be taught at these grades, the elaboration of that content as shown by the increased number of objectives of fifth over fourth grade, and in its assumptions about the level of sophistication for the teaching of content. All but 1 rural school had separate fourth- and fifth-grade classes. Due to their small enrollments, the other 19 rural schools had combined 3/4 and 5/6 cross-grade classes. All 9 urban schools had self-contained classes for each grade.

We surveyed and interviewed every principal from these 29 schools, the 57 fourth- and fifth-grade teachers whose classrooms had been selected for the study, the fourth- and fifth-graders in those classrooms, and as many of the heads of their respective households as we could find. A by-school breakdown of our sample comprises Tables 5.1 and 5.2.

Table 5.1

Number and Median Age of Students and Number of Heads of Households, Teachers, and Principals in the Fourth-Grade Sample

Type of Location	School	Students				Head of Household	Teachers	Principals
		Female	Median Age	Male	Median Age			
	CDA01	10	10	18	10	20	1	1
	CDA02	17	10	9	10	22	1	1
	CDQ01	17	9	13	10	28	1	1
	CDQ02	18	10	14	10	27	1	1
Urban	CDQ03	15	11	14	10	28	1	1
	CPA01	15	9	29	10	30	1	1
	CPA02	18	10	13	10	25	1	1
	CPC01	41	10	0		37	1	1
	CPQ01	19	10	15	10	31	1	1
	STQ01	3	12	9	11	10	1	1
	STQ02	11	11	2	NA	7	1	1
	STQ03	4	14	7	13	9	1	1
	STQ04	2	9	5	11	6	1	1
Rural	STQ05	9	11	5	11	13	1	1
Quechua	STQ06	7	11	7	11	12	1	1
	STQ07	12	11	7	11	14	1	1
	STQ08	5	12	12	13	16	1	1
	STQ09	7	12	9	12	15	1	1
	STQ10	11	11	3	10	13	1	1
	STA01	5	11	4	10	6	1	1
	STA02	3	11	2	10	3	1	1
	STA03	3	11	13	10	11	1	1
	STA04	7	10	8	9	12	1	1
Rural	STA05	3	10	8	11	7	1	1
Aymara	STA06	5	11	5	11	7	1	1
	STA07	7	12	5	9	11	1	1
	STA08	8	10	5	10	11	1	1
	STA09	7	11	7	11	13	1	1
	STA10	3	9	5	10	6	1	1
All Schools		292	11	253	10	450	29	29

NA = Not available.

Approximately 60 more females than males participated in the study. Twenty-five more fourth- than fifth-graders participated. Since these differences in participation are so small relative to the larger sample size and since we tend to consider the fourth- and fifth-grade results separately in order to look for cross-grade patterns, we did not think that differential sample size would threaten bias in the study results.

Table 5.2
Number and Median Age of Students and Number of Heads of Households,
Teachers, and Principals in the Fifth-Grade Sample

Type of Location	School	Students				Head of Household	Teachers	Principals
		Female	Median Age	Male	Median Age			
Urban	CDA01	11	11	21	11	27	1	1
	CDA02	15	11	7	11	17	1	1
	CDQ01	10	11	14	11	23	1	1
	CDQ02	12	10	11	12	22	1	1
	CDQ03	14	11	22	12	32	1	1
	CPA01	24	11	16	11	25	1	1
	CPA02	16	11	13	11	23	1	1
	CPC01	41	11	0		32	1	1
	CPQ01	10	11	16	11	23	1	1
Rural Quechua	STQ01	11	11	10	11	13	1	1
	STQ02	5	11	7	11	9	1	1
	STQ03	4	13	4	13	7	1	1
	STQ04	6	12	3	12	5	1	1
	STQ05	0		6	12	4	1	1
	STQ06	8	13	6	12	12	1	1
	STQ07	4	12	8	13	12	1	1
	STQ08	6	14	6	13	8	1	1
	STQ09	7	12	8	12	15	1	1
	STQ10	8	13	2	12	8	1	1
Rural Aymara	STA01	4	10	5	11	6	1	1
	STA02	6	12	4	12	6	1	1
	STA03	8	10	7	11	11	1	1
	STA04	7	12	8	10	13	1	1
	STA05	6	12	8	12	11	1	1
	STA06	1	NA	14	11	13	1	1
	STA07	12	12	5	11	17	1	1
	STA08	5	12	4	11	7	1	1
	STA09	7	12	7	13	10	1	1
	STA10	2	11	8	11	9	1	1
All Schools		270	11	250	11	420	29	29

NA = Not available.

Data Gathering

We gathered a broad range of data for the larger study (Cueto and Secada 2001) from which this chapter is taken. In the following narrative, we describe the sources of the data for this particular chapter.

Indicators of Student Poverty in Schools. Specially trained adults weighed and measured students for their height. A child's height-to-age and weight-to-height ratios, when measured against international norms, provide indicators of that child's relative nutrition. Individuals whose height-to-age ratio or a weight-to-height ratio is 2 or more standard deviations below international norms are considered to suffer *growth retardation* or *acute malnourishment*, respectively. While the causes of growth retardation can vary for individual children (e.g., due to illness or heredity), when growth retardation affects an entire population of children, it is likely to have been caused either by an epidemic or from a low-quality diet (i.e., one low in proteins and certain vitamins and minerals) throughout the population. A child who is acutely malnourished suffers from both stunted growth and being severely underweight relative to her or his actual height. Acute malnourishment entails more than a low-quality diet; it also entails inadequate caloric intake. If large numbers of children within a population have a weight-to-height ratio that is 2 or more standard deviations below international norms, then it is likely that the given population suffers from widespread acute malnourishment.

Each head of household (that is, each child's principal caretaker) was asked to report on her or his level of education, principal source of income, and income level. In addition, each head of household responded to questions on their home's flooring, water source, access to public sewage, electricity at home, and number of people sleeping in a single room. In Peruvian research, three or more people sleeping in a room is considered an indicator of overcrowded living conditions.

Indicators of Basic Resources Needed for Opportunity to Learn. There is a lively debate among economists and educational policymakers on the monetary resources that are needed to ensure educational opportunity (Reimers 2000). Money, like time, is an empty resource, and what is important is what one does with that money and time. However, the situation in Peru's altiplano is very different than in the worlds inhabited by those who engage in debates about fiscal resources. First of all and as will be documented later in this chapter, schools in Puno lack many of the basic amenities that are taken for granted in the world's developed nations. In the absence of compelling evidence that things like access to electricity, potable water, and public sewage-disposal systems do not matter for providing educational opportunity, we rely on a different test for the importance of these kinds of resources: Let those people who think these things do not matter send their children to these schools. No one, to our knowledge, has ever taken up that challenge. Hence, we documented the distribution of these resources among the schools in our sample.

At each school, we gathered information on: the make of the building's roof, the availability of water via a public system that would provide potable water (as opposed to wells that, in some cases, required the use of a bucket), access to a public sewage-disposal system (as opposed to toilet facilities that, in some cases, were little more than latrines or outhouses), electricity, phone, and the availability of chalk and blackboard. Under the assumption that children's chances of learning are hurt when they are not in school, we checked school records for the start and the end dates of each school's academic year.

Each selected teacher was asked whether he or she spoke, read, and/or wrote

Spanish, Aymara, and/or Quechua. A teacher's non-Spanish-language skills are an important opportunity-to-learn resource, especially in the rural areas where another language is the primary language for everyday home and economic interactions, since it would enable a teacher (and the larger school) to communicate with children, with their principal caretakers, and with others (such as bus drivers and/or building maintenance and repair personnel) whose dominant language is not Spanish.

Each classroom was visited four times—for a complete day each time—during the latter part of the academic year. During that visit, teachers were asked to teach mathematics so that the specially trained observers could rate the classroom's mathematical instruction environment along three scales (see below). As a result of our asking teachers to teach mathematics during our observations, we did not obtain a good indication of how much time is spent on mathematics instruction during a *typical* day. However, we did obtain information on how much time, in a typical day, is actually used on academics.

The typical school day is supposed to last from 8:00 A.M. until 1:00 P.M., with half an hour devoted to morning recess. Usually, schools provide children with a snack during recess time; otherwise, children are assumed to come to school having eaten breakfast and to have lunch when they arrive home. We computed the amount of time that was spent on academics during a typical school day by keeping track of what occurred during that day and subtracting noninstructional time (e.g., time spent on transitions, recess beyond its scheduled 30 minutes, student assembly, and students just sitting around and waiting for instruction) from the maximum of four and a half hours that are available for instruction during a school day. The most frequently observed instructional activities included teachers lecturing and answering student questions, students copying work from the board into their notebooks, students working in their workbooks or notebooks, and students working at the board.

Indicators of Opportunity to Learn Mathematics: Curriculum Coverage. While the Ministry of Education provides mathematics workbooks for each student, the primary source for content coverage are teachers' classroom lectures with chalkboard explanations that students record in their notebooks. We collected the mathematics notebook for each classroom's highest-achieving boy and girl (as nominated by the teacher) on the assumption that their notebooks would provide the most comprehensive overview of the year's content coverage. The Peruvian national curriculum, as passed by an act of that country's congress, was used to create a three-dimensional framework for analyzing each grade's content coverage.

The superordinate headings along the first dimension of content coverage included number sense, computation, geometry, measurement, data analysis, algebra, and set theory. Number sense, computation, geometry, measurement, data analysis, and algebra are all found in Peru's most recently promulgated national curriculum. While set theory appeared in previous curricula, it was deleted from the most current one. Set theory emerged as a major heading because of its presence in students' notebooks and in spite of its absence from the official curriculum. Number sense and computation could be thought of as covering the content of arithmetic; the latter five represent content that was seldom (if ever) taught in the past and for whose inclusion the most recent national curriculum was designed. These seven content strands were further broken down into sub-headings that were based on that grade's specific objectives as found in the national curriculum (see Gómez and Steinþórsdóttir 2001). In this chapter, we report results only for the major headings due to the strength of the findings and to the limited variation in content coverage that was found within the sub-headings.

Along the second dimension were included five broad cross-cutting process objectives: the memorization of facts (for example, number facts) and/or definitions; the acquisition of procedures *without* connection to underlying concepts; the acquisition of procedures *with* connections to underlying concepts; the exploration (primarily informal) of mathematical ideas; and the solution of real-life (or realistic) problems. The memorization of facts and the acquisition of procedures without connections to underlying concepts are content that, traditionally, are taught and learned by rote. In contrast, the acquisition of procedures *with* connections to underlying concepts is content that deepens student understanding. The exploration of mathematical ideas and the solution of real-world (or realistic) problems are content that encourages students to engage in higher-order thinking. That is, students are expected to analyze problems and situations, to provide justifications for their problem solutions, and/or to compare their reasoning with one another. In a word, when exploring situations and solving problems, students go beyond merely repeating something they have learned and create something that, to them, may be new.

A third dimension of the notebook analysis—which we report only anecdotally here—focused on whether an answer or problem solution was right or wrong.

Each entry in a given notebook was classified using the above framework. That is, an individual computation was coded as a single entry, as was the complete solution to a single problem. For a given year's total, we counted the total number of entries per cell and converted those totals into percentages. Each classroom's content-coverage rates were the average of the rates computed for its highest-achieving girl and boy. We did not analyze these data based on gender since such differences would probably be due to differences in the individual student's school attendance or in copying from the board and, most likely, would not be due to differential treatment of boys and girls in a given classroom.

Indicators of Opportunity to Learn Mathematics: Quality of Instruction. Teachers were asked to teach mathematics during each day that they were observed. The intellectual quality of the classroom processes during mathematics instruction was scored using methods originally developed for observing American mathematics classrooms in restructured schools (Newmann and Associates 1996; Newmann, Secada, and Wehlage 1995).

Every 15 minutes spent on mathematics instruction, specially trained observers rated the classroom's learning environment along a 5-point scale for each of three dimensions. The first scale focused on whether the classroom was a *psychologically safe* place where students could take intellectual risks without fear of putdowns and gratuitous comments. A classroom received a score of 1 if it was an unsafe place to learn mathematics. This score was awarded if the teacher put students down for errors or if students often interrupted one another. A classroom scored a 3 along this dimension if the teachers ensured that it was safe and comfortable for students to take intellectual risks when doing mathematics. That is, the teacher encouraged children to try hard and children would seldom—if ever—put one another down or interrupt with one another's efforts. A classroom scored a 5 along this dimension if students actively supported one another and encouraged each other to try hard to understand the mathematics content of the lesson.

The second scale for the quality of mathematics instruction focused on the *depth of understanding* to which the day's content was developed. A score of 1 was awarded if content was covered superficially and trivially. A 3 was scored when the teacher made a conscious effort to cover content in some depth, for example, when she or he tried to explain the reasons as to why an algorithm works the way that it works. However, there was no evidence that any student actually grasped (or even tried to grasp) the point of the explanation. An observation scored 5 on the depth scale when there was evidence that most of the students engaged in at least one sustained effort to understand something in depth; no classroom met this demanding criterion on depth.

The third dimension focused on the extent to which students analyzed the lesson's topic in order to better understand it. *Mathematical analysis* requires higher-order thinking where the content of that thinking is mathematics. Mathematical analysis entails the learning and/or production of new knowledge and insights as opposed to the rote learning of prespecified lists of information. Mathematical analysis takes place when students draw distinctions between things, discuss solutions, justify answers, generalize rules, make elaborate explanations, and/or apply what they know to new settings. Mathematical analysis can occur when students explore mathematical topics, solve real-world problems, or apply mathematics to realistic settings.

An observation scored 1 on *mathematical analysis* when it was focused almost exclusively on the rote learning of established content. A 3 was scored when the teacher expended substantial effort in trying to engage students in making contrasts, explaining their reasoning, or some other activity requiring higher-order thinking. A score of 5 would be awarded to an observation if there was at least one occurrence where most of the students engaged in mathematical analysis (for example, discussing their solution to a problem) for a substantial amount of time; not a single classroom observation met this demanding standard for mathematical analysis.

It may help to think across the scales. A score of 1 for each of the dimensions was low and awarded to a classroom that was unsafe (the teacher or students put other students down), where the mathematics was covered superficially, or where students were treated as if they were expected to repeat what was being taught by rote. A 3 was the highest that a classroom could score based solely on the teacher's efforts. That is, a 3 was scored when the teacher treated students well and encouraged them to take intellectual risks, provided elaborate explanations of the content, or encouraged students to analyze and think about a topic so as to better understand it. While a 5 was never awarded to a classroom in this study, it could have been achieved by a classroom where most of the students (i.e., about 80% or more of the students) were engaged in a given activity for more of the time (i.e., about 80% or more of the time). That is, a class environment could score a 5 if students actively encouraged one another to try hard and to take risks, if students treated the content in great depth, or if they focused on elaborating the content, drawing distinctions, and making connections in the mathematics that was being taught.

All classroom observers were mathematics teachers who had received three full days of training on making school visits and on using the observation scales prior to making their observations. Beyond learning the proper protocols for entering schools and classrooms—for example, introducing themselves to the teacher and explaining to curious children what they were doing—the observers watched videotapes of mathematics instruction conducted by teachers who were not in our sample so that they could discuss the intent of each scale and how to use it. Training also included visits to classrooms for real-time training that was followed by postobservation debriefing among the observers, a discussion of difficulties that they encountered during their observations and a consensus on how to resolve those difficulties, and discussion of how their observations should be translated into numeric ratings. By the end of three days of training, all observers had achieved over 90% interrater agreement on each of the observation protocol's sections. We dropped those observers who had failed to achieve a minimum of 90% agreement with the rest of their colleagues and/or those who, based on their participation in the discussions, had failed to understand how to implement the classroom observation protocols.

RESULTS

Poverty in Puno's Schools

Most students live in households whose head has not completed secondary school, who is engaged in fishing or agriculture, and whose median salary is less than U.S.$75 per month (see Table 5.3). These depressed earnings are reflected in the kinds of homes where students live. Over half live in homes

Table 5.3
Indicators of Student Poverty as a Function of School Locale

	Urban	Rural Aymara	Rural Quechua
Infrastructure of students' homes			
Percent of homes with dirt floors	42	72	97
Percent of homes without public water	44	72	86
Percent of homes without public sanitation systems: that is, with cesspits, latrines, etc.	49	86	93
Percent of homes without electricity	34	63	99
Percent of homes with 3 or more persons per room	24	46	43
Household socioeconomic conditions			
Percent of households whose heads have received no formal education	2	10	9
Percent of households whose heads have received less than secondary education	65	95	97
Percent of households whose heads are engaged in agriculture and fishing	43	79	84
Median monthly income for household heads in U.S. dollars	74	17	13

with dirt floors, that lack access to public water systems, that lack access to public sewage-disposal systems (i.e., that rely on latrines and outhouses), and that lack electricity (Table 5.3). A third of the students live in overcrowded homes (Table 5.3). Between 25% and 55% of the students suffer from a low-quality diet as shown by their low height-to-age ratios (i.e., students in Puno tend to be short for their ages; see Table 5.4), though almost no students are acutely undernourished. Hence, these students are likely to go to school from what would be considered stressful situations.

Moreover, poverty is unevenly distributed (see Tables 5.3 and 5.4) in Puno. Almost no head of household has finished secondary school in the rural schools, while at least one third have finished in the urban settings; these differences might be expected to translate into parental pressure on students to stay in school and familial ability to help students with their schoolwork. While the median monthly salary for the head of household is almost U.S.$75 in the urban districts, it drops to less than U.S.$20 in the rural districts. These are the same areas in which the dominant economic activity entails fishing or agriculture; hence, people might be expected to eke out a subsistence living and to engage in barter and trade for other needed commodities. These are also the areas in which between one third to over one half of the students suffer from low-quality diets.

Table 5.4
Percent of Students Suffering from Acute Malnourishment (Weight-to-Height Ratio) and Growth Retardation (Height-to-Age Ratio)

	4th grade			5th grade		
	Urban	Rural Quechua	Rural Aymara	Urban	Rural Quechua	Rural Aymara
Acute malnourishment*						
Female	1	0	0	0	0	0
Male	0	0	0	0	0	0
Growth retardation**						
Female	25	48	35	23	38	35
Male	25	54	43	36	50	42

*Weight-to-height ratio is 2 or more standard deviations below international norms.
**Height-to-age ratio is 2 or more standard deviations below international norms.

The vast majority of rural students (over at least 60% in each category), though more so in the Quechua than the Aymara zones, live in homes with dirt floors, lacking public water and sewage, and lacking electricity. In contrast, less than half of the urban students lack these amenities. More so in rural than in urban homes, students are likely to live in overcrowded conditions. Finally, as evidenced by their differentially low height-to-age ratios, rural boys are more likely than rural girls to suffer from growth retardation; that is, they are more likely to have relatively low-quality diets and, as a result, to be short for their age.

Basic Educational Resources

Physical Resources. Most schools in our sample reflect the overall poverty found in Puno (Table 5.5). Schools tend to have sheet metal roofing, lack access to public water and sewage systems, and lack telephones. Lack of resources, moreover, is concentrated in rural as opposed to urban schools, with the lack somewhat greater in the Quechua as opposed to Aymara zones. This is reflected in the large disparity between urban and rural schools on access to public water, sewage, and electric systems—utilities that are difficult to install and maintain due to the great costs associated with infrastructure development. A relatively easy-to-provide resource, the chalkboard, can be found in good working order across all schools; not reflected in Table 5.5 is the fact that all but one school had a blackboard in good condition in *either* fourth or fifth grade (if not in both).

Throughout Peru, in spite of the quick spread of cell phones that can be found on Lake Titicaca on the floating islands known as "los Uros" that date to pre-

Table 5.5
School Characteristics

Type of Location	Urban	Rural Aymara	Rural Quechua
Percent with sheet metal (zinc/calamine) **roof**	67	100	100
Percent with public water	67	10	10
Percent with public sewage	56	10	0
Percent with electricity	89	40	0
Percent with telephone	22	0	0
Percent with blackboards in good condition **in both classrooms**	67	70	80
Median number of elementary students	349	89	79
Median number of teachers	15	4	3
Median student-to-teacher ratio	26	18	25

Columbian times, schools in our sample had no phones. The relatively small number of teachers found in rural schools—with a median number of 4 per school versus a median number of 15 teachers per urban school—is due to their relatively low student enrollments and reflected in the cross-grade classrooms that they teach. Once again, however, rural Quechua students—whose median pupil-teacher ratio of 25 rivals that of their urban cohorts—are in relatively more crowded classrooms than their Aymara peers, who have a median pupil-teacher ratio of 18.

Table 5.6 shows that, based on teachers' self-reports, there is a substantial match between teachers' linguistic skills and where they are teaching. For example, the first languages of the urban, rural Quechua, and rural Aymara teachers tend to be the dominant languages of their regions: 72% of teachers in the urban schools have Spanish as their first language; 72% of teachers in the rural Quechua schools have Quechua as their first language; and 70% of the teachers in rural Aymara schools have a matching first language. Though less than an ideal of 100%, 78% of the teachers in rural Quechua schools report that they can speak Quechua fluently, and 70% are fluent in Aymara in that region. As regards teachers possessing the more advanced linguistics skills of reading and writing Quechua and Aymara—skills that are necessary for the proper implementation of bilingual instruction—rates drop to less than 50%. Since these data are based on teacher self-report, they are likely to overestimate the levels of the linguistic resources that are available in Puno's schools.

The presence of Aymara- and Quechua-speaking teachers does not mean that students are receiving language-enhanced educational opportunities. As might

Table 5.6
Percent of Teachers Whose First Language Is Spanish, Quechua, or Aymara and Who Read, Speak, and Write a Non-Spanish Language

	Language	Urban	Rural Quechua	Rural Aymara
	Spanish	72	22	25
Teacher's first language	Quechua	17	72	5
	Aymara	11	6	70
Language the teacher speaks fluently	Quechua	33	78	15
	Aymara	28	6	70
Language the teacher reads fluently	Quechua	0	50	0
	Aymara	0	0	35
Language the teacher writes fluently	Quechua	0	33	0
	Aymara	0	0	15

Note: Based on teachers' self-reports.

be expected from the low rates of teacher written fluency, the student notebooks showed virtually no Quechua or Aymara in work that went beyond the writing of numbers. However, contrary to what might be expected given the high levels of teacher-reported oral fluency, our observers reported virtually no cases of either Quechua or Aymara being spoken within instructional settings; observers did not note language use during recess or during other noninstructional times.

Our data shed some light on the reasons why teachers across settings teach almost exclusively in Spanish. Students might pressure their teachers to use Spanish. Over 90% of the students in each of the different kinds of schools reported that it is *very important* to learn Spanish; in contrast, less than 40% of the students in Puno's urban and rural Quechua schools thought it was very important to learn to read or to write in their native language, and an even lower

Table 5.7
Number of Days the School Was Open during the Year 2000

	4th grade			5th grade		
	Urban	Rural Quechua	Rural Aymara	Urban	Rural Quechua	Rural Aymara
Minimum	117	115	101	53	117	129
Median	138	144	141	149	142	150
Maximum	156	169	155	164	169	159

17% of the Aymara students thought it was very important to learn to read or write Aymara.

Parents might also communicate similar educational priorities to their children and to the teachers. Heads of households across all three zones—94% in urban areas, 93% in rural Quechua, and 98% in rural Aymara—reported wanting their children to learn Spanish. Between 39% and 45% of the household heads reported wanting their children to learn how to speak or to read/write their native languages in school.

Teachers reported a pattern of educational language-learning objectives that mirror those of their students and parents. In the urban, rural Quechua, and rural Aymara schools, 95%, 87%, and 92% of the teachers want their children to learn Spanish. In contrast, between 28% and 48% of the teachers hold similar objectives for their students' learning of Quechua and Aymara.

Academic Instructional Time. Table 5.7 and Figure 5.1 illustrate the small amount of time that is actually devoted to academics in Puno. Table 5.7 shows that schools throughout Puno reported being in session for substantially less than a possible 180 days of instruction. One fifth-grade teacher was not assigned until mid-October to the urban school that reported 53 days of instruction for its fifth-graders. The main reason that a class did not meet for a particular school was that the teacher had failed to show up—something that, due to the unavailability of phones at schools, people did not realize would happen until well into the day.

Figure 5.1 shows that the average classroom spends a little over two hours on academics out of a day that has four and a half hours of time that is scheduled for academics. While there is some variability, the best-case scenario of over three hours of academic time in some urban and rural Aymara schools is balanced by worst cases of less than an hour actually spent on academics in urban and rural Quechua schools. Beyond the loss of time due to overlong recess or transitions, teachers would sometimes arrive late at school because the bus had been delayed or broken down, or they would leave school early because they had a medical or other appointment.

Recall that these findings are based on four observations per classroom toward the end of the school year—a time when one would expect teachers to feel

Figure 5.1
Mean Amount of Academic Instructional Time, +/−1 Standard of Deviation

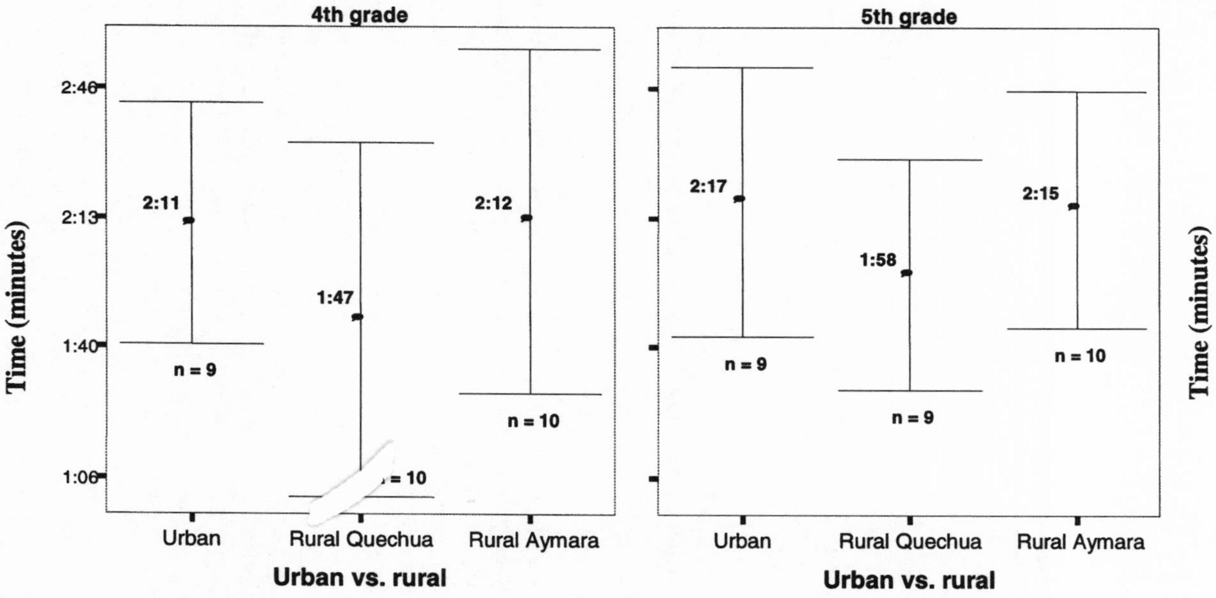

Table 5.8
Percent of Student Notebook Entries That Reflect Specific Mathematical Content

Mathematical Topic	4th grade			5th grade		
	Urban	Rural Quechua	Rural Aymara	Urban	Rural Quechua	Rural Aymara
Number sense	16	18	24	31	26	26
Computation	64	77	72	61	57	57
Geometry	0	1	0	0	1	1
Measurement	2	2	0	1	7	3
Data analysis	0	0	0	0	0	9
Algebra	0	0	1	4	6	4
Set theory	4	3	2	2	3	1

pressure to complete the year's content coverage. What is more, these observations excluded days when school was not in session because the teacher was absent from school.

The relatively low time that was spent on academic activity should not obscure the fact that rural Quechua schools spend approximately 30 minutes less on academics than either their urban or rural Aymara counterparts.

Curriculum Coverage

As seen in Table 5.8, the vast majority of notebooks reflect an almost single-minded emphasis on arithmetic, that is, on number sense and computation (the first two rows). An average of 90% of fourth-grade and 87% of fifth-grade notebook entries reflect this emphasis. This shift from fourth to fifth grade is reflected in a *slightly* greater emphasis that is placed on the nonarithmetic topics of geometry, measurement, data analysis, algebra, and set theory in fifth grade.

Table 5.8 also shows urban-rural differences in content emphasis, but they are not systematic. While 80% of the entries in the urban fourth grade reflect arithmetic content (number sense and computation), over 95% of the rural notebooks reflect this emphasis. Somewhat surprisingly, the differences are reversed in fifth grade, where 92% of the urban student notebook entries are arithmetic versus 83% for the rural student notebooks.

Table 5.9 reflects a uniform emphasis on rote skills development across school setting (urban, rural Aymara, and rural Quechua). Overall, 87% of the fourth-grade entries are focused on either memorization or the development of procedures (such as algorithms) without connections to underlying conceptions. This rate increases so that, in fifth grade, 84% of the entries reflect this emphasis. In fourth and fifth grades, respectively, 8% and 6% of the notebook entries reflect processes that could be said to promote the development of student understanding of mathematics by either *deepening* that understanding through practice on

Table 5.9
Percent of Student Notebook Entries That Reflect Mathematical Processes

Mathematical Processes	4th grade			5th grade		
	Urban	Rural Quechua	Rural Aymara	Urban	Rural Quechua	Rural Aymara
Memorization*	14	16	11	10	15	11
Procedures without connections to underlying concepts*	62	77	81	84	79	83
Procedures with connections to underlying concepts**	4	3	8	4	1	3
Exploration of mathematical concepts***	0	0	0	0	0	0
Real-life or realistic problems***	5	4	1	1	4	2

*Corresponds to rote skills development.
**Corresponds to instruction that could promote depth of understanding.
***Corresponds to instruction that could promote mathematical analysis.

procedures *with* connections to underlying conceptions and/or by enhancing students' engagement in mathematical analysis through the exploration of mathematical topics and the solution of real-world (or realistic) problems. No pattern of consistent differences could be found across school settings on these latter curricular emphases.

Our method of counting every notebook entry as a single item is likely to overestimate the emphasis on rote skills development. A page devoted to computations might take as much class time and require as much intellectual work on the part of students as a page devoted to the solution of a single problem. However, *each* computation would be counted once, while the problem would also be counted a single time. In spite of this methodological weakness, we are confident in our findings since they were replicated through classroom observations. We also found many errors in almost every notebook. While error-pattern analysis is just beginning, our initial impressions are that students showed most of their errors on content involving fractions and decimals.

Hence, our analysis of the highest-achieving students' notebooks indicates that the dominant mathematics content that students encounter is arithmetic with an emphasis on rote skills development. We may be overestimating the emphasis on rote skills development due to our method for analyzing the notebooks, and there may be some variation on content emphasis because we did not collect student workbooks that are provided by the Ministry of Education. It may be possible, for instance, that students devoted more time to geometry than could be caught in the notebooks since workbooks provide ready-made figures that students would not need to draw in their books. However, a recent analysis of curricular emphasis found in mathematics workbooks provided to native speak-

Table 5.10
Mean (and Standard of Deviation) for Classroom Observation Scales

Scale	4th grade			5th grade		
	Urban	Rural Quechua	Rural Aymara	Urban	Rural Quechua	Rural Aymara
Physical safety	2.97	3.00	2.41	2.86	2.95	2.46
	(0.77)	(0.17)	(0.4)	(0.56)	(0.07)	(0.45)
Depth of knowledge	1.66	1.16	1.23	1.59	1.25	1.31
	(0.91)	(0.31)	(0.43)	(0.93)	(0.27)	(0.56)
Mathematical analysis	1.49	1.09	1.04	1.43	1.17	1.10
	(0.85)	(0.11)	(0.07)	(0.8)	(0.19)	(0.16)

ers of Quechua across four nations—one of which is Peru—indicates a similar set of emphases.

Quality of Instruction

Intellectual Safety in the Classroom. Table 5.10 shows that, in urban and rural Quechua schools, teachers maintained an intellectually safe environment during mathematics instruction. Since a score of 3 is based on the teacher maintaining a relatively safe environment with minimal student intrusion, the variability found in urban fourth and fifth grades indicates that, in some classrooms, students will sometimes encourage and help one another, yet in other classrooms, they will put one another down. The low variability in the rural Quechua schools indicates that the students neither help nor hinder one another during mathematics. In contrast, the relatively low rating for intellectual safety in the rural Aymara schools suggests that either students or teachers in those classrooms are more likely to put one another down than in other schools. Our data do not reveal whether teachers intervene in cases of student putdowns.

Depth of Understanding. Table 5.10 shows that, on average, mathematics is treated in a relatively superficial manner across fourth- and fifth-grade classes. That scores hover near an absolute floor of 1 indicates that rarely (and then it would seem, almost by accident) do teachers go into greater depth of coverage than simply to present material.

Urban classrooms reported somewhat higher scores on the depth scale—ranging from an average of .2 to .5 of a point greater than in the rural classrooms. The urban classrooms also show greater variability on the depth scale than do rural classrooms. These differences are due to the fact that in some urban classrooms teachers seem to treat content in greater depth than their colleagues.

Recalling that a score of 4 requires some evidence of student contribution to the topic being treated in depth, we found no evidence that students treated content in much depth. This finding is consistent with student notebooks having relatively very few entries where procedures were connected to underlying concepts, that is, where procedures were treated in any depth (Table 5.9).

Mathematical Analysis. Table 5.10 also reveals that teachers seldom promoted and that students even more seldom engaged in higher-order thinking. Average scores for mathematical analysis—that is, for evidence that mathematics classrooms are places where students are encouraged to engage in higher-order thinking skills of reasoning, of drawing distinctions, of discussing why something may or may not be true, and of similar thought processes—hover near an absolute floor of 1. In rural schools, teachers seldom, if ever, try to engage students in analyzing the mathematical content that they encounter. The slightly higher score of just below 1.5 in urban fourth and fifth grades and the greater variability in these grades are due to the fact that some teachers would sometimes try to engage students in higher-order thinking or provide reasons for why something was true. Under the assumption that exploration of mathematical topics and the solution of real-life (or realistic) problems would draw upon similar processes of mathematical analysis, these findings are consistent with what was revealed by the students' notebooks (Table 5.9).

DISCUSSION

When we began this study, we could not have foreseen the political changes that have swept through Peru whereby the newly elected president has pledged to focus on issues of social justice and on the development of opportunity for the nation's indigenous peoples. Our results document some of the great challenges that Peru faces from both perspectives, that of social justice and that of socially enlightened self-interest.

The poverty that Puno's students face at home is pervasive and worse in its rural (as opposed to urban)—especially, Quechua-speaking—areas. Our findings suggest that the effects of poor nutrition, while great throughout Puno, are a greater problem among rural boys than rural girls.

Schools lacked access to public utilities that are uniformly common across most developed world nations and in the world's large urban centers such as Lima. Upgrading those facilities requires substantial investments in infrastructure development. What is easy to provide has already been taken care of.

Inequalities and Social Justice

We found a persistent pattern of inequality, differentiating the urban from rural schools on basic infrastructure such as access to public utilities for potable water, sewage disposal, electricity, and phone. What is more, rural Quechua schools lacked these utilities at greater rates than did the Aymara schools. While language resources seemed to be distributed where they might help to overcome inequalities due to language-use mismatches, neither the Aymara-speaking nor the Quechua-speaking teachers reported reading or writing skills adequate to conduct instruction via those languages—findings supported by our failure to find evidence in students' notebooks or in their classrooms for any use of either language for instructional purpose. What is more, we found a strong set of converging desires among students, their parents, and teachers for the students to learn Spanish—Peru's dominant language. It may be that the learning of Spanish is the more salient goal, over and above the use of indigenous languages. These findings replicate Hornberger's (1987) finding that bilingual instruction is unevenly implemented, in part, at least, due to similar social pressures.

While there was no consistent pattern differentiating schools on the number of days that they were in session, there was a clear pattern whereby schools in rural Quechua areas devoted less time to academics than did the other schools. Our curricular analyses revealed no consistent pattern of differential coverage of mathematics. On the other hand, our observations found that rural Aymara classrooms were less safe, intellectually, than either urban or rural Quechua classrooms and that urban classrooms provided somewhat greater opportunities for students to cover content in depth and to engage in higher-order thinking than did rural classrooms.

In summary, we found that rural schools provide their students with a lower quality of opportunity to learn mathematics than do urban schools. It struck us that there are some relatively inexpensive things that could be done to address some of these inequalities: provide incentives to increase the number of days that schools are in session to at least 150, provide schools with cell phones so that teachers can call when they will be late or will not be coming, discourage teacher absence but also plan for ways of responding to it, monitor that teachers spend more school time on academics, and fix some chalkboards. Our findings on language-use patterns are ambivalent since it may be the case that teachers are doing what parents and their children expect them to do, which is to teach in Spanish.

But, also, we realize that some very expensive decisions need to be made. The provision of basic public utilities within schools requires the provision of those utilities within the region. The provision of incentives to increase the literacy skills match between Quechua- and Aymara-speaking teachers and their schools and the professional development that these teachers will need in order to use those skills during instruction are not likely to come cheaply. Sustained professional development so that teachers cover a more balanced mathematics curriculum, as envisioned by the national curriculum, and so that teachers teach in ways that encourage depth and/or mathematical analysis are not likely to be cheap investments either.

Social justice issues are certainly more expansive than portrayed in this study. For example, had we compared Puno to Lima, it is likely that we would be reporting cross-site differential opportunity to learn and be calling for steps to equalize those differences across regions. What is more, historically based concerns for social justice would have arisen, had we studied cross-generational differences in opportunities to learn mathematics that have been provided to Quechua and Aymara speakers and to their children. Our study did not take either of these tasks. However, we do provide another no less politically compelling warrant for action on opportunity to learn mathematics: the argument of socially enlightened self-interest.

Socially Enlightened Self-Interest

As noted above, a society can ill afford to undereducate its children because of the social consequences of such failure. On this basis, we would call for massive efforts to upgrade the physical plant, increase instructional time, make more use of Aymara and Quechua, have more balanced curriculum coverage, and improve the quality of instruction that all Puno students experience.

Low-quality educational facilities, for example, are likely to worsen the ill effects of poverty on children. We saw children with respiratory infections, evidenced by runny noses, trying to copy mathematics from blackboards in ill-lit, cold, and clammy classrooms. Children from multiple classrooms stood outside with a principal, her own class in abeyance, while waiting to determine if school would be held because their teacher was late or maybe not coming. When a social system displays such distress, its infrastructure needs focused attention.

Peru's national curriculum calls for deemphasis in number sense and computation and a more balanced representation of mathematics content to include geometry, data analysis, measurement, and algebra. The curriculum also calls for deemphasis in rote learning to focus more on ensuring the development of deeper student understanding of mathematics. Our analysis of student notebooks and our observations of mathematics classrooms shows that in spite of widespread teacher-training efforts, practices in Puno have scarcely budged from the stereotypes of conventional practices. Content remains limited to arithmetic, it is taught by rote, and in some cases, it is taught in settings where students risk putdowns for or interference with their efforts to understand.

However, we would resist efforts to portray teachers or other school personnel as villains. There can be villains only when people behave purposefully to deny opportunity to others. We saw, rather, that teachers worked hard and often at the limits of their own knowledge and skills under stressful conditions. For example, can we really blame someone for being late to work when the day's only bus is late or breaks down, when they get sick from an illness brought to school by their students, when they are assigned to a school and do not understand the language that the students speak, or when they are short tempered because they are trying to teach in spite of being ill? Rather, we view our results as showing the crisis in Puno's overall educational system.

In further analyses of these data, we plan to link our opportunity to learn indicators more explicitly to student achievement (Andrade 2001). Yet we also think that we could learn from the cases at the upper ends of our opportunity to learn indicators. Some schools were in session for well over 150 days; in some classrooms, instructional time was over three hours; and in some classrooms, mathematics instruction showed some depth and provided some opportunities for students to engage in mathematical analysis. These cases could shed light on ways by which to aim efforts to improve students' opportunities to learn mathematics.

Finally, there have been many successful efforts to improve mathematics instruction in developed nations. We end this chapter with the tantalizing question: Could we learn anything from those efforts? Or is it the case that there is no way of adapting professional development for teachers who teach in the distressed areas of the world so that efforts to improve the material resources that are made available can proceed apace with efforts to improve the professional lives of teachers and the quality of the instruction that their children receive?

ACKNOWLEDGMENTS

This work was commissioned and sponsored by the World Bank and by the Partnership for Sustainable Strategies on Girls' Education through a grant to GRADE (Grupo de Análisis para el Desarollo). Additional support in the development of this chapter was provided to Walter Secada by the School of Education, the Graduate School, and the National Center for Improving Student Learning and Achievement in Mathematics, all at the University of Wisconsin at Madison. All findings and conclusions are those of the authors. No endorsement by the World Bank, GRADE, or the University of Wisconsin at Madison should be inferred. The notebook analyses, on which the curriculum coverage section is based, were conducted by Olof Bjorg Steinthorsdottir of the University of Wisconsin at Madison and Cristina Gomez of the University of Alabama.

REFERENCES

Andrade, Fernando. (2001). Mutivariate Analysis for Mathematics Achievement. In Santiago Cueto and Walter Secada, *Mathematics Learning and Achievement in Quechua, Aymara and Spanish Boys and Girls in Bilingual and Spanish Schools in Puno, Peru* (Research report submitted to the World Bank). Washington, DC: World Bank.

Banco Central de Reserva. (2001). *Memoria 2000*. Lima, Peru: Author.

Bowles, Samuel. (2000). *Persistent Inequality in a Competitive World: Causes, Consequences, Remedies*. Santa Fe, NM: Economics Program, Santa Fe Institute, December.

CEPAL. (2001). *Anuario estadístico de América Latina y el Caribe*. Santiago de Chile: Comisión Económica para América Latina y el Caribe.

Coleman, James. (1968). The Concept of Equality of Educational Opportunity. *Harvard Educational Review*, 38, 7–22.

Cuanto. (2000). *El Perú en números*. Lima, Peru: Author.

Cueto, Santiago and Secada, Walter G. (2001). *Mathematics Learning and Achievement in Quechua, Aymara and Spanish Boys and Girls in Bilingual and Spanish*

Schools in Puno, Peru. Research report submitted to the World Bank. Washington, DC: World Bank.

Fennema, Elizabeth, and Leder, Gilah (Eds.). (1990). *Mathematics and Gender.* New York: Teachers College Press.

FONCODES. (2000). *Mapa de Pobreza 2000.* Lima, Peru: Author.

Gómez, Cristina, and Steinþórsdóttir, Ólöf. (2001). Enacted Curriculum in Mathematics: Students' Opportunity to Learn. In Santiago Cueto and Walter Secada, *Mathematics Learning and Achievement in Quechua, Aymara and Spanish Boys and Girls in Bilingual and Spanish Schools in Puno, Peru.* Research report submitted to the World Bank. Washington, DC: World Bank.

Hornberger, Nancy. (1987). Schooltime, Classtime and Academic Learning Time in Rural Highland Puno, Peru. *Anthropology & Education Quarterly,* 18, 207–221.

Howe, Kenneth R. (1997). *Understanding Equal Educational Opportunity: Social Justice, Democracy and Schooling.* New York: Teachers College Press.

INEI. (2001). *Perú. Compendio Estadístico.* Lima, Peru: Author.

Ministerio de Educación. (2000a). *Boletín UNEBI No. 2.* Lima, Peru: Author.

Ministerio de Educación. (2000b). *Estructura curricular básica de educación primaria de menores. Programa curricular de primer ciclo de educación primaria de menores.* Lima, Peru: Author.

Ministerio de Educación. (2001). *Boletín UMC* (Vols. 7–15). Lima, Peru: Author.

Moen, Phyllis, Dempster-McClain, Donna, and Walker, Henry A. (1999). *A Nation Divided: Diversity, Inequality and Community in American Society.* Ithaca, NY: Cornell University Press.

Newmann, Fred M., and Associates. (1996). *Authentic Achievement: Restructuring Schools for Intellectual Quality.* San Francisco, CA: Jossey-Bass.

Newmann, Fred M., Secada, Walter G., and Wehlage, Gary G. (1995). *A Guide to Authentic Instruction and Assessment: Vision, Standards and Scoring.* Madison: Center on Organization and Restructuring of Schools, Wisconsin Center for Education Research.

Rawls, John. (1971). *A Theory of Justice.* Cambridge, MA: Harvard University Press.

Reimers, Fernando (Ed.). (2000). *Unequal Schools, Unequal Chances.* Cambridge, MA: Harvard University Press.

Saavedra, Jaime. (2001). Las familias y el financiamiento de la educación pública en el Perú. *Análisis y Propuestas* (Lima, Peru: GRADE), 4, 1–8.

Secada, Walter G. (1989–1991). Agenda Setting, Enlightened Self Interest, and Equity in Mathematics Education. *Peabody Journal of Education,* 66(2), 22–56.

Secada, Walter G. (2001). *Conceptions of Equity.* Paper presented at the conference *Equitable Education: Utopia or Realism?* Bodo, Norway, June 13–15. To appear in the conference *Proceedings,* published by Nordland Research Institute.

Secada, Walter G. (2002). Conceptions of Equity. In Karl Jan Solstad (Ed.), *Equitable Education: Utopia or Realism?* (pp. 17–33, NF—report no. 7-2002). Bodo, Norway: Nordlands Forskning [Nordland Research Institute].

Secada, Walter G., Gamoran, Adam, and Weinstein, Matthew. (1996). Pathways to Equity. In Fred M. Newmann and Associates, *Authentic Achievement: Restructuring Schools for Intellectual Quality* (pp. 228–244). San Francisco, CA: Jossey-Bass.

Smith, Adam. (1904). *An Inquiry into the Nature and Causes of the Wealth of Nations* (Edwin Cannan, Ed.). London: Methuen. Available online at http://www.econlib.org/library/Smith/smWN1.html.

Tilly, Charles. (1998). *Durable Inequality*. Berkeley: University of California Press.

Unidad de la Medición de la Calidad Educativa (UMC) and GRADE. (2000). Resultados de las pruebas de matemática y lenguaje. ¿Qué aprendimos a partir de la Evaluación CRECER 1998? *Boletín CRECER 5/6*. Lima, Peru: Ministerio de Educación.

Unidad de la Medición de la Calidad Educativa (UMC) and GRADE. (2001). El Perú en el primer estudio internacional comparativo de la UNESCO sobre lenguaje y matemática y factores asociados en tercer y cuarto grado. *Boletín UMC 9*. Lima, Peru: Ministerio de Educación.

World Bank. (1999). *Peru Education at a Crossroads: Challenges and Opportunities for the 21st Century*. Report No. 19066-PE. Vol. I. Washington, DC: Author.

Chapter 6

Teachers' Beliefs about Teaching Mathematics to Students from Socially Disadvantaged Backgrounds: Implications for Social Justice

Robyn Zevenbergen

INTRODUCTION

Within the mathematics education literature, there is a substantive body of research into teachers' beliefs. A considerable amount of this literature explores what teachers believe about different aspects of mathematics and mathematics education. This literature consists of projects such as the beliefs teachers hold about teaching and learning (Prawat 1993), preservice teachers' beliefs about various aspects of mathematics education (Raymond 1997; Vacc and Bright 1999; Verschaffel, de Corte, and Borghart 1997), and the mismatch between beliefs and actual practice (Perry, Howard, and Tracey 1999). These themes are recurring ones in the literature on teacher beliefs and focus primarily on aspects of teaching and learning mathematics without considering implications.

In contrast, and not always related to mathematics education, a further component of the literature on teacher beliefs explores the interaction between beliefs and the outcomes for students. For example, in their seminal study, Rosenthal and Jacobson (1969) demonstrated the power of teacher beliefs in bringing about particular outcomes in the classroom. In their study, students were randomly assigned to groupings that were labeled as if representing the ability of the students. The authors noted that as a consequence of the teachers believing that the students in any one group were of a particular ability, they interacted with the students and held very different expectations of the students. Subsequently, these qualitatively different experiences for the students produced results confirming the random groupings rather than the true abilities of the students being identified. This powerful study alerted educators to the importance of teachers' beliefs about students' perceived abilities and how such perceptions can become self-fulfilling prophecies.

Within the mathematics education literature and more recently than Rosenthal and Jacobson's study, Walkerdine (1984) noted the powerful influence of teachers' beliefs about how students learned—in this case, through Piagetian constructs. Within her study, she demonstrated how discourses framed how teachers organized and assessed student learning. These discourses also provided a lens for interpreting behavior and learning. Ultimately, the behaviors exhibited by the young children were interpreted by the teachers within Piagetian terms so that the teachers' views of Piagetian frameworks for "natural child development" were reinforced. In their comprehensive study of UK primary school teachers, Askew and colleagues (1997) claimed that one of the key features of effective teachers of numeracy is that they believe that all students can succeed in numeracy. In contrast to earlier studies where the focus had a greater emphasis on the negative impact of teachers' beliefs and student achievement, Askew et al.'s study showed the impact of the positive influence that teachers' beliefs can have on student performance. These studies, among a plethora of similar studies, have indicated that the beliefs teachers hold about students and learning impact significantly on learning and schooling outcomes.

Within this context, teachers' beliefs about students and learning can influence considerably how students will be perceived, their actions interpreted, subsequent interactions, and ultimately the outcomes for students. As such, questions need to be posed as to teachers' beliefs about particular students in terms of their social backgrounds and ultimately whether such views could reinforce the differential outcomes. In generic studies of schooling, it has been noted that some teachers hold particular views about their students, their families, and their living conditions, yet when questioned as to whether or not they have visited the students' homes in order to make such claims, there was no basis upon which to make the claims they did (Dent and Hatton 1996). In this study, it was clear that the teachers made assumptions about the children's home circumstances that were interpreted as the root of problems and behaviors being observed in school. Dent and Hatton's (1996) work indicates that some of the teachers they studied held stereotypical views of students living in poverty and that such views can provide a halo effect for other aspects of students' lives. Freebody, Ludwig, and Gunn (1995) found similar stereotypical comments from teachers in literacy classrooms where they were working with children from socially disadvantaged backgrounds. In their study, teachers often held similar assumptions about the lived circumstances of their students without having any real evidence upon which to make such claims. These studies raise questions as to whether or not teachers make stereotypical judgments of their students without having any real sense of their students' family circumstances.

In extending this work, other studies have explored the models teachers use to explain student performance. In her study of teachers' and students' beliefs about poverty and the impact on schooling, Chafel (1997) noted that respondents tended to adopt a victim-blaming approach to the issue. This view of educational underachievement places the blame of failure on those most at risk of failing in schools.

These research projects raise questions about the beliefs that teachers of mathematics hold toward students from socially and economically disadvantaged backgrounds. Research in mathematics education suggests that teachers' beliefs impact on how they organize, interpret, and position students in terms of learning mathematics. More generally, educational research has suggested that teachers often hold conservative views for explaining the relationship between social background and learning outcomes. Given that the process of teacher education is one of enculturation into the middle-class values of the schooling system, it would not be unreasonable to expect that many teachers will hold the values that are part of the middle-class value system of schooling. As such, questions as to whether or not they are cognizant of the issues of cultural incongruence between the value systems of the home and those of the school need to be asked. Indeed, as earlier research cited indicates, it is possible that teachers may hold stereotypical views of students from socially and economically disadvantaged backgrounds similar to those noted by Dent and Hatton (1996) and Freebody, Ludwig, and Gunn (1995) when thinking about mathematics. The intersection of this general educational research with mathematics education needs further exploration to identify synergies and differences.

Starting from the cited research, this chapter explores teachers' beliefs about the teaching and learning of mathematics for students from socially and economically disadvantaged backgrounds. It is suggested, on the basis of the evidence in the literature, that teachers may hold stereotypical views of student learning and the cultural backgrounds of the students and as such may be at risk of attributing lack of success in school mathematics to perceived or imagined qualities of the student and/or family background.

The theoretical approach taken in this chapter uses the tools offered by French sociologist Pierre Bourdieu to understand the ways in which teachers frame student learning and, more particularly, student success. It is proposed that through the processes of teacher education, both preservice and in-service, teachers are exposed to practices that facilitate the construction of a teaching habitus. Bourdieu (1979a, p. viii) defines the construct of habitus as being a "system of durable, transposable dispositions which functions as the generative basis of structured, objectively unified practices." Within the context of mathematics teachers, Gates (2001, p. 22) argues more specifically that a mathematics teacher's habitus "will be at the root of the ways in which teachers conceptualise themselves in relation to others, how they enact and embody dominant social ideas as well as how they transform and adapt them." In terms of this chapter, I seek to argue that through teacher education teachers have been exposed to practices that facilitate the development of a particular habitus, which in turn provide a particular lens for seeing and viewing the world. As I have argued elsewhere (Zevenbergen 1994, 1997), this habitus is dominated by psychological viewpoints, and as such teachers tend to focus on the individual. The research reported in this chapter extends this work to encompass teachers' beliefs about the mathematical learning of students from socially disadvantaged backgrounds. As the data used in this chapter demonstrate, this individualistic viewpoint is framed predominantly within deficit models.

THE PROJECT

The following sections discuss mathematics teachers' beliefs about students from socially disadvantaged backgrounds and the relationship between socio-economic background and school mathematics. Using survey and interview data collection methods, teachers from 15 schools participated in the study to examine their beliefs about teaching and learning in mathematics when that learning is focused on students from socially disadvantaged backgrounds. A total of 50 teachers participated in the survey, of which 20 volunteered to participate in one-on-one interviews. Schools from the South-East Queensland region of Australia participated in the study. Schools were selected on the basis of their being part of a national project (The Disadvantaged Schools Project), which is a federally funded program aimed at supporting students from socially and economically disadvantaged backgrounds. Strict guidelines have been established by the relevant funding authorities as to which schools are eligible for funding so that those schools in receipt of government funding can be assumed to have significant numbers of students who are classified as socially and economically disadvantaged. Fifteen schools were represented in the survey and 9 in the interviews.

The questions posed in the survey and interview specifically targeted the teaching of mathematics to students from socially disadvantaged backgrounds. Specifically, teachers were asked about the challenges, dilemmas, and pleasures of working with this cohort of students. The teachers had been working with this cohort of students for varying lengths of time. Some were novices with less than 3 years of experience, while others had more than 15 years of experience. However, regardless of years of experience, level of schooling (primary or secondary), gender of teacher, or the school in which they taught, all teachers but one held very similar views of teaching in these schools and these students.

Extreme stereotypical views of socially disadvantaged families were not common in the responses offered by the teachers. However, there were hints as to how some of the teachers viewed the issue of social reproduction. For example, the comment offered by Margaret (below) suggested that the cycle of poverty and social class was inextricably bound to lives of crime and that the school could have some, albeit minor, role in breaking this cycle by intervening early in the lives of the children from these families:

Margaret: Children who don't succeed or who are expelled or whatever and then they go to jail and we are spending thousands and millions on these people. If you got them right at the beginning, you wouldn't wipe everything out, but you could wipe a fair bit of it out and you would be able to do something.

While this view is extreme in its links with incarceration, it suggests that some teachers hold very moralistic views of social class and how students from the working class and/or poverty are circumscribed with many other attributes. In other words, the teacher's habitus provided a particular way of viewing families from socially disadvantaged backgrounds. Comments passed by the teachers referred to other aspects of the students' lives including stereotypical views of single-parent (to be read as mother) families; excessive violence in the homes; attitudes of not caring about their children; children being poorly fed or ne- glected. Sometimes riders were added to their comments whereby they recog- nized that the perceived plight of the students was also found in more affluent settings:

Megan: These kids have very sad lives. I mean, how can they cope with maths or any other subject when they are not fed properly or they know that when they get home their manic-depressive father is waiting to belt them up? This might happen in middle-class families, but not like it happens here. It is just a daily event, whereas in nice areas this is not the norm.

Evident in many of the comments, such as the one above, are value-laden words such as *nice* or *good* being used to describe the children and families from middle-class backgrounds, whereas negatively laden words were used to de- scribe the students and families from working-class backgrounds. A common framework used to describe the life circumstances of the students was that of Maslow's hierarchy of needs. Teachers often framed their perceptions of the families within this legitimated model, tending to describe families as being deficit in their provision of the basic needs of the students. Families from working-class backgrounds were described as not meeting the basic needs of their children, whereas this was not attributed to more affluent and middle-class families.

DEFICIT MODELS OF EXPLAINING DIFFERENCE

Common to most of the comments offered by the teachers were deficit views of education and student performance. Students and their families were typically described in terms of lacking particular attributes or dispositions. Teachers would describe their observations of the students in terms of lacking some innate qualities or experiences that hindered their capacity to undertake mathematics. This view has been well documented in other studies (Connell, White, and Johnston 1991; Daniels and Lee 1989). Typical of these comments is that of Barbara (below) who is quite open in her belief that the students from socially disadvantaged backgrounds were lacking in many of the core characteristics needed for mathematics and school in general:

Barbara: Working in schools like this can be very disheartening at times. No matter how hard you try, you just can't help them. They are lacking in so many things—things that will help them with maths but also just plain old manners on how to behave and interact. The parents just don't know how to help their kids. They can't read, they can't do the maths, and most of them don't care. They would prefer to be at the pub or at Bingo. I feel sorry for the kids, as you know they are never going to get anywhere, no matter how hard I try.

Similarly, Michelle offered deficit frameworks for students' poor performance in mathematics:

Michelle: It is hard work with these kids. They come to school but don't have any of the skills or abilities that you take for granted that a good student would have. These kids, mostly, don't know how to read, they can't write their names or numbers, they don't know basic things like colors or shapes, so you spend a lot of time teaching them things that they really should know before they come to school. I mean, how can parents talk to their children without using things like colors—go and get your red jumper. I think they know the differences in colors, but they are not able to talk about them because they don't have the language or the knowledge. They just don't have any of the things that you expect normal children to have when they start school. This makes it very difficult to learn mathematics. We have to go way back to what you would think a three-year-old would know.

These comments represent common themes in the teachers' views about the teaching of mathematics to students from socially disadvantaged backgrounds. As can be seen in Michelle's comment, she describes the lack of knowledge as being something inferior, as opposed to different, from that of middle-class— or in her words, *normal* or *good*—children. She sees the parenting as deficit in that she proposes that the modes of interaction between child and parent are restricted since she sees the parents as not using the rich language typically used by middle-class parents. She sees that this places the children as being delayed in their cognitive development by a number of years.

The comments offered here are representative of those offered by most of the teachers. Typically, they commented that the failing or underachievement of students from socially disadvantaged backgrounds was predominantly due to deficiencies in particular areas—mathematics, social skills, language, and so on. Typically, this was framed as lacking in terms of poor parenting practices and deviant family life so that the students were seen to have quite negative home lives. This is discussed in greater detail in the following section, as there were many facets of the students' lives that were seen to be deficit, and these deficiencies were seen to be what contributed to students' underachievement in school mathematics.

Families, Communities, and Cultural Capital

All but one of the teachers passed many comments about the effect of impoverished communities on students' capacities to succeed in school mathematics. While various derivations of the theme were evident in the comments offered, it was clear that the teachers felt that the communities from which the students came held them back in significant ways. While some of the comments offered were subtle, others were far more overt and placed blame for the underachievement of the students with the parents, families, and communities. There was little or no recognition that the family backgrounds were very different from those of the teachers and that what was seen as legitimate knowledge and practices within the school setting were very particular worldviews.

Overall, comments suggested that the students from socially disadvantaged backgrounds had poverty in their experiences that influenced their capacity to undertake and/or understand the concepts that were being developed in mathematics. The perceived poverty of these experiences was seen to impact negatively on the learning experiences of the students. Bourdieu's notion of cultural capital is central to this aspect of mathematics. The experiences of students become embodied so that they have very different habitus upon which to draw. These experiences, which are representations of cultural and historical events, become part of the habitus upon which the students can draw when in the classroom. For students whose experiences are closely aligned to the practices that are valued within the classroom, there is greater opportunity for them to use such experiences in responding to demands within this context. This is summed up effectively:

[T]hose coming from a cultural background (often expressed in language) which is closest to the orthodox school culture, will have a whole set of productive and receptive schemes of thought and valuing which will render the pedagogic process less problematic. The reverse is also true. (Grenfell and James 1998, pp. 164–165)

For those students whose culture is closer to the orthodox school culture, there is greater opportunity to *trade* their cultural knowledge for school success. Thus culture becomes a form of capital that can be exchanged for rewards. Hence, the notion of cultural capital becomes important. The structuring practices of school and the classroom differentially acknowledge and reward different aspects of culture so that the cultural dispositions and attributes that students bring to the classroom can be exchanged for academic rewards. For example, students who have been exposed to rich experiences with the language and practices of counting or spatial concepts (as noted by Michelle earlier) are more likely to be positioned better than those students whose experiences have included boxing and fishing. This is not to say that the latter activities are inferior; only that they are not legitimized through the mathematics curriculum and hence are not as valued within the classroom. That is, they are not part of the orthodox school culture. As such, particular cultural practices will position some students better than others in terms of learning and achieving in mathematics. This Bourdieu refers to as cultural capital—differential acknowledgment of cultural background in exchange for academic rewards. Through his detailed work on patterns of consumption and society, Bourdieu (1979b) shows the different preferences of social classes in their patterns of consumption and dispositions. One of the key aspects of cultural capital is linguistic capital since particular forms of language are recognized and legitimated in and through school mathematics (Zevenbergen 2001). Here, the language that the student brings to school is important, and this aspect of schooling and mathematics has been well documented (Cooper and Dunne 1999).

In considering the construct of cultural capital, the different experiences of students position them differently in relation to the practices within school. Those students for whom there is a greater synergy between the cultural practices of the school and home have a greater chance of educational success, with the inverse also being the case. Paul notes this when he makes the following comments regarding the experiences of students:

Paul: Poor children often do not have a chance to deal with distance in mathematics. Thirty kilometers means nothing to some children who have never left the area. Never traveled to Sydney, for instance. One girl in our class has just come back from Europe, and there are others who have never been to Brisbane or the Gold Coast. Now, you are looking at a map and you are trying to explain concepts of a thousand kilometers, and it means nothing. Whereas children in the same group. [*Pause*] It might well be affluence or it might be priorities.

In this context, Paul recognizes that the experiences of the students will offer greater or lesser opportunities for success in mathematics. Hence, these out-of-school experiences can be forms of capital that may enhance the success of students. Some teachers recognized that the impoverished experiences of the socially disadvantaged students engendered a greater risk of failure since they were not aware of the contexts or knowledge being presented.

Cultural capital also refers to the dispositions that are developed toward schooling as embodied in the habitus. Studies have shown that many families can have very different dispositions toward schooling, depending on the experiences of the previous generations. In their well-cited studies of schooling, authors (Connell et al. 1982; Willis 1977) have shown that families from different social classes value schooling differently. Such orientations have been developed through the familial and personal experiences of schooling. Often parents from working-class families have been excluded from the schooling process—either overtly or covertly—so that school becomes an alien experience and is hence at risk of being rejected as a valued or useful part of their lives. Most of the teachers in this study offered similar views of educational reproduction. However, the converse can also be true where some parents also recognize education to be a path out of the poverty trap. The communities within which the students grew up were seen to provide very particular views of the world that inhibited their capacity to learn and relate to schooling. In the comments below, the teachers claim that the families and peers provided experiences that facilitated the construction of a legitimate negative attitude toward school mathematics. The strong comment offered by Peter in the second comment listed below where he claims that their parents were "dropouts themselves" suggests that he has particular views of the parents' educational backgrounds and their orientation to school.

Naomi: I think their belief that they can't do this mathematics stuff comes from a variety of places. I really do. I think it comes from home, other people around them like their peers, and from the general community they are from.

Peter: The students come from families that really don't care about school. Most of them are dropouts themselves, so school has no place in their lives. Many of the kids will say that their parents hated school and were no good at maths, so they believe it is their gene pool.

However, not only were the familial experiences seen to provide restrictive views of education that inhibit success in school mathematics; there was also the overt statement claiming a biological predisposition to learning mathematics. The final comment made by Peter in reference to the *gene pool* of the students also confirms a dominant view in education that students from socially disadvantaged backgrounds often have lower ability than students from more advantaged backgrounds. Many of the teachers passed comments about the poor or inferior abilities of these students, indicating their acceptance of the innateness of the concept and its potential to be part of the genetic makeup of students. When questioned further about the notion of ability, Sandra offered the following comments supporting a biological determinist viewpoint.

Sandra: It is often frustrating working with these kids in this school. No matter how hard I try, or how hard they try, they just don't seem to get it. They just don't have the ability needed to cope with maths. In one way it is not surprising because when you see their parents, they are not very bright—I mean, some of them have difficulty doing the reading with the kids, so I have to give them other things to do when they want to help out in class.

Sandra confirms the well-entrenched belief of natural abilities and their heredity among families. Notions of ability and intelligence have long permeated educational discourses, and their influence is very strong (Seldin 2000). Here it can be seen that these discourses have been incorporated into the teacher's habitus, and in turn provide a lens for her interpretation of why the students are not able to cope with the mathematics that she is teaching. Rather than seeing lack of success in mathematics as being something inherent in the structuring practices of schooling, it was seen as something innate in the student.

Peers, Role Models, and Significant Others

There are other members of the community who contribute to the success, or lack thereof, of students as they pass through school and mathematics. Teachers commented on the role of peers in the construction of attitudes and dispositions toward mathematics. These teachers had acknowledged the powerful influence of the peer group in their communities and that the counterschool and counter-achievement ethos within the groups facilitated a rejection of school mathematics. Comments of *nerds* and *stiffs* were passed about peers who attempted to engage with mathematics so that students who wanted to be accepted by their peer groups needed to reconcile their actions with the group. In the second comment below, Bob goes on to elaborate that the peer pressure in these communities was stronger than what he had observed in other nondisadvantaged schools.

Ross: Any kid who tries to work is called a "stiff," and it just pulls them down to the same level.

Bob: The kids here are fighting a losing battle. They have to be tough with their mates, and that means rejecting school. I try hard to tell them that is not the way it is, but they believe that school is for nerds, and maths is the worst subject of all to like because then you are a king-size nerd. You can't fight the peer pressure in schools like this—it is so strong.

The peer group was seen to be an important part of the students' lives, and where these, as suggested by Ross, "pulled students down," the peer group was described in pejorative terms. It was seen as a culture of mediocrity that hindered the students' progress through school. These types of comments reinforce the view that the social environment of the students was counterproductive to success in mathematics. While the power of the peer group is widely recognized within the literature on youth and schooling (Mac an Ghaill 1995), Bob's comment suggests that it is even more powerful among socially disadvantaged youth, thereby further limiting their potential for success.

While peers were seen to exert a powerful influence over the students, comments about the lack of human resources, such as role models, were also noted. As Kerry (below) comments, lack of role models or heroes or mentors within the communities was an endemic cause for the cycle of failure:

Kerry: One of the big differences in teaching these kids from middle-class kids is that they have no motivation in them. There is no future. What has the world got for me. They have no mentor, they have no hero, they have no role model, and all of this means that this concept of failure is never ending.

Implicit in Kerry's comment is the recognition that students do not have significant others to whom they can aspire. They are exposed to endless cycles of poverty from which there is little hope of escape. Rather than place the blame on families, she looks more widely into the community and the structuring practices within those communities. This view was in contrast to many of the others where the teachers focused more specifically on parents and immediate families and recognized that the lack of interest and support from parents also served to act as a model for the students. These comments offered support for the general perception among the teachers that this cohort of students lacked the human resources to see successful members of their communities and, as such, could not relate to the notion of success in mathematics since it was an alien concept—something foreign to them—as there were no people within their communities with whom they could relate.

Resourcing and Technology

The notion of cultural capital was also implicit in comments teachers made in relation to computers. Implicitly, some teachers recognized that the experiences of the home are differentially recognized and rewarded within school. Focusing on computers and the interest that socially disadvantaged students had in them brought to the fore two issues—first was access to computers; the second related to the interrelationship between students and computers. Technology is being hailed as a tool for improving learning, yet little is really known about how this can be achieved and if it is differentially accessible. In terms of the types of interactions students had with computers, the teachers claimed that there was little difference in orientation toward computers—students were not scared of them. The two teachers' comments offered below illustrate the different understandings that teachers have of students' access to computers in the homes. In the first case, Marilyn proposes that all students have access, and it is a priority. However, Margaret questions the responses made by her students. Margaret's initial reaction confirms Marilyn's experiences but suggests that her students may see computers as being video games, and the like, rather than the technological tools that are being used in the classroom.

Marilyn: These kids are all exposed to video games so are not phased by computers. They have no fear of them—Can I handle it or not? The thing is, I have to stop them from pressing buttons. No, I don't think they are disadvantaged in that area, and it is amazing how you can ask kids who you think come from a poorer area, who has a computer, and it's amazing how many have. It seems to be a priority over so many other things.

However, a number of the teachers believed that the access to computers was not always as indicated and that often what was seen as "computer" by the students was not the "computer" valued within the school system but rather a game device:

Margaret: They enjoy playing with computers. When I asked who had computers, they nearly all put their hands up. But then I realized they thought Segas were computers. That is what they call a computer. They do like the games. It does turn them on, and if you look at these Time Zone places [*arcade game alleys*] they are full of kids from these poorer areas. They spend all their money there because there is big excitement.

The discrepancy between these two experiences suggests that the responses offered by students should not be taken at face value. Again, this suggests that what teachers see as legitimate forms of knowledge (in this case, computers) may be different from what the students see as computers (in this case, interactive games).

Margaret suggests that experiences with computer games are not as valued in school as more formal computer skills. However, she also comments further on the dispositions the students have toward the "excitement" offered by these games. As both teachers' comments indicate, the focus was on playing games; hence, their experiences were not positioning them well for the practices that they would encounter within the classroom context. Hence, students came to school with very different expectations of what a computer was, and while they responded that they had access to them, their experiences were not those legitimated through the curriculum.

Again, there is some indication in the comments offered by Margaret insofar as her assumptions about the values of socially disadvantaged students where she states that the students spend "all of their money" in arcade game alleys. Spending time in arcade game alleys is not a middle-class value and, from this viewpoint, is not seen to cultivate the valued dispositions needed for success in school. Explicit recognition of the bias in the school curriculum vis-à-vis socially legitimate knowledge and experiences did not appear in the comments offered by the teachers.

In terms of access to other forms of technology, such as calculators, teachers commented that the students either did not have them or, when they did, they would damage them so that they were unusable.

Melanie: We have class sets of calculators, but they are always going missing. The kids take them. Sometimes we find them in the school yard, but most of the time, they just take them, so we never have a full class set. I don't know why they do it, as they would never use them at home. It is just like they have to take stuff because they don't have it.

Robert: We tried to get class sets of graphics calculators, but the kids would just wreck them. They'd pull the buttons off or smash the displays so that they were wrecked. They nick [*steal*] the batteries so you never can use the ones that you have for the class anyway. This is really frustrating, as they have no respect for other people's property. You might start the year off with a full set, but by the end of the year, you are lucky if a quarter of them are left or usable.

The implicit acknowledgment of the dispositions of the students toward resources—in this case, calculators—suggests the teachers' recognition of a value system of the students that was incongruent with those of the teachers. The comments offered here indicate the frustration of both primary and secondary teachers with the use of calculators within the classroom. Both comments indicate that they have difficulties with the students' [ab]use of school property. In subtle ways, they also suggest that the students have a lack of respect for property that is not theirs. The blame for the abuse of the school equipment is seen to be a characteristic of the students.

Lower Standards for Students

The habitus of the teachers, as represented through their comments, indicates that they are disposed toward believing that the backgrounds of the students impact negatively on their capacity to learn. Many of the teachers suggested that the experiences of the students positioned them in ways inferior to the curriculum and assessment that they would encounter in the mathematics classroom. This meant that they were seen to be struggling with the substantive content being covered, and as such, expectations lowered for them. Many of the teachers passed open comments that they had to have lower standards for these students.

Mitch: The kids have a lot of trouble understanding what is expected of them and what they have to do. Because they don't know very much and are often off-task, I find that I have to lower my expectations of what I can get them to do. When I first started here, I thought I would be able to get them to do the same work, but they were just too slow, so I had to make things go at a very different pace.

Julie: I would say that the big problem with maths is accepting a lower standard. Basing it on my observations, they are achieving at a lot lower standard. I can't pinpoint it exactly—the inability to work cooperatively, the inability to sit and listen for any length of time, you know for longer than five minutes. Their inability to stay on task. Their inability to share resources when doing hands-on work.

Both Mitch and Julie state that they have lower expectations of these students in mathematics. In part, this is because they believe that the students have inferior experiences and cannot cope with the work being asked of them. Julie goes on to add that other social skills militate toward having lower expectations since they are unable to work effectively. In the comments offered by teachers, there was a dominant view that teachers had to lower their expectations for these students since they were unable to cope with the work. The lowered expectations can be seen to be incongruent with the outcomes of the Askew et al. (1997) study where one of the key indicators of an effective teacher of numeracy was the belief that all students could be successful. Comments such as these indicate that teachers felt that they needed to have lower expectations of their students.

Behavior Problems

Many of the teachers' comments to date have indicated their concerns about behavior management in these schools and classes. In nearly all of the comments offered, teachers commented that the classes tended to be a lot noisier and on task less often. Behavior management was seen to be a big issue when working with the students. The students were seen to be the root of the problem in that they did not have the same (expected) control on their behavior.

Helen: I have worked in these schools a number of times, and it is always the same. They don't know how to behave, they want to try and get your attention, you know, no social skills. You seem to spend most of the lesson on managing their behavior rather than teaching them anything.

Bruce: There are more suspensions here than my last schools. I think the kids don't want to be here, so they misbehave. They want to get you upset so you spend your maths lesson trying to teach them manners and courtesy but no maths.

Behavior management was a recurring theme in what teachers felt were issues that prevented them from achieving what they intended. From the comments here, Helen indicates a common theme in the responses where she says that the students "don't know how to behave," suggesting that there is an appropriate way to behave. The comment is located within a deficit view of the students in that they lack the social knowledge for what is seen to be appropriate behavior. In contrast, Bruce recognizes a social dimension to behavior and describes the misbehavior in terms of resistance rather than deficit but with the net effect that the behavior detracts from the potential to cover set curriculum. When asked what they could ask for to help them work more productively with the students, one teacher suggested the following:

Ross: If I could have something to change the outcomes for these kids it would be to have a big policeman at the door that [*sic*] could discipline the kids instantly and put them back into the classroom. That way behavior management would be taken care of instantly. At the moment if I want to discipline a child, it's to the office.

From Ross's comment, the notion of behavior management in this form arises from his earlier comments that the students were "here and now" students, by which he meant that his students were in need of immediate feedback—hence, his comment about the immediacy of discipline from a "big policeman." It potentially raises a further concern that teachers were feeling overwhelmed by what they saw as the problem—that they were required to undertake disciplinary measures rather than teach (as in Bruce's comment above).

SEEING THE ISSUE FROM A DIFFERENT STANDPOINT

At the beginning of this chapter, I noted that the comments offered by many of the teachers were of recurring themes. These tended to place the root of the problem with the students and the families. However, there was one dissenting voice, and it is to this voice I now turn. Kerry's comments throughout the interviews indicated a very different way of seeing the issues in her school. Her comments indicated an engagement with theories of social and cultural reproduction. Rather than see the students and the families as the root of underachievement, she was more critical of the practices within schools and the wider society. In the preamble to the quote cited below, Kerry had been commenting on the teachers who can successfully work with the students, who have significant success in relating to and raising the levels of achievement for their students. Her views were markedly different from the other teachers in this study. In these comments, she notes there are few behavior problems in the classes; the students are engaged and keen to be in the classes. What she saw as the fundamental issue for schools to address when working with students from socially disadvantaged backgrounds was respect:

Kerry: It's another that I would identify—respect. They [*the disadvantaged kids*] need to be respected, and they are not getting it.

From many of the comments that the teachers passed about the students, it could be asked whether there was a deep understanding of issues of curriculum relevance or challenge for the students. Kerry raised her concerns about the lack of understanding among many teachers of the strengths that the students bring to schools and their dismissal of many of these attributes. Indeed, the comment of respect raises an important consideration: Do teachers respect the home cultures and their manifestations in the classroom, or are these cultures denied legitimacy?

In contrast to the other comments offered by teachers, Kerry demonstrated an understanding of the reproductive mechanisms of schooling not articulated by the other teachers. She voiced concerns of how systemically the students are excluded from the school and how parents' cultural capital (or lack of it) prevents them from actively challenging the processes of exclusion and how the system relies on this in order to reproduce the status quo:

Kerry: I think that there is such a smorgasbord in schools these days that something has to go. And, cruel as it may seem, people from low SES [*socioeconomic*] backgrounds are the least likely to make waves if they are the ones to go. That's nasty I know, but in this world of economic rationalism, that is what is happening. Like if your child or mine was failing, we would be on the phone, but these parents don't have the knowledge about phoning up. They are powerless.

Unlike other teachers who spoke of restricted resources and other negative aspects of teaching in these environments, Kerry expressed a greater awareness of the needs of the students. She identified that these needs were not related to psychological models of basic needs but more social, that is, needs of identity. She spoke of how she enacted practices within the classroom to support the students' sense of identity. That she lived out basic ideals of respect and trust are evident in the practice she described below and in marked contrast to the earlier comments regarding the use of calculators in schools.

Kerry: I lend the kids the calculators. They have them for a year and then give them back. I never have any problems getting them back. The thing is, if you like these kids and they know that you are helping them and not in a condescending manner, they respect that and they live up to your expectations. With these kids, I don't ask questions about who needs to use my calculators; I just leave them because they are in Grade 11. Saving face is important.

Her description of the way she sees the world is very different from the practices described by many of the other teachers. Two key points can be identified. First is her notion of expectations and how this applies to technology (calculators). In her comments on expectations, there is a strong sense of reciprocity—she has high expectations of the students, and they live up to her expectations because of her respect for them. Not only is respect evident in her comment but a deep understanding of the students—she does not ask questions about needs; she just leaves the calculators so that there is no shame in needing one. Unlike the earlier comments from teachers who had lower expectations of the students and suggested that the students had little respect for school property, Kerry's experiences are somewhat different. Unlike the other teachers in this study who were critical of the students' lack of respect for school equipment, Kerry's experience suggests that the students respected the calculators and did not damage them, and she had full return rates for calculators borrowed.

CONCLUSION

In conclusion, the comments offered by the teachers highlight the discourses they use when talking about the students with whom they work. Most of the comments offered by the teachers drew heavily on conservative models for understanding pedagogy and curriculum in mathematics. There was a heavy emphasis on deficit models and a pathologizing of students and families. The views expressed by many of the teachers suggest that they have particular views on how they see the background of students impacting on and influencing learning and teaching mathematics. The constructions that these teachers have of students learning mathematics raise questions as to how entrenched are such views and the impact that such views may have on the success of students from socially disadvantaged backgrounds. In light of earlier research on the influence that teachers' beliefs have on the construction of success, concerns need to be raised as to whether some teachers may be creating environments that hinder the potential for success for many students. This is not to say that it is a conscious decision but rather one that remains at the level of ideology and hence not rendered available to critique.

Earlier research on teachers' beliefs has suggested the powerful influence such beliefs have on how learning is organized and assessed. In the responses offered by the teachers in this research, there is a potentiality for their practices to be framed by their beliefs and thereby hinder the mathematics learning for their students. Indeed, as many explicitly noted, their expectations of these students were lowered, thus exposing students to a restricted curriculum. Thus, it becomes important for educators to consider the beliefs that are held about learners and the impact this potentially has for learning and learning outcomes.

The views expressed by the teachers in this cohort have serious implications for preservice education and professional development of teachers. Where beliefs of teachers reflect an ideology of deficit and biological determinism, as evident in the comments posed by most of the teachers in this study, there are serious implications for students from socially disadvantaged backgrounds. As the studies cited early in this chapter indicate, teachers' beliefs impact significantly on the outcomes for students. In terms of equity and social justice, teachers who hold beliefs of students from socially disadvantaged backgrounds based in deficit models may engender practices that reinforce the status quo and therefore are at risk of ensuring that the students are locked into practices of social reproduction. For example, in considering the dominant belief of the teachers in this study that students were in some way deficient, the literature on beliefs would suggest that practices are then implemented that reflect this belief. As such, practice potentially engenders the reification of disadvantage. If teachers hold beliefs within a deficit framework, then it may not be unreasonable to expect that such beliefs filter through to practice. Indeed, this was evident in some of the comments offered by the teachers here in terms of their lower expectations of the students. Indeed, if teachers have lower expectations, then it is highly likely that curriculum will be offered that is somewhat inferior to other less-disadvantaged cohorts of students. In so doing, social differences become educational differences.

In closing, the one teacher (Kerry) who had a more systemic view of educational success and failure in school mathematics raised an important consideration that moved blame away from the students and their families. She raised questions as to whether teachers understood the differences in the cultures that students bring with them to school and whether such differences are respected at a level that allows a sense of justice for all students to pervade the classrooms. Her comments and experiences were often the antithesis of those offered by the other teachers, yet her school is one of the most disadvantaged in the region. Her habitus provided a different lens for seeing and interacting with her students, and thus her experiences were quite different from those described by the other teachers. Perhaps there is a greater role in teacher education—preservice and in-service—to raise ideological critiques in order to challenge beliefs about learners, their backgrounds, and the impact of the same on success in mathematics. As the comments posed by the majority of teachers in this study suggest, there is a dominance of views that focus attention on students and families as being deficient in ways that hinder success. In contrast, the one dissenting voice identified ways in which schooling and curriculum also have a considerable role to play in how success in mathematics evolves and how, as a consequence of their backgrounds, some students will have greater or less chance of being successful within that system.

REFERENCES

Askew, M., Brown, M., Rhodes, V., Johnson, D., and Wiliam, D. (1997). *Effective Teachers of Numeracy: Report of a Study Carried out for the Teacher Training Agency 1995–6*. London: School of Education, Kings College.

Bourdieu, P. (1979a). *Algeria 1960: The Disenchantment of the World, the Sense of Humour, the Kabyle House or the World Reversed*. Cambridge: Cambridge University Press.

Bourdieu, P. (1979b). *Distinction: A Social Critique of the Judgement of Taste* (1984 ed.). Cambridge, MA: Harvard University Press.

Chafel, J.A. (1997). Societal Images of Poverty: Child and Adult Beliefs. *Youth and Society*, 28(4), 432–467.

Connell, R.W., Ashendon, D.J., Kessler, S., and Dowsett, G.W. (1982). *Making the Difference: Schools, Families and Social Division*. Sydney: George Allen & Unwin.

Connell, R.W., White, V.M., and Johnston, K.M. (Eds.). (1991). *Running Twice as Hard: The Disadvantaged Schools Program in Australia*. Geelong: Deakin University Press.

Cooper, B., and Dunne, M. (1999). *Assessing Children's Mathematical Knowledge: Social Class, Sex and Problem Solving*. Buckingham, UK: Open University Press.

Daniels, H., and Lee, J. (1989). Stories, Class and Classrooms: Classic Tales and Popular Myths. *Educational Studies*, 15(1), 3–14.

Dent, J.N., and Hatton, E. (1996). Education and Poverty: An Australian Primary School Case Study. *Australian Journal of Education*, 40(1), 46–64.

Freebody, P., Ludwig, C., and Gunn, S. (1995). *Everyday Literacy Practice in and out of Schools in Low Socio-economic Urban Communities*. Brisbane: Griffith University—Centre for Literacy Education Research.

Gates, P. (2001). Mathematics Teachers' Belief Systems: Exploring the Social Foundations. In M. van den Heuvel-Panhuizen (Ed.), *Proceedings of the 25th Conference of the International Group for the Psychology of Mathematics Education* (3: 17–24). Utrecht: International Group for the Psychology of Mathematics Education.

Grenfell, M., and James, D. (1998). *Bourdieu and Education: Acts of Practical Reason*. London: Falmer Press.

Mac an Ghaill, M. (1995). *Making of Men: Masculinity, Sexuality and Schooling*. Buckingham, UK: Open University Press.

Perry, B., Howard, P., and Tracey, D. (1999). Head Mathematics Teachers' Beliefs about the Learning and Teaching of Mathematics. *Mathematics Education Research Journal*, 11(1), 39–53.

Prawat, R.S. (1993). Teachers' Beliefs about Teaching and Learning: A Constructivist Perspective. *American Journal of Education*, 100(3), 354–395.

Raymond, A.M. (1997). Inconsistency between a Beginning Elementary School Teacher's Mathematics Beliefs and Teaching Practice. *Journal for Research in Mathematics Education*, 28(5), 550–576.

Rosenthal, R., and Jacobson, L. (1969). *Pygmalion in the Classroom*. New York: Holt, Rinehart and Winston.

Seldin, S. (2000). Eugenics and the Social Construction of Merit, Race and Disability. *Journal of Curriculum Studies*, 12(2), 235–252.

Vacc, N.N., and Bright, G.W. (1999). Elementary Preservice Teachers' Changing Beliefs and Instructional Use of Children's Mathematical Thinking. *Journal for Research in Mathematics Education*, 30(1), 89–110.

Verschaffel, L., de Corte, E., and Borghart, I. (1997). Preservice Teachers' Conceptions and Beliefs about the Role of Real-World Knowledge in Mathematical Modeling of School Word Problems. *Learning and Instruction*, 7(4), 339–359.

Walkerdine, V. (1984). Developmental Psychology and the Child-Centred Pedagogy: The Insertion of Piaget into Early Education. In J. Henriques, W. Holloway, C. Urwin, C. Venn, and V. Walkerdine (Eds.), *Changing the Subject: Psychology, Social Regulation and Subjectivity* (pp. 153–202). London: Methuen.

Willis, P. (1977). *Learning to Labour: How Working Class Kids Get Working Class Jobs*. Aldershot: Gower.

Zevenbergen, R. (1994). Psychologising Educational Difference. In G. Bell, B. Wright, N. Leeson, and J. Geake (Eds.), *Challenges in Mathematics Education: Constraints on Construction* (2: 717–724). Lismore: The Mathematics Education Research Group of Australasia.

Zevenbergen, R. (1997). Psychologising Difference in Mathematics Education. *Chreods*, 11, 37–46.

Zevenbergen, R. (2001). Mathematics, Social Class and Linguistic Capital: An Analysis of a Mathematics Classroom. In B. Atweh and H. Forgasz (Eds.), *Socio-cultural Aspects of Mathematics Education: An International Perspective* (pp. 201–215). Mahwah, NJ: Lawrence Erlbaum.

Chapter 7

Gender-Related Differences in Working Style during Cooperative Learning in Secondary School Mathematics: A Malawian Case Study

Panji Catherine Chamdimba

INTRODUCTION

Malawi, formerly called Nyasaland, is a landlocked developing country situated in southern Africa. It borders Tanzania, Mozambique, and Zambia and has a land area of 118,484 square kilometers (45,747 square miles). The 1998 population census showed that it has a population of about 9.8 million people, with an annual growth rate of 3.2%, of which 51% are female. Chichewa is the national language, and English is the official language and the medium of instruction from year five of schooling onward. Malawi's economy is based on agriculture, the main export crops being tobacco and tea. Its social and economic development plans are supported mainly through donor aid, notably from the International Monetary Fund and the World Bank. As in many countries, the Malawi government recognizes education as an important factor in the economic and social development of the country. One of the problems faced by the Malawi education system is its sharply pyramidal structure. It is a four-cycle structure, and it includes an eight-year primary cycle, a two-year junior secondary school cycle leading to a further two-year senior secondary cycle, and finally, tertiary education. Due to limited resources, the government uses highly selective national examinations to control access to each successive level. For example, about 7% of the students sitting primary school leaving examinations enter secondary school, and only about 6% of the students completing secondary school go on to university. At each level, the participation of girls drops considerably compared to that of boys. For instance, the 1999 statistics from the Ministry of Education showed that the number of girls and boys enrolling in year 1 of primary was about equal, but the proportion of girls dropped to 42% by the time they completed year 8 of primary. According to the Ministry of Education

(1997), some of the reasons for the gender disparity in participation have included: (1) Parents/guardians who could not afford to pay school fees and other costs for both sons and daughters opted to send boys rather than girls, (2) children walk long distances to school, and under these conditions, boys are naturally more physically fit than girls to persevere. In order to alleviate this inequality, the government of Malawi has implemented a number of strategies including

1. introduction of free primary education in 1994 in order to address the economic obstacle to girls' access to education;
2. recent upward revision of the quota policy for selection of girls into secondary school from 33% to 50%—efforts are still under way to realize this;
3. removal of restrictions with respect to subject combinations that barred some girls from science and technical subjects; and
4. implementation of a scholarship program between 1987 and 1994 by the University of Malawi (with funding from the U.S. Agency for International Development [USAID]) for female students who opted to study subjects such as engineering, mathematics, physics, chemistry, and law, subjects not traditionally studied by females in Malawi.

In addition, the government is currently implementing the Girls' Attainment in Basic Literacy and Education (GABLE) program (again with funding from USAID). Under the program,

1. GABLE is paying school fees for all girls attending public secondary schools;
2. a Social Mobilization Campaign (SMC) targeting families and community leaders such as chiefs and religious leaders is being implemented to try to change their attitudes about females in society; and
3. GABLE is publishing short biographies of Malawian women in important positions and occupations, especially in the nontraditional fields, to provide role models for the girls.

All of the above policies represent a response to equal access. They are merely aimed at increasing numbers of females without addressing the causes of poor performance or poor persistence. Implicit in such efforts is the argument of fairness that women constitute 50% of the population of Malawi and must therefore have 50% representation in all subjects at all levels of education. As important as many of these strategies may have been, arguments that are focused on fairness alone lose force when such efforts continue to be counteracted by the twin problems of high dropout and low achievement. The available statistics show that gender inequity in enrollment and achievement at all levels still exists. Table 7.1 summarizes the situation at primary level. Table 7.1 shows that the number of girls and boys sitting the Primary School Leaving Certificate (PSLCE) has increased over the years. This is possibly due to the increase in

Table 7.1
Primary School Leaving Certificate (PSLCE) Performance by Gender, 1984–1994

	GIRLS			BOYS		
	Sat	Passed	Percentage	Sat	Passed	Percentage
1984	21,837	13,490	61.8	58,137	43,140	74.2
1986	25,779	16,045	62.2	62,675	45,860	73.2
1987	27,446	17,423	63.5	64,917	48,514	74.7
1991	32,316	29,608	91.6	66,845	63,005	94.3
1993	32,663	18,077	55.3	63,771	42,341	66.4
1994	42,692	32,628	76.4	64,821	52,068	80.3

Source: Khembo 1995, p. 3.

population from 8 million in 1987 to 9.8 million in 1998 (1987 and 1998 population census). There is, however, gender disparity in both entries and pass rates in favor of boys for all the years. The low number of females entering for the PSLCE is mainly due to lower retention rates. More girls than boys drop out of school before they reach the final year of primary (Malawi Government 1996). Several studies on Malawi have also shown that girls lag behind boys in achievement in all subjects, the gap being widest in mathematics (Chimwenje 1998; Hiddleston 1990; Kadzamira 1987, 1988; Khembo 1991). The picture of the achievement of females in selected subjects at the secondary school leaving examinations is given in Table 7.2.

The data in Table 7.2 show that boys achieve better than girls in all subjects. As in primary school, the situation is worse in mathematics and some art subjects. The gender gap is still narrowest in Chichewa. Table 7.2 also shows that the gender gap in terms of the proportion of students obtaining distinctions (grades 1–2) is widest in mathematics and geography. This contrasts with the achievement of girls in mathematics in a number of other countries. For example, in New Zealand, the proportion of girls obtaining top grades (1–3) in mathematics is much higher than that of the boys (Harker 2000); in the United Kingdom, girls now attain the same proportion of grades A–C as boys, although gender differences still exist among students obtaining A grades (Boaler 1997; Younger and Warrington 1996).

My basic contention in this chapter is that the girls' poor performance in general and mathematics in particular should be a cause for concern if social justice is to be promoted in Malawi. The social injustices against women arise in the fact that the girls' low score in mathematics places them at a great disadvantage since the requirements for most of postsecondary training and employers demand a good pass in mathematics. Since the number of girls sitting the national examinations at each level has been lower than boys and the latter

Table 7.2
Percentage of Students Obtaining Distinctions and Credits in Malawi School Certificate of Education (MSCE) Examinations in Selected Subjects for the Years 1994 to 1996

Subject	Sex	% Grades (1–2) (Distinction)			% Grades (3–6) (Credit)		
		1994	1995	1996	1994	1995	1996
Mathematics	M:	7.60	9.72	8.67	32.17	29.9	19.48
	F:	0.01	1.84	3.56	12.97	13.86	15.73
Biology	M:	1.20	0.02	1.13	21.73	3.06	23.53
	F:	0.03	0.00	0.03	12.74	3.10	14.28
Chichewa	M:	2.60	0.59	0.84	60.53	52.92	25.60
	F:	0.66	0.32	0.61	50.85	27.15	44.64
English	M:	0.30	0.67	0.60	24.82	7.07	31.61
	F:	0.18	0.33	0.45	25.36	17.83	28.20
Geography	M:	8.81	1.41	25.11	37.27	34.27	63.10
	F:	0.97	0.08	1.38	41.02	10.03	19.78
History	M:	0.26	3.07	4.50	15.89	34.25	35.14
	F:	0.00	1.65	1.97	7.24	11.25	32.23

Source: Chimwenje 1998, Appendix 1, pp. 10–15.

as a group have performed better than the former, more boys are selected into successive levels of education than girls despite the positive affirmation policy. This has tended in part to limit girls' participation at the tertiary level. This state of affairs is a recipe for most of the injustices against women in the sense that the bargaining power of women as a group for social/economic resources tends to be marginalized compared to their male counterparts as a result of the girls' low levels of education. Any attempt therefore to improve equality of access to education by boys and girls in Malawi must also be committed to providing equal opportunity for achievement and persistence between boys and girls. Hence, the current equity strategies need to be complemented with efforts within school to provide girls with positive learning experiences that will boost their achievement and morale.

Recent research from other countries suggests that cooperative learning has considerable potential for promoting a learner-friendly classroom climate and enhancing achievement of girls (Boaler 2000; Rogers 1995; Solar 1995). Given this background, it seemed important to investigate whether cooperative learning would improve the learning of girls in mathematics in Malawi, thus helping to redress inequity in mathematics education via a pedagogical strategy.

Although cooperative learning has been extensively researched (Cohen 1994; Johnson and Johnson 1999; Webb 1995), relatively few studies have isolated gender as a factor for investigation. The few studies that have isolated gender on cooperative learning have done so as part of broader studies and usually as an afterthought (Busato et al. 1995) or looked at the academic and attitudinal benefits of cooperative learning (Boaler 1997, 2000). Relatively few studies have investigated the influence of gender on student-student interaction during small groups (but see, e.g., Barnes 2000; Webb 1995). Barnes investigated the influence of gender on power relationships during collaborative group discussions. Further, most of the studies have been conducted in the developed countries. Thus, the possible influence of gender on specific group processes and interactions within cooperative learning groups has seldom been investigated, certainly not in Malawi. Consequently, this chapter contributes to the literature on gender and mathematics by focusing on the student-student interaction of three Form 3 classes, comprising 48 girls and 102 boys, during cooperative learning mathematics lessons in one secondary school in Malawi.

DESCRIPTION OF THE STUDY

The study was conducted in a government, coeducation, and boarding secondary school in Zomba Urban, Malawi, and involved one female mathematics teacher and 150 Form 3 (year 11) students in three classes (Form 3E, Form 3N, and Form 3W). I observed 105 mathematics lessons during a three-month period, usually taking the role of a participant observer. I used a variety of data collection methods such as observation notes, interviews, conversations, students' journals, students' questionnaire, and researcher's field notes. The experience of incorporating cooperative learning into mathematics teaching was novel for the teacher and the students in Malawi (Chamdimba 2002).

To prepare students and the teacher for the innovation, the following steps were taken: First, a teacher's guide on how to incorporate cooperative learning into mathematics teaching was sent to the teacher three months prior to the data collection phase. This advance timing was to give the teacher and the students ample time to experiment with cooperative learning before I commenced classroom observations. It also gave students opportunity to practice some cooperative learning skills. Much research has shown the importance of training students in cooperative learning skills for cooperative learning to be productive (Sharan 1980).

Second, after three months of experimenting with cooperative learning, a professional development workshop was organized, and the sample teacher, together with 14 other teachers, participated in the workshop. They shared their experiences, conceptions, and concerns about incorporating cooperative learning into their teaching. Any misconceptions the teachers had about cooperative learning were discussed, and a shared understanding was negotiated at this stage.

There was some evidence that as a result of the experimentation phase, as well as her participation in the teacher development workshop, the teacher's conception of cooperative learning groups broadened to include some aspects of cooperative learning that were missing in her prior practice. For example, her use of cooperative learning broadened to include a variety of activities other than revising and practicing mathematics as previously conceived. During the data collection phase, I asked the teacher to make her own decisions about how to assign students to groups. She decided to assign students into cooperative-base groups (Johnson and Johnson 1999) of the same gender but with mixed ability. She explained that she had decided to form separate groups of boys and girls because she noticed during the initiation stage that girls were passive when placed in mixed gender groups. The base groups lasted for the whole term. There was a total of 31 groups (11 groups of girls and 20 groups of boys). Students were mostly working in these groups, although the teacher would at times ask the students to work with peers of their own choice (self-selection groups) or those sitting next to them (seating arrangement groups). A question-naire was administered to students toward the end of the research period to determine their feelings toward cooperative learning.

RESULTS

An analysis of lesson observation notes indicated that three broad sequential categories characterized her teaching: Introduction, Example(s), Class Exercise(s). Typically, she introduced the topic by explaining the content of the lesson and defined some new terms. Next, she had the example(s) to be worked out. The students were then given exercises based on the example through which they practiced the topic. Within this broad framework, the teacher used a combination of teaching approaches in a single lesson. For instance, she would introduce a lesson using a lecture method, work out an example using a question/answer method, and let the students work on class exercises in cooperative learning groups. However, there was always a particular approach that took most of the class time, and this was almost inevitably either the "whole class question/answer" variation of a direct teaching approach or "cooperative learning approach." This led me to distinguish between two main approaches: question/answer and cooperative learning, depending on whichever approach dominated the lesson. For the purposes of this chapter, I shall limit most of my discussion to the student-student interaction during the cooperative learning approach.

I should, however, mention that the data revealed that the students' experiences of the question/answer teaching approach negatively affected the mathematics learning of both boys and girls. For example, almost all students expressed either through their journal entries or during interviews their lack of understanding of the mathematics they encountered during the question/answer teaching approach. For example, responding to an open journal prompt given to students soon after a question/answer lesson—"What did you like/not like about the way we worked today?"—36 out of 50 (72%) students commented on their lack of understanding. Even the 14 students who commented that they had understood the lesson remarked in their journals that they didn't learn in class; they had practiced the problem in the textbook before coming to class. They attributed their lack of understanding to the fast pace of question/response and feedback (14 students), the teacher's inability to handle their questions and answers properly (7 students), and their need to be involved enough to stop them from sleeping in such hot weather (6 students).

Further, although the whole class question/answer approach affected all students, there was evidence suggesting that this approach inhibited girls more than boys in the learning of mathematics. For example, I observed that during question/answer lessons, more than half of the girls were quiet during the lesson and were usually looking down, avoiding being picked by the teacher to answer a question. The majority of activities involved students going to write their answers on the chalkboard. Boys jumped over desks quickly to go in front to the chalkboard, but it was culturally unacceptable for girls to jump over desks. This discouraged girls from participating during such lessons. The girls also said that the whole class question/answer approach silenced them, because they did not feel "psychologically safe" to participate. One girl stated, "If we were working in our groups, I would have asked my friends, but since it was in a large group, I felt ashamed to ask the teacher because I was afraid of being laughed at by my friends." The girls' fear of asking or answering questions during a whole class discussion session also seemed to be influenced by some of the boys' behaviors. When the girls contributed to class discussion, the boys tended to display antagonistic behaviors that tended to silence some of the girls. For instance, on my first day of classroom observation, I observed that there was a particular girl about whom the boys jeered, moaned, or made some negative remarks each time she made a contribution toward class discussion. On one occasion, as she was trying to make a contribution, almost all the boys and some girls jeered and laughed at her, correcting her "broken English," so much so that she could not continue giving her contribution. On another occasion during the same lesson, as she was making her contribution, they jeered at her again, but this time the teacher intervened to allow her to finish explaining. At the end of the lesson, I asked the teacher why the boys were behaving that way toward that particular girl. The teacher replied: "She is a new student from another school. The students say that she is very vocal, so the boys want to put her down." The teacher's comment suggested that the boys had established a "classroom culture" that expected the girls to be silent during whole class discussion. With respect to the cooperative learning approach, the results from the questionnaire and interviews indicated that all students preferred this to the "whole class question/answer" approach. However, the working style of the boys was qualitatively different from that of the girls. This showed in their (1) cooperative group strategies, (2) student-student power relations, and (3) preferences for group composition. I discuss these differences in turn below.

Cooperative Group Strategies

I noted during classroom observations that the strategies employed by girls when working on a group task were different from those employed by boys. Excerpts of the field notes I took while observing a group of girls in 3N and a group of boys in 3W working on the same activity are given below to illustrate the differences in group strategies employed by boys and girls. The notes are presented in columns for easy comparison.

Lesson with 3N, 7/09/99, 10.40–12.00

There are 4 girls, call them G1, G2, G3, and G4. G1 picks the notebook and says the theorem she wants to write aloud, in a question form and as if uncertain. She makes gestures as if seeking for group's approval/correction. The other girls approve it, so she writes the theorem on the group's paper and she passes it to G2. G2 does the same and passes the paper to G3, and so on.

Lesson with 3W, 7/09/99, 14.10–15.30

There are 5 boys in this group. Call them B1, B2, B3, B4, and B5. B3 (I learnt later from the teacher that he was the brightest in the group) says, "Let us have everyone write 2 theorems each; then we will proceed from there." B1 writes down the theorems on the paper. He does not first seek approval from the group members in the way the girls I observed in 3N did. He passes the paper to the next boy. They do this quietly and individually. The other boys in the group are not even looking at what is being written. They are simply waiting for their turn to come.

This excerpt reflects the typical working styles of girls' and boys' cooperative groups that I observed. Most often, I noted that the strategies of solving the mathematical activity for many of the boys seemed to be that of working through the given activities as quickly as possible. They seemed to achieve this by avoiding discussion as much as possible. For instance, the statement "Let us have everyone write 2 theorems each; then we will proceed from there" could be interpreted as a strategy to minimize discussion. This sort of behavior was particularly common among groups that had in them the "top-achieving boys." In most cases, this meant that interruptions by lower-achieving group members for explanations or clarifications were only entertained after the answer was produced. This is illustrated in the excerpt below:

[A] group of 6 boys was about to plot the points they had worked out for the graph $y = x + 3$. When it came to plotting $(-3,0)$ only one boy GU knew where to plot the point. After some discussion, three other boys understood the concept while the other two boys were still lost. GU says: "Because we are running out of time, the few of us who know how to do it let's go on and we will explain to you afterwards." (lesson with 3N, 9/09/99, 7.30–8.10)

This tendency of the more competent students to go on to completion and then explain to others afterward contrasted with how most girls worked. The girls' strategy for working seemed to be that of all moving together. They seemed to be less concerned about working quickly and finishing the task than with involving everyone in the group in doing the given task. Consequently, instead of avoiding discussions, as the boys did, the girls tended to initiate discussion as much as possible. They usually did so by verbalizing their ideas in a question form and as if uncertain. I observed that this sort of "tentative behavior" displayed by girls seemed to serve three purposes: It seemed to be used (1) to make a contribution without the exercise of power over others, (2) to make sure that everyone else in the group understood what was being put forward before moving on, or (3) when the contributor was not sure of the idea and was using the group to test her ideas or thoughts. As the presenter verbalized the idea aloud and noticed through gestures that some members of the group seemed lost, they would discuss the idea until they reached a shared understanding before they would move on to the next idea. This was not perceived as beneficial by some boys, possibly because they felt that they were being slowed down, as illustrated by one boy's questionnaire response: "Girls tend to insist for explanation of the problem step by step; therefore this makes the group to spend a lot of time on a problem."

Student-Student Power Relations

During my lesson observations, I noticed on many occasions that for both boys' and girls' groups, the more able students in the groups, regardless of gender, usually assumed leadership roles. The difference was in the way they exercised their leadership powers. The girls were often tentative and negotiating when leading the group, usually presenting their ideas in a question form as though they were unsure. At times, they deliberately gave an incomplete idea to allow the other members to fill in so that the idea looked as if it came from all of them. For example, a group of four girls was working on a group task, involving calculating values of missing angles and sides for the given pairs of similar triangles. The group initially considered using the Pythagorean theorem, but after some discussion, they realized that it would not lead to the desired solution. In trying to suggest to her group mates that the missing sides could be calculated using the ratio property of similar triangles, the highest achiever in the group was observed as follows:

Writes a set of three parallel horizontal lines and another set of three vertical parallel lines and asks in an uncertain manner: "Is the symbol for similar triangles this [*pointing to horizontal lines*] or this [*pointing to vertical lines*]? Immediately, the other girls completed the symbol by arranging the letters of the given triangles in the right order and it became obvious to all of them that they needed to use the ratio of the sides, and one by one started contributing their ideas.

In the excerpt above, the group leader's use of an incomplete symbol for similar triangles gave other students an opportunity to contribute toward the solution. This seemed to promote a sense of shared ownership of whatever they were producing, rather than individual success or failure. The excerpt below from my field notes illustrates this team spirit in girls of the "we-succeed-or-fail together" approach/strategy:

A group of 4 girls had just finished plotting the given points on the graph paper. They plotted one of the points wrongly. They had plotted (0, 3) instead of (3, 0). The teacher pointed to the wrong point and asked them: "What are the coordinates of this point?" They all said, "Ah we have made a mistake." They corrected it. The teacher moved on to another group. The girl who had plotted the wrong point said, "So I am the one who made the mistake." The other three girls all said at once in an assuring way, "No, it is all of us, not just you!"

The statement "it is all of us" demonstrates that team spirit is involved. Generally, the high-achieving girls tended to take the role of facilitator rather than posing as someone who knew better than the rest.

Boys, on the other hand, led their groups in a controlling manner. The most competent student's role in the majority of boys' groups resembled that of the teacher's role in a teacher-centered classroom. In most cases, they were teaching their peers, endorsing or rejecting ideas from their group mates. The excerpt below from my observation notes illustrates this point:

There are 4 boys in a group. Call them B6, B7, B8, and B9. B6 is the highest achiever in the group and he automatically assumes a leadership role.

B6: In whose notebook are we going to write?

B7: Mine.

B6 [*In a commanding tone*]: So you will be our secretary.

B6 works out the problem by himself, while others are listening, and dictates the solution step by step for B7 to write down. They move on to question 2. B6 grabs the notebook from B7 and quickly copies down the diagrams for Q2 and hands back the notebook to B7.

B7 [*Directing the question to B6 for approval*]: Can I label this triangle ABC instead of XYZ since XYZ is already used in Q1?

B6: Yes.

And continues to dictate the solution for Q2.

In the excerpt above, although there were four boys in the group, the interaction/ conversation was only between two, B6 and B7, and it was mainly a one-way conversation from B6 to B7. B6 related to his group mates in an authoritative manner. His group mates were simply listening to his teaching, obeying instructions from him such as "you will be the secretary" and "you write this," and so on. He had to endorse (or reject) whether B7 could use different letters for the triangle in Q2. Such roles are characteristics of teachers in a teacher-centered classroom.

Preferences for Group Composition

Another observed gender difference related to the preferences for group composition held by boys and girls. I observed on several occasions that when students were allowed to choose with whom to work, the majority of the girls would cluster around boys, especially high-achieving boys, while boys usually formed groups with students sitting next to them. Further evidence of the different priorities held by boys and girls regarding with whom to work was revealed by the students' responses to the questionnaire item "Would you prefer to work in a girls only/boys only group, or in a group of mixed boys and girls? Give some reasons." A total of 53 boys and 30 girls responded to the question. Some 80% of the girls preferred to work in mixed gender groups, compared with about 40% of boys. The girls' preference for mixed gender groups seemed to be influenced by their classroom experiences that boys were more capable of getting better marks in mathematics. The 24 girls all stated that they preferred to work in groups with boys because the likelihood of solving the given problem was higher if they had boys in the group than if the group was composed of girls only. Typical comments from the girls were: "When girls fail to solve the problem, boys can do it"; "A lot of boys do better in maths"; "When we have boys in the group we solve problems very easily."

This belief that boys knew more mathematics than they did was evident throughout the research period. Another instance of this belief came from an interview:

Panji: You mentioned that some girls are shy. What about yourself?

EC: In my opinion, I can't be shy because I know that boys can help me more than girls because boys know more things than girls.

Panji: Do you think boys know more maths than girls?

EC: No, it's not all of them, but there are more boys who know maths than girls.

The most prevalent reason given by boys (11 out of 32) for their preference to work in a boys-only group was that it allowed them to meet and discuss mathematics at any time and any place, which was not possible due to boarding rules if they had girls in the group. Other reasons given by boys included: Less work is achieved because girls are playful during group discussions (9 out of 32), boys or girls are shy in the presence of the opposite sex (9 out of 32), and one boy wrote, "In a boys-only group, you can work hard to compete with the fellow boys, while if it includes girls, it gives you a false impression that you are doing well just because you see that you do better than the girls." In general, the reasons given seem to suggest that boys felt that having girls in their groups would generally slow them down in doing mathematics. This was consistent with their working strategy described above.

DISCUSSION AND CONCLUSION

In this chapter, I have indicated that current Malawi government strategies for enhancing participation of girls in education (and mathematics) focus on increasing numbers without paying attention to the classroom environment to reduce dropout and raise achievement. This study sought to enhance the learning of girls in mathematics from a pedagogical perspective. Data analyses revealed evidence (not presented in this chapter) that the whole class question/answer teaching approach commonly used in Malawi for mathematics teaching disadvantages girls in their learning of mathematics. All girls stated that they preferred the cooperative learning approach because they felt safer to contribute their ideas or ask questions for clarification in a small cooperative group rather than in front of the whole class.

The evidence reported in this chapter relates to the differences in working styles between boys and girls during cooperative learning. The boys preferred to work quickly through the given tasks with a minimum of discussion. Speed, rather than discussion, was the focus for many boys. This tendency was most acute among the highest-achieving boys. The girls, on the other hand, were more concerned with discussion and clarification among the group members than the speed at which the task was done. These differences support previous claims that males and females have different ways of coming to know (Becker 1995; Belenky et al. 1986). The finding of this study that girls had a tendency to initiate discussions more than the boys during cooperative tasks supports Becker's notion that women are more connected knowers than males. A possible interpretation for this tendency for girls is that discussions allowed the girls to listen to alternate methods of solution, and through the sharing of ideas, they constructed the mathematics together. This seemed to have a positive effect on their self-perception of mathematical ability. The teacher had remarked on several occasions that she had noticed that the girls had gained confidence as a result of working in groups. She commented, "The girls are now able to put up their hands and give their ideas even when they are not necessarily correct." This gain in confidence possibly resulted from making a contribution in small groups without being laughed at. However, in the classroom context in which they were working, the strategies adopted by girls were less rewarding than those used by boys. On many occasions, the girls lost some marks because they spent a lot of time on discussion and were unable to complete their tasks in the given time. Such experiences probably convinced most girls that it was beneficial for them to work with boys because it gave them the opportunity to earn high group marks. The 80% of girls who stated in their questionnaire response that they preferred to work in groups with boys did so despite their awareness that working with boys was not necessarily beneficial for their individual learning. An informal interview I had with a group of seven Form 3W girls about midway through the data collection period was particularly revealing in this respect. I started with an open-ended question: "I would want you to comment on the type of group discussions that we have had so far since the beginning of the term or even from last term." In the course of the conversation, one girl said:

Gin: We learn more when we are working in groups with girls only because when we are discussing in a group with boys, we don't think because we think boys know more maths than girls. And if a boy gives a point, we think it's just because he is a boy, and we just sit waiting for the boys to give points. But when we are only girls in a group, we are forced to think and when one girl gives a point we get encouraged and say to ourselves, "Ah! Even this girl can give a point, which means I can also think of one." And that way we see that we are able to solve the problem.

The above comment also shows that their experience of working in groups helped them to discover that they were capable of contributing to the process of solving mathematical problems. The finding that most girls preferred to have more time for discussion suggests that the present teaching method that puts emphasis on speed of production of the final correct answer disadvantages girls. By focusing on the final correct answer, girls are denied the opportunity to explore different viewpoints. Teachers must ensure that small group tasks are allocated reasonable time to allow maximum discussion among students. It is not inconceivable that time invested in developing understanding at this stage of schooling could lead to more rapid development of mathematics ideas later.

The boys were more controlling when leading a group discussion, while the girls were negotiating, trying to include everyone, when leading the group. The resulting effect was that some of the boys, especially those working in groups with top students, lost their self-perception of mathematics competence, as remarked by the teacher during an informal conversation: "MM was a competent boy, but ever since he started working in EM's group, I have noticed that his confidence and performance in mathematics has gone down." The findings of this study suggest that Malawian boys do not naturally work cooperatively, even when they are physically placed in groups. They appear to need to be taught cooperative skills for cooperative learning to be productive. Teachers need to monitor boys carefully to make sure that everyone in the group has the opportunity to contribute ideas. The high-achieving boys need to be convinced of the importance of listening to others' viewpoints about solving the problem.

In conclusion, the findings of this study indicate that the cooperative learning approach (using single-sex groups) enabled the girls to develop a positive attitude toward mathematics learning. It is not possible, however, on the basis of this study to comment on the impact of cooperative learning on the achievement of girls in the public examinations. This aspect was not part of the focus of the study, and indeed it is questionable whether such an impact can be determined within a short term (Rogers 1995). To examine the long-term effects of cooperative learning on the achievement of girls in the Malawian context, a longitudinal study is needed.

REFERENCES

Barnes, M.S. (2000). Effects of Dominant and Subordinate Masculinities on Interactions in a Collaborative Learning Classroom. In J. Boaler (Ed.), *Multiple Perspectives on Mathematics Teaching and Learning* (pp. 145–169). Westport, CT: Ablex.

Becker, J. (1995). Women's Ways of Knowing in Mathematics. In P. Rogers and G. Kaiser (Eds.), *Equity in Mathematics Education: Influences of Feminism and Culture* (pp. 175–185). London: Falmer Press.

Belenky, M., Clinchy, B., Goldberger, N., and Tarule, J. (1986). *Women's Ways of Knowing: The Development of Self, Voice, and Mind.* New York: Basic Books.

Boaler, Jo. (1997). *Experiencing School Mathematics: Teaching Styles, Sex and Setting.* Buckingham, UK: Open University Press.

Boaler, Jo. (2000). *So Girls Don't Really Understand Mathematics? Dangerous Dichotomies in Gender Research.* Paper presented at the ICME9 Conference, Tokyo.

Busato, Vittorio V., Ten dam Geert, Den Eeden, and Terwel, Jan. (1995). Gender-Related Effects of Co-operative Learning in a Mathematics Curriculum for 12–16 Year-Olds. *Journal of Curriculum Studies,* 27(6), 667–686.

Chamdimba, P.C. (2002). *Cooperative Learning: A Possible Strategy for Improving the Learning of Girls in Secondary School Mathematics in Malawi?* Ph.D. thesis, University of Waikato, New Zealand.

Chimwenje, C. (1998). Effectiveness of Distance Education in Malawi: Student Outcomes. Paper presented at a Distance Education for Mzuzu University Workshop, Lilongwe Hotel, Malawi.

Cohen, E. (1994). Restructuring the Classroom: Conditions for Productive Small Groups. *Review of Educational Research* 64(1), 1–35.

Harker, R. (2000). Achievement, Gender and the Single-Sex/Coed Debate. *British Journal of Sociology of Education,* 21(2), 203–218.

Hiddleston, P. (1990). *Differences between the Results of Boys and Girls in Subjects of the Primary School Leaving Certificate Examinations.* Zomba: University of Malawi.

Hiddleston, P. (1995). The Contribution of Girls-Only Schools to Mathematics and Science Education in Malawi. In P. Rogers and G. Kaiser (Eds.), *Equity in Mathematics Education: Influences of Feminism and Culture* (pp. 147–152). London: Falmer Press.

Hyde, K.A.L. (1992). *Female Education in Malawi: Problems, Priorities and Prospects.* Paper presented at the Educational Research in Malawi: Problems and Priorities

Conference of the Centre for Educational Research and Training, Chancellor College, University of Malawi, August 23–27.

Johnson, D., and Johnson, R. (1999). *Learning Together and Alone: Cooperative, Competitive, and Individualistic Learning.* Boston: Allyn and Bacon.

Kadzamira, E. (1987). *Sex Differences in the Performance of Candidates in the Malawi Certificate of Education in Mathematics and Science Subjects.* Zomba, Malawi: Malawi National Examination Board, RTC 21/87.

Kadzamira, E. (1988). *Sex Differences in the Performance of Candidates in Languages and Humanities Subjects at MSCE Level 1982–1986.* Zomba, Malawi: Malawi National Examination Board, RTC 6/88.

Khembo, D. (1991). *Comparison of Examination Results over Time.* Master's thesis, University of London.

Khembo, D. (1995). *Disparities in Access to and Achievement in Education.* Zomba, Malawi: Malawi National Examination Board, RTC May/95.

Malawi Government. (1995). *The Policy and Investment Framework for Education (1995–2005).* Lilongwe: Ministry of Education.

Malawi Government. (1996). *Malawi Capacity Building Assessment.* Lilongwe: Ministry of Education.

Ministry of Education. (1997). *A Position Paper of the Ministry of Education: The Education of Girls in Science, Technology and Mathematics.* Paper presented at the Regional GASAT Conference, Lilongwe, Malawi, October 20–24.

Ministry of Education and Culture. (1985). *Education Development Plan 1985–1990: A Summary.* Lilongwe: Planning Division of Ministry of Education and Culture.

Rogers, P. (1995). Putting Theory into Practice. In P. Rogers and G. Kaiser (Eds.), *Equity in Mathematics Education: Influences of Feminism and Culture* (pp. 175–185). London: Falmer Press.

Sharan, S. (1980). Cooperative Learning in Small Groups: Recent Methods and Effects on Achievement, Attitudes, and Ethnic Relations. *Review of Educational Research,* 50(2), 241–271.

Solar, C. (1995). An Inclusive Pedagogy in Mathematics Education. *Educational Studies in Mathematics,* 28, 311–333.

Webb, N. (1995). Testing a Theoretical Model of Student Interaction and Learning in Small Groups. In R. Hertz-Lazarowitz and N. Miller (Eds.), *Interaction in Cooperative Groups: The Theoretical Anatomy of Group Learning* (pp. 102–119). Cambridge: Cambridge University Press.

Younger, M., and Warrington, M. (1996). Differential Achievement of Girls and Boys at GCSE: Some Observations from the Perspective of One School. *British Journal of Sociology of Education,* 17(3), 299–313.

Chapter 8

Choosing Maths/Doing Gender: A Look at Why There Are More Boys Than Girls in Advanced Mathematics Classes in England

Heather Mendick

INTRODUCTION

Debates on education and equity have a long history, with a shifting focus from class to gender and then to "race." In this chapter, as in much current research, there is a growing understanding of multiple positionings and the joint articulation of these differences, with others like hetero/sexuality and dis/ability, to produce disadvantage. However, underlying the work there remains a tension between deterministic approaches that emphasize the role of education in reproducing the structural inequalities that exist within society and more optimistic approaches that stress student and teacher resistances. This is one version of the classic sociological opposition between structure and agency, and intertwined with it is the question of why members of oppressed groups appear "freely to choose" educational paths and behaviors that ultimately serve to reproduce their oppression. Tackling this question regarding class, Bourdieu (1984) used his formulation of habitus, while Paul Willis, through a cultural studies approach, sought to explain how working-class boys get working-class jobs (Willis 1977).

This chapter starts from a parallel question in the area of gender and education, asking why a disproportionate number of girls opt out of powerful areas of the curriculum. These areas include science, technology, and mathematics, the latter, as Sells (1980) pointed out, functioning as a "critical filter" controlling entry into a large number of high-status areas of academia and employment. After critically reviewing the early research in the area of gender and mathematics, I outline a poststructuralist framework that deals with some of the problems related to this work and that also enables a deconstruction of the structure/agency opposition. I then move on to a discussion of the study and my methodology, before looking in detail at interviews with three of the boys. They are representative of a strand of male students who opt to study mathematics beyond the compulsory stage, even though they do not enjoy it. Simon (all students and the school involved have been made anonymous) chooses it, in spite of the way its curriculum violates his notions of "common sense," in order to prove his worth to potential employers; James also uses it as a way of securing his future within the labor market; while Michael uses the reputation of mathematics as a hard subject to prove his intelligence to those around him. Intellect, rationality, and wage earning are central features of masculinity in contemporary society, and so, I argue, these students are using the social power of maths as a way of confirming their masculinity; in choosing maths they are simultaneously doing gender. In the concluding section, I set these stories in the context of those of the other boys and girls that I interviewed and discuss some of the implications of these students' stories for mathematics pedagogy.

GENDER AND MATHEMATICS EDUCATION RESEARCH: OLD AND NEW DIRECTIONS

The research stimulated by the debate on gender and mathematics education during the 1970s and 1980s looked at the role of stereotyping in curriculum materials and in the views of teachers, parents, and peers, the organization of schooling, male dominance of classroom space, and female lack of confidence and maladaptive patterns of attribution (see Burton 1986, for a discussion of this research). However, the male dominance of advanced maths courses persisted despite all attempts to shift it. In fact, between the years 1994 and 2001 the proportion of the total number of 17- and 18-year-olds entered for Advanced (A)-level mathematics in England who are male showed very little change, dropping only slightly from 65% to 63% (Government Statistical Service 1995, 1996, 1997, 1998, 1999, 2000, 2001). This greater participation of males in maths courses becomes more pronounced as you go up the levels from A-level to undergraduate and then to postgraduate and is also reflected in the larger number of men than women working in mathematically oriented fields. There is a similar pattern of gendered participation in maths in other countries (Boaler [2000] has recent statistics on the situation in America, while Hanna [1996] contains slightly older data from a range of countries).

Dunne and Johnston (1994) argue that the failure of the feminist interventions was at root a theoretical one. They divide the early research on gender and maths into three categories: work that provides a quantitative documentation of gender differences, that which offers biological explanations for these differences, and that offering sociological explanations for them. The crucial point for my analysis here is that while the biological determinist and the social constructionist positions appear to be radically opposed, Dunne and Johnston's poststructuralist feminist critique identifies two major assumptions that they both share and leave unexamined. First, "the power and position that mathematics holds as a discipline inevitably remains inviolate in the gender and school mathematics research, where the implicit message seems to be that all will be well once sufficient (but clearly not all) girls have access to the power and privileges of maths" (1994, p. 222). And second, gender categories are seen as natural and to preexist the research. For example, even some of the most radical approaches, such as those advocating single-sex schooling and a girl-centered curriculum, which extol feminine qualities and values over masculine ones, function to reinforce the idea of male and female as binary oppositional categories and emphasize gender differences over similarities. As Walkerdine (1998, p. 23) argues, "[T]he reification of the categories 'girl' and 'boy' produces explanations which favour sex-specific characteristics, so that more complex analyses of masculinity and femininity are impossible." We need to engage with these two taken-for-granted assumptions, of maths as legitimately powerful and gender as naturally binary.

To do this I adopt the poststructuralist position of Dunne and Johnston, Walkerdine, and others that acknowledges a dialectic of structure and agency, rather than viewing them as mutually exclusive forces.

Poststructuralist theory argues that people are not socialised into the social world, but that they go through a process of *subjectification*. In socialisation theory, the focus is on the process of shaping the individual that is undertaken by others. In poststructuralist theory the focus is on the way each person actively takes up the discourses through which they and others speak/write the world into existence *as if it were their own*. (Davies 1993, p. 13; emphasis in original)

Discourses are structures of language and practice through which objects come into being. These knowledges about objects are powerful because they determine what can be said about something as well as who can say it, and even what can be thought or imagined. It is within a range of discourses of mathematics, femininity, masculinity, and schooling, among other things, that an individual's educational choices and experiences are constituted. The dominant discourses of maths that thread through the narratives of Simon, James, and Michael are maths as "hard," maths as currency in the labor market, and maths as boring and irrelevant. It is how they work and are worked by these discourses in constructing their gendered, classed, and "raced" identities on which I focus in this chapter.

RESEARCH SETTING AND METHODOLOGY

Simon, James, and Michael were all in the second term of an Advanced Supplementary (AS)-level maths course at Grafton School in London when I interviewed them. AS-levels are normally studied between the ages of 16 and 18 and are designed to follow on directly from the GCSE (General Certificate of Secondary Education) that young people take at age 16+, the examination with which compulsory schooling ends. Students normally choose four subjects to study and then drop one at the end of their first year, continuing with the remaining three to A-level in the following year. The students at Grafton were originally taught in one group, but due to the larger-than-expected size of this group, about three weeks into the course, they were split into two sets. The students were allocated to a group by their "ability" as measured by their GCSE grade. GCSEs were originally graded with a single letter from G to A, but subsequently an additional grading (A*) was introduced to recognize exceptional achievement above the level of grade A. GCSE mathematics can be entered at one of three different tiers (higher, intermediate, and foundation), each associated with a different syllabus; the grade ranges A*–D, B–F, and D–G, respectively, are available at each level. The entry level, as well as the grade attained, were crucial in the Grafton setting process. The "top" set included all those who obtained an A*, A, or high B on the higher-level GCSE exam; Simon and James were in this group, and it continued to be taught by the same three teachers as the original group. This group contained five girls and nine boys. The "bottom" set contained mostly students who had obtained a pass at the intermediate level GCSE exam (although three students had a B grade at the higher level); Michael was in this group, and I took them for all their lessons. This group contained six boys and three girls. The class and "race" mix of the maths AS-level cohort reflected that of the school as a whole, being ethnically diverse and predominantly working class.

The extracts below are drawn from individual semistructured interviews, which lasted between 25 and 40 minutes in length. These were conducted as part of an ongoing study of students' experiences of maths, gender, and subject choice at 16+. The study combines student interviews with three weeks of observations in the maths lessons attended by the research participants. Twelve self-selecting students (7 boys and 5 girls) are involved at Grafton, and a further 18 and 13 students, respectively, at the other two sites, Westerburg Sixth Form College and Sunnydale Further Education College. Students were asked

- to describe a typical maths lesson and what they had enjoyed most and least during the year;
- about the different learning styles used in their classes and about which of their subjects was most similar to maths and which most different from it;
- to give the reasons for their subject choices and what they hope to do when they leave the sixth-form; and
- about their feelings on gender.

The interviews were first analyzed by looking at a variety of themes. Two of these, students' reasons for choosing maths and their views on other people's image of maths, were used as a starting point for developing narratives from the data. These themes involved the students in defining themselves against other people and thus enabled me to focus on the way the students speak about who they are. After completing the individual stories, I developed connections between them such as the ones discussed in this chapter. I view "the processes of interviewing and of being interviewed [as] not simply about the giving and receiving of information but at least as much about speaking identities into being, solidifying them and constantly reconstituting them through the stories we tell ourselves and each other" (Epstein and Johnson 1998, p. 105). Unconscious factors form an important part of this process, "the elements of phantasy, the rush of desire and/or disgust, of who we desire and who we wish to be—in psychoanalytic terms, the cathexis of object choice and identification" (p. 116; see also Hunt 1989, for a detailed exploration of the role of unconscious factors within the interview). Identity is an important metaphor for understanding the "complex topography of choice" (Maguire, Macrae, and Ball 1998, p. 182) that "is powerfully driven by the idea of being with other people who are 'like me' " (p. 187). Identity can be conceptualized as a "like me" / "unlike me" filtering device that people use to help them organize the vast quantities of information with which they are required to deal (Jackson and Wain 2000).

Davies (1989, p. 19) points out that gender is a central part of anyone's identity, for "competent social membership presumes gender" and moreover a gender that is binary being "defined in terms of male and female as opposite and antithetical." Since all socially competent members of society must demonstrate that they have located themselves relative to the categories of male and female, their subject choices are one of the ways in which they can do this; that is, they are a form of "gender category maintenance work" (see Hughes [2001] and Whitehead [1996] for examples of other studies on subject choice at 16+ that argue this). The need continually to be working on one's identity demonstrates both its role in organizing our experience and its unstable and fragmented character; an identity is always in process and never attained (this is something that has been discussed extensively in the literature; e.g., Flax 1990; Griffiths 1995; Hall 1996). Many writers have stressed that this insecurity applies particularly to masculinity, the achievement of which can never be taken for granted. "Masculinity is something that we have to be constantly trying to prove. It isn't anything that we can feel easy or relaxed with because we have to be constantly vigilant and on guard to prove, for instance, we are not 'soft' or 'sissies' " (Seidler 1997, p. 39). Gender is a project and one that is achieved in interaction with others. What follows is a reading of three male students' experiences of maths as part of their performance of masculinity in the face of the constant threat of its loss (see Redman and Mac an Ghaill 1997 for a fascinating Lacanian psychoanalytic theorization of this threat).

SIMON'S STORY

Simon's mother is an English housewife. His father arrived in this country on a boat from Hong Kong and then worked in nightclubs. Simon is studying business, information technology (IT), geography, and mathematics. Simon's interview was the longest individual interview that I did. He appeared very relaxed and discussed all the topics I asked about at length, needing very little prompting from me. In this story I look at the way he positions himself as a business-oriented representative of "common sense" in his views on maths teaching, and his subject choices, performing a masculinity tied to the new vocationalism within the curriculum.

I begin with his views on maths since these mark out clear differences for him between it and his other subjects. Simon's favorite maths lessons are those "where you go in there knowing nothing and you go out knowing much more about that [topic]"; he enjoys the buzz of understanding. His experiences, more than those of any of the other interviewees, resemble those of the girls in Boaler's (1997) study who found their "quest for understanding" frustrated within procedural maths lessons. "They wanted to locate the rules and methods within a wider sphere of understanding. Thus they wanted to know *why* the methods worked, *where* they came from and *how* they fitted into the broader mathematical domain" (Boaler 2000, p. 33; emphasis in original).

Simon wants "To understand like, not just the answer's this because it's this, or *e*'s infinity because of this, whatever, yeah. It's better to understand why it is like that. 'Cos when you understand why it is like that, not just know that it is that, then you can learn easier." He links this explicitly to the pace of the lessons and the way one topic rapidly becomes another and then another. He insists, "You've gotta make sure that everybody understands, yeah, the whole topic, yeah, before you move on, because when you move on and people get left behind, yeah, I think that's when you start getting problems." He has a very clear agenda about how to improve maths teaching and speaks authoritatively about it. His agenda, which is also reminiscent of the girls Boaler interviewed, includes not just a slower pace to lessons but also more participation and connection to real life. This latter point comes out most strongly in his response to my question:

Heather: What do you think other people not doing maths think about it?

Simon: They think to themselves that it's a really boring, pointless subject. . . . But to be honest, you won't never use it in your life, like if you're gonna be an accountant after maths, you might do a bit of maths, but it's not gonna be nothing near the stuff. Like there's a lot of pointless stuff. . . . I reckon people view that [*pause*] maths being really difficult. And that's why they think it's boring. Because they don't understand it. That's why they've got a lot of bad experiences because the teacher just said "3 + 3 = 6" and that's it. . . . And the sum of the triangle, I mean Pythagoras' theorem, is *a* plus *b* equals *c* squared. And they, they just don't know why, why you're doing that. You know what I mean? Does it work in real life? Have you checked it out or got a real-life example? Have you got a triangle that you've actually measured and that you can tell that it's actually right? . . . You could be lying. 'Cos generally a lot of what the maths teacher says you don't understand anyway, so they could just go on and on, yeah, something that's completely lies. And they will think to themselves it's maths. "Obviously I don't understand it 'cos it's hard."

Simon clearly wants many shifts in mathematical pedagogy including a move to a more democratic classroom in which the students can challenge the teacher's statements. The changes he wants to make suggest he holds an epistemological position that sees mathematical truths as less absolute than most people's. However, this is complicated by his belief that discussion is inappropriate in maths classrooms, because, "well, you do the discussion, but if you know the answer you know the answer, and then there's nothing to discuss." He feels this even though he finds this a productive approach to learning in other subjects. As he puts it, "When you're talking with someone else, you get ideas, so it's better." So for Simon, introducing real life and common sense into maths classrooms will displace the power and authority of the teacher but not of the mathematics itself.

Thus Simon feels there are fundamental things that mark out mathematics from other forms of knowledge and hence affect the way it is best communicated. Looking in more detail at the way he speaks about these differences, he describes geography as "not really a hard intellectual subject," while of business, he says: "It's not that much; it's not that really demanding, I think. I think maths is more really demanding. It's more. You can either get it right or wrong, but in other subjects, it's more of a gray area. You know what I mean? . . . [Business] is not something that can be put in a textbook, I don't think. You couldn't teach someone how to be a good businessman." He connects studying geography and business, his intended career and the subject that he enjoys the most, to the kind of person he is. With geography, "it's the way that I think; it's really straightforward . . . because it's more like real life." While business is like law, which he wishes he had taken, because "I can understand that stuff. . . . I understand why it's gotta be there and why. I don't know, I just find it's interesting and I just wanna know about it." It is clear from his interview that it is what Simon reads as the commonsense aspects of business and geography (and law) that enable him to identify with them and, conversely, the absence of these from his maths lessons that seems to prevent him from identifying with it. The tenuous nature of his affiliation with maths is evident in the extrinsic motivation for his choice to pursue maths:

Simon: I chose maths because I think it sounds good when you say you're doing maths. And also because it's, it's the most challenging subject . . . that and physics, I reckon, and chemistry. They're like the most challenging subjects, and [*pause*] generally if you can do something like that you are an intelligent person. . . . Also because in maths, when you're applying for jobs, if you say you got maths, they always automatically assume that your common sense is good and that you're generally smart. Not just that you know how to work out an equation or whatever. They generally think you're smart, and they think you're hardworking 'cos they know that maths is a hard subject. So I thought that, in terms of getting a job, that it would be a good idea to take it.

It is clear that Simon is constructing himself as a "doer" rather than a "thinker"—someone concerned with the concrete rather than the abstract. As such he fits a pattern identified by Mac an Ghaill (1994 p. 63) in his study of masculinities and schooling that he named the "New Enterprisers": "[W]orking within the new vocationalist skilling regimes of high-status technological and commercial subject areas, the New Enterprise students were negotiating a new mode of school student masculinity with its values of rationality, instrumentalism, forward planning and careerism." What is interesting is the way that Simon works geography and maths, both traditional academic disciplines, into his narrative. In the former case, Simon reads geography as vocational in almost the same terms as business and IT, something that I think can be attributed to the very dynamic and practical way in which it is taught at Grafton. However, with maths, something that Simon clearly sees as very disconnected from real life, it is the earning power in the labor marketplace that he will get by succeeding in it, that enables him to tie it to his view of himself. This pattern of the discourse of the possibility of economic empowerment through studying maths, overriding discourses of maths as irrelevant and uninspiring, recurs in a slightly different form in James's story.

JAMES'S STORY

James is in the second year of his postcompulsory education. He is repeating his mathematics AS-level and is also in the second year of his A-levels in physics and sports studies. This year he has supplemented his original subject choices with a fourth subject, performing arts. James is white and tells me that his mother is not engaged in paid labor and his father is a fire engineer. From his interview it seems that James takes a highly pragmatic approach to life. The centrality of this to his identity is demonstrated by his answer to the question I put forth:

Heather: What do you think other people who are not doing maths think about the subject?

James: Yeah, a lot of people ask me, um, like, "Oh, what A-levels are you doing?" And I sort of say maths and physics and they go, "Ooh, tough" sort of thing. . . . "You must be clever" sort of thing. So I mean, I think there's a general consensus that it's very hard. But I don't actually think it's that hard. I mean, it's just [*pause*] if you listen, take the notes, and just make sure you learn everything and revise a lot, I mean it's not that hard. And I think that's the same for most subjects; as long as you listen, do the work, and revise, then, then you can probably do any subject.

Here he describes other people's views of maths as being very different from his; he rejects an academic identity based on being *clever* in favor of one founded on hard work. There is no mystery to doing well at maths for James. That it is just a matter of application is something he demonstrated in his GCSE approach. This consisted of getting the notes in class and then working through past papers: "I mean, I had a folder like that fat [to illustrate this point, he holds his hands horizontal, one above the other and separated by several inches] basically of past papers of every question that had ever come up sort of thing, and I just gone through every single one."

James's pragmatic approach is very different to the "laddish" behavior that researchers such as Francis (2000) and Epstein (1998) have found in their studies of compulsory schooling. Within this boys' antischool culture, hard work, far from being extolled as a virtue, is equated with effeminacy. Status is gained through a range of competitive and aggressive behaviors tied to sport, particularly football, and disruptive behavior; a studious identity becomes a difficult one for a boy to occupy, carrying with it the risk of being labeled as a "boffin," as "gay," or even as a "girl." The only acceptable way for a boy to succeed is through "effortless achievement" (Mac an Ghaill 1994, p. 67). However, Mac an Ghaill also found a small group of boys, whom he labeled the "Academic Achievers," who had a "positive orientation to the academic curriculum" (p. 59) and were "in the process of equipping themselves for social mobility and a middle-class post-school destination" (p. 62), based on a traditional working-class work ethic. Moreover, the work done on masculinities in post-16 education suggests that such positions become more secure for boys who continue beyond compulsory education, since the move from year 11 to year 12 "marks a key cultural transition that involves young people in new social relations (in particular those of the labour market) and requires new forms of identity to handle them" (Redman and Mac an Ghaill 1997, p. 169). Power et al. (1998, p. 143) also relate this to an evolution in the lived relationship between school and work: "[I]t may be that, at this level, as career aspirations begin to take on more substance and significance, 'hard work' is an acceptably masculine attribute because it becomes more closely connected to entry to male professional status" Connell (1989, p. 1995) explicitly connects this shift to the way power operates within society, since hegemonic masculinity, the repository of social and economic power, is not located in aggressive, antiinstitutional, macho forms of masculinity but is tied to rationality and technical/scientific knowledge. Technical expertise is central to advanced capitalism, and men, through "the mechanism of academic credentials" (p. 296), can invest time and accept a subordinate position within training, in return for a secure employment future. I think that James's investment in technical rationality and achieving qualifications is apparent in his investment in working hard. It also helps to explain his preference for "traditional" chalk and talk methods of teaching, as he says: "I like, um, when we do, we talk about a topic and then the teacher does, works through an example on it. And then you've got a worked example that you can apply to every other question, sort of thing. I like that." And for learning individually: "I always work by myself. I mean, if I'm stuck I talk to someone else and then and talk through it, and, but generally I just work on my own. I find it easier that way." For James, "the central themes of masculinity here are rationality and responsibility rather than pride and aggressiveness" (p. 297). Connell's work suggests that this is the default position for middle-class boys who construct their life course through their family's relationship to the educational system. However, such an identity is less secure for the working-class pretenders, such as James, than for the middle-class boys who inhabit it. This perhaps explains why his investment in rationality and qualifications translates into subject choices based on instrumentalism rather than enjoyment. I conclude my story of James by looking at these in greater detail.

Academic studies, with perhaps the exception of sports studies, do not seem to be a locus of pleasure for James. When asked for a maths topic, lesson, or anything that he has enjoyed this year, he selects, after a long pause and a prompt from me, that morning's lesson, because "it's just that everything seemed to click. I seemed to remember everything, and it all just went really well." Subjects seem to be almost entirely a means to an end for James. This is clearly demonstrated in the explanation he gives for his decision to take physics and maths:

James: My form tutor basically said to me a good A-level to take would be physics. It's really hard, but it's sort of, it's, if I come out of it and I pass, I would think that like I worked really hard to get that pass 'cos it's so hard. So he said it's quite rewarding; so I thought OK. But he said it would be wise to take maths with physics because there's so much overlap and it would be, it would just be very helpful.

As a result of this he had to drop the more vocational media studies in favor of the more academic mathematics, since they clashed. When I ask him how he felt about leaving media studies, he recalls:

James: Um, I was happy in the subject, but I was looking at more in the long run, as in I'm not interested in the media either, anything like that, so I thought maths. And maths is more, sort of, you can apply it to more than you can with media. Maths is sort of used everywhere like, sort of thing. Whereas media is really specific. I thought maths it's more of a benefit in the long run [*pause*], so it would be a disadvantage dropping it.

Although James speaks of maths being more applicable and widely used than media studies, he combines this with a strong dislike of questions that require him actually to apply his knowledge to "realistic" contexts. The following is part of his explanation as to why he prefers maths to physics: "I don't like the real-life situations 'cos it clouds your judgment. You think about irrelevant things and you, you're talking about bridges and whatever. Clouds, clouds your brain really, and you can't really think. Whereas maths you just [*pause*] do maths." This could represent a rejection of the very contrived nature of what passes for a "realistic" context in examinations. However, his interview does not contain any criticism of this—simply a statement that "they'll relate it to a real-life situation," while his use of phrases like "physics they'll give you a shape, but indirectly" and it "clouds your brain" (in the quote above) lead me to think it is more likely that he dislikes the way these contexts make it more difficult for him to recognize the specific piece of technical knowledge being tested. As a result, I think his reference to the wider applicability of maths than media earlier indicates the way that maths can guarantee access to a wider range of careers, rather than a sense that he will have greater opportunity later in life to use the actual mathematical skills he is studying. This orientation around the future even affects his selection of sports studies as his favorite subject, " 'cos that's obviously what I want to do most; so that's what's my favorite." He has built a masculine identity project around considerations of what is "more of a benefit in the long run" and around his participation in the traditional goals of schooling, working hard, and following an academic trajectory. However, this is a path that, as mentioned earlier, is far from a perfect fit. Mathematics did not work out for James the first time around, and in fact he did not return to Grafton after the summer holidays, having found himself a job with training. The way in which working-class boys attempting complicity with the goals of a middle-class educational system often experience failure is also a theme of Michael's story.

MICHAEL'S STORY

Michael, a working-class African Caribbean student, is studying for AS-levels in mathematics, geography, and IT, as well as resitting his GCSE in English in order to improve his grade D. Michael has struggled with maths this year and plans to repeat the AS-level course next year rather than progress to the A2 modules, as he had previously planned to do. He had problems making the step up from GCSE (where he obtained an intermediate grade C) to AS-level. He highlights particular problems with the pace of the work, with the amount of material that has to be memorized, and with negotiating the variety of methods available for tackling each problem. When I ask him what he has enjoyed least about maths this year, he says, "Only just loads of writing and equations and having to remember most of it and copy it." Here, as elsewhere in the interview and in my classroom interactions with Michael, I get a strong sense of how frustrating Michael has often found the process of learning maths. This is a frustration that he nicely captures in his explanation of the connection between "learning what" and "understanding why" in maths: "You have to learn what you're doing before you can understand it, but if you learn it and don't understand it, there's no point, so it's just a Catch-22."

He has very different feelings toward maths than toward geography and IT, differences that illuminate the nature of his identification with maths. For Michael, geography and IT relate more directly to his experience of everyday life; there is "just more thinking about normal situations than with maths. . . . But maths, more [*pause*] it depends what you're going into after school with maths, but when you're actually doing it, you don't think you're going to need it further on. So that's why; it's just different." I ask if this makes maths more difficult or less interesting. Michael opts for the latter, seeing the disconnection of maths from everyday life as very demotivating: "It's probably just that that makes you lose your interest and, which makes you wanna just give up and stop working." Another difference that Michael raises in his interview relates to why he chose these subjects. While he speaks of enjoying geography and IT, his motivation for selecting maths is more extrinsic:

Michael: It's 'cos GCSE. Throughout all of my lessons I was on the C/D borderline, so I had to work hard to get my Cs and I thought if I could do A-levels, like I could even prove more that, yeah, I've done maths, something that's really hard and no one likes doing, and passed it, so it would be like I've achieved something. And it hasn't happened, but at least I tried. I know I have tried, so it's not that bad.

So while Michael speaks of enjoying the challenge of doing maths, this is very different to enjoying doing maths. This is evident in the excerpt below:

Heather: So did you prefer doing GCSE, or do you prefer doing A-level?

Michael: [*Pause*] Probably A-level 'cos it's much more of a challenge. Although that's a problem. The challenge can be too great and you fall behind. Like in the other class [*the original class before the setting was introduced*] that's what happened to me. So it's just a good challenge. That's why I chose it. I thought it would look good first [*pause*] in my CV, or anything to have A-level maths, and also it'd be a challenge to prove everyone wrong.

Certain aspects of Michael's identification with maths are apparent in this answer. He is well aware that maths has a reputation as a difficult subject, and it is this that leads him to identify it as a challenge; he is using this status of maths as "hard" as a way of gaining personal power, providing him with the external validation of his "ability" that he needs to prove wrong those who do not believe in him. *Hard* is a relational term existing in binary opposition to *easy, soft*, and *yielding*, an opposition that parallels the associated one of masculine to feminine. Thus, it is the societal valuation of maths that makes an A-level in it the object of Michael's desire. It will enable him to prove himself. When I ask for whom this proof is required, he says, "Everyone," and then elaborates: "Most of the time some of the teachers, some of my friends, 'cos some of them think, you know, I'm not too bright at some subjects, and [*pause*] even my parents sometimes just to say I've tried. Well, I've tried it. Just showing that you can have tried something, even though I haven't done it, I've tried and know, you see, I can try something else." I ask:

Heather: Is the omission of yourself from the list of people to whom you are proving yourself significant? Are you also proving anything to yourself?

Michael: Yeah, I am proving it to myself, as [*pause*] I'm trying to build up myself more, but [*pause*] sometimes I think I have to prove it to myself, but sometimes I know I say,

"Yes, I may not be good at it, but I know what I know." But people don't know what I know, so it's to really, it's like, um, if you know it all in your mind and you don't have the [*pause*] GCSEs and A-levels, then people don't think you are that bright, so it's really having it down on paper that counts so that's what I was trying to prove to them. And once again it didn't work.

These passages conjure an image of Michael against the world. Competition, as Seidler (1997, p. 173) argues, is a central part of many men's masculinity projects: "The competitive institutions of advanced capitalist societies mean that men are locked into competitive relationships with each other. Often we can only feel good about ourselves at the expense of other men." However, the deep way in which Michael internalizes other people's views of himself, transforming them into action, is perhaps also a response to his experience of racism and the objectification and othering that are a part of racism's psychic assault on black people (Fanon 1986). I return to this aspect of Michael's identity work in the concluding section when I look at it in the context of what the girls told me.

In what follows I break Michael's struggle down into three aspects, highlighting the identity work that he engages in through each. First, Michael constructs himself as aware that he is not academically brilliant but that he is confident and comfortable with his own understanding and "ability." This sense of "knowing his place" surfaces when I ask how he felt about the "ability" setting that took place at the start of the year:

Michael: I can understand why they split us up in the first place. Because, um, they either work at a different pace to us or not or try more challenging, because they got higher grades, it's more, [*pause*] it's really common sense really to have the brighter people doing much harder work than us, even though we are going for the same thing. If we're doing different methods, then we'll probably get the same, so it's really no biggy to me.

However, beneath the happy contentment that Michael expresses here there lurks a quiet resignation. This resignation is clearer in this next statement where he reflects on his future: "I was hoping to go on to university, but that looks like a grim outlook right now. So I'll probably just start working."

Second, there is a dissonance between his and other people's views of him; Michael believes strongly that he is better academically than all his significant others—friends, family, teachers—think he is. This is manifest in his transformation of the question. "What do other people not doing maths think of the subject?" into "What do they think of you for doing the subject?"

Michael: They think it's one of the most difficult lessons that you can do in A-level, and what makes it worse is that when they hear what I got in GCSE, they go, "Oh, you're mad for doing it 'cos it's so hard." So people's impressions of maths A-level is just [*pause*] a subject you don't wanna take 'cos it's so hard.

The way he personalizes the issue of the public image of maths further demonstrates how important it is to the way he is constructing himself. Finally, he
has a passionate desire to gain the kind of external validation the world demands
in order that they should see Michael as he sees himself.

There seems to be an odd combination of success and failure within Michael's
account of his mathematical career. He seems to have a sense that his scheme
for proving himself based on achieving success in A-level maths has failed but
that, despite this, it does not affect what he knows about himself; also, that it
was being brave enough to make the attempt that really mattered and what he
has learned about himself through it. However, his earlier conflation of examination success with "ability," his morphing of people with "higher grades" into
"brighter people" quoted above, suggests how difficult it is for people like Michael who accept the terms of the conventional schooling project, along with
its definitions of success and failure, to maintain confidence in themselves when,
in those terms, they fail. It is in narratives like Michael's that the structural
failure of schooling to meet the needs of working-class and African Caribbean
boys is individualized; the political is made personal. In the final section of this
chapter I will further draw out the political implications of these stories.

CONCLUSIONS: THINKING BEYOND GENDER BINARIES

Returning to the issues with which I began, what might these three stories
tell us about the reasons for the gender imbalance in the participation in postcompulsory maths in England? Simon, James, and Michael show us how they
negotiate educational choices, using the available discourses on maths and other
subjects to construct an identity, in such a way as to feel powerful. For these
boys maths is a powerful choice because its social construction allows it to
function in their masculinity projects as a way of proving their "abilities" to a
range of others, from friends to future employers. This raises three questions
relating back to the analysis of Dunne and Johnston (1994) discussed earlier.
Why is maths a more powerful proof of ability than other subjects? How is this
need to assert one's intellect and forge a high-status employment trajectory gendered? And what are the implications for maths teaching and learning?

Taking a poststructuralist approach, the power of mathematics as a subject,
and hence its authority in saying something about oneself, is not fixed and
natural but is a contingent product of the discourses through which it is constituted. These discourses produce it as objective, absolute, abstract, "hard," a
means of controlling our environment, and an essential prerequisite for entry
into the economically lucrative fields of science and technology. Also, these
discourses are gendered. It is useful here briefly to examine the way the girls
talked about their choice of mathematics. While the boys fell into two groups,
four students, including the three discussed above, who did not like maths but
took it anyway, and three others, who did express feelings of enjoying maths
and for whom this seemed to be an important part of their identification with

it, the girls' responses were more heterogeneous. One girl had chosen mathematics solely on the basis of her GCSE result in it. While encouragement from teachers was mentioned by three of the other four girls as an important factor either in their initial decision to take maths or in their decision to continue with it into the following year, this was mentioned by only one of the boys. Career ambitions also played a role in two of their responses, but in the specific sense of their needing maths in order to secure entry to particular professions (architecture and banking) rather than in the more vague sense of improving their general employment prospects through studying it, which features in the boys' narratives. Some of the girls also relished the challenge of doing maths, and for one, Julie, this was the main reason she gave me for taking maths. I have discussed Julie's motivations in more detail elsewhere (Mendick 2002). Here it is pertinent to note that she, and some of the other girls, use the challenge mathematics offers in a more private way than the boys discussed above. So that while, for example, Michael's aim in taking maths is the public display of his intellect to others rather than to himself, Julie's is the more private goal of proving something to herself; and she even reveals to me that she does not share this ambition with her friends. Thus Julie seems to be concealing any aspects of herself that could mark her out publicly as different from her friends.

However, I would argue that both boys' and girls' subject choices represent attempts by young people to occupy powerful subject positions and that the gender differences are a reflection of the way that, in general, girls' femininity projects and boys' masculinity projects make available different ways of being powerful. As Nazima (also from Grafton) persuasively puts it:

Nazima: This is also what I think it is. When you study English, right, you somehow have power [*pause*]. You do. And I think, a lot of girls [*laughs*], I'm sounding really feminist here, aren't I? I think a lot of girls tend to have, like power, 'cos when you, when you know English you have power over virtually anything, even boys, men. Like when I, when I do English now I say things to boys and they're like [*whispered*], "What's she talking about?" . . . So it's power, I mean English gives you more power in stuff like that, whereas technology just gives you the brains to do this and to do that. It's not that girls aren't interested in money. We are. But we just like the power side of everything.

Further, I would be surprised if there are not also many girls who use maths in similar ways to those explored in this chapter. When I talk about masculinity, I use it in the relational way that Connell (1995) does to refer to a configuration of practice within a gender regime. This stresses that while the discursive construction of masculinity and femininity is tied to the reproductive arena via a system of binary thought, this can be powerfully replaced by a fluid understanding of gender, in which dichotomies become continua and differences overlap. Thus masculinity is found in the actions of girls and women, just as femininity is found in those of boys and men. The stories here provide many examples that are best read through such an antiessentialist lens: Simon's "quest for understanding," James's conscientious and hardworking approach, and Michael's sensitive internalization of other people's views of him are all commonly located within the academic literature as feminine traits. They also provide evidence for the way other factors such as class, "race," ethnicity, and sexuality intersect with gender, further undermining a binary model of gender difference. The way that people take up the available discursive subject positions as their own is also a psychic process, albeit a socially embedded one. People choose subjects in response to fears, desires, anxieties, and other unconscious drives (Shaw 1995). However, as this chapter also demonstrates, the access to the different available masculine and feminine subject positions and even the workings of the unconscious, while complex, remain highly dependent on a person's assigned gender, and this is a significant source of inequality. On this issue, Michael's response when I asked him to help me to respond to a reviewer's comment on this chapter and explain in what way his need to prove himself differed from similar sentiments expressed by Julie is revelatory. He was unable to explain this difference but was angry about the comment and insistent that there was a difference. Perhaps this difference is in the public rather than private way in which this aspect of his identity is framed, as I argued earlier. But perhaps it is gendered simply because for Michael this is something that he experiences and performs as masculine.

I would like to finish by arguing that making a wider range of subjectivities available to a wider range of individuals would be a way of tackling educational inequity. This carries implications for mathematics pedagogy; to do this we need maths reform work that shifts the discursive invention of maths from that of a subject of abstract rules and absolutes to that of a more relational and collaborative discipline. This is something that would also help stem the tide of students rushing away from the subject at the first opportunity. The identifications that Simon, James, and Michael form with maths are temporary ones; for them maths is a popular choice but not a popular subject. We also need gender reform work that rejects the fashionable polarized "Mars and Venus" versions of gender that naturalize dominance as difference and that does not dictate to girls or try to change them but works with both boys and girls, acknowledging the complexities of their lived identities. However, these two cannot be separated since, as these interviews further demonstrate, maths and gender are mutually constitutive; maths reform work is gender reform work. Reflecting on the wider social implications of such reform work, if, as I argue, in choosing maths students are doing gender, and doing class and "race," this implicates maths in preserving masculinity and capitalism and white supremacy as sources of power and domination (see also Frankenstein 1995; Shelley 1995). So higher maths remains a masculine domain, not only in the sense that it is numerically dominated by men but also in the way that it serves to support the current gender regime— "the capacity of certain men to control social resources through gender processes—and the kind of society being produced by that power" (Connell 1995, p. 205). And this really matters, for while male control is only one force shaping the world, it is one that must be challenged because it influences "issues about violence, inequality, technology, pollution and world development. Masculinity politics concerns the making of the gendered power that is deployed in those issues. It is a force in the background of some of the most fateful issues of our time" (p. 205).

ACKNOWLEDGMENTS

I would like to thank Debbie Epstein, Leone Burton, Dennis Atkinson, and two anonymous reviewers for their helpful comments on an earlier draft of this chapter. I would also like to thank Goldsmiths College and the Economic and Social Research Council for funding the research on which this chapter is based.

REFERENCES

Boaler, Jo. (1997). *Experiencing School Mathematics: Teaching Styles, Sex and Setting.* Buckingham, UK: Open University Press.

Boaler, Jo. (2000). *So Girls Don't Really Understand Mathematics? Dangerous Dichotomies in Gender Research.* Paper presented at the ICME9 Conference, Tokyo.

Bourdieu, Pierre. (1984). *Distinction.* London: Routledge.

Burton, Leone. (1986). Introduction. In L. Burton (Ed.), *Girls into Maths Can Go* (pp. 1–20). London: Cassell.

Connell, Robert W. (1989). Cool Guys, Swots and Wimps: The Inter-Play of Masculinity and Education. *Oxford Review of Education*, 15(3), 291–303.

Connell, Robert W. (1995). *Masculinities.* Cambridge: Polity Press.

Davies, Bronwyn. (1989). *Frogs and Snails and Feminist Tales: Preschool Children and Gender.* Sydney: Allen and Unwin.

Davies, Bronwyn. (1993). *Shards of Glass: Children Reading and Writing Beyond Gendered Identities.* Sydney: Allen and Unwin.

Dunne, Mairead, and Johnston, Jayne. (1994). Research in Gender and Mathematics Education: The Production of Difference. In P. Ernest (Ed.), *Mathematics, Education and Philosophy: An International Perspective* (pp. 221–229). London: Falmer Press.

Epstein, Debbie. (1998). Real Boys Don't Work: "Underachievement," Masculinity and the Harassment of "Sissies." In Debbie Epstein, Janette Elwood, Valerie Hey, and Janet Maw (Eds.), *Failing Boys? Issues in Gender and Underachievement* (pp. 96–108). Buckingham, UK: Open University Press.

Epstein, Debbie, and Johnson, Richard. (1998). *Schooling Sexualities.* Buckingham, UK: Open University Press.

Fanon, Frantz. (1986). *Black Skin, White Masks.* London: Pluto Press.

Flax, Jane. (1990). *Thinking Fragments: Psychoanalysis, Feminism, and Postmodernism in the Contemporary West.* Berkeley: University of California Press.

Francis, Becky. (2000). *Boys and Girls and Achievement: Addressing the Classroom Issues.* London: Routledge/Falmer.

Frankenstein, Marilyn. (1995). Equity in Mathematics Education: Class in the World Outside the Class. In Walter G. Secada, Elizabeth Fennema, and Lisa Byrd Adajian (Eds.), *New Directions for Equity in Mathematics Education* (pp. 165–190). Cambridge: Cambridge University Press.

Government Statistical Service. (1995). *Statistics of Education: Public Examinations GCSE and GCE in England 1994*. London: Her Majesty's Stationery Office.

Government Statistical Service. (1996). *Statistics of Education: Public Examinations GCSE and GCE in England 1995*. London: Her Majesty's Stationery Office.

Government Statistical Service. (1997). *Statistics of Education: Public Examinations GCSE and GCE in England 1996*. London: Her Majesty's Stationery Office.

Government Statistical Service. (1998). *Statistics of Education: Public Examinations GCSE/GNVQ and GCE in England 1997*. London: Her Majesty's Stationery Office.

Government Statistical Service. (1999). *Statistics of Education: Public Examinations GCSE/GNVQ and GCE in England 1998*. London: Her Majesty's Stationery Office.

Government Statistical Service. (2000). *Statistics of Education: Public Examinations GCSE/GNVQ and GCE in England 1999*. London: Her Majesty's Stationery Office.

Government Statistical Service. (2001). *Statistics of Education: Public Examinations GCSE/GNVQ and GCE in England 2000*. London: Her Majesty's Stationery Office.

Griffiths, Morwenna. (1995). *Feminisms and the Self: The Web of Identity*. London: Routledge.

Hall, Stuart. (1996). Introduction: Who Needs "Identity"? In Stuart Hall and Paul du Gay (Eds.), *Questions of Cultural Identity* (pp. 1–17). London: Sage.

Hanna, Gila (Ed.). (1996). *Towards Gender Equity in Mathematics Education: An ICMI Study*. Dordrecht: Kluwer Academic Publishers.

Hughes, Gwyneth. (2001). Exploring the Availability of Students' Scientist Identities within Curriculum Discourse: An Anti-Essentialist Approach to Gender-Inclusive Science. *Gender and Education*, 13(3), 275–290.

Hunt, Jennifer C. (1989). *Psychoanalytic Aspects of Fieldwork*. London: Sage.

Jackson, Carolyn, and Wain, Jo. (2000). The Importance of Gender as an Aspect of Identity at Key Transition Points in Compulsory Education. *British Educational Research Journal*, 26(3), 375–391.

Mac an Ghaill, Mairtin. (1994). *The Making of Men: Masculinities, Sexualities and Schooling*. Buckingham, UK: Open University Press.

Maguire, M., Macrae, S., and Ball, S. (1998). "Race," Space and the Further Education Marketplace. *Race, Ethnicity and Education*, 1(2), 171–189.

Mendick, Heather. (2002). *Narratives of Gender and Maths*. Paper presented at the Mathematics Education and Society Conference (MES3), Helsingor, Denmark.

Power, Sally, Whitty, Geoff, Edwards, Tony, and Wigfall, Valerie. (1998). Schoolboys and Schoolwork: Gender Identification and Academic Achievement. *International Journal of Inclusive Education*, 2(2), 135–153.

Redman, Peter, and Mac an Ghaill, Mairtin. (1997). Educating Peter: The Making of a History Man. In Deborah Lynn Steinberg, Debbie Epstein, and Richard Johnson (Eds.), *Border Patrols: Policing the Boundaries of Heterosexuality* (pp. 162–182). London: Cassell.

Seidler, Victor Jeleniewski. (1997). *Man Enough*. London: Sage.

Sells, Lucy. (1980). The Mathematics Filter and the Education of Women and Minorities.

In Lynn H. Fox, Linda Brody, and Dianne Tobin (Eds.), *Women and the Mathematical Mystique* (pp. 66–75). Baltimore: Johns Hopkins University Press.

Shaw, Jenny. (1995). *Education, Gender and Anxiety*. London: Taylor & Francis.

Shelley, Nancy. (1995). Mathematics: Beyond Good and Evil. In Gabrielle Kaiser and Pat Rogers (Eds.), *Equity in Mathematics Education. Influences of Feminism and Culture* (pp. 247–262). London: Falmer Press.

Walkerdine, Valerie. (1998). *Counting Girls Out* (2nd ed.). London: Falmer Press.

Whitehead, Joan M. (1996). Sex Stereotypes, Gender Identity and Subject Choices at A-Level. *Educational Research*, 38(2), 147–160.

Willis, Paul. (1977). *Learning to Labour: How Working Class Kids Get Working Class Jobs*. London: Gower Publishing.

Chapter 9

Constructing Difference: Assessment in Mathematics Education

Dylan Wiliam

INTRODUCTION

Since the pioneering work of Maccoby and Jacklin (1974), there has been a great deal of research on sex differences in mathematics. Most of this research has treated these differences as substantial, as more or less real and in some way inherent, innate, or even inherited, and has focused either on measuring the size of the difference or on exploring possible causes such as differences in brain physiology, child-rearing practices, or biases in processes of schooling.

This chapter will challenge the prevailing view. In the first section, I show that differences between males and females are in fact extremely small—of an order that most statisticians would regard as negligible—and in the second section, I argue that these differences are not in any sense "natural" but rather are constructed through the social processes that have shaped what we choose to call mathematics. Since the results of assessments in mathematics have profound consequences for the lives of students, adopting a particular definition of mathematics is therefore a moral, as much as an epistemological, enterprise, which is discussed in the third section, and this is examined through the key concept of validity in the fourth section. In the final section, I develop a principle for the use of assessments in selection, based on the idea that if we cannot make selections fairly, we should make them at random.

THE (MIS-)USE OF STATISTICAL SIGNIFICANCE TESTING

If we test a sample of students and find that the average scores of the males are higher than those of the females, the first question that arises is, Can we take this difference seriously? After all, it could be that the achievement of males and females in the whole population is equal but that the males who were selected for inclusion in the sample just happened, by chance, to be of higher attainment than the females. By using straightforward principles of statistics, we can calculate the probability that a specified difference between males and females emerges just through the vagaries of random sampling (this, of course, requires that our sample was, indeed, random, which, as we shall see below, is often not the case).

Suppose we have a mathematics test on which we know that the scores for a population of students range from around 20 to 80, with an average of 50 (more precisely, the mean of the population is 50 and its standard deviation is 15). If we choose 15 students from this population at random, then the average score of these 15 students is unlikely to be exactly 50. Sometimes we will get an average above 50, and sometimes we will get less than 50. If we repeated this process of drawing samples of 15 students at random from the population, then approximately 10% of the time the average score of the sample of 15 students will be over 55, and conversely, 10% of the time, the 15 students will average less than 45 on this test. This is why if we tested a class of 15 males and 15 females from this population, and found that the males averaged 5 points higher than the females, it would not be safe to conclude that the males in the population were actually performing higher than the females. It could be simply that the 15 males who were selected to "represent" the males in the population were not, in fact, representative.

For this reason, we use statistical significance testing to tell us how likely a given result is to arise by chance. If the males outscored the females by 5 marks, we can calculate that such a result (i.e., a difference of 5 marks either way between males and females) could have arisen by chance with a truly random sample with a probability of around 20%. We would almost certainly attribute this to random variation and conclude that we had no grounds for deciding that males in the population have higher attainment than the females. If, however, the 15 males in our sample outscored the females by 13 marks, such a result would arise by chance just one time in a thousand in a population where the average scores of males and females were exactly equal. In this case, we would probably decide that it was not reasonable to hang on to the idea that the males' performance across the whole population was the same as that of the females. In the language of statistical significance testing, we would reject the null hypothesis (i.e., that the males and the females in the population had equal scores, on average) and instead decide, on the basis of our sampling, that the males in the population from which the sample was drawn did have higher scores than the females. However, it is important to realize that we have not established that the males in the *population* outscore the females by 13 marks. All we have shown is that it is highly unlikely (one in a thousand unlikely) that the scores of the males and the females in the population are equal. In fact, statistical significance tells us nothing about the size of the difference between males and females—only that it is likely there is a difference (more precisely: that it is unlikely there is *no* difference). This is because statistical significance testing mixes up two quite different elements: the size of the differences between groups and the faith we can have in the conclusion that the difference is real, as opposed to an artifact of our sampling.

Where we draw the line that marks the boundary between acceptance and rejection—effectively equivalent to determining the strength of evidence we require—however, is not clear. We would probably not regard a result that could occur with a probability of 20% as evidence that our null hypothesis had to be rejected but would do so if our observed result only occurred one time in a thousand. The value generally used is 5%, but this is quite arbitrary. In some cases, it might be justifiable to use a higher figure, such as 10%, and in many other cases, it would be appropriate to require a much heavier burden of proof, for example, by setting our cutoff at 1% or even lower.

As we saw, a difference of 5 marks is not significant across a group of 30 students, but using the conventional 5% cutoff, the same 5-mark difference *would* be significant across a group of 100 students. In fact, if we had a group of 10,000 students, with equal numbers of males and females, then a difference between males and females of just half a mark would be statistically significant. In other words, with such a large sample, we can be sure that the difference between males and females is unlikely (i.e., less that 5% likely) to have arisen by chance. The difference between males and females would therefore be *statistically significant*, because we can be reasonably sure that it is really there and not just some fluke in our sample, but it is not a *large* difference.

Much early research on sex differences in mathematics (and, in my view, too much recent research) has used statistical significance as the primary tool for investigating the size of differences in performance between males and females. Instead, we need to focus not on the level of statistical significance but on the *size* of the differences.

Of course, we cannot use differences in marks or scores to indicate the size of differences because, as Willingham and Cole (1997) note, a difference of 1 mark between males and females on (say) the 5-point scale of the Advanced Placement (AP) examination is a far greater difference than a one-mark difference on the 200 to 800 scale used in the Educational Testing Service's SAT. The solution is to divide the difference in scores between males and females by a measure of how spread out are the marks for the whole group (the rationale for this is that the measure of spread provides some sort of a standardized "measuring stick" for the data). The most generally used measure of spread is the standard deviation of the scores. The resulting quantity is variously called the standardized effect size or the standard difference and is generally denoted *d* or *D*. Conventionally, positive values of D denote differences where females outscore males. Willingham and Cole (1997) provide the standard sex difference for 75 national surveys of students undertaken in the United States at the end of schooling (grade 12). An analysis of these results, given in Table 9.1, shows that the effects for each group of tests are very variable.

Table 9.1
Values of Standard Difference Found in 75 Grade 12 Tests in the United States

Type	Number	Mean	Range	H-spread*
Verbal: writing	2	+0.57	+0.54 to +0.59	–
Verbal: language use	6	+0.43	+0.33 to +0.53	0.11
Verbal: reading	10	+0.20	+0.00 to +0.46	0.15
Verbal: vocabulary/reasoning	8	+0.06	–0.07 to +0.21	0.08
Mathematics: computation	2	+0.18	+0.17 to +0.19	–
Mathematics: concepts	14	–0.11	–0.28 to +0.15	0.16
Natural science	7	–0.17	–0.36 to +0.17	0.16
Social science	3	+0.02	–0.15 to +0.20	0.16
Geopolitical	5	+0.20	–0.43 to –0.12	0.12
Study skills	4	+0.20	+0.06 to +0.30	0.14
Perceptual processing	4	+0.31	+0.23 to +0.42	0.12
Spatial skills	2	–0.14	–0.25 to –0.03	–
Short-term memory	2	+0.23	+0.18 to +0.27	–
Abstract reasoning	2	+0.10	–0.03 to +0.23	–
Mechanical/electronics	4	–0.93	–1.25 to –0.78	0.18
Total	75			

*The hinge-spread, or H-spread, of the data is the difference between lower and upper hinges of a set of data, where the hinges are the median values of the lower and upper halves, respectively, of the data (including the median where there are an odd number of data values) when the data are arranged in order. As the number of data increases, the H-spread approaches the value of the interquartile range and thus provides a measure of the dispersion of the data values.

Source: Willingham and Cole 1997.

How these standard differences should be interpreted is a matter of some controversy. Cohen (1988) proposed that absolute values of D (i.e., ignoring plus and minus signs) from 0.20 to 0.49 be classed as small, 0.50 to 0.79 as medium, and those of 0.80 or more as large. Glass, McGaw, and Smith (1981), however, suggest that there can be no hard-and-fast rules about such interpretation, and Abelson (1995) points out that apparently small effects can be very noteworthy if produced by small interventions or in areas where previous research has failed to find any effect at all.

As might be expected, the research studies reviewed by Willingham and Cole indicate clear differences in favor of females in language and language-based subjects and differences in favor of males in natural science, spatial skills, and mechanical comprehension. In mathematics, males outperform females in math-

Table 9.2
Variation of Overlap with Standard Difference (D)

D	0.0	0.1	0.2	0.3	0.4	0.5	0.6	0.7	0.8	0.9	1.0
Overlap	100%	96%	92%	88%	84%	80%	76%	73%	69%	65%	62%

ematical concepts, but surprisingly perhaps, females outperform males in computation. However, it is important to note two cautions in interpreting these data.

First, the effect sizes are very small—as noted above, effect sizes below 0.20 are regarded as negligible by many authors—and the differences that are found between males and females are much smaller than the variation within males and within females. One way to look at this issue is to consider the "overlap" between the populations. If it were the case that all females outscored all males, then the overlap would be 0%, and if the standard difference were zero, the overlap would be 100%. Table 9.2 shows how the overlap in populations varies with the size of the standard difference, D. A standard difference of +0.2 means that 92% of students are in the region of overlap, and in fact the proportion of the data in the overlapping region does not fall below 50% until D reaches a value of 1.4. A graph of the overlap for values of D up to 4.0 is shown in Figure 9.1.

Second, the *range* of values of D in the studies is large, even within each of the 15 categories. For example, in the 14 studies on mathematics concepts, the average effect was − 0.11 (in favor of males), but the values of D ranged from −0.28 to +0.15. This variation is puzzling, because if there was a difference between males and females in mathematics, the estimates of the size of these differences should be consistent. There are three possible sources of the variation in effect sizes.

The first is differences in the sample—the students who elect to take a particular test might not be representative of the population they are meant to represent. The obvious example here would be the Armed Services Vocational Aptitude Battery (ASVAB) that is designed to provide vocational guidance for Armed Services Personnel. While it is taken by both males and females, far more males took the test, and for this reason the ASVAB data used by Willingham and Cole were adjusted to be representative of a national sample of young adults. However, such weighting can do nothing about the fact that the females taking this test are not likely to be as representative of the whole female population as the males.

The second source of difference is that of differences between populations. Even if a sample of students is representative of a population, such as the cohort of 18-year-olds in school, it might be that the population of males differs systematically from that of females (e.g., if more females stay on at school). Willingham and Cole state, however, that the data they analyzed were based on

Figure 9.1
Variation of Overlap with Standard Difference (D)

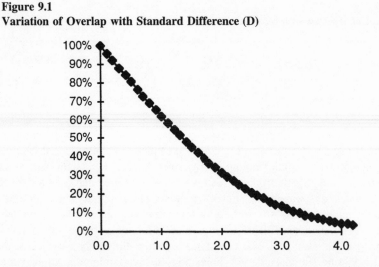

representative samples and populations, so we are led to the conclusion that it is a third source of difference—the definition of mathematics employed in the construction of the test (what Willingham and Cole term "construct differences")—that is the most important determinant of the size (and even the direction) of any sex differences.

It would be tempting to conclude that it was the type of mathematical concepts that were being tested that was causing this difference, but in fact the most extreme values of D found in the "mathematics: concepts" category are for two tests that would appear to be measuring the same thing: the ASVAB Test of Arithmetical Reasoning (D = −0.28) and the Differential Aptitude Test (DAT) of Numerical Reasoning (D = +0.15). We are led to the conclusion that the size of the sex differences found on mathematics tests tells us more about the kind of mathematics being tested than it does about the respective capabilities of males and females.

While the overlap between males and females is considerable even for quite large values of D, it is important to bear in mind that this will not be the case at the extremes. If we look only at the top so-many percent of the population, quite small differences between males and females become very pronounced. Table 9.3 shows the variation in the proportion of males in the top 50, 20, 10, 5, 1, and 0.1% of the population according to the value of the standardized difference D. For example, as we saw in Table 9.2, a standardized difference of −0.8 means that the overlap between males and females is 69% of the two populations. If we look only at the top 50% of the combined population of males and females, then we can see from Table 9.3 that 65.5% will be male, and so 34.5% will be female—in other words, there are almost 2 males for every female. If we look, however, at the top 1% of the same population, we

Table 9.3
Variation in the Proportion of Males in Selected Proportions of Population, According to Standardized Difference (D)

| D | \multicolumn{6}{c}{Proportion of Population} |
	top 50%	top 20%	top 10%	top 5%	top 1%	top 0.1%
–0.0	50.0	50.0	50.0	50.0	50.0	50.0
–0.1	52.0	53.5	54.4	55.2	56.6	58.4
–0.2	54.0	57.0	58.7	60.2	63.1	66.3
–0.3	56.0	60.4	63.0	65.1	69.2	73.6
–0.4	57.9	63.8	67.1	69.8	74.7	79.8
–0.5	59.9	67.1	71.0	74.2	79.7	84.9
–0.6	61.8	70.3	74.7	78.2	84.0	89.1
–0.7	63.7	73.3	78.2	81.9	87.6	92.2
–0.8	65.5	76.3	81.4	85.1	90.6	94.6
–0.9	67.4	79.0	84.3	87.9	92.9	96.2
–1.0	69.2	81.6	86.9	90.4	95.0	97.5

can see that 90.6% will be male, and only 9.4 percent will be female, resulting in nearly 10 males for every female.

The situation is further complicated by evidence that there may be differences in the variability of the performance of males and females. If the scores of females are less variable than the scores of males, then this will tend to increase the proportion of males in the highest-achieving segments of the population even if there is no overall difference in the means of males and females. The effect of this can be seen clearly in Table 9.4, which reproduces the same analysis as that in Table 9.3, but based on a population in which the variability (measured as standard deviation) of females is 90% that of males—this was the figure found by Cleary (1992) on "almost all tests" (p. 54), although the National Assessment of Educational Progress (NAEP) found that the standard deviation of female scores was around 95% of those for males in mathematics. In contrast with Table 9.3, the top 1% of the population contains approximately 2 males for every female even when there is no overall sex difference, and when D is −0.8, the top 1% of the combined population now contains approximately 27 males for every female.

Whether the performance of males really is more variable than that of females is far from clear. It is certainly the case that on some tests (e.g., the Iowa Test of Basic Skills) the scores of males are more variable than those of females. However, there are many tests that have found little or no evidence of greater male variability. It therefore seems that, just like the sex differences discussed

Table 9.4
Variation in the Proportion of Males in Selected Proportions of Population,
According to Standardized Difference (D) When Female Variance Is 90% That of
Males

D	Proportion of Population					
	top 50%	top 20%	top 10%	top 5%	top 1%	top 0.1%
–0.0	50.0	53.1	55.9	58.9	66.0	75.5
–0.1	52.1	56.7	60.6	64.2	72.4	81.9
–0.2	54.2	60.5	65.0	69.3	77.9	87.1
–0.3	56.3	64.0	69.2	74.0	82.8	90.9
–0.4	58.3	67.5	73.4	78.3	86.9	93.9
–0.5	60.4	70.9	77.2	82.3	90.2	95.9
–0.6	62.4	74.1	80.7	85.7	92.9	97.4
–0.7	64.4	77.2	83.9	88.6	94.9	98.3
–0.8	66.3	80.1	86.8	91.2	96.4	98.9
–0.9	68.2	82.8	89.3	93.2	97.5	99.3
–1.0	70.1	85.3	91.4	94.9	98.3	99.6

above, differences in variability are the result of differences in construct definition. Define mathematics one way, and you get males outscoring females at the mean, and with greater variability in their scores, so that the more selective the sample being taken, the more extreme male superiority appears to be. However, define mathematics in another way, and you will find no difference in either the means or the variability of male and female scores.

CAUSAL EXPLANATIONS?

Although the differences between male and female performance in mathematics are small, they are nonetheless widespread, and so females are systematically disadvantaged where particular levels of performance or competence are required. What is rather surprising is that while many practitioners have been concerned over the last 30 or so years to do something about these differences, it appears that academics have been more concerned with finding their causes. While at first sight, this might seem sensible, in fact little progress has been made in understanding what causes these differences.

Perhaps nowhere else in educational research have correlations been pressed into service as causal explanations as readily as they have in the field of sex differences. It is almost as if the normal rules of caution, rigor, and parsimony are suspended and "anything goes." Dozens of more or less unsupported claims are made about the origin of such sex differences as have been found, even though, as noted above, these differences appear to have more to do with the instruments used than the nature of mathematics itself.

The earliest explanations were biological, arguing that male brains were more suitable for academic work (and particularly mathematics) than those of females. There are undoubtedly differences between males and females in how the brain is organized, particularly in the way the cognitive functions are distributed between the left and right sides of the brain (hemispherical specialization) but because we understand so little about how the brain does what it does, these explanations cannot count as causes. For example, damage caused by stroke or trauma to particular parts of the brain has predictable consequences, and from this it is tempting to conclude that the part of the brain affected is responsible for the affected capabilities. But this does not follow. If we have trained a frog to leap in response to a particular sound, the fact that it cannot do so when we cut its legs off does not mean that the frog hears through its legs!

These biological explanations have been given a renewed lease on life by the upsurge of interest in evolutionary psychology. While it is probably unexceptionable to claim that the development of human brains, and some aspects of behavior, have been influenced by evolutionary pressures, there are some who believe that such things as our sexual behavior, moral behavior, and psychiatric disorders (Ridley 1993; Stevens and Price 1996; Wright 1995, respectively) are all the result of evolutionary adaptation to situations pertaining hundreds of thousands of years ago and are therefore, in some sense, "hardwired" into the brain. One of the most far-fetched explanations of this type is that superior male performance on spatial tasks is the result of evolutionary selection, whereby males, who went hunting for animals, needed to develop greater spatial capability than the females who remained behind and raised crops. In the first place, the anthropological evidence for this division of roles is very thin, but, second, it has been shown that the need to forage for edible plants, which do not move, can place greater demands on spatial processing and memory than does hunting (Eals and Silverman 1994). In fact, the evidence on sex differences in spatial abilities is very complex. There is a body of research that shows that tasks involving the mental rotation of three-dimensional objects show marked sex differences in favor of males. Linn and Petersen (1985) found a mean effect, $D = -0.73$ across a number of studies, although most of these studies were conducted on small, academically advanced, self-selected samples of students. However, females outperform males on recall of spatial arrays (McBurney et al. 1997), and in some cultures, such as the Inuit, women outperform men on most spatial tasks (Berry 1966, 1971). Most important, what is lacking is any kind of plausible mechanism that explains why, apart from in the polar regions, running around after wild animals might provide an evolutionary pressure to select for people who can mentally rotate three-dimensional objects. Since we do not understand how these component skills are deployed in advanced mathematical reasoning, these "explanations" are no more than fanciful speculation.

The strongest evidence against the idea that sex differences in mathematical performance are largely genetic or innate, however, is their mutability. Alan Feingold examined the performance of males and females on the SAT from 1947 to 1983, and while the differences apparent in Table 9.1 (i.e., female superiority in language, male superiority in mathematics) were found, the size of the differences declined markedly over the period studied (Feingold 1988). Hyde, Fennema, and Lamon (1990) and Linn (1992) found that sex differences in a range of achievement tests had halved over the latter half of the twentieth century. A meta-analysis of 98 studies on sex differences in mathematical tasks conducted between 1974 and 1987 (Friedman 1989) also found decreasing sex differences over time, and although the average effect favored males, the size of the effect was very small, and a 95% confidence interval for the effect size included zero.

However, even these small differences have to be viewed with suspicion. As noted earlier, studies of mathematics achievement have used a range of different tasks and have found that males outperform females on some, that females outperform males on others, but that "on average" males outperform females. However, the fact that the "average" effect favors males just means that more of the tasks that favor males were used. In other words, the generally perceived superiority of males in mathematics is just the result of the preferences of researchers in their choice of what is to count as mathematics. We are rightly suspicious of researchers who use "opportunity samples" of subjects in their research, because of the potential for bias. Accepting at face value, and weighting equally all research studies into sex differences in mathematics, would be to accept a poorly understood opportunity sample of *studies*.

As with the biological side of the debate, there are many possible explanations of sex differences in mathematics education. When the same child is dressed as a boy, s/he is encouraged to play with masculine toys such as tools and trucks and is left alone, whereas when dressed as a girl, s/he is encouraged to play with dolls and is spoken to frequently (Rogers 1999, pp. 96–97). The superiority of females with language may also, therefore, be simply the result of early experience rather than being innate. Valerie Walkerdine has suggested that the crucial influence is that of the tendency of young girls to be more compliant and obedient than young boys (Walden and Walkerdine 1985; Walkerdine 1988; Walkerdine & Girls and Mathematics Unit 1989). This leads to greater success in the short term, in the rote aspects of mathematics common in the elementary school curriculum such as computation, but in the long term leads to problems, when the ability to create one's own strategies becomes important, as is arguably the case for more advanced mathematics. This theme was taken up by Fennema and Carpenter (1998) in a study of students learning mathematics in grades 1, 2, and 3. They found that 42 of the 44 boys had used at least one self-invented algorithm by the end of the teaching experiment, compared with 30 of the 38 girls, which just reaches statistical significance (Fisher's exact test, required because two of the expected cell counts are around 5, gives a probability of

0.039, while chi-square gives a value of 0.023). Now while this result is statistically significant, it must be borne in mind that had just 3 more girls invented their own algorithms and 3 fewer boys done so, then the proportion of boys and girls inventing their own algorithms would actually have been equal. While the statistical calculations tell us that the observed result is unlikely if there is no difference between girls and boys, this requires us to assume that the sample of boys and girls was truly random. This is difficult to justify, since the students in each grade were taught by the same teacher, in the same school, and their experiences are likely to have been more similar than would be the case with a genuinely random sample. In fact, a hierarchical linear model, which respects the multilevel structure in the data, suggests that the difference is *not* statistically significant.

From this, Fennema and Carpenter go on to argue that girls' adherence to taught strategies indicates a lower level of conceptual understanding. However, if girls are more compliant than boys, as seems to be widely accepted, then it could easily be that the greater use of teacher-taught strategies could be a matter of choice by the girls, rather than a matter of inability (Boaler 2002).

I have explored this study in some depth, not because it is a particularly egregious example but because it illustrates the complexities of interpreting findings and of disentangling the influences of the many forces at work on learners developing competence in mathematics.

COMPETING IMPERATIVES

The foregoing has shown that sex differences in mathematics achievement are small, diminishing, and most important, socially constructed. Different definitions of mathematics lead to differences in the relative success of males and females. Even the assumed advantage that multiple-choice items confer on males depends on the kinds of items. For example, Beller and Gafni (1996) found that the male superiority over females was greater on constructed-response (CR) items than multiple-choice (MC) items, although this appears to have been an artifact of the fact that the CR items were harder than the MC items, and the males performed better overall (which was, of course, in turn, an artifact of the definition of mathematics employed). Constructed-response items do generally favor females, but then it would be astounding if they did not, because of assumed superior linguistic functioning. Moreover, the size of the advantage that constructed-response items confer on females is highly variable. For example, in the United States, both Kansas and Kentucky have statewide assessment programs for grade 12 (i.e., 18- to 19-year-old) students that involve both multiple-choice and constructed-response items. In Kansas, the multiple-choice items favor males ($D = -0.22$), while the constructed-response items favor females ($D = +0.14$), so that the difference between the two formats represents a swing of 0.36 standard deviations. In Kentucky, the same pattern is found—multiple-choice items favor males and constructed-response items favor females—but the sizes of the effects are much smaller; -0.02 and $+0.04$, respectively. Even the size of the advantage that constructed-response items confer on females, therefore, depends on the definition of mathematics used.

All this shows that there cannot be a "mathematics degree zero" in the sense that Barthes (1984) talked about "writing degree zero"—there is no "natural" choice of mathematics that we can use for our assessments. So how can we choose? In the final sections of the chapter, I want to argue that all the issues discussed above can be subsumed within the key concept of validity and that the choices about definitions of mathematics can be viewed in terms of conflicting concerns about the meanings and consequences of test results.

THE VALIDITY OF EDUCATIONAL ASSESSMENTS

Validity was seen originally as a property of a test—a test was valid to the extent that it tested what it purported to test. However, a test may be more valid for one group than another—a particular mathematics test may involve complex language and so would tell us little of the mathematical abilities of poor readers but might work quite well for fluent readers. A further complication is that while a test may have been developed and administered for one purpose (e.g., to determine the achievement of a student), the results are often used in other ways (e.g., to determine how good is the teacher of a particular class). For this reason, it is widely agreed now that validity is not a property of a test but a property of the use to which the information arising from the test is put.

Within this, of course, there are competing priorities. Professional mathematicians have a legitimate interest in determining what is to count as mathematics at school, but this influence has not always been productive. For example, at the famous Royaumont Seminar in 1959, a group of mathematicians decided that the best way to organize and teach school mathematics was with the structures that professional pure mathematicians used, such as set theory (Organisation for European Economic Co-operation Office for Scientific and Technical Personnel 1961). While the resulting "modern mathematics" may have been a useful platform for the ablest students, there can be little doubt that the abstract, decontextualized axiomatic approach used was alienating for many students. It also seems likely that a disproportionate number of students alienated by a decontextualized approach would have been female (see, e.g., Boaler 1997; Gilligan 1982), and so the move away from such approaches will have been a contributory factor in the reduction of sex differences over recent years.

Other stakeholders will have other priorities for the curriculum. The "industrial trainers" (Williams 1960) will want school mathematics to have a strong vocational strand, while others may stress the increased control over one's life that mathematical competence may bring. These are concerns with the content of the assessment (what is sometimes called "content validity"), where the primary aim of the assessment is to certify the achievement of an individual in mathematics (and so is, essentially, retrospective).

The other main use that is made of the results of mathematics assessments is prospective: using the results of one assessment to predict how well an individual will do in the future. Success in mathematics at one level of the educational system does correlate positively with success at the next level, although nowhere near as strongly as is often supposed (correlations as low as 0.3 are common). It might be supposed that choosing items that predict future performance well might offer the possibility of an objective choice of mathematical content (in other words, a "mathematics degree zero"), but since the content of the mathematical curriculum at the next level is just as arbitrary as that at the prior level, then this is really no more than a self-fulfilling prophecy. Here, I should make clear that the term *arbitrary* does not mean "capricious" but rather that the mathematics curriculum is the result of competing and conflicting forces and that different resolutions of these conflicts would result in different curricula.

In response to this, our search for a "mathematics degree zero" might focus not on predicting success on harder *mathematical* content but so that we can predict other, *nonmathematical*, performance. In fact, success at mathematics does predict future performance levels in a range of other activities and occupations, but there is little evidence that this is causal. Our current measures of mathematics performance tend to correlate better with measures of general intellectual aptitude than any other school subject. However, this again leads us to define mathematics in a particular way. If we include mathematical content that helps us to predict general job performance, we are likely to pick out those aspects of mathematics that are strongly related to general intellectual functioning—in which case, why not use an IQ test? Indeed, while many authors seem to regard the high correlation of mathematics scores with IQ scores as appropriate (Newton, Tymms, and Carrick 1995), it could be argued that in order to be really useful mathematics assessments should *not* correlate well with IQ.

These debates can be best understood not as arguments about the technical merits of rival assessments but as arguments over the value implications of different definitions of what is to count as mathematics. Mathematics has high status as a subject precisely because it correlates so well with IQ test scores, and because it is a subject in which it is easy to create large differences in performance between individuals—see Wiliam, Bartholomew, and Reay (2002) for an extended discussion of this point. It could even be argued that the preeminence of mathematics in the curriculum as a high-status subject arises because it is the subject with the greatest sex differences in favor of males. After all, being able to use a typewriter was a high-status occupation when typewriters were first developed and at a time when almost all typewriter operators were male but declined in status as typewriter operation became feminized. Similarly, medicine, while still a high-status profession in the West, declined in status in the USSR as the profession became dominated by women. In the same way, I would argue that the superior performance of males in mathematical subjects is not a *cause* of male supremacy in politics, employment, and elsewhere but a *consequence*. In other words, our definitions of mathematics are precisely those that keep males outperforming females. Changes in the definition of mathematics that reduce, remove, or even reverse sex differences are criticized as "dumbing down" the mathematics curriculum, but these criticisms can equally well be viewed as laments for the loss of power (witness the arguments about the "dumbing down" of mathematics brought about by the introduction of school-based performance assessments in the national school leaving examination in England and Wales). The struggles over what is to count as mathematics (in other words, its value implications) are important because assessments send messages about what is and is not important in mathematics education. The result is that teachers and students change what they do.

These four aspects of validity—content considerations, predictive utility, value implications, and social consequences—have been integrated by Samuel Messick (1989) into a unified model of validity argument. The important feature of this model is that validating an assessment requires attention to all aspects:

Unified validity does not imply answering only one overarching validity question or even several questions separately or one at a time. Rather, it implies an integration of multiple supplementary convergent and discriminant forms of evidence to answer an interdependent set of questions. (Messick 1997, p. 59)

In validating an assessment, therefore, as well as asking the traditional questions about the relevance and representativeness of the content, and its utility for prediction, we must explore the value implications of adopting the assessment and assess the likely social consequences. We must then attempt to reconcile the competing imperatives suggested by these different aspects.

For example, as we saw above, being able to rotate three-dimensional shapes mentally shows a considerable sex difference in favor of males. Should such items be used in mathematics tests? (Note that this is not the same question as whether these items should be taught to students.) Professional mathematicians might posit an *epistemological imperative*, arguing that omitting such items un-derrepresents the construct of mathematical competence, and such items must be included. Such items might also be favored by those with a *utilitarian imperative*, since they are likely to discriminate strongly between candidates and thus contribute to predictive validity. However, such items could well have a disproportionate impact on females. Including such items would lower the scores of females relative to males, and in the absence of evidence that the particular skill of mentally rotating three-dimensional shapes is relevant to future performance, even in mathematics, then a *moral imperative* would require omitting the item.

RANDOM JUSTICE[1]

The tensions between the conflicting imperative discussed above are exacerbated when tests are required to fulfill many functions. Odd though it may seem, it is possible to ameliorate the tension by introducing a degree of randomness into the use that is made of test results. The principle is illustrated by means of an example. In almost all countries, entry into medical education is highly competitive. In most countries, selection is based on scores on school examinations or some other assessment, more or less well designed to assess aptitude for medical education. Let us assume, therefore, that 10% of the applicants would be able successfully to train as a doctor but that only 1% of the applicants can be admitted. How should we use the results of our test? In the anglophone countries, the typical approach is to accept the highest-scoring 1% of the applicants on the assessment. The effect of this is to magnify any sex differences in selection. To see why, look back at Table 9.3. If there is a standardized mean difference (D) of 0.5 in favor (say) of males (assuming equal variances), then males will form at 71% of the top 10% but just under 80% of the top 1% (and of course these trends are even more marked for larger values of D, or if the variance of the lower-scoring group is smaller, as in Table 9.4). Restricting our selection to the top 1% has increased the proportion of males accepted for medical education, even though we have no evidence that they will do better. In contrast, in many countries in continental Europe, the selection procedure discards any "surplus achievement" beyond the minimum threshold and instead proceeds by randomly selecting from the 10%, whom, after all, we know could all train successfully as doctors.

In the assessment literature, it is conventional to distinguish between recruitment and selection. *Recruitment* is the process of identifying all suitable applicants (i.e., in our medical example, this would mean identifying the 10% of applicants who could train successfully as doctors). *Selection* refers to the process of selecting from these the appropriate individuals whom we will actually train as doctors. It may be that certain subgroups (e.g., males, females, ethnic minorities, students with disabilities) are underrepresented in the recruitment group, and we must be sure that such underrepresentation cannot be ameliorated by suitable adjustment of the training and working environment. For example, students requiring wheelchair access might be denied a place at medical school, not because they could not become good doctors but because they would not be able to satisfy the particular requirements of a medical training program. It is also necessary to ensure that any adjustments in the nature of the work for which students are being trained are made that would reduce underrepresentation. However, given these conditions, and once the recruitment group is well defined, we can frame the conclusion of the argument above in terms of the following principle:

> The representation of subgroups in the sample selected must be the same as that in the recruitment group.

Any selection process that increases the underrepresentation of any subgroup (when compared with the recruitment group) is unjust and unjustifiable.

Another example here is that of the use of aptitude tests in selection to higher education in the United States. The scores obtained on the SAT by students from some ethnic minorities are below that of whites, which is cited by some as evidence of bias in the test. But it is also the case that the same ethnic minorities do less well in higher education. However, the crucial evidence of bias is that the standardized difference in SAT scores is approximately twice that of scores in higher education, which implies that using the SAT for selection increases the underrepresentation of those ethnic minorities (Hakel 1997). A fairer approach would be to identify the minimum score required on the SAT in order to succeed in higher education (using difference cut-score for different subgroups) and, if this process identifies more suitable candidates than can be admitted, making any further selection by lottery.

This seems counterintuitive—we seem to be throwing away information. But if we do not have specific evidence that surplus achievement beyond the threshold required (i.e., to be counted in the recruitment group) produces greater performance, then it makes sense to disregard that evidence, even when working with a utilitarian imperative. When the importance of having doctors (to choose just one example) who adequately represent the communities they serve is factored in, then the moral imperative is compelling. It is just an application of the general principle that if you cannot make a selection without introducing bias (in the sense of unjustifiable difference), then random selection is the only fair way.

CONCLUSION

In this chapter, I have argued that differences between the scores of males and females on mathematics tasks have always been small when compared to the variability of males and of females (i.e., that the variation between each group is small compared to the variation within the group). The small differences have been regarded as much larger than they are primarily because of an over-reliance on statistical significance as a measure of effect size. When the empirical evidence on sex differences in mathematics is viewed in terms of the overlap between populations, even the largest differences found in practice mean that 90% of the population is in the region of overlap, and only 1% of the variation (variance) in scores is attributable to sex. More important, the size, and even the direction, of these sex differences depends on the mathematical tasks and items used. Even the "pernicious hypothesis" (Noddings 1992) that males are more differentiated than females can be seen to be the result of choices made about what is to count as mathematics.

Given these competing definitions of mathematics, it is tempting to try to arbitrate between them and to attempt to locate "mathematics degree zero," but the search is doomed to failure since there can be no such thing. Mathematics curricula are "objects of history" (Cherryholmes 1989, p. 116)—the outcomes of social contestations about what is to be included—and even the high status of mathematics in many contemporary societies may be simply a reflection of previous male dominance.

However, even if there were some absolute definition of mathematics, and even if we accepted the essentialist arguments that attempt to show that males are "naturally" better than females at certain things, this would tell us nothing about how to use assessments of mathematics for selection, because one cannot deduce an "ought" from an "is." An epistemological imperative encourages us to shape our assessments according to existing notions of what mathematics "should" be, while a utilitarian perspective would require us to look at the utility of these assessments for prediction. However, a moral imperative requires us to consider the social consequences of such actions. For example, even if it were agreed that mental rotation was an essential part of mathematics, and even if it were essential to the task for which we are selecting, we should not accept male superiority in this task. Instead, we should do whatever needs to be done to mitigate its effect.

Finally, in moving from recruitment to selection, we should introduce no additional discrimination. Surplus achievement beyond the minimum required for whatever is the object of selection should be used only when there is no difference in representation in subgroups. If there is a difference, then random selection from the recruitment group is the only fair way. Social justice sometimes requires random justice.

NOTES

I am grateful to Jo Boaler and an anonymous reviewer for helpful comments on an earlier draft of this chapter, although, of course, the responsibility for any remaining errors lies with me.

1. This phrase is taken from Duxbury (1999).

REFERENCES

Abelson, R.P. (1995). *Statistics as Principled Argument*. Hillsdale, NJ: Lawrence Erlbaum Associates.

Barthes, R. (1984). *Writing Degree Zero & Elements of Semiology* (Annette Lavers and Colin Smith, Trans.). London: Jonathan Cape.

Beller, M., and Gafni, N. (1996). *Can Item Format (Multiple-Choice vs Open-Ended) Account for Gender Differences in Mathematics Achievement?* Jerusalem, Israel: National Institute for Testing and Evaluation.

Berry, J.W. (1966). Temne and Eskimo Perceptual Skills. *International Journal of Psychology*, 1, 207–229.

Berry, J.W. (1971). Ecological and Social Factors in Spatial Perceptual Development. *Canadian Journal of Behavioral Science*, 3, 324–336.

Boaler, J. (1997). *Experiencing School Mathematics: Teaching Styles, Sex and Setting*. Buckingham, UK: Open University Press.

Boaler, J. (2002). Paying the Price for "Sugar and Spice": Shifting the Analytical Lens in Equity Research. *Mathematical Thinking and Learning*, 4(2/3), 127–144.

Cherryholmes, C.H. (1989). *Power and Criticism: Poststructural Investigations in Education*. New York: Teachers College Press.

Cleary, T.A. (1992). Gender Differences in Aptitude and Achievement Test Scores. In Educational Testing Service (Ed.), *Sex Equity in Educational Opportunity, Achievement, and Testing: Proceedings of a 1991 ETS Invitational Conference* (pp. 51–90). Princeton, NJ: Educational Testing Service.

Cohen, J. (1988). *Statistical Power Analysis for the Behavioural Sciences*. Hillsdale, NJ: Lawrence Erlbaum Associates.

Duxbury, N. (1999). *Random Justice: On Lotteries and Legal Decision Making*. Oxford: Oxford University Press.

Eals, M., and Silverman, I. (1994). The Hunter-Gatherer Theory of Spatial Sex Difference: Proximate Factors Mediating the Female Advantage in Recall of Object Arrays. *Ethology and Sociobiology*, 15, 95–105.

Feingold, A. (1988). Cognitive Gender Differences Are Disappearing. *American Psychologist*, 43, 95–103.

Fennema, E., and Carpenter, T.P. (1998). New Perspectives on Gender Differences in Mathematics: An Introduction. *Educational Researcher*, 27(5), 4–5.

Friedman, L. (1989). Mathematics and the Gender Gap: A Meta-analysis of Recent Studies on Sex Differences in Mathematical Tasks. *Review of Educational Research*, 59(2), 185–213.

Gilligan, C. (1982). *In a Different Voice*. Cambridge, MA: Harvard University Press.

Glass, G.V., McGaw, B., and Smith, M. (1981). *Meta-analysis in Social Research*. Beverly Hills, CA: Sage.

Hakel, M.D. (Ed.). (1997). *Beyond Multiple-Choice: Evaluating Alternatives to Traditional Testing for Selection*. Mahwah, NJ: Lawrence Erlbaum Associates.

Hyde, J.S., Fennema, E., and Lamon, S.J. (1990). Gender Differences in Mathematics Performance: A Meta-analysis. *Psychological Bulletin*, 107, 139–155.

Linn, M.C. (1992). Gender Differences in Educational Achievement. In Educational Testing Service (Ed.), *Sex Equity in Educational Opportunity, Achievement, and Testing: Proceedings of a 1991 ETS Invitational Conference* (pp. 11–50). Princeton, NJ: Educational Testing Service.

Linn, M.C., and Petersen, A.C. (1985). Emergence and Characterisation of Sex Differences in Spatial Ability: A Meta-analysis. *Child Development*, 56, 1479–1498.

Maccoby, E.E., and Jacklin, C.N. (1974). *The Psychology of Sex Differences*. Stanford, CA: Stanford University Press.

McBurney, D.H., Gaulin, S.C.G., Devineni, T., and Adams, C. (1997). Superior Spatial Memory of Women: Stronger Evidence of the Gathering Hypothesis. *Evolution and Human Behaviour*, 18, 165–174.

Messick, S. (1989). Validity. In R.L. Linn (Ed.), *Educational Measurement* (pp. 13–103). Washington, DC: American Council on Education/Macmillan.

Messick, S.J. (Ed.). (1997). *Alternative Modes of Assessment, Uniform Standards of Validity*. Mahwah, NJ: Lawrence Erlbaum Associates.

Newton, D., Tymms, P.B., and Carrick, N. (1995). Is the GCSE Fair? Examination Success and Cognitive Style. *British Journal of Curriculum and Assessment*, 6(1), 21–25.

Noddings, N. (1992). Variability: A Pernicious Hypothesis. *Review of Educational Research*, 62(1), 85–88.

Organisation for European Economic Co-operation Office for Scientific and Technical Personnel (Ed.). (1961). *New Thinking in School Mathematics*. Paris: Organisation for European Economic Co-operation.

Ridley, M. (1993). *The Red Queen: Sex and the Evolution of Human Nature*. London: Penguin.

Rogers, L. (1999). *Sexing the Brain*. London: Weidenfeld and Nicholson.

Stevens, A., and Price, J. (1996). *Evolutionary Psychiatry: A New Beginning*. London: Routledge.

Walden, R., and Walkerdine, V. (1985). *Girls and Mathematics: From Primary to Secondary Schooling*. London: University of London Institute of Education.

Walkerdine, V. (1988). *The Mastery of Reason: Cognitive Development and the Production of Rationality*. London: Routledge.

Walkerdine, V., and Girls and Mathematics Unit (Eds.). (1989). *Counting Girls Out*. London: Virago.

Wiliam, D., Bartholomew, H., and Reay, D. (2002). Assessment, Learning and Identity. In R. Zevenbergen and P. Valero (Eds.), *Researching the Socio-political Dimensions of Mathematics Education: Issues of Power in Theory and Methodology*. Dordrecht: Kluwer Academic Publishers.

Williams, R. (1961). *The Long Revolution*. London: Chatto & Windus.

Willingham, W.S., and Cole, N.S. (Eds.). (1997) *Gender and Fair Assessment*. Mahwah, NJ: Lawrence Erlbaum Associates.

Wright, R. (1995). *The Moral Animal: Why We Are the Way We Are*. London: Little, Brown.

Chapter 10

First Results of a Study of
Different Mathematical Thinking
Styles of Schoolchildren

Rita Borromeo Ferri and Gabriele Kaiser

INTRODUCTION

> My previous teacher explained fast and much and did not make any draw-
> ings. And then one time I got a six[1] for a maths test and then I only got a
> four and then I thought, "I don't know maths." And if I don't understand
> just a bit of it, I understand nothing at all, and I would like to understand
> everything from the beginning, each small step the teacher does. And that
> I couldn't cope with. My new teacher always makes a drawing, and now I
> understand how to come to the result, not like only by formulae and cal-
> culation and for the first and third test I got a one.
>
> Sarah, 15 (Original in German translated by authors)

From this student's statement, it is clear that Sarah has certain preferred kinds
of explanations for mathematical methods. One can infer from this that there
are kinds of explanations that cause young people to understand mathematical
methods well and others through which they only understand a little. Sarah
shows that explanations of mathematical facts through drawings, meaning pic-
torial representations, are apparently much more helpful to her than an exclusively analytic-algorithmic way of proceeding.

Of course, this does not mean that the teacher's explanation was faulty or
bad. On the contrary, this statement suggests another question: Has Sarah been
disadvantaged by the way of teaching and thinking of her previous teacher
because her own way of thinking did not correspond with that of the teacher?
How many girls and boys in her class experienced the same problem, or are
there girls or boys who do not cope with the teacher's thinking style?

Traditionally, many psychologists and pedagogues share the opinion that success and failure of learning are exclusively caused by individually different learning abilities, although the question how it comes that pupils of one teacher are considered as being intelligent and of another one as being not intelligent remains still unanswered. Similarly, it remains still unanswered why the same pupil produces mediocre results in a multiple-choice task, while within a project he or she produces extraordinary results.

During the last decades, empirical cognitive-psychological studies made it clear that thinking styles, learning styles, and cognitive styles are strongly influencing performance in many fields and therefore are fundamentally determining pupils' great differences in performance. Sternberg and Zhang (2001) point out that these new approaches that clearly distinguish thinking and learning styles and cognitive styles from the construct of abilities make prediction or explanation of academic success possible in ways that go far beyond the concept of "ability." Furthermore, they point out that the pedagogical relevance of these approaches "is also of interest, because when teachers take styles into account, they help improve both instruction and assessment. Moreover, teachers who take styles into account can show sensitivity to cultural and individual diversity that is so often absent in the classroom" (2001, p. viii). Sternberg and Zhang also indicate that there has never been such diversity among our pupils, in both individual and cultural respects. They show that for teaching to be adequate for this population of pupils it must respect different styles of thinking, learning, and cognition.

With this in mind, in this chapter based on the construct of mathematical thinking style, we show that diversity in learning mathematics exists in classrooms and is influenced by different mathematical thinking styles. In addition, we demonstrate that many problems of learning mathematics are caused by differences in thinking styles of teachers and pupils, as was pointed out by Sternberg and Zhang: "[T]here is quantitative evidence that teachers tend to think students are better matches to their own styles than the students really are. Perhaps as consequence, the teachers evaluate more positively students who match their own style of thinking, regardless of the students' abilities or achievements" (2001, p. viii). In similar ways, textbooks may cause problems, as they play an important role in mathematics teaching and normally follow one mathematical thinking style.

In our study, of which the first results are presented below, we refer to various descriptions of mathematical thinking styles, especially to a schema of Leone Burton outlined in various publications (e.g., 1995, 1999). She proposes a visual, an analytic, and a classificatory style that she identified in an empirical study with practicing male and female mathematicians. In our study we asked, can similar thinking styles also be identified and reconstructed empirically with 15- to 16-year-old students at the lower secondary level? Are there other thinking styles that are specific to schoolchildren or students while learning mathematics?

We are not primarily focusing on gender differences. On the contrary, the study aims to broaden that discussion toward a claim for social justice for young people of different gender and cultural backgrounds participating in school education. We are proposing that generally education, and specifically mathematics education, should take into account the heterogeneity of learning preconditions, such as ways of thinking and thinking styles. The significance of this dimension has been pointed out, among others, by Christine Keitel in her book *Social Justice and Mathematics Education*, where she writes:

Gender, social, and cultural dimensions are very powerfully interacting in conceptualizations of mathematics education, in attitudes towards and perceptions of mathematics and education, in policy issues concerning organizations, curriculum and assessment, as well as in research approaches and intervention programs with inclusiveness perspective. (Keitel 1998, p. v)

Our study was guided by the following research questions:

• Global: Can various thinking styles of 15- to 16-year-old students at the end of compulsory school education be distinguished and reconstructed?
• If so, which different styles of thinking can be reconstructed with these young people?
• What are the connections between their problem-solving strategies in solving mathematical problems and their mathematical thinking styles?
• How far do the observed young people show distinct preferences for certain thinking styles in solving different problems, and how far do they choose a variety of thinking styles?

CURRENT DISCUSSION ON STYLES OF MATHEMATICAL THINKING

At present, the discussion about the construct of "style" mainly takes place in the field of cognitive psychology. There are only a few approaches with reference to mathematics. The extensive works of Sternberg are basic, including the readers edited by him (see Sternberg and Ben-Zeev 1996; Sternberg and Zhang 2001), to which we will refer more extensively below. Sternberg describes a long research tradition of cognitive psychology on the theoretical construct of style, but there has, as yet, been no consensus about the definition. As one possible reason, among others, he posits the strong connection to abilities and personality traits, together with the related problem of distinction between abilities and styles. Empirical problems arose because of the dependence on instruments on which the identification of styles was based, which made generalization impossible. A further difficulty arose because it was necessary to differentiate styles from strategies, which are more strongly task and context dependent and which are positioned on a higher plane of consciousness. Sternberg and Grigorenko (2001) discuss a range of empirical studies from the 1970s and 1980s that afterward showed that the identified styles were abilities or could not be replicated in other studies. In their overview of the development of the discussion about styles, Sternberg and Grigorenko present the following uncontentious characterization of style: "reference to habitual patterns or preferred ways of doing something (e.g., thinking, learning, teaching) that are consistent over long periods of time and across many areas of activity" (p. 2). Furthermore, they point out that styles applied in various situations may render better or worse performance. However, basically, no style produces better performances than others, because, if it did, the underlying construct would more represent an ability than a style. In his summary of the current discussion about styles, Sternberg (2001a) emphasizes the aspect of choice as a characterization of styles, which, in his opinion, can lead to satisfying theoretical constructs. He says: "Individuals have preferences for certain styles" (p. 250 f). Styles do not represent personality traits, but "they represent choices in the face of environmental stimuli" (p. 251). In principle, pupils can choose any style. They make their choice dependent on situation and circumstances. In Sternberg's opinion, the emphasis on choice and decision distinguishes the old cognitive styles movement, reflecting abilities, from current approaches.

For teaching and learning research, it is interesting to distinguish between learning styles, thinking styles and cognitive styles as described by Sternberg (2001b):

Learning styles might be used to characterize how one prefers to learn. . . . Would one rather learn about it visually . . . or auditorily? . . . Or perhaps one would prefer an active form of learning . . . versus a passive form. . . .

Thinking styles might be used to characterize how one prefers to think about material as one is learning it or after one already knows it. For example, would one rather think about global issues or local issues? . . .

Cognitive styles might be used to characterize ways of cognizing the information. For example, does one tend to be a splitter . . . or [known] as a lumper? . . . The cognitive styles tend to be closer to personality than are the other types of styles. (p. vii)

First, we would like to discuss thinking styles, which, following Sternberg (1997), we take as preferred ways of thinking or as preference in the use of the "abilities" one has. That means that thinking styles are not viewed as being unchangeable, but they may change, depending on time, environment, and life demands. Sternberg states that thinking styles are acquired at least partly through socialization. There is almost no study on the theoretical construct of mathematical thinking styles, especially no empirical one. However, one can find quite a lot of work that refers to the concept of mathematical thinking (among others, compare the anthology of Sternberg and Ben-Zeev 1996), but among that work, few aspects are held in common. In part this is due to the dependence of the described abilities on their related mathematical subject area. Sternberg (1996) describes this situation as follows: "In other words, mathematical thinking, like game, does not seem to be a classically defined concept with a set of defining features that are necessary and sufficient" (p. 304). Therefore, Sternberg suggests that mathematical thinking be described as a set of prototypes, for which the characterizing qualities of each single prototype must be developed so that they can be distinguished from characterizations of other prototypes. In this way, mathematical thinking in algebra, for instance, may be characterized differently from that in calculus, but probably there are characterizing features, like spatial visualization, that play a role in several mathematical subject areas. Sternberg describes various approaches to develop prototypes of mathematical thinking, as, for instance, psychometrical approaches that regard the human intellect as a map divided into different regions and that classify abilities by analyzing how many, and how far, can penetrate different mathematical subject areas.

Anthropological approaches give special emphasis to the construct's reliance on culture and context (see Saxe et al. 1996), while approaches of a more mathematical kind are stressing elements of mathematical working and affective aspects, such as self-confidence or mathematical creativity (see Dreyfus and Eisenberg 1996). The studies of Schoenfeld, who worked extensively, theoretically as well as empirically, on the learning of mathematical thinking and its necessary preconditions, also come under this approach. Schoenfeld (1994) develops a broad and age-independent description:

Learning to think mathematically means (a) developing a mathematical point of view—valuing the processes of mathematisation and abstraction and having the predilection to apply them, and (b) developing competence with the tools of the trade and using those tools in the service of the goal of understanding structure—mathematical sense-making. (p. 60)

This work deals with the construct of mathematical thinking more from an ability-oriented perspective and is therefore not very helpful in developing characterizations of mathematical thinking styles.

In the discussion within mathematics there can be found some approaches that seem to be useful to develop descriptions of mathematical thinking styles. In 1892, in German, Klein constructed a typology of three different thinking styles. He outlined this typology in connection with an opening for a new professor. He pleaded for a policy of appointing mathematicians to German universities who would utilize various thinking styles in order to promote mathematics and its applications generally. In 1892, in a letter to Althoff, assistant secretary of state in the Prussian Department of Spiritual, Educational, and Medical Affairs, Klein distinguished the following types of mathematicians:

1. The philosopher who constructs on the basis of concepts
2. The analyst who essentially "operates" with a formula
3. The geometer whose starting point is a visual one ("Anschauung") (quoted from Tobies 1987, p. 44, original in German, translated by the authors)

This classification was based on observations in cooperation with other mathematicians and not based on empirical studies (and therefore it should be regarded more as anecdotal knowledge). The following famous mathematicians were classified by Klein as follows:

- Type 1: Karl Weierstraß and Georg Cantor
- Between Types 1 and 2: Leopold Kronecker
- Type 2: Georg Frobenius
- Type 3: Sophus Lie, his own

For details, we refer to Tobies (1987), who analyzed the discussion historically.

A similar typology, restricted to visual and analytic thinking styles, is found in Hadamard (1945): *The Psychology of Invention in the Mathematical Field.* His study is guided by the question of how, when working on mathematical problems and from a psychological point of view, abstract ideas for mathematical solutions arise. For this, Hadamard referred to psychological research from the beginning of the last century where mathematicians were asked how they found the solutions of mathematical problems and which working and thinking style they applied. In particular, the relations between consciousness and unconsciousness, mathematical dreams, signs, and words played a central role and were discussed with, as an example, the discovery of the Fuchs functions by Poincaré (see Hadamard 1945, pp. 11 ff). Hadamard's description of studies by the psychologist Ribot on problem-solving processes of mathematicians is interesting because he distinguished two mathematical thinking styles: "Some of them (the mathematicians) have told him that they think in a purely algebraic way, with the help of signs; others *always* need a 'figured representation,' a 'construction,' even if this is 'considered as pure fiction' " (Hadamard 1945, p. 86).

In her well-founded study on mathematics and its epistemology, Leone Burton recently characterized mathematical thinking styles. Based on a theoretical model developed earlier, she interviewed 35 male and 35 female mathematicians working at universities in England, Scotland, and Ireland and asked them about various aspects of their professional activities. She makes clear: "In particular, although mathematicians research very differently, their pervasive absolutist view of mathematical knowledge is not matched by their stories of how they come to know, nor of how they think about mathematics" (1999, p. 87).

Leone Burton asked the research mathematicians to describe mathematical problems on which they were working and how they were solving them. She analyzed these data to see whether the thinking styles documented in scientific literature could be reconstructed. Unlike Hadamard, but similar to Klein, she identified three, and not two, styles of thinking:

Style A: Visual (or thinking in pictures, often dynamic),

Style B: Analytic (or thinking symbolically, formalistically), and

Style C: Conceptual (thinking in ideas, classifying) (1999, p. 95).

She categorized nearly a third of the mathematicians as having only one thinking style, while most of them moved between two styles, and only a few used all three styles of thinking. She gave the following examples of the statements of the mathematicians that caused her to categorize them as users of two styles:

Style A/B: "I think very visually and I mostly only have recourse to algebra when I have to work out a proof rigorously."

Style A/C: "I cannot imagine thinking in a way that is completely non-visual. . . . Depending on what the problem is but usually I am trying to count how many different orbits there are so things fall into classes so you can move within a class."

Style B/C: "I am not a very visual person. I think in terms of equations but I think it is problem driven. I don't think I can ever deal with solid geometry problems. If I am looking for a taxonomy, I use hierarchies, classificatory pictures." (p. 95)

No significant gender- or culture-related differences could be found. Therefore, she could not support, for example, the widespread assumption that "visual thinking" is a predominantly male characteristic. However, from the point of view of mathematics didactics, she raised some alarming doubts concerning her results. Most of the scientists who did not have a visual thinking style were conscious of the fact that other thinking styles exist. But many of the other mathematicians assumed that every mathematician thinks about mathematics or is practicing it in the same way that they do. This can have strong effects, as Leone Burton points out, on teaching and learning mathematics. She writes that

most of my participants did not appear to realise that thinking and learning styles go very closely hand-in-hand—a lecturer with one dominant style is likely only to be communicating fluently with those students who share that style. (p. 96)

We have presented this classification of thinking styles in detail because our study, as already mentioned, proceeded—among others—from Leone Burton's. We hoped to answer the still unaddressed question of whether these thinking styles can be reconstructed similarly, or be further differentiated, with students of mathematics.

The works of Skemp (1987) and Fischbein (1987) seemed also to be of importance to our study. In his book *The Psychology of Learning Mathematics*, Skemp differentiated between various kinds of pictures individuals possibly use in thinking. For this, in his opinion, two kinds of symbols, visual and verbal ones, are used as mental pictures in practicing mathematics. Visual and verbal pictures he distinguished as follows: "So by 'verbal' we shall mean both the spoken and the written word. Visual symbols are clearly exemplified by diagrams of all kinds, particularly geometrical figures" (1987, p. 66).

Furthermore, he was concerned with determining within which category central algebraic symbols should be classified. And he observed a stronger proximity of algebraic symbols to verbal symbols than to diagrams and geometrical figures. For Skemp, mathematics cannot rely on verbal symbols—including algebraic symbols—in contrast to visual symbols, although a drawing or graph can sometimes explain much more than a long verbal explanation.

A contrary position to that of Skemp was developed by Fischbein (1987) in his work on intuition in science and maths. He demonstrated the great importance of intuition in the development of mathematics and recognized a close connection between intuition and visualization. He referred to the distinction between geometricians and analysts made by Poincaré. Fischbein states:

Intuition, as we have frequently emphasized, implies a kind of empathy, a kind of cognition through direct, internal identification with a phenomenon. A visual representation with its rich, concrete details mediates such a personal involvement generally much better than a concept, or a formal description. (p. 104)

The literature on mathematical thinking often points to mathematical thinking as taking place while solving mathematical problems. Mathematicians have been interviewed about how they solve problems, or people have been observed while solving problems. This is based on the assumption that in autonomous problem-solving processes individual strategies and ways of thinking are of great importance. Therefore, the reconstruction of problem-solving processes and the applied problem-solving strategies of students is essential to the identification of their underlying thinking styles, because—as already explained—strategies and styles are strongly related to each other. Therefore, we consider briefly problem solving and problem-solving strategies.

Schoenfeld, whose studies decisively influence the discussion about problem solving, gives the following description:

The difficulty with defining the term problem is that problem solving is relative. . . . Of the definitions in the Oxford English Dictionary, the one I prefer is the following: "Problem: A doubtful or difficult question; a matter of inquiry, discussion, or thought; a question that exercises the mind." (Schoenfeld 1985, p. 74)

Problem-solving strategies were specified by Stebler (1999) in her extensive empirical research about autonomous problem solving. She said:

Strategies are hierarchically organised sequences and practical activities which have the purpose to optimise target-oriented behaviour (cognitive strategies) or to watch it (meta-cognitive strategies). (p. 74; translation by authors)

The connection of problem-solving strategies to meta-cognition in mathematics lessons was addressed by Goos, Galbraith, and Renshaw (2000), who examined senior secondary school students' self-controlled meta-cognitive strategies while solving problems individually. The examination of notes from the problem solving as well as of the students' questions strongly demonstrated successful self-control but also gave reason for doubting if control was adequate or even seemed to be missing. To identify characteristic types of meta-cognitive failure for any kind of solving strategy, the difference between two key elements of effective self-control must be emphasized. These are being able to notice mistakes and other difficulties during the process and being able to correct and overcome them.

Finally we turn to the discussion about cognitive and learning styles whose concepts and constructs seem to be suitable to make our construct of mathematical thinking styles more precise and detailed. Distinctions between cognitive and learning styles are not homogeneous, which is pointed out by Adey et al. (1999) in their elaborate literature report on learning styles and strategies. Altogether, this overview reflects the discussion with all its uncertainties and controversies. Riding, for instance, at first defined his theoretical approach as learning style, as cited in Adey et al. (1999), while in his recent work he refers to cognitive style. In the following, we present Riding's approach in more detail because his dimensions show a strong proximity to ours. Riding (2001) distinguishes between two groups of dimensions that describe the theoretical construct of cognitive style:

the wholist-analytic style dimension of whether an individual tends to organize information in wholes or parts, and the verbal-imagery style dimension of whether an individual tends to represent information during thinking verbally or in mental pictures. (p. 48)

Riding shows that, on the one hand, these dimensions have a bipolar character and that, on the other hand, each dimension is a continuum and therefore can have various intermediate positions. These two dimensions he describes in more detail:

- The Wholist-Analytic Dimension influences the way an individual gets, organizes and uses information. "Wholists" tend to overlook situations as a whole from a global perspective, i.e. they look at a situation within the framework of its superordinated context. In contrast to that "Analytics" tend to look at situations as a collection of parts and tend to concentrate on few of them. They analyse a situation due to its components, which enables them to discover similarities and differences.
- The Verbal-Imagery Dimension refers to the way that information is represented: "Verbalizers" get their information through spoken words and associate verbally. "Imagers" work with pictures and associate mentally.

This description shows the proximity to learning styles that makes it difficult to distinguish cognitive styles from learning styles.

An approach to learning styles, which is extremely influential in the cognitive psychology discussion, was developed by Kolb. It is included in Adey et al. (1999). Kolb also distinguished between two bipolar dimensions: from concrete experience to abstract conceptualization and from active experimentation to reflective observation. Therefore, he distinguished four types of learning styles reflecting these features.

- Diverging: People with this learning style are best at viewing concrete situations from many points of view; they perform better in situations that call for generation of ideas.

- Assimilating: Individuals with this learning style are best at understanding a wide range of information and putting it into concise, logical form; they are less focused on people and more interested in ideas and abstract concepts.

- Converging: Persons with this learning style are best at finding practical uses for ideas and theories, solving problems, and making decisions based on finding solutions to questions.

- Accommodating: People with this learning style learn from primarily "hands-on" experience. Their tendency may be to act on "gut" feelings rather than on logical analysis (see Kolb, Boyatzis, and Mainemelis 2001).

This approach also describes dimensions, which seem to be interesting for further analyses of our own data.

In our study, we have analyzed "mathematical thinking styles" from a mathematical and didactic perspective, based on empirical studies about the solving of mathematical problems. In this way, we locate our research mainly in the field of didactics of mathematics and refer only in parts to the field of cognitive psychology.

EMPIRICAL APPROACH AND DESIGN OF THE STUDY

The study was designed as a comparative case study. Based on definitions of case study methods, the study was aimed less at generalization than at generating hypotheses for further study. This meant that the study design was less broad, which would have claimed a greater number of cases, but concentrated on analyses in depth. Generalization going beyond the sample, the aim of much research, was only conditionally possible. In particular, it is important to note that the results obtained from this study are strongly dependent on age.

The study was qualitatively oriented, utilizing grounded theory (cf. Strauss and Corbin 1990) and focusing on interpretation of the data. The methods of data collection were interviews with teachers and students, observation of problem-solving processes, and stimulated recall (see Wagner, Uttendorfer-Marek, and Weidle 1977). As a basic strategy of data interpretation, decomposition of the text, not dependent on the underlying sequencing and encoding of the material but aimed at categorization and possibly theory formation, was used. This so-called theoretical encoding procedure, which at first was worked out with in vivo codes and then with methods of selective and axial encoding, was aimed at conceptualizing data and phenomena through segmentation. The multiple decomposition, conceptualization, and recomposition of the data in a new way constituted, following the approach of Strauss and Corbin (1990), the central process by which theories were constructed from data. For these analyses, the software tool ATLAS.ti was used.

Before starting the theoretical encoding procedure, first the problem-solving processes for each task from all participating pupils have to be reconstructed. During this procedure the problem-solving processes were examined for code words indicating an analytical, visual, or conceptual thinking style. Pupils, for instance, trying to find a formula or to write down their ideas of solution in the form of an equation very often used words or expressions such as *formulae, write down–checking off, tabular, equations* [Formeln, aufschreiben-weghaken, tabellarisch, Gleichungen]. Pupils with a preference for a visual thinking style mostly used expressions such as *imagine, picture, graphic component, turn around in one's head* [vorstellen, Bild, graphische Komponente, im Kopf drehen].

It is extremely important that all the statements of the pupils that refer to thinking styles are viewed in the whole context, including all the pupils' actions, descriptions, and paraphasings of events during the problem-solving process. Therefore, the problem-solving process became more transparent (see design below) by the stimulated recall and was taken into account, together with the interviews, because through questions concerning image and attitude toward mathematics hypotheses about thinking styles could be put on a solid base.

The first codes have been done manually, working through the text. The following coding is done, as already mentioned, with ATLAS.ti. The problem-solving process plays an important role in the reconstruction. We have divided the process into four phases, given examples, and tried to subsume all codes referring to visual, analytic, and various "mixed types" under the "thinking style codes." Already in this stage, it became clear that our classification of thinking styles went beyond those developed by Burton and Klein. Our data did not allow us to develop codes for the classificatory style of Burton or Klein but led us more closely to the classification given by Hadamard. In accordance with the descriptions found in the literature, we could reconstruct so-called mixed types, who incorporate elements of different thinking styles. In further analyses the different usage of the concept "to see" will be more differentiated and clarified by referring to Skemp's and Fischbein's definitions.

Altogether 12 students, 6 boys and 6 girls in years 9 and 10, 15 and 16 years old, participated in the study. Eight students came from the higher-type secondary schools (so-called Gymnasium); 4 came from the higher level of comprehensive schools. The schools are situated in middle-class areas as well as those with a predominantly lower-class population. Ten students grew up monolingual in German, while 2 students had a multicultural background. The students were chosen by their teachers because of their mathematical performance and their communication readiness as well. During the problem-solving process, the 6 pupils from each year group were arranged in pairs, a pair of boys, a pair of girls, and a mixed pair. The students were used to working together during lessons.

For the reconstruction of different thinking styles of male and female students, we developed a design that made clear different views and levels of reflection about problem-solving processes. For each session, we used the following Three-Step Design:

Step 1: Problem-solving process. Each pair of students solved four problems, one after another. They were free to decide how far to work together. The working process was videotaped.

Step 2: Stimulated recall. Afterward, each student was shown, individually, a videorecording of Step 1. Beforehand, the students were asked to stop the video when they had ideas, approaches, or considerations with respect to the solving of the problem in order to describe them. We also stopped the video at selected points where we wanted to know what was going on in their heads. This phase of stimulated recall was tape-recorded.

Step 3: Individual interview. Each student was interviewed about his or her judgments about the problem-solving tasks, about the problem-solving process of each task, and about questions concerning their mathematics teaching and their image of mathematics. The interviews were taped-recorded.

There were two sessions for each pair.

Following Schoenfeld's (1985) method, used in many of his empirical studies, we decided to use the pair-protocol method instead of individual sessions, although we focus on the reconstruction of individual thinking styles. In the literature it is pointed out, repeatedly, that if problem solving is done in pairs, the process is more clearly verbalized and therefore can be reconstructed by the researcher more easily. And meta-remarks about the procedure used and the underlying strategies are more intense. Goos (1994) refers to how pair sessions ease the burden:

Pair protocols are more likely to capture a complete record of students' typical thinking than single protocols because, first, two students working together produce more verbalisation than one and, second, the reassurance of mutual ignorance can alleviate some of the pressure of working under observation. (p. 145)

Besides problem solving in pairs and videotaping, individual stimulated recall carried out directly after the problem solving seemed to be a promising method for the reconstruction of thinking styles. Wagner, Uttendorfer-Marek, and Weidle (1977) made clear:

Our experiences show that with this method many thoughts and considerations can be reproduced, although not completely and not without adulturation. . . . It is the aim of the stimulated recall to report plans, goals and decision making processes. (p. 248; translation by authors)

The subsequent individual interview is meant to give insight into the students' image of mathematics and their school experiences in learning mathematics (see the interview questions in the appendix at the end of this chapter).

In the problem-solving sessions, items from other studies were adapted, or we developed the problems. Before the problems were used in the study, 16 suitable tasks were pretested in several classes of years 9 and 10. The pupils classified them following grades of difficulty and interest. The evaluation identified 8 tasks that were used for this study. The tasks originated from various topic areas and admitted or even demanded different problem-solving strategies (e.g., graphic-visual, numeric or algebraic-algorithmic, trial-and-error method).

When constructing the problems, it was difficult to develop problems that needed a thinking style Klein called "the philosopher," which starts from a concept, or the thinking style Leone Burton classified as conceptual, which uses ideas to think and classify but that did not go beyond the mathematical level of 15- to 16-year-old students. We are assuming that a reason for this may be that this thinking style is settled on a metalevel of thinking requiring a high degree of reflection; students at the end of the lower secondary school level might be quite overburdened by such a demand. Further studies with other problems will be needed in order to clarify this open question.

In the following analysis, we are using two problems from the four:

The Birthday Party

> Eight persons are gathered at a birthday party. Everybody wants to clink their glass exactly once with each other. How many glasses will be clinked?

From the literature it was clear that such well-known problems demand combinatorics. However, algorithmic and graphical ways of solving were possible, as there is the successive calculation of number of clinking glasses, or a graph can be constructed. Therefore, this task enabled us to reconstruct how far visual, analytic, or conceptual ways of thinking were used.

A second problem used in the chapter is:

A Magic Figure

> You see a magic figure containing 9 fields. Place the numbers 1–9 into the figure in such a way that on each axis you get the sum s = 18. Each number may only be used once. Is there more than one solution ?

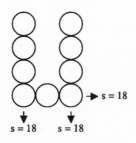

This problem directly followed the clinking glasses problem. The fields created a graphic component for the task and provoked a visual approach as the emerging symmetry of numbers got a special emphasis for further solutions. On the other hand, the task could be approached analytically by separating and adding up the numbers so that the graphic component did not have any influence.

Additionally, with this task, we could find out to what degree visual or analytical ways of problem solving were applied.

In this chapter, we are not dealing explicitly with the other problems, so we refrain from a complete description and restrict ourselves to a few short remarks (the complete list of problems used in the first session can be found in the appendix). In a further task, spatial abilities were demanded: Three cubes were shown from three different perspectives. The letters U, V, W, X, Y, and Z were written on the faces of the cubes. The students had to determine which face was opposite to the letter Y. It was interesting, with this task, to see how extensively the students needed all three cubes to find the solution, or if they produced sketches, what kind. The last problem was a task adapted from the Fibonacci-sequence. First, the rule for construction of a Fibonacci-sequence was shown in an example. The students were asked to determine a Fibonacci-sequence whose fifth term is the number 50. This problem was the most complex, as very different solving strategies could be applied, and it was one of the few problems that tried to provoke conceptual approaches. Not all students could solve it, and some produced incomplete solutions.

These problems were given in the first session; in the second session, further problems were given. These problems are not discussed because this part of the study has not yet been analyzed. When the students were finished, interviews were held with their teachers. These interviews focused on the problems given to the students, their solution strategies, and the image of mathematics teaching held by the teachers. These parts of the study, not yet evaluated, are intended to give insight into the lessons to which the students refer in their statements.

FIRST RESULTS

First we describe our global results and then add detailed data to provide exemplifications. The results are tentative, and we are aware that we might well need to revise a few of the hypotheses, a fact that is not unusual for studies with a case study character, broadly structured but going into more depth and therefore not easily generalized.

Global Results

The data analyzed so far allow us to assert the following hypotheses.

1. It is possible to reconstruct mathematical thinking style as a distinct psychological construct. The distinctions and descriptions developed so far fulfill the criteria for a style; that is, the dimensions are unrelated to one another, are distinct from "ability," vary in dependence on the problem, and are independent of mathematical success in the problem solving.

2. An empirically grounded description of the characteristics of the visual and the analytic thinking style can be developed. In accordance with the approach of grounded theory, we developed the following descriptions of visual

and analytic thinking styles using our empirical data. We characterize analytical thinking style as a formula-oriented way of mathematical thinking when solving mathematical problems. That means that information from the text of a given problem, from a graph or something similar, is expressed by means of equations. Usually there are connections made to already known formulae that are used to solve the problem. In addition, the analytical thinking style exhibits a preference for analyzing a situation in its parts.

We characterize visual thinking style as a strongly image-oriented way of thinking when solving mathematical problems. That means that information from a given problem is sketched, drawn, or graphed, or mental images are used and described, often in connection with actions. Mental imagery may be used without drawing sketches on a paper or something similar, meaning that the mathematics is worked on mentally. The visual thinking style includes the preference for a holistic procedure.

3. It is possible to reconstruct preferences for analytic and visual mathematical thinking styles with young people. Distinct differences in students' thinking styles while working on a task were observed. Even within a pair of students working together to solve a problem, fundamental differences of strategies and thinking styles during the problem-solving processes became clear. Based on our descriptions of the different mathematical thinking styles, the preferred thinking styles could be reconstructed as using either the features of the analytic thinking style or the features of the visual thinking style.

4. "Polar types" can be reconstructed, that is, students strongly favoring one thinking style. Also "intermediate types" can be reconstructed, that is, students have a preference for using both thinking styles. For some students, one thinking style seems to be dominant. Using our descriptions, analytic and visual thinking styles were identified. Furthermore, there were students we characterized as an intermediate type, that is, choosing both of these thinking styles depending upon the problem or the situation.

5. Despite a strong variation in the problems—when considering all the problems used—distinct preferences in the thinking style of a single student can be reconstructed. As already described, the problems were chosen to promote analytic or visual thinking. Despite the differences, the reconstructed approaches of single students showed relatively stable preferences. It was of central importance if a preference for certain mathematical topic areas existed, such as geometry that might help to solve a more visual problem.

6. In this study the "conceptual" or "philosophical" thinking style could not be identified. As already discussed, we are assuming that a reason for this may be that this thinking style is settled on a metalevel of thinking requiring a high degree of reflection and therefore might be more appropriate at a university level. Because the results of this type of empirical research rely heavily on the problems used, further study with other problems is necessary.

Detailed Results

We now put the global results into concrete terms by using detailed descriptions from the study. For this we concentrate on three students, who serve as prototypes for the reconstructed thinking styles: Saskia, Hanna, and Tim. The descriptions are put into concrete terms using student statements from the interviews, the problem-solving processes, and stimulated recall. For the sake of clarity and to preserve meaning, we give both a translation of the quoted statements of the pupils and the original German.

1. Saskia is an example of someone with a preference for the analytic thinking style. In the following we exemplify characteristics of the analytic thinking style using the problem solving and stimulated recall of Saskia. We were able to reconstruct Saskia's distinct preference for the analytic thinking style on three levels:

(a) Dominance of equations and variables. Typical of Saskia's problem solving, and her underlying strategies, was the application of equations she usually tried to create at the beginning. In doing so she explicitly used the concept of variable.

(b) Focusing on formulae. The procedure was explicitly aimed to create formulae or to use already known formulae. She looked for rules and patterns. She tried to recognize a system in the problem solution.

(c) Minor importance of visual imagination. Saskia's problem solving showed that she hardly used visual images. The imagination she brought into play always related to acts.

To sum up, her approach can be characterized as dominantly static.

Using the example of the clinking glasses problem, we exemplify these characterizations:

Saskia started by drawing a sketch making eight crosses that represented the eight persons:

```
X   X   X   X   X   X   X   X
1   2   3   4   5   6   7   8
```

The crosses X were not interpreted visually by Saskia but each as an algorithmic variable, which was meant to serve to find or to apply a suitable formula. In the following extract, Saskia and her partner are solving the problem:

Saskia: A formula, we need a formula.

Hanna: Well?

Saskia: Let's go through it systematically. Writing down eight persons and then always crossing one off?

Hanna: Can we do that?

Saskia: We can do what we like!

Hanna: Let's write down everything.

Saskia: Okay, let's write simply X and something similar.

Saskia: Eine Formel, wir brauchen eine Formel.

Hanna: Also?

Saskia: Machen wir das jetzt systematisch durchgehen. Acht Leute aufschreiben und dann immer weghaken?

Hanna: Kann man's machen?

Saskia: Wir können machen was wir wollen!

Hanna: Schreiben wir alles auf.

Saskia: Okay schreiben wir einfach x und so was.

Saskia did not directly construct a formula from the crosses she had drawn. Rather, she developed various "equations" in order to make clear who clinked his or her glass with whom:

$$1 = 7$$
$$2 = 6$$
$$5 = 5$$
$$4 = 4$$
$$5 = 3$$
$$6 = 2$$
$$7 = 1$$
$$8 = 0$$

In Figure 10.1 we reconstruct Saskia's problem-solving process of the clinking glasses task through the explanations during the solution process and through the stimulated recall. Saskia's other problem-solving processes showed hardly any visual elements; the analytic thinking style remaining dominant. In Figure 10.2 we reconstruct the problem-solving process in another example, the task with the magic figure. Saskia's explanations of her image of mathematics and her emotions about mathematics, which became clear in the interview, confirmed her characterization as a student with a preference for an analytic thinking style. This preference could be reconstructed on three levels:

- Preference for algorithm
- Connection of mathematics and formulae
- Aversion to geometry

In the interview, when asked what mathematics meant to her, she said:

Figure 10.1
Saskia's Problem-Solving Process and Thinking Style Codes (Birthday Party)

Phases	Statements	Thinking style codes
READING AND UNDERSTANDING THE PROBLEM Task read		
FIRST IMPRESSIONS TO SOLVE Constructs a product (8 x 8), multiplicative-subtractive procedure	*Interviewer*: After reading the problem, did you have an idea directly how to solve it? *Saskia*: Yes, you could say eight times eight and then always minus one, because you always have one less. (stimulated recall)	**analytic approach**
SEARCHING FOR IDEAS Searches for a formula, tries to be systematic	*Saskia*: A formula, we need a formula. *Hanna*: Well? *Saskia*: Let's go it through systematically. Writing down eight persons and then always cross one off. (problem-solving process)	**analytic procedure**
CREATING SOLUTIONS Draws a sketch using variables and develops "equations"	x x x x x x x x $\quad$ 1 = 7 1 2 3 4 5 6 7 8 $\quad$ 2 = 6 $\qquad$ 3 = 5 $\qquad$ 4 = 4 $\qquad$ 5 = 3 $\qquad$ 6 = 2 $\qquad$ 7 = 1 $\qquad$ 8 = 0 (problem-solving process)	**analytic execution**
CHECKING RESULTS Solves through "sketch of variables" and by developing equations and using a calculator	*Saskia*: OK, we have got 28 clinking glasses. (problem-solving process)	**analytic solution**

Saskia: Yes, one always must think in formulae, I think, because somehow mathematics always has to do with formulae; even if a teacher does not say so at the beginning, it always has to do with mathematical formulae!

[Ja, man muss immer mit Formeln denken, denke ich, weil Mathe hat immer irgendwas mit Formeln zu tun, auch wenn das kein Lehrer am Anfang sagt, das hat immer irgendwas mit Matheformeln zu tun!]

Figure 10.2

Saskia's Problem-Solving Process and Thinking Style Codes (A Magic Figure)

Phases	Statements	Thinking style codes
READING AND UNDERSTANDING THE PROBLEM Task read		
FIRST IMPRESSIONS TO SOLVE - Writes down numbers and crosses off (system) - Remembers something similar (crossword puzzle)	*Interviewer:* What were your ideas? *Saskia:* Yes, at first writing down the numbers and crossing numbers off, that it goes slowly down one by one and the high numbers cannot stay in a row. (stimulated recall)	**analytic approach**
SEARCHING FOR IDEAS - Puts the high numbers into order into the two lower edges - Construction of a division equation for the horizontal row	*Saskia:* Here high number must be put in, at any case [pointing at both lower edges of the magic figure]. (problem-solving process) *Saskia:* We must divide eight by three numbers. *Hanna:* Why eight? *Saskia:* Yes, because nine to eighteen is nine we must . . . (problem-solving process)	**analytic procedure** - Formulalike procedure
CREATING SOLUTIONS - Figure drawn and separation of numbers is registered following trial and error - First, put 9 into the low edge, then turn into the middle place - Numbers exchanged	*Interviewer:* What do you mean by exchanging the two numbers? *Saskia:* Yes, first we had nine there and . . . *Interviewer:* Like this, on the left. *Saskia:* Yes, and then we exchanged and then it worked better with these numbers. *Interviewer:* That means at first the nine was first at the left edge or what and then you turned it to the middle? *Saskia:* Yes, turned into the middle, because it was too high. (stimulated recall) *Saskia:* I always try out somehow, to come to a result. *Interviewer:* Mm. (interview)	**analytic execution** - Search for patterns
CHECKING RESULTS - 1. and 2. solution found by trial and error - Then starting a systematic approach	*Interviewer:* Did you already realize what must be the next numbers or what you had to do? *Saskia:* Actually yes, because we must . . . we could not turn/change so much. There remained two possibilities and that was easy. (stimulated recall)	**analytic solution** - Recognizes pattern after two solutions

Later she said:

Saskia: I don't like geometry at all. It is the worst thing that exists. One should not have invented it.

[Mm auf gar keinen Fall mag ich Geometrie. Ist das Schlimmste was es gibt. Das hätte man nicht erfinden dürfen].

2. Hanna is an example of someone whose preference is for a visual thinking style. Hanna was Saskia's partner in the problem-solving sessions. Hanna's preference for the visual thinking style became apparent on two levels:

(a) Use of mental models. Typical for Hanna's problem-solving processes and the underlying strategies was that she used mental models, situated images together with graphic representations.

(b) Action orientation. In her problem-solving approaches, Hanna combined her visual imagination with actions, through which algorithmic aspects became obvious.

To sum up, this kind of procedure is characterized as being dynamic.

To illustrate these characterizations, we once more use the example of the clinking glasses. At the beginning, Hanna and Saskia together used one sheet of paper to note their solutions. As already mentioned, Saskia made crosses symbolizing persons without connecting them because she did not consider it necessary; by comparison, Hanna interpreted these crosses as points of a graph and, therefore, proposed to draw connecting lines between the crosses. The following extract from the transcript demonstrates Hanna's and Saskia's different meanings for the crosses:

Saskia: Okay, let's simply write down X or something like that.

Hanna: You just can, just make eight points and then we connect them or somehow like that.

[*Saskia*: Okay schreiben wir einfach x und so was.

Hanna: Kannst doch einfach mach doch einfach acht Punkte und dann verbinden wir das irgendwie so.]

Because Saskia did not draw connecting lines on the paper, Hanna drew them on the table, while often supporting her explanations by some hand gestures.

Hanna: Well, if eight people clink their glasses, one does not always clink his glass with one's own but with other people's glasses. [*While making a gesture as if clinking glasses*]

Saskia: Yes, then it gets more and more less, or not?

Hanna: Because it is as if I clink my glass with yours then we have both and then, well, if now I make a row and put myself and clink my glass with yours and with the other seven, six, who are there too and then I stand aside or at an edge and then it's your turn and you go through the row, then I am not there anymore. [*Making hand gestures and with her fingers drawing lines on the table*]

[*Hanna*: Also wenn acht Leute anstoßen dann stößt man ja nicht immer mit sich selbst an sondern immer mit den anderen. (*Macht dabei Handbewegungen, als wenn man Gläser zusammenstößt*)

Saskia: Ja dann wird das immer weniger oder nicht?

Hanna: Weil das ist ja, wenn ich mit dir anstoße dann ham wir beide ja und dann also wenn ich jetzt so ne Reihe mache und stell mich jetzt und stoß mit dir an und dann anderen sieben sechs die da noch stehen und dann stell ich mich irgendwie an den Rand oder an ne Ecke und dann bist du dran und gehst dadurch, dann bin ich ja nicht mehr dran. (*Macht dabei Handbewegungen und zeichnet mit dem Finger Linien am Tisch nach*)]

It became clear that the drawing had a fundamentally different meaning for Hanna and Saskia. For Hanna's visual thinking, the drawing functioned as a medium for the problem solving, while, for Saskia, it was a method of notation, to note results or intermediate steps which could not be interpreted independently.

Hanna's problem-solving process with respect to the clinking glasses problem can be reconstructed, as shown in Figure 10.3. As with Saskia, other problem-solving processes hardly contained analytic elements, and the visual thinking style remained dominant. Figure 10.4 illustrates another example. From Hanna's statements on her understanding of mathematics, it became clear that she did not relate mathematics exclusively to numbers but that the connection between mathematics and reality, especially in geometrical applications, was also of importance to her. In the interview, she answered the question of what mathematics meant to her:

Hanna: Mathematics, that is calculation, numbers, well, I don't know, sometimes and somehow something to do with measuring or so for building houses. . . . Yes, I like geometry. Well it is more fun to me because one can make drawings.

[*Mathematik, ja halt rechnen, Zahlen also ich weiß nicht manchmal so irgendwie was mit vermessen oder so zum Häuser bauen. . . . Ja Geometrie find ich gut also das bringt mir auch mehr Spaß als also weil man da halt was zeichnen kann.*]

3. Tim is an example of someone with a preference for an analytic-visual thinking style. Unlike Saskia and Hanna, whose thinking style can, more or less, be characterized as "polar types" because they mainly prefer one thinking style, Tim showed a preference for features of both, the visual as well as the analytic thinking style. However, the analytic part was more strongly evident and could be found on the following levels:

• Dominance of algorithmic, iterative solution strategies. Characteristic of his solution approaches was a step-by-step procedure based on algorithms.

Figure 10.3
Hanna's Problem-Solving Process and Thinking Style Codes (Birthday Party)

Phases	Statements	Thinking style codes
READING AND UNDERSTANDING THE PROBLEM Problem read		
FIRST IMPRESSIONS TO SOLVE - Associates with similar problem - Envisions the situation of people clinking glasses	*Hanna*: Well, if eight people clink their glasses, one does not always clink his glass with one's own but with other people's glasses. [while making a gesture as if clinking glasses]	**visual/dynamic/ situative approach**
SEARCHING FOR IDEAS - Represents people for illustration	*Interviewer*: Hm. What was your idea on how to do it? *Hanna*: Well, if one writes it down separately then one can see it better and more clearly.	**visual approach**
CREATING SOLUTIONS Connects points representing people for the solution	*Saskia*: OK, let's simply write down X or something like that? *Hanna*: You just can, just make eight points and then we connect them or somehow like that.	**visual execution**
CHECKING RESULTS Solves by imagined connecting lines and adding up	No explicit wording, because the solution was articulated by the partner.	

- High value of a systematic approach. Tim always searched in his solution trials for a system on which the problem was based. And by recovering a pattern, he tried to come to a generalized approach for the solution.
- Usage of mental models. In his solutions, Tim used mental models, visual images. These visualizations did not have a value of their own and did not function as solution strategies but as notation of results.

Altogether his method of approach had to be characterized as dynamic. He seemed to be strongly influenced by his school experiences, which he confirmed in the stimulated recall. Additionally, we illustrate these characterizations with a quotation from the transcript of Tim's stimulated recall where he described his approach to this problem:

Interviewer: You just said system. What do you mean by system?

Figure 10.4

Hanna's Problem-Solving Process and Thinking Style Codes (A Magic Figure)

Phases	Statements	Thinking style codes
READING AND UNDERSTANDING THE PROBLEM Problem read		
FIRST IMPRESSIONS TO SOLVE - Remembers something similar (riddle) - Tries	*Interviewer*: What were your first ideas? *Hanna*: Then I thought now it is exactly the same as with these riddles. There are riddles where one always must, for it always becomes a square or so, and so I have thought, well, I just should try out all that. (stimulated recall)	**visual/analytic approach**
SEARCHING FOR IDEAS - First solves by trial and error	*Interviewer*: What was going on in your head? *Hanna*: Then I just tried all numbers. (stimulated recall)	
CREATING SOLUTIONS - Draws fields and tries -Exchanges numbers and incorporates graphic components of the figure	*Interviewer*: Mm, to turn it around. *Hanna*: Yes, then I had somehow; then one has *seen* it, because we have drawn it like that and then we *have seen it somehow*; if we leave the row like that, always the same number at the right side and the same number at the left side, and just changed one with the other, because then we always have the opposite number. (stimulated recall)	**visual components**
CHECKING RESULTS - After finds the 2nd solution, becomes more systematic and faster in finding 3rd and 4th possibility	*Hanna*: And after the second time we have turned it, it was logical somehow that one does the same with the remaining two. (stimulated recall)	**visual/analytic solution**

Tim: If you receive a task of which you know that you have already done it, you always try to remember, because in school we always take the most logical way and the most simple way ... there is always such a scheme for special tasks ... and that was it. I searched for this scheme and then I knew and finally I got the solution.

[*VL*: Du sagtest gerade System, was meinst du denn mit System?

Tim: Wenn man irgendwie ne Aufgabe kriegt von der man weiß, dass man sie gemacht hat, versucht man sich ja immer daran zu erinnern, weil in der Schule machen wir ja den logischsten Weg und den einfachsten Weg ... es gibt ja immer son Schema für bestimmte Aufgaben . . . und das war halt, dass ich dieses Schema gesucht hab und dann hab ich auch gewusst also bin ich schließlich zur Lösung gekommen sozusagen.]

Again, in Figure 10.5 we exemplify Tim's problem-solving process with the clinking glass problem. Problem-solving processes with other problems clearly showed visual elements too, example, with the magic figure, for which we reconstruct Tim's solution process in Figure 10.6.
Tim's image of mathematics matches the characterization of his thinking style—containing visual as well as analytic elements. Therefore, Tim regards mathematics as a science of numbers but also as a science of geometrical figures. In the interview, he said:

Tim: Maybe somehow on the one hand it is a science of numbers but on the other hand something like geometry or, yes, hmm, that not only numbers but, for instance, geometrical figures, that's how I would understand it.

[Vielleicht irgendwie einerseits diese Lehre von Zahlen aber andererseits auch so was wie Geometrie oder ja halt ehm das nicht nur die Zahlen sondern auch zum Beispiel ehm geometrische Figuren oder so also so was würde ich drunter verstehen.]

CONCLUSION

Analyses until now have demonstrated that preferences for two of the different thinking styles with 15- to 16-year-old students based on Leone Burton's (1999) classification can be reconstructed, although preferences for the conceptual thinking style were not found. This might be a function of the problems used, or it might be a function of the specifics of the thinking style as already mentioned. Further studies with other problems are necessary to clarify this. In addition, the question of the relation between problem-solving strategies and mathematical thinking style, raised at the beginning, has not been answered so far. Our present analyses did not reveal distinct patterns, but these might become noticeable after further work.

Specific gender peculiarities or patterns cannot yet be discerned. However, in the problem-solving processes, some social differences have become obvious: The pairs of girls normally communicated with each other more intensely than the boys did. One mixed pair showed competitive behavior, which was mentioned obliquely by Nic in the stimulated recall:

Interviewer: Is there still anything else unclear, or why did you just look that way?

Nic: No, I don't know, somehow I have, I think, I believe that then I thought that once more she was quicker than me because always when I started something new she had already finished it and then at the end I did it that way because she was always two steps ahead.

[*VL*: War da irgendwie noch was unklar du gucktest da gerade so?

Nic: Nee ich weiß nich irgendwie ich hab eher ich dachte glaub eher dass ich da dachte jetzt war sie schon wieder schneller als ich weil immer wenn sie wenn ich was Neues

Figure 10.5

Tim's Problem-Solving Process and Thinking Style Codes (Birthday Party)

Phases	Statements	Thinking style codes
READING AND UNDERSTANDING THE PROBLEM Item read		
FIRST IMPRESSIONS TO SOLVE Remembers similar item	*Tim*: . . . Yes, at first we were considering how have we done it two or three years ago. Yes, that was actually the first idea.	analytic approach
SEARCHING FOR IDEAS Searches for a scheme of calculation	*Tim*: . . . It was just so that we searched for this scheme.	analytic approach
CREATING SOLUTIONS Sums up the number of clinks of glasses; becomes clear through the "pyramid calculation"	*Tim*: And this number of clinks is added and then one gets twenty-eight. "pyramid calculation": 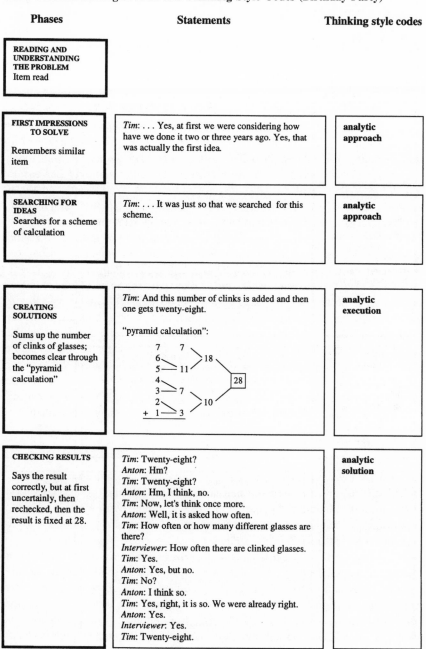	analytic execution
CHECKING RESULTS Says the result correctly, but at first uncertainly, then rechecked, then the result is fixed at 28.	*Tim*: Twenty-eight? *Anton*: Hm? *Tim*: Twenty-eight? *Anton*: Hm, I think, no. *Tim*: Now, let's think once more. *Anton*: Well, it is asked how often. *Tim*: How often or how many different glasses are there? *Interviewer*: How often there are clinked glasses. *Tim*: Yes. *Anton*: Yes, but no. *Tim*: No? *Anton*: I think so. *Tim*: Yes, right, it is so. We were already right. *Anton*: Yes. *Interviewer*: Yes. *Tim*: Twenty-eight.	analytic solution

Figure 10.6
Tim's Problem-Solving Process and Thinking Style Codes (A Magic Figure)

Phases	Statements	Thinking style codes
READING AND UNDERSTANDING THE PROBLEM Task read		
FIRST IMPRESSIONS TO SOLVE - Tries	*Interviewer*: Did you have a special idea how to tackle this item? *Tim*: No, at first I just looked it through, I would say, well, by trying. (stimulated recall)	
SEARCHING FOR IDEAS - First, tries solutions by thinking possibly, by mentally using graphical representations, no evidence provided	*Interviewer*: What did you have in your mind then? *Tim*: Yes, at first I thought I have got it and then it does not work and then I tried *in my head* to get it just like this to make it work. (stimulated recall) *Tim*: Yes, we have seen that there were four empty fields, two times four empty fields, and therefore we have seen that in the four empty fields there must be put in, if possible, the smaller numbers, probably together with the nine.	visual/ analytic
CREATING SOLUTIONS - Searches for the solution more systematically, again supported by graphic component, no evidence provided	*Tim*: There was the change, I believe. Well, I just think, because when I have these five, six, seven, *then I have seen* that the edges if they together make nine, that's good and that has been the case when I have crossed out this equation I have got to the result. (stimulated recall)	visual/ analytic
CHECKING RESULTS - Solves last two possibilities by a systematic procedure	*Tim*: Yes, at the beginning it was difficult, because after that it was actually very simple; it was just to insert. *Interviewer*: Mm. *Tim*: Not really thinking, right. (stimulated recall) *Tim*: It was more like a calculation; if one has understood the principle, then one only had to calculate . . . but somehow I found it more interesting because here some of the numbers were taken away and also here were some of such fields. *Interviewer*: Mm. *Tim*: Yes, that is not so graphic, somehow, that there are figures, functions or so, but it is something totally different, that there are fields lined up. (interview)	visual/ analytic

angefangen hatte hatte sie das dann schon fertig und dann hab ich es am Ende so gemacht dass sie immer zwei vorgegangen ist.]

Furthermore, even these first results, as presented above, indicate a high didactic relevance in this kind of study. A teacher has a mathematical thinking style of his or her own of which, usually, s/he is not aware. However, this thinking style is the basis of the teaching and is therefore simultaneously structuring it. Therefore, students whose mathematical thinking style is different from that of the teacher may experience greater difficulties in lessons than students whose thinking style is similar to the teacher's. This is pointed out by Sarah's statement, recorded at the beginning of the chapter. These results are in accordance with evidence reached in other empirical studies such as that by Zhang and Sternberg (2001) who emphasize: "Findings from a third study indicated that teachers inadvertently favored those students whose thinking styles were similar to their own" (p. 204). Therefore, we must take seriously a student's complaint that a particular teacher's teaching style hinders their appropriation of the subject matter. This does not mean that the teacher teaches badly, but it does indicate an incongruence between the teacher's and the student's thinking styles. Naturally, many students who have had only one mathematics teacher over many years are "stamped" by that teacher's style of teaching, so that some problems may vanish or become temporarily invisible, or the student might consider themselves not to be "mathematical."

Students do have different mathematical thinking styles; some report being unable to participate in lessons with the same intensity as some of their peers. To realize equal opportunities for all students, teachers need to become conscious of their own mathematical thinking styles as well as those of their students and to become aware of strategies to address the existing heterogeneity. Riding (2001) makes a plea for programs that raise "the awareness of teachers of their own cognitive style and of ways of broadening their teaching styles to suit the needs of a wider range of pupils" (p. 69).

This does not mean that teachers should or could change their own mathematical thinking styles. However, they must be aware that some students may experience difficulties in learning from someone with a different mathematical thinking style. Adey et al. (1999) contend that teachers should not try to fit their teaching to each child's style, which would be impossible anyway. They emphasize that teachers and students should become aware of different styles and that teachers should encourage students to use a wide variety of styles. "Students need to learn both how to make the best of their own style and also how to use a variety of styles" (p. 49).

The presence of various thinking styles, found in every class, and reflection on one's own, should become a theme in the education of mathematics teachers. Young teachers, whose own thinking styles have been shaped by the academic teaching style which they have experienced and then pass on in the school, need sensitivity to the fact that students might not share their mathematical thinking style and consequently problems of understanding may occur.

Simultaneously, students learning mathematics should be offered the chance to learn in a way that more closely matches their own thinking style, either through differentiated teaching material or through differentiated methods of explanation by the teacher. Diversity—not only in connection with mathematical thinking styles but in general—is needed in mathematics teaching.

We close this chapter with a statement by another student—Natalie—who expressed the difficulties she experienced with a kind of teaching that always allows only one way:

Natalie: Formulae I just learn by heart and do not always understand them, because it does not help me. I know the visual connection, but the formula, no, that does not suit me.

[Formeln lerne ich halt nur auswendig und verstehe sie nicht immer, weil mir das nicht viel bringt. Ich weiß, wie es bildlich zusammengehört aber formelmäßig, nein, das liegt mir nicht.]

APPENDIX

Tasks of the First Session

1. A Birthday Party. Eight persons are gathering at a birthday party. Everybody wants to clink his glass exactly once with each other. How many glasses will be clinked?

2. A Magic Figure. You see a magic figure containing nine circles. Place the numbers 1–9 into the figure in such a way that on each axis you get the sum s = 18. Each number may be used only once. Is there more than one solution?

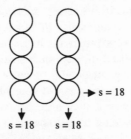

3. Below are shown three cubes. On the cubes' sides are written the letters U, V, W, X, Y, Z. Which letter is written on the side opposite of the letter Y?

4. Around the year 1200 a well-known mathematician, Leonardo from Pisa, also named Fibonacci, invented the following sequence of numbers: 1, 1, 2, 3, 5, 8, 13, ...

Summing up the two preceding numbers of the sequence, one receives the succeeding number as the next term of the sequence. The first two numbers of such a sequence are to be defined and may thus be chosen freely; that is, they may also be different numbers.

Following problem:

The 5th term of such a Fibonacci sequence should be 50!

How many similar sequences are there that comply to the above written formation law?

(All numbers of such sequences should be natural numbers.)

Write down all the sequences you find!

Questions from the Interview

- What did you think of the problems? Did you enjoy solving them?
- How do you assess the problems? Were they easy, average, or difficult?
- Do you like such problems? Which problem would you not have calculated and why?
- How would you have modified the problems, in order to find them enjoyable?
- Which kind of problems do you like in the mathematics lessons?
- Do you prefer a certain way of solving or tackling problems? If so, were you able to use it to solve problems?
- Describe what mathematics means to you!
- Are you also interested in mathematics (besides school)? If yes, for what? If not, why?
- Describe briefly themes and activities from your mathematics lessons that you enjoy or you do not enjoy and try to explain the reasons why!

NOTE

1. Six is the worst mark in a 1–6 assessment scale usual in German teaching.

REFERENCES

Adey, Philip S., Fairbrother, Robert W., Wiliam, Dylan, Johnson, Barbara, and Jones, Carys. (1999). *A Review of Research Related to Learning Styles and Strategies.* London: King's College, London Centre for the Advancement of Thinking.

Burton, Leone. (1995). Moving Towards a Feminist Epistemology of Mathematics. *Educational Studies in Mathematics,* 28(3), 275–291.

Burton, Leone. (1999). Mathematicians and Their Epistemologies—and the Learning of Mathematics. In Inge Schwank (Ed.), *European Research in Mathematics Education Vol. I* (pp. 87–102). Osnabrück: Forschungsinstitut für Mathematikdidaktik.

Dreyfus, Tommy, and Eisenberg, Theodore. (1996). On Different Facets of Mathematical

Thinking. In Robert Sternberg and Talia Ben-Zeev (Eds.), *The Nature of Mathematical Thinking* (pp. 253–284). Mahwah, NJ: Lawrence Erlbaum.

Fischbein, Efraim. (1987). *Intuition in Science and Mathematics.* Dordrecht: Reidel.

Flick, Uwe. (2000). *Qualitative Forschung.* Reinbek: Rowohlt.

Goos, Merrilyn. (1994). Metacognitive Decision Making and Social Interaction during Paired Problem Solving. *Mathematics Education Research Journal,* 6(2), 144–165.

Goos, Merrilyn, Galbraith, Peter, and Renshaw, Peter. (2000). A Money Problem: A Source of Insight into Problem Solving Action. *International Journal for Mathematics Teaching and Learning,* April 13. Available online at http://www.ex.ac. uk./cimt/ijmtl/ijmenu.htm.

Hadamard, Jacques. (1945). *The Psychology of Invention in the Mathematical Field.* Toronto: Princeton University Press.

Keitel, Christine. (1998). An Introduction: Social Justice and Mathematics Education: Gender, Class, Ethnicity and the Politics of Schooling. In Christine Keitel (Ed.), *Social Justice and Mathematics Education* (pp. v–viii). Berlin: Freie Universität Berlin.

Kolb, David A., Boyatzis, Richard E., and Mainemelis, Charalampos. (2001). Experiential Learning Theory: Previous Research and New Directions. In Robert Sternberg and Li-Fang Zhang (Eds.), *Perspectives on Thinking, Learning, and Cognitive Styles* (pp. 227–247). London: Lawrence Erlbaum.

Riding, Richard. (2001). The Nature and Effects of Cognitive Style. In Robert Sternberg and Li-Fang Zhang (Eds.), *Perspectives on Thinking, Learning, and Cognitive Styles* (pp. 47–72). London: Lawrence Erlbaum.

Saxe, Geoffrey, Dawson, Venus, Fall, Randy, and Howard, Sharon. (1996). Culture and Children's Mathematical Thinking. In Robert Sternberg and Talia Ben-Zeev (Eds.), *The Nature of Mathematical Thinking* (pp. 119–144). Mahwah, NJ: Lawrence Erlbaum.

Schoenfeld, Alan H. (1985). *Mathematical Problem Solving.* New York: Academic Press.

Schoenfeld, Alan H. (1992). Learning to Think Mathematically: Problem Solving, Metacognition, and Sense-making in Mathematics. In Douglas A. Grouws (Ed.), *Handbook for Research on Mathematics Teaching and Learning* (pp. 334–370). New York: Macmillan.

Schoenfeld, Alan H. (1994). *Mathematical Thinking and Problem Solving.* Hillsdale, NJ: Lawrence Erlbaum.

Skemp, Richard. (1987). *The Psychology of Learning Mathematics.* Hillsdale, NJ: Lawrence Erlbaum.

Stebler, Rita. (1999). *Eigenständiges Problemlösen: Zum Umgang mit Schwierigkeiten beim individuellen und paarweisen Lösen mathematischer Problemgeschichten— theoretische Analyse und empirische Erkundungen.* Wien: Lang.

Sternberg, Robert. (1996). What Is Mathematical Thinking? In Robert Sternberg and Talia Ben-Zeev (Eds.), *The Nature of Mathematical Thinking* (pp. 303–318). Mahwah, NJ: Lawrence Erlbaum.

Sternberg, Robert. (1997). *Thinking Styles.* New York: Cambridge University Press.

Sternberg, Robert. (2001a). Epilogue: Another Mysterious Affair at Styles. In Robert Sternberg and Li-Fang Zhang (Eds.), *Perspectives on Thinking, Learning, and Cognitive Styles* (pp. 249–252). London: Lawrence Erlbaum.

Sternberg, Robert. (2001b). Preface. In Robert Sternberg and Li-Fang Zhang (Eds.), *Perspectives on Thinking, Learning, and Cognitive Styles* (pp. vii–x). London: Lawrence Erlbaum.

Sternberg, Robert, and Ben-Zeev, Talia (Eds.). (1996). *The Nature of Mathematical Thinking*. Mahwah, NJ: Lawrence Erlbaum.

Sternberg, Robert, and Grigorenko, Elena. (2001). A Capsule History of Theory and Research on Styles. In Robert Sternberg and Li-Fang Zhang (Eds.), *Perspectives on Thinking, Learning, and Cognitive Styles* (pp. 1–21). London: Lawrence Erlbaum.

Sternberg, Robert, and Zhang, Li-Fang (Eds.). (2001). *Perspectives on Thinking, Learning, and Cognitive Styles*. London: Lawrence Erlbaum.

Strauss, Anselm L., and Corbin, Juliet M. (1990). *Basics of Qualitative Research*. London: Sage.

Tobies, Renate. (1987). Zur Berufungspolitik Felix Kleins. Grundsätzliche Ansichten. *NTM-Schriftenreihe Geschichte, Naturwissenschaft, Technik* (Medizin), 24(2), 43–52.

Wagner, C. Angelika, Uttendorfer-Marek, Ingrid, and Weidle, Renate. (1977). Die Analyse von Unterrichtsstrategien mit der Methode des, "Nachträglich Lauten Denkens" von Lehrern und Schülern zu ihrem unterrichtlichen Handeln. *Unterrichtswissenschaft*, 3, 244–250.

Zhang, Li-Fang, and Sternberg, Robert. (2001). Thinking Styles across Cultures: Their Relationships with Students' Learning. In Robert Sternberg and Li-Fang Zhang (Eds.), *Perspectives on Thinking, Learning, and Cognitive Styles* (pp. 197–226). London: Lawrence Erlbaum.

Chapter 11

Mathematics Participation, Achievement, and Attitudes: What's New in Australia?

Helen J. Forgasz, Gilah C. Leder, and Jan Thomas

INTRODUCTION

In this chapter, we present and discuss recent findings on the participation rates and achievement levels of male and female grade 12 mathematics students in the state of Victoria, Australia. Data gathered from students in a separate study in which current beliefs about the gender stereotyping of mathematics are explored are also presented. Collectively our data challenge some past assumptions that females are disadvantaged with respect to mathematics learning. We argue, however, that it is too simplistic to assume that males are now the educationally disadvantaged group and refer to the broader social context and political climate to support our claim.

Gender equity issues have been on the Australian national educational agenda for more than 25 years. The policy initiatives of the 1980s (e.g., Commonwealth Schools Commission 1987) required state governments to address identified areas of female disadvantage. The resulting initiatives appear to have had some measure of success, as can be seen from data reported in this chapter and by enrollment trends in senior secondary mathematics courses. Many of the trends, especially in advanced courses, are connected to an increased female enrollment (Dekkers, Malone, and de Laeter 2000). In recent years, there has been growing concern that males are now the educationally disadvantaged group. This trend is also apparent in the United Kingdom. The hysteria associated with recent achievement data can be gauged from the following report from the *Guardian*, reprinted in an Australian newspaper: "The education secretary said he would give schools 'ammunition' to tackle the poor performance of boys, amid a wave of concern about the gender gap in education, which is set to be heightened by recent examination results that showed girls achieving more A grades than boys at A-level *for the first time*" (Woodward 2000, p. 4; emphasis added).

In Australia the gender gap in both participation and achievement has a long history. Teese (2000) reported 1947 results showing a pass rate in pure mathematics of 60% for girls and 55% for boys but noted that boys had a much greater level of participation. At the beginning of the 2000s a serious malaise seems to be gripping Australian science that may have serious implications for mathematics education for all students. The professional communities of scientists and mathematicians have increasingly voiced their concerns about the declining numbers of graduate and postgraduate students in the physical sciences and mathematics. They have condemned the lack of employment opportunities open to talented, enthusiastic young researchers who leave the country to take advantage of lucrative opportunities offered elsewhere (Thomas 2000) and have drawn attention, in a variety of publications, to the long-predicted critical shortage of appropriately qualified mathematics and science teachers (Jones 1998; Thomas 2000). Only recently have national and state governments acknowledged this situation. However the depth of the problem, and a shortfall in appropriately qualified mathematics teachers in many Western nations, suggests that this will not be easily solved even if immediate action is taken. This has long-term implications for access to careers dependent on mathematics.

In this chapter, we focus on mathematics and related careers and present data on the participation rates and performance levels of grade 12 students enrolled in mathematics subjects in the years 1994 to 1999 in one of Australia's most populous states, Victoria. The data are examined in conjunction with recent findings from a study in which a new instrument was used to determine grade 7–10 students' beliefs about the gender stereotyping of mathematics. Within the wider social and political context in which the data were gathered, our interpretation of the findings challenge the assumptions underpinning some claims of male educational disadvantage.

The Social, Political, and Educational Context for This Study

In recent years in Australia, as in the United Kingdom (Weiner, Arnot, and David 1997), when high-stakes examination results have been made public, newspaper headlines commonly proclaim that "girls are (now) outperforming males" (e.g., Milburn 2000; Zevenbergen 1998). Do the facts support the inference made that girls are now more successful educationally than boys? In Victoria, females, on average, have outscored males in grade 12 results since 1944 (Commonwealth Schools Commission 1975). What is different from the past is that females are now achieving higher average grades than males in traditionally male disciplines including mathematics and physics. However, as shown later in the chapter, a higher proportion of males than females continue to be awarded the highest grade in mathematics. Based on current participation rates in mathematics at the school level, at the tertiary level, and in the workforce, and on well-publicized differences in earnings capacity (Carson 2000; Maslen 1998; see also Figure 11.2), we contend that females clearly have some way to go to benefit from their improved mathematics achievement levels.

Recent controversial Australian reports and inquiries into boys' education (e.g., O'Doherty 1994; Standing Committee on Employment, Education and Workplace Relations 2000) have drawn attention to aspects of school life, educational outcomes, and societal expectations that appear deleterious to boys' learning and future lifestyles. For example, compared to girls, boys are reported to have poorer attitudes to learning, higher representation in remedial programs, greater literacy difficulties, more behavior problems, and higher rates of school suspensions; to choose more traditional and narrower curriculum options; to be reluctant to be seen to excel except in sport; and to display a detrimental overestimation of their abilities.

Factual distortions, however, have fueled the "what about the boys?" debate in academic circles and in the public sphere (e.g., Ludowyke and Scanlon 1997; Messina 1997). In some quarters, reactions have been particularly negative and destructive. It has been suggested that the emphasis on girls' educational needs in recent years was not only at the expense of boys but that boys regressed educationally as a consequence. Few would dispute that there are some pressing issues with respect to boys' education. However, it is wrong to imply that they have arisen largely as a consequence of efforts directed toward redressing clearly identified female disadvantage. The vast majority of the boys' issues raised are not new (see Francis 1977). They have only recently received serious and consistent attention (e.g., O'Doherty 1994). In the past, the areas in which girls outperformed boys were not considered particularly important, nor did society seriously challenge boys' behaviors. Hence, these *boys' issues* received scant mainstream research or media attention. Connell highlighted the critical role of the educational process in reproducing masculinities and the importance of curriculum in addressing "the diversity of masculinities, and the intersections of gender with race, class and nationality" (1995, p. 239).

In the United Kingdom, similar concerns about boys' disadvantages have been voiced. A complex set of school-related and external factors linked to male underachievement in the British General Certificate of Secondary Education (GCSE) was identified by Younger and Warrington (1996) and included teacher attitudes, concerns with image and masculinity, acceptable social behavior, peer pressure, and parental expectation.

The media can be strong shapers of public opinion (Leder 1995). What do people—including students and their parents—infer from headlines proclaiming girls' superiority in mathematics? If the public believes it true that mathematics is no longer a predominantly male domain, is there research evidence that such previously strongly held beliefs have changed? Taken together, what can be deduced from trends in contemporary enrollment and achievement data in mathematics? How do students perceive mathematics and themselves as learners of mathematics? What are the postschool options of males and females in pertinent mathematics and science-related career paths? How well qualified are male and female school leavers to embark on tertiary studies and careers that require a sound mathematical background? We set out to gather the necessary data to provide some answers to these questions.

Beliefs about the Stereotyping of Mathematics

Recent research studies (see, e.g., Forgasz, Leder, and Gardner 1999; Watt 2000) have indicated that many people, both males and females, reject the notion that mathematics is a male domain and do so because they believe that women are higher achievers in mathematics than men. These changing perceptions raise questions about the conceptual frameworks that underpin some common attitude scales, including the Mathematics as a Male Domain (MD) subscale of the Fennema-Sherman Mathematics Attitude Scales (Fennema and Sherman 1976), an instrument frequently used to measure attitudes toward mathematics and in research on gender issues. When the scale was developed, there was no apparent allowance for beliefs that mathematics might be considered a *female* domain. This assumption was consistent with prevailing Western societal views of the 1970s but may no longer be true today (Forgasz, Leder, and Gardner 1999).

Two forms of a new survey instrument have been developed and trialed: Mathematics as a Gendered Domain and Who and Mathematics. The aim of both versions of the instrument was to measure the extent to which students stereotype mathematics as a gendered domain—that is, the extent to which they believe that mathematics may be more suited to males or to females or be regarded as a gender-neutral domain.

An important difference between the two versions was in the response formats used. For the Mathematics as a Gendered Domain scale, a traditional Likert-type scoring format was adopted—students indicated the extent to which they agreed (or disagreed) with each statement presented. A 5-point scoring system was used—strongly disagree (SD) to strongly agree (SA). A score of 1 was assigned to the SD response and a score of 5 to SA. This version of the instrument consisted of 48 items. There were three subscales: Mathematics as a Male Domain, Mathematics as a Female Domain, and Mathematics as a Neutral Domain. The 16 items making up each subscale were presented in a random order.

An innovative response format was adopted for the Who and Mathematics version of the instrument. Thirty statements were presented. For each statement, students had to select one of the following responses:

BD—boys definitely more likely than girls
BP—boys probably more likely than girls
ND—no difference between boys and girls
GP—girls probably more likely than boys
GD—girls definitely more likely than boys

In developing the items, we drew on the Fennema-Sherman Mathematics Attitudes Scales and on previous research findings about gender issues in mathematics learning. We devised items related to ability, career, general attitude, environment, peers, effort, and task; trialed the items extensively; and rejected items that were unsatisfactory psychometrically or in other ways. Subsequently we administered the questionnaires to approximately 1,600 students from eight schools situated in the metropolitan and country regions of Victoria. At each school, approximately half of the students completed each version of the questionnaire. In the next section we report gender trends elicited by the Who and Mathematics instrument. Comparable findings were obtained from the Mathematics as a Gendered Domain scale but are not reported here.

THE STUDY

The Who and Mathematics Instrument

Sample Size. The instrument was administered to 861 Victorian high school students (402 females, 436 males, 23 unknown) equally distributed across grade levels 7 to 10.

Analyses. In order to interpret the response patterns to items, the categories were scored as follows: BD = 1, BP = 2, ND = 3, GP = 4, and GD = 5.

Statistical analyses included the following:

- Mean scores for each item were calculated. Thus, a mean score < 3 meant that, on average, the students believed that boys were more likely than girls to match the wording of the item, and mean scores > 3 meant that they believed girls were more likely than boys to do so.

- One-sample t-tests were conducted to test whether mean scores were significantly different from 3. Items for which students essentially believed that there was no difference between girls and boys with respect to the wording of items were thus identifiable.

- Independent groups t-tests, by gender, were used to explore for gender differences in the responses to each item.

Results. Predicted directions of students' responses based on previous research findings (Pred) are shown in Table 11.1. Also shown are the findings from the present study (Find).

The Entire Cohort. As can be seen in Table 11.1, there were only eight items for which the responses were consistent with previous findings. These items were largely related to the learning environment and to peers. For example, boys were believed to be asked more questions by the teacher (Item 3), to distract others from their work (Item 16), to tease both boys (Item 21) and girls (Item 30) who did well in mathematics, and to like using computers to work on mathematics problems (Item 24). That students' beliefs on so many items were inconsistent with previous findings implies a fairly recent change in gendered

Table 11.1

Predictions Based on Previous Research (Pred) and Findings from the Present Study (*Find*)

ITEM	Pred	*Find*	ITEM	Pred	*Find*
1 Mathematics is their favorite subject	M	*F*	16 Distract other students from their mathematics work	M	*M*
2* Think it is important to understand the work in mathematics	F	*F*	17* Get the wrong answers in mathematics	F	*M*
3* Are asked more questions by the mathematics teacher	M	*M*	18 Find mathematics easy	M	*F*
4* Give up when they find a · mathematics problem is too difficult	F	*M*	19* Parents think it is important for them to study mathematics	M	*nd*
5* Have to work hard to do well in mathematics	F	*M*	20* Need more help in mathematics	F	*M*
6 Enjoy mathematics	M	*F*	21 Tease boys if they are good at mathematics	M	*M*
7* Care about doing well in mathematics	M/F	*F*	22* Worry if they do not do well in mathematics	M/F	*F*
8* Think they did not work hard enough if do not do well in mathematics	M	*F*	23* Are not good at mathematics	F	*M*
9* Parents would be disappointed if they did not do well in mathematics	M	*F*	24 Like using computers to work on mathematics problems	M	*M*
10* Need mathematics to maximize future employment opportunities	M	*M*	25 Mathematics teachers spend more time with them	M	*nd*
11 Like challenging mathematics problems	M	*nd*	26* Consider mathematics to be boring	F	*M*
12 Are encouraged to do well by the mathematics teacher	M	*nd*	27* Find mathematics difficult	F	*M*
13 Mathematics teachers think they will do well	M	*F*	28 Get on with their work in class	F	*F*
14* Think mathematics will be important in their adult life	M	*F*	29* Think mathematics is interesting	M	*F*
15* Expect to do well in mathematics	M	*F*	30* Tease girls if they are good at mathematics	M	*M*

Notes: Items for which one-sample t-tests revealed that the mean score for the entire cohort was not a statistically significant difference from 3 are shown as **nd** in the findings column; using independent groups t-tests, statistically significant gender differences in mean scores were found for items marked with an asterisk (see Figure 11.1 also).

perceptions related to mathematics education. In the past, boys were generally believed to have more natural ability for mathematics than girls and were considered to enjoy mathematics and find it more interesting than did girls.

The findings reveal that, on average, students now consider boys more likely than girls to give up when they find a problem too challenging (Item 4), to find mathematics difficult (Items 27 and 18), and to need additional help (Item 20). Girls were considered more likely than boys to enjoy mathematics (Item 6) and to find mathematics interesting (Item 29).

Gender Differences. We also analyzed the mean scores for each item by gender. Male and female students were consistent in their beliefs about which group (boys or girls) was more likely to match the wording for the majority of the items (22 out of 30). The data are graphically illustrated in Figure 11.1. Note that the items for which "no difference" between girls and boys were found for the entire cohort are shown in Figure 11.1 (and in Table 11.1) with "(nd)" beside the item number (Items 11, 12, 19, and 25).

It can also be seen in Figure 11.1 that statistically significant gender differences were noted on 19 items (2–5, 7–10, 14, 15, 17, 19, 20, 22, 23, 26, 27, 29, and 30)—the items are marked with an asterisk in Figure 11.1 (and also in Table 11.1). For many of these items, the gender differences found indicated that although both male and female respondents held beliefs in the same "direction," one group or the other held a more extreme view with respect to particular items. As an example, consider Item 30—"Tease girls if they are good at mathematics." The bars in Figure 11.1 indicate that the female respondents believed more strongly than did the male respondents that boys are more likely than girls to do the teasing (both means < 3).

For Item 19—"Parents think it is important for them to study mathematics"— the mean score for the entire cohort was not statistically significantly different from 3—indicated by (nd) next to the item number. However, a statistically significant gender difference in mean scores was found revealing that males responded in the "boys" direction (mean score < 3) and females in the "girls" direction (mean score > 3).

In summary, the changing beliefs expressed by the students in our sample about the importance of mathematics and perceptions of learners of mathematics were elicited by a carefully devised and trialed instrument that contained new items as well as, where appropriate, items used and validated in earlier work. The attitudes and values elicited by the students appear to challenge historical stereotypes about mathematics and perceptions of learners of mathematics and appear consistent with the now prevalent perceptions of boys as the educationally disadvantaged group. In the next sections we explore current patterns of enrollment in various educational settings as well as occupational pathways and rewards.

Who Studies What?

Across Australia today statistics indicate that more females than males now complete grade 12 and participate in higher education. The apparent retention rate to grade 12 in 1998 was 71.6%: 77.7% for females and 65.9% for males (Australian Bureau of Statistics [ABS] 1999c).

In 1997 there were 659,000 students enrolled in undergraduate and postgraduate higher education courses: 358,700 females (54.4%) and 300,200 males (ABS 1999a). In the Vocational Education and Training (VET) sector in June 1997, however, there were 1.41 million "clients": 733,000 (52%) males and 676,700 females. There has also been a decline in tertiary mathematics enrollments, particularly in higher-degree courses, and mathematics departments are under strain (Forgasz 1999).

Figure 11.1
Who and Mathematics: Mean Scores by Gender for Grade 7–10 Students

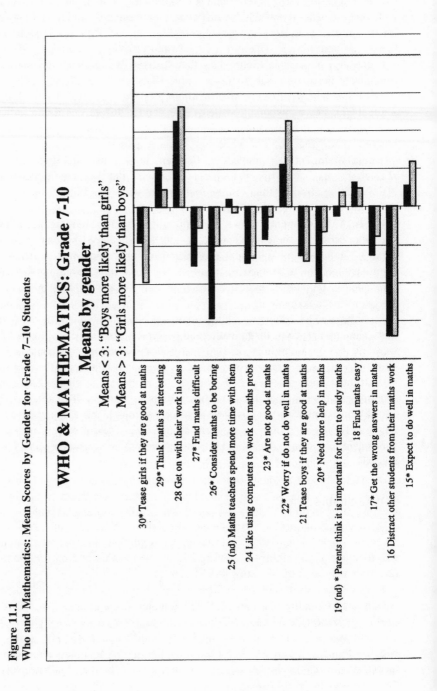

WHO & MATHEMATICS: Grade 7-10
Means by gender

Means < 3: "Boys more likely than girls"
Means > 3: "Girls more likely than boys"

30* Tease girls if they are good at maths

29* Think maths is interesting

28 Get on with their work in class

27* Find maths difficult

26* Consider maths to be boring

25 (nd) Maths teachers spend more time with them

24 Like using computers to work on maths probs

23* Are not good at maths

22* Worry if do not do well in maths

21 Tease boys if they are good at maths

20* Need more help in maths

19 (nd) * Parents think it is important for them to study maths

18 Find maths easy

17* Get the wrong answers in maths

16 Distract other students from their maths work

15* Expect to do well in maths

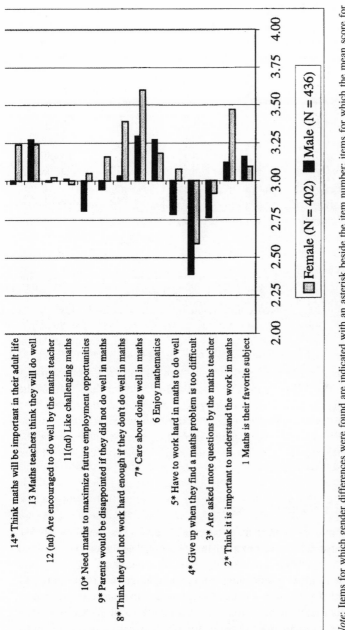

14* Think maths will be important in their adult life

13 Maths teachers think they will do well

12 (nd) Are encouraged to do well by the maths teacher

11(nd) Like challenging maths

10* Need maths to maximize future employment opportunities

9* Parents would be disappointed if they did not do well in maths

8* Think they did not work hard enough if they don't do well in maths

7* Care about doing well in maths

6 Enjoy mathematics

5* Have to work hard in maths to do well

4* Give up when they find a maths problem is too difficult

3* Are asked more questions by the maths teacher

2* Think it is important to understand the work in maths

1 Maths is their favorite subject

2.00   2.25   2.50   2.75   3.00   3.25   3.50   3.75   4.00

☐ Female (N = 402)   ■ Male (N = 436)

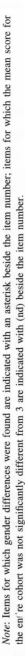

Note: Items for which gender differences were found are indicated with an asterisk beside the item number; items for which the mean score for the enf're cohort was not significantly different from 3 are indicated with (nd) beside the item number.

Figure 11.2
Percentage of Female Enrollments in Victorian Certificate of Education (VCE)
Mathematics Subjects, 1994–1999

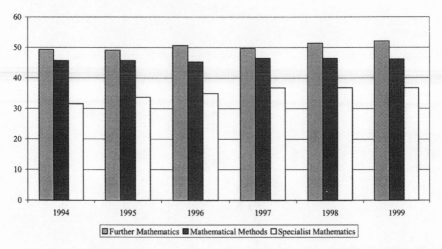

Gender differences in participation rates in some disciplines persist, however. At school, in higher education, and in the VET sector, more males are enrolled in science and technology-related courses and more females in the humanities and social sciences. Enrollment data, for the period 1994–1999, for the high-stake, final year of school examination—the Victorian Certificate of Education (VCE)—are also instructive. From 1994 to 1999, about 54% of all VCE students were female. An analysis of the enrollment patterns for the three mathematics subjects offered revealed that in each year (1994–1999) fewer than 53% of the cohort in each subject was female. In other words, compared to their proportion in the overall cohort, more males than females were studying each of the mathematics subjects. For the most challenging subject, specialist mathematics, the proportion of females was least; it was highest for the least challenging subject, further mathematics. See Figure 11.2.

Who Reaps the Rewards of Education?

In educational and employment domains considered high status in Australia, males continue to dominate and prosper. In Australia, legislation was enacted during the 1970s and 1980s to protect against discrimination, including sex discrimination. The workplace was included, and employers are required to pay men and women equally according to the job done. Yet there is a high disparity in earnings favoring males. Among full-time adult workers in Australia in May 1998 "the ratio of female to male average weekly total earnings for full-time adult employees was 80.6%. It was highest for the Professionals occupation group (85.0%) and lowest for Tradespersons and related workers (72.3%)" (ABS

Figure 11.3
Average Weekly Total Earnings for Full-Time Adult Employees by Occupation Group and Gender

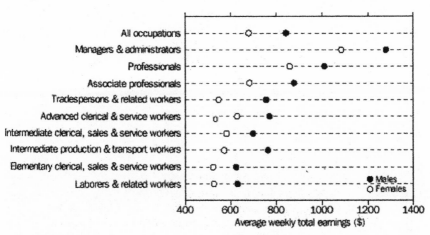

Source: ABS 1999b.

1999b). The average weekly total earnings for full-time adult employees by occupation group and gender are shown in Figure 11.3.

Males work more overtime hours than females. This, however, only partially explains the discrepancy in pay levels. Among graduates moving from their courses into their chosen career areas, males' commencement rates are generally higher than females'. The commencement (annual) salaries (in Aus$) of 1998 graduates are reported in *Grad Stats* (Grad Stats 1999). For the 23 fields listed, the average salary for males (M) was $32,500 and for females (F), $30,000. Fifteen of the listed fields could be classified as mathematics and science related. Of these, males' commencement salaries were higher than females' in nine areas including: *Mathematics*: M: $35,500, F: $33,000; *Physical Science*: M: $33,700, F: $31,700; *Medicine*: M: $45,000, F: $42,000; *Optometry*: M: $42,200, F: $39,200; *Dentistry*: M: $48,000, F: $42,000. Females had higher commencement salaries in four fields, for example, *Earth Sciences*: M: $33,000, F: $37,000; *Engineering*: M: $35,000, F: $36,000; *Pharmacy*: M: $24,000, F: $24,800. In *Computer Science* ($35,000) and *Biological Science* ($30,000), the commencement salaries were the same for males and females. The financial rewards for women in the Earth Sciences and Engineering are of interest. These have traditionally been male-oriented disciplines both at the tertiary level and in the workplace. Young women who have taken up these areas have tended to be exceptionally resilient and high achievers. Employers now seem to be recognizing, in line with current community expectations, that women should be part of all professions. There is little evidence that this is having much effect on employment in the university sector where Ph.D. studies are required. This was documented for advanced-level mathematics in a report that showed almost equal numbers of men and women at the Honors level but men dominating after that (National Committee for Mathematics 1996).

In contemporary Australia, it would appear that despite females' readiness to stay at school longer and to gain entry into tertiary studies in higher numbers than males, participation rates in mathematics and science-related courses are higher for males, particularly as the level of the degree pursued increases, and inequities persist in the financial rewards of the educational enterprise. Can these discrepancies be explained by school performance in mathematics, so often used as a critical filter to educational and career options?

Who Shines in Mathematics?

To explore this question, we again turn to the VCE examination, to which reference has already been made in an earlier section of this chapter. A brief overview of the VCE offers a useful context for our next set of data.

Background to the VCE. The VCE was introduced for English and mathematics in 1991 at grade 11 in all Victorian secondary schools, after 10 pilot schools had trialed the new curricula in 1990. By 1992 the VCE was fully implemented into schools across Victoria. From its inception, the VCE was envisaged as a two-year course that spanned grades 11 and 12, served as a common credential for completing secondary school, and thus replaced the collection of alternate certificates that had evolved over time to cater to students with diverse aspirations and abilities. Its assessment format symbolized and reinforced real structural changes in postcompulsory education in Victoria. Briefly, the VCE was expected to encourage innovative teaching practices at all levels of secondary school through a broadening of the assessment tasks and to provide an extensive curriculum to allow all students, not just those intending to go on to tertiary education, an opportunity to remain within the mainstream school and examination structure. Consistent with this philosophy, a wide range of mathematics subjects was initially offered.

As reported by Leder, Brew, and Rowley (1999), a careful examination of the VCE mathematics data for 1992 revealed a significant link between the format of the Common Assessment Task (CAT) and student performance on that task. Specifically, for the VCE mathematics subjects available that year, females, on average, performed better than males on the two newly introduced CATs, which were longer term and open-ended, required a sustained commitment particularly out of school hours, had a much stronger verbal component for their presentation, and were initially assessed by teachers within the school. On the other hand, males, on average, did better on the two rigidly timed, more traditional CATs done under strictly supervised examination conditions. Boys' consistently poorer performance on particular assessment tasks attracted considerable attention.

The introduction of the VCE, and its innovative CATs that required sustained effort in and out of school, met widespread resistance. Two waves of major modifications in the curriculum and assessment format occurred. These changes resulted in a movement back toward the pre-VCE mathematics curriculum—a much reduced and more hierarchical subject selection with a greater emphasis on examinations. By 1994, the VCE mathematics subjects available to students had been reduced from six to three. Assessment tasks were changed so that two traditional, strictly timed tests contributed two thirds of the final mark in each of these subjects, with an extended task—an investigative project—contributing the remaining third. This last task continued to be teacher assessed, on the basis of assessment advice and externally provided marking schemes (Leigh-Lancaster 2000). Between 1994 and 1999 there were relatively few changes to the mathematics subjects offered in the VCE and to the assessment of these subjects. This allowed a careful examination of overall patterns of participation and performance by gender over this period.

Performance Data—An Average Picture. To accommodate different distributions of results across all subjects offered in the VCE, a Study Score, with a mean of about 30 and a standard deviation of about 7, is calculated for each VCE subject. Study Scores are used to determine students' tertiary entrance scores (known as ENTERs), which are used for selection into the various tertiary courses. Study Scores, by gender, are not available to the public. We requested and obtained relevant data from the Board of Studies (BOS), Victoria, Australia.

For each of the VCE mathematics subjects at the grade 12 level offered in the years 1994–1999, the three separate CAT scores were used to calculate the Study Scores. BOS (Victoria) publishes results for each CAT using grades (A^+, A, B^+, B, ... E, UG [ungraded], and total—see Figure 11.5) and the proportions of male and female students obtaining each grade. The mean raw scores for each CAT are not publicly available. These data were requested and received from BOS (Victoria).

The three VCE grade 12 mathematics subjects offered in the period 1994–1999 were:

- Further Mathematics—the least demanding option
- Mathematical Methods—the subject listed most frequently as a prerequisite for tertiary courses
- Specialist Mathematics—the most demanding (calculus-based) option

Performance data for each of the three VCE mathematics subjects for the period 1994–1999 are shown in Table 11.2. Study Score data are presented, as well as mean raw scores for each of the CATs converted into percentages for ease of comparison since the maximum possible raw score for particular CATs was not the same each year.

The Study Scores shown in Table 11.2 reveal the following:

Table 11.2
Mean Study Scores and Mean CAT Scores in Grade 12 VCE Mathematics
Subjects by Gender, 1994–1999

YEAR	SUBJECT	CAT 1 (%)		CAT 2 (%)		CAT 3 (%)		STUDY SCORE[1]	
		M	F	M	F	M	F	M	F
1994	Further Mathematics	54.2	61.5	38.1	38.8	32.9	33.2	29.28	30.76
	Mathematical Methods	72.0	75.5	64.4	63.6	53.3	49.3	30.14	30.17
	Specialist Mathematics	77.1	79.1	58.2	63.6	43.4	45.7	29.77	30.53
1995	Further Mathematics	50.7	57.6	50.0	51.6	37.9	37.4	29.36	30.64
	Mathematical Methods	64.1	67.6	56.2	54.8	36.5	32.6	30.04	29.97
	Specialist Mathematics	75.9	76.5	51.2	52.5	39.2	42.3	29.79	30.40
1996	Further Mathematics	58.4	59.9	50.0	52.2	42.6	44.5	29.03	30.88
	Mathematical Methods	64.0	66.0	50.9	48.9	42.0	38.9	30.10	29.89
	Specialist Mathematics	76.0	77.8	50.8	51.8	42.7	42.6	29.88	30.21
1997	Further Mathematics	51.2	59.9	41.4	42.6	33.6	37.0	30.13	30.94
	Mathematical Methods	68.0	70.4	55.8	54.3	44.5	40.7	30.13	29.86
	Specialist Mathematics	79.3	80.6	45.1	45.5	43.9	44.0	29.93	30.11
1998	Further Mathematics	52.6	61.9	46.1	48.6	55.8	41.6	30.03	30.82
	Mathematical Methods	65.0	67.0	47.6	45.9	41.7	40.0	30.03	29.98
	Specialist Mathematics	79.1	81.1	51.8	52.8	38.8	39.1	29.83	30.30
1999	Further Mathematics	56.4	64.6	51.7	53.5	36.6	38.2	29.37	30.92
	Mathematical Methods	69.3	72.2	55.8	55.1	38.1	36.6	29.90	30.14
	Specialist Mathematics	72.7	74.9	49.4	50.5	40.2	41.9	29.78	30.39

[1]To two decimal places to capture small differences masked if data are presented to one decimal place.

- Further Mathematics—girls outperformed boys in each of the years from 1994 to 1999
- Mathematical Methods—very little difference in performance of girls and boys, with the exceptions of 1994 and 1999, boys did slightly better than girls
- Specialist Mathematics—girls performed slightly better than boys in each of the years from 1994 to 1999

Entry to university in general, and to specific courses in particular, has become highly competitive. In high-demand courses very small differences in tertiary entrance scores can affect success in tertiary selection. Study Scores, which determine the overall tertiary entry score, are critical. It is noteworthy, then, that for Mathematical Methods, the mathematics subject most frequently cited as a prerequisite study for tertiary courses, there were no consistent differences in favor of boys or girls across the six years. For Further Mathematics, the least difficult VCE mathematics study and the subject with the highest female participation rate, females' mean Study Scores were consistently higher than those of males. A similar pattern of higher mean Study Scores for females was found for Specialist Mathematics, the most demanding of the VCE mathematics options and, coincidentally, the one with the lowest female participation rate.

The data in Table 11.2 reveal the following with respect to the three CATs in each VCE mathematics subject:

- Further Mathematics—girls consistently do better than boys on CAT 1 (extended task) and CAT 2 (examination: multiple choice—facts, skills, and applications), with an inconsistent pattern for CAT 3 (examination: answers require worked solutions to analytical questions)
- Mathematical Methods—girls' mean scores are consistently higher than those of boys for CAT 1; for CATs 2 and 3 the pattern is reversed, with boys, on average, consistently scoring higher than girls
- Specialist Mathematics—girls, on average, consistently perform better than boys on each of the three CATs, with the results for CAT 3 in 1996 being the only exception.

Thus, for each subject, and in each year, girls do better than boys on CAT 1—an extended assessment task, done partly at school and partly at home. On CAT 2, a timed multiple-choice examination, boys do better than girls in Mathematical Methods—the subject consistently taken by most boys. For the other two mathematics subjects, girls do better than boys on CAT 2. A complex pattern of gender differences was found across the subjects for CAT 3. The pattern varied for Further Mathematics, with boys doing better in some years, girls in others. In Mathematical Methods, boys consistently did better than girls on CAT 3 (an examination with questions requiring extended written answers), while girls performed better than boys in Specialist Mathematics CAT 3 each year, except in 1996.

Performance Data—The Extremes. It is also helpful in this analysis to consider the distribution of scores within the two groups. This can be done conveniently by inspecting the standard deviations as a measure of spread of the Study Scores for females and males in each of the three VCE mathematics subjects. The data for Specialist Mathematics for each of the years from 1994 to 1999 are shown in Figure 11.4. A higher standard deviation for males than for females was also found for Further Mathematics and for Mathematical Methods and for each of the CATs in each of the three mathematics subjects for each of the years from 1994 to 1999.

The data in Figure 11.4 indicate that proportionally more males than females are likely to obtain extreme scores, both the highest and the lowest; that is, proportionally more males than females are likely to perform very well and overly poorly, at least as indicated by standard deviation, a measure of spread.

Figure 11.4
Specialist Mathematics: Standard Deviations of Study Scores by Gender, 1994–1999

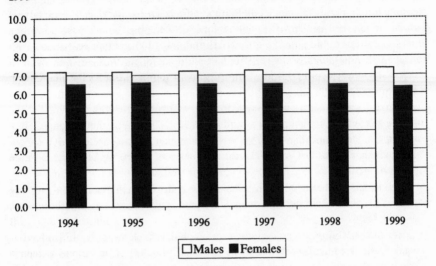

☐Males ■Females

Consider, for example, the CAT results by grade obtained (A⁺ to E) for males and females in Mathematical Methods in 1997 that are shown in Figure 11.5. It can be seen that for each of the three CATs there was a higher proportion of males gaining an A⁺ grade. In that year, the mean score for females was higher than for males on CAT 1, although the males' mean scores for CATs 2 and 3 were higher than females'.

In summary, it would appear that females' achievements in grade 12 level VCE mathematics subjects are generally superior to males', at least when mean scores are considered.

CONCLUSION

The statistical significance of many of the gender differences in stereotyping of dimensions of mathematics learning, identified from the Who and Mathematics instrument, warrants some generalizations of the findings beyond the specific sample in the study. However, further research is needed to determine to what extent the findings are replicated in other Australian states, among subgroups of the Australian school population (e.g., extremely high achievers, students from a non-English-speaking or socioeconomically disadvantaged background) and among students in other societies around the world.

As noted earlier, females remain at school longer, participate in greater numbers in tertiary studies generally, and outperform males on average in school-level mathematics. In what can be considered a part of the *backlash* against feminism and its achievements, these results have been interpreted to mean that

Figure 11.5
1997 Mathematical Methods CATs 1, 2, and 3 Results by Grade Obtained:
Percentages of Males and Females

1997 Mathematical Methods CAT 1

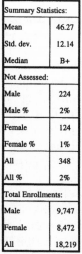

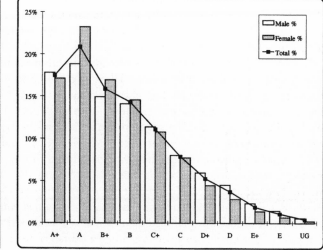

1997 Mathematical Methods CAT 2

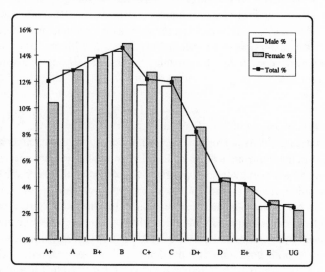

Figure 11.5 (continued)

1997 Mathematical Methods CAT 3

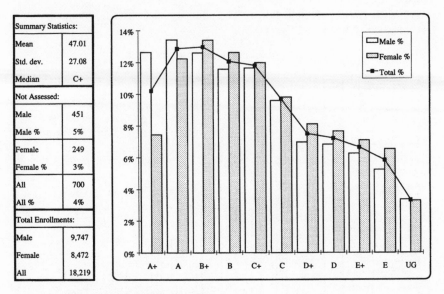

Summary Statistics:	
Mean	47.01
Std. dev.	27.08
Median	C+
Not Assessed:	
Male	451
Male %	5%
Female	249
Female %	3%
All	700
All %	4%
Total Enrollments:	
Male	9,747
Female	8,472
All	18,219

Source: Extracted from Board of Studies 1998.

males are now the disadvantaged group with respect to mathematics education. Yet male dominance in the mathematics and physical science fields and related careers seems to persist.

There are many disadvantaged students in mathematics education in Australia. Teese (2000) showed the extent to which socioeconomic and school-related factors can affect performance. The VCE data highlight the interaction between mode of assessment and student performance. The initiatives taken in the 1980s did influence the participation of girls but not of all girls. Students' perceptions about gender and mathematics learning also appear to be changing. Naive views that males are now a disadvantaged group will do little to alleviate the problems. Difficulties experienced by this group must, however, be confronted. At the same time it is important to address some of the bigger issues that affect the participation and achievement of both males and females. Critical to this is solving the problem of appropriately qualified teachers at every level from early childhood to university. Like many countries, Australia is facing an economic divide in terms of access to a quality mathematics education, which has more to do with the interactions of gender, social, ethnic, and socioeconomic factors than with gender alone. Ill-informed reports of male disadvantage divert focus from more important debates.

It is clear that female disadvantage in mathematics still exists within the university sector, the next generation of academics, and in related professional spheres. Unless there is action to address females' lower participation rates in school-level mathematics courses, in Ph.D.s, and in postdoctoral positions, mathematics will remain essentially a male domain. The current state of university mathematics (Thomas 2000) does little to encourage women's participation, but there also appear to be other barriers that need to be identified and addressed.

REFERENCES

Australian Bureau of Statistics (ABS). (1999a). *Education and Training in Australia* (ABS Catalogue No. 4224.0). Canberra: ABS.

Australian Bureau of Statistics (ABS). (1999b). *Employee Earnings and Hours, Australia May 1998* (ABS Catalogue No. 6306.0). Canberra: ABS.

Australian Bureau of Statistics (ABS). (1999c). *Schools Australia 1998* (ABS Catalogue No. 4221.0). Canberra: ABS.

Board of Studies. (1998). *Statistical Information Victorian Certificate of Education Assessment Program 1997* (CD-ROM). Carlton, Victoria: Author.

Carson, Andrea. (2000). Female Pay Scales Fail to Keep Up. *The Age*, 3, May 12.

Commonwealth Schools Commission. (1975). *Girls, Schools and Society*. Canberra: Author.

Commonwealth Schools Commission. (1987). *A National Policy for the Education of Girls in Australian Schools*. Canberra: Author.

Connell, Robert W. (1995). *Masculinities*. St. Leonards, Australia: Allen and Unwin.

Dekkers, John, Malone, John, and de Laeter, John. (2000). Mathematics Enrolments in Australian Upper Secondary Schools: Trends and Implications. In Jack Bana and Anne Chapman (Eds.), *Mathematics Education beyond 2000* (1: 220–227). Perth: Mathematics Education Research Group of Australasia.

Forgasz, Helen J. (1999). Challenges Facing Tertiary Mathematics: Lecturers' Views. *Australian Senior Mathematics Journal*, 13(1), 26–33.

Forgasz, Helen J., Leder, Gilah C., and Gardner, Paul L. (1999). The Fennema-Sherman "Mathematics as a Male Domain" Scale Re-examined. *Journal for Research in Mathematics Education*, 30(3), 342–348.

Francis, Babette. (1977). *Committee on Equal Opportunity in Schools: Minority Report*. Melbourne: Government Printer.

Grad Stats. (1999). Graduate Starting Salaries. *Grad Stats*, 4, 5–8. Available online at http://www.gradlink.edu.au/gradlink/studfrm3.htm.

Jones, Carolyn. (1998). Teacher Supply Crisis Is Looming. *The Age*, 3, October 28.

Leder, Gilah C. (1995). Learning Mathematics: The Importance of (Social) Context. *The New Zealand Mathematics Magazine*, 32(3), 27–40.

Leder, Gilah C., Brew, Christine, and Rowley, Glenn. (1999). Gender Differences in Mathematics Achievement—Here Today and Gone Tomorrow? In Gabriele Kaiser, Eduardo Luna, and Ian Huntley (Eds.), *International Comparisons in Mathematics Education* (pp. 213–224). London: Falmer Press.

Leder, Gilah C., and Forgasz, Helen J. (2000). *Mathematics: Behind the Stereotypes*. Paper presented at ICME9 (Gender and Mathematics Working Group), Tokyo, July–August.

Leigh-Lancaster, David. (2000). An Overview of Coursework Assessment-VCE Mathematics Units 3 and 4. *Vinculum*, 37(2), 4–9.

Ludowyke, Jeremy, and Scanlon, John. (1997). *Improving the School Performance of*

Boys. North Melbourne, Victoria: Victorian Association of State Secondary Principals.

Maslen, Geoff. (1998). The New Professionals. *The Bulletin*, November 17, 21–24.

Messina, Alex. (1997). Boys Trail Further Behind in VCE. *The Age*, July 7, A3.

Milburn, Caroline. (2000). Alarm Grows at Student Fail Rates. *The Age*, 1 and 8, August 5.

National Committee for Mathematics. (1996). *Mathematical Sciences: Adding to Australia*. Canberra: Australian Government Publishing Service.

O'Doherty, Stephen. (1994). *Inquiry into Boys' Education 1994. Challenges & Opportunities: A Discussion Paper*. Sydney: Ministry of Education, Training and Youth Affairs, NSW.

Standing Committee on Employment, Education and Workplace Relations. (2000). *Inquiry into the Education of Boys*. Available online at http://www.aph.gov.au/house/committee/edt/eofb/index.htm.

Teese, Richard. (2000). *Academic Success & Social Power*. Melbourne: Melbourne University Press.

Thomas, Jan. (2000). *Mathematical Sciences in Australia: Looking for a Future*. Canberra: Federation of Australian Scientific and Technological Societies.

Watt, Helen M.G. (2000). Exploring Perceived Personal and Social Gender Stereotypes of Maths with Secondary Students: An Explanation for Continued Gender Differences in Participation? Paper presented at the annual conference of the Australian Association for Research in Education, Sydney, December.

Weiner, Gaby, Arnot, Madeleine, and David, Miriam. (1997). Is the Future Female? Female Success, Male Disadvantage, and Changing Gender Patterns in Education. In Albert H. Halsey, Hugh Lauder, Phillip Brown, and Amy Stuart Wells (Eds.), *Education, Economy, Culture and Society* (pp. 620–630). Oxford: Oxford University Press.

Woodward, Will. (2000). UK Secretary Acts on Gender Imbalance. *Education Age*, 4, August 30.

Younger, Mike, and Warrington, Molly. (1996). Differential Achievement of Girls and Boys at GCSE: Some Observations from the Perspective of One School. *British Journal of Sociology of Education*, 17(3), 299–313.

Zevenbergen, Robyn. (1998). Gender, Media, and Conservative Politics. In Christine Keitel (Ed.), *Social Justice and Mathematics Education. Gender, Class, Ethnicity and the Politics of Schooling* (pp. 59–68). Berlin, Germany: Freie Universität Berlin.

Part III

Computers and Mathematics Learning

Chapter 12

Toys for Boys?

Leigh Wood, Dubravka Viskic, and Peter Petocz

INTRODUCTION

The teaching and learning of mathematics are increasingly dependent on technology. Computer programs have become an integral part of mathematics education at all levels but most especially at the tertiary and pretertiary levels. Graphing packages are widely used at the secondary level, as are those that investigate the foundations of calculus, such as A Graphic Approach to the Calculus (Tall, Blokland, and Kok 1985). At the tertiary level, computer algebra systems such as Mathematica and Maple have become essential tools for university mathematics, and statistics packages such as Minitab and SPSS are a sine qua non for data analysis and display. The Internet and e-mail are widely used for finding information and for communicating with fellow students and teachers. Mathematics education is very different technologically from what it was even 10 years ago.

We perceive a major shift in the practice of mathematics that has occurred in the last 10 to 20 years with the improvement in computer technology (see, e.g., Horgan 1993). The shift in statistics practice came earlier. While there are still theoreticians, the vast majority of mathematicians in academia and industry now work either numerically or analytically with computing tools (*Mathematical Sciences: Adding to Australia* 1996). Presently, there is significant controversy about how much theory, algebraic skills, and computer skills students need, or in fact which packages should be taught (see, e.g., Holton 2001). These details are insignificant in comparison to larger pedagogical issues. The professional practice of mathematics and statistics has changed; the teaching and learning must also change to reflect this transformation in practice.

But have these changes favored the sexes differentially? In particular, have they continued the historical disadvantages faced by women who want to study mathematical sciences? Are these new technological tools merely "toys for boys"? In this discussion, we wish to review the current evidence for the impact of technology, particularly computing technology, on the participation and success of women in mathematics. We also wish to offer some recent evidence from some of our own courses in mathematics and statistics at the tertiary and pretertiary level.

PHILOSOPHY: "THINK GLOBAL, ACT LOCAL"

The catch-cry of the environmental movement "think global, act local" is also an apt description of appropriate action for teaching and learning. What happens in the classroom matters: It matters to individual students and to groups within the class (Petocz and Reid 2002). Many studies show that how teachers interact with students and how teachers structure assessment does affect students' learning (Biggs 1999; Brown, Bull, and Pendlebury 1997; Smith and Petocz 1994; Smith et al. 1996). In our classrooms, we have endeavored to create an atmosphere where sex differences between students in their learning were not apparent, by the use of inclusive assessment practices, by careful choice and development of teaching materials, and by monitoring the reactions of target groups to teaching and learning methods. While we are concentrating on technology in this chapter, this is but one component in the teaching and learning process.

Globally, the classroom cannot be dissociated from the culture in which it resides. So external factors such as attitudes to women and education, mandated assessment schedules, and textbooks can and do influence what happens in the classroom. An education system that leaves little room for inclusive assessment and society's attitudes toward women, mathematics, and education in general can adversely influence student learning (Burton 1990). When the global and local work together, then inclusive education is likely to offer a richer and more satisfying experience of mathematics to the students (Risvi 2000; Sadiki 2001).

BACKGROUND

Computer and communications technology are here to stay, and they have already had significant influence on mathematics learning and teaching. How does this affect the mathematics classroom? Will women be adversely affected by this change? In many Western countries—Britain, the United States, Australia, and others—women have been less inclined to study mathematics and seemed to perform less well in this subject. The evidence for this is wide: historical overviews are given in Reeves (1992) and Mangione (1995), and a good summary of the international perspective is given in Burton (1990). Indeed, all the "Women in Mathematics" initiatives are predicated on this sex imbalance in mathematics study. In Australia, even 10 years ago, boys were studying mathematics at higher levels in the secondary schools and achieving better results than girls. At the university level, men were studying mathematical subjects to higher levels (honors and research degrees) and obtaining more first-class honors degrees and 10 times as many research degrees in mathematics (see, e.g., Petocz 1996).

Against this background, the present situation is not quite as clear-cut, as there is evidence that women are achieving equality in at least some aspects of mathematics education. Some recent American studies continue to demonstrate sex inequalities in the use of technology, particularly computers, in mathematics education (Owens and Waxman 1998). However, other reports indicate that girls approach the use of technology in the same way as do boys, particularly if they are in a single-sex environment (Craig 2000). In Australia, girls at secondary school have increased their participation in the highest level of mathematics courses and have raised their levels of performance to a point where people are discussing whether boys should have access to special help (Coupland and Wood 1998). While participation at the highest levels of university mathematics is still chosen by more men than women, many Australian undergraduate mathematics courses have roughly equal numbers of the sexes.

A recent monograph (Galbraith and Haines 2000) discusses the interaction between computer mathematics and computing. Galbraith and Haines found that women exhibited a confidence level in computing consistently lower than men. This occurred on every item of their confidence and motivation scales. Even though female confidence (as measured by items used by Galbraith and Haines) may be lower, the question remains as to whether increasing use of technology in mathematics education will have an impact on learning of mathematics. Does lower confidence with technology translate to lower performance in mathematics learning using technology? Does increasing use of technology favor men at the expense of women? Or has it helped to balance the previous sex inequalities in participation and achievement? Or has it made no difference at all?

AIMS AND METHODS

The authors of this chapter, two women and one man, have been involved in various aspects of mathematics education and research over the past decade at several of Sydney's five universities and pretertiary educational institutions. We are joint authors of a mathematics textbook written for a university preparation course for mature-age students (Petocz, Petocz, and Wood 1992). We monitor our teaching and learning in a variety of ways, depending on the student group. With the introduction of technology into the teaching and learning of mathematics in our classrooms we wanted to monitor any possible adverse effects. Data are also collected on other variables, such as age, language, and ethnic background and socioeconomic group, as these variables have been shown to influence learning and attitudes to learning. Only the data on sex are reported here.

Within this aim of monitoring the teaching and learning of our students, we report here on three relevant sets of data that we have collected:

- *Differential equations*. For the differential equations class, data were collected in order to design individualized assignments that would be relevant to the needs of the individual students in the class. This was done early in the semester and so reflects the attitudes that students bring to the class rather than those developed in the class.
- *Statistics 1*. The Statistics 1 data were collected at the end of the subject. This is a first-year subject and is the students' introduction to statistics and to the use of a statistical package (Minitab). The aim of the data collection was to monitor the learning in the subject, particularly in relation to the laboratories. Since the subject runs each semester, the student feedback at the end of one course is used to inform any modifications for the next course.
- *Preparatory mathematics*. The data collected for this subject consist of extended student comments collected as part of group or solo projects on various mathematical topics. The aim of the data collection was to encourage students to reflect on their learning and, as a byproduct, for the teacher to obtain more insight into the learning of her students.

These three sets of data were collected from quite different classes, using a variety of methods and for a variety of reasons. Yet each sheds light on the question of whether technology has different effects on the learning of women and men. The net effect of several small and statistically inconclusive studies can be a conclusion that is more definite than any of the individual studies. In our investigation, we have combined the (quantitative and qualitative) information from three of our recent classes. Overall, the conclusion seems to be that the women and men in our classes do not hold different opinions about the uses of technology in mathematics and statistics education.

Preliminary Data

In 1997, one of us (Wood) gave an informal questionnaire to a second-year class studying differential equations. In this questionnaire, students were asked how much *Mathematica* (a computer algebra system) they would like in their next assignment. They were also asked about topics and style options for the assignment. The questionnaire is presented in Figure 12.1.

The results of the questionnaire helped in the design of assignments that correlated with the students' interests and perceived skills in *Mathematica* and communication (style). In terms of wanting to work in groups, 40 students stated yes, 7 said no, and 3 said maybe. Considering the *Mathematica* question, the women stated that they wanted significantly less *Mathematica* than the men (statistics: 31 men, 20 women, difference of 1.0 on a 5-point scale, $t = 2.84$ on 48 df, $p = 0.006$). The numbers here are interesting: For mostly *Mathematica* and three-fourths *Mathematica* there were 15 males and 1 female. Possible im-

Figure 12.1
Questionnaire of Student Preferences

Options for assignment.

Use of Mathematica
I would prefer an assignment that used:

mostly *Mathematica*
¾ *Mathematica*
½ *Mathematica*
¼ *Mathematica*
almost no *Mathematica*

Topic Choice
I would prefer an assignment that included:

	Yes	Maybe	No
Chaos			
Financial applications			
Population applications			
Graphical applications			
Theory			
Electrical applications			
Mechanical vibrations			
Other ...			

Style
I would prefer an assignment where I could:

	Yes	Maybe	No
use *report format*			
use *essay format*		.	
research topic in library			
find my own examples			
Other ...			

I would like to work in a group (maximum 3). Yes/No

plications are that female students were less confident, felt less competent with *Mathematica*, or just didn't like using it. Another possibility is that our teaching methods for introducing *Mathematica* had not been successful, particularly for female students.

Therefore, these (statistically and practically) significant sex differences led to the investigation on which we are reporting here, using forms of questions appropriate to the different courses. In each case, students were asked about their attitudes toward the computer technology being used in their classes. These were a second-year differential equations class, a first-year statistics class, and a university preparation class for mature-age students, all from the 1999 aca-

Figure 12.2
Questionnaire for Differential Equations Course

Group	Preferred group size	1, 2, or 3
q1	I like to do assignments that are theoretical	1 = agree
q2	I like to do assignments that relate to real problems	2 = neutral
		3 = disagree
q3	I like to do assignments that use *Mathematica*	
q4	I like to work in a group where the others do the *Mathematica*	
q5	I think students in the same class doing different assessment is unfair	
q6	I like to have a choice of assessment tasks	
q7	I like to have a choice in the weighting of assessment tasks	
q8	I think the lecturer should make all the decisions about assessment	
q9	I think the whole class should have the same assessment	
q10	I like to have detailed individual feedback on my assessment	
q11	I like to have a few general comments on my assessment	
Comp	I have access to a computer at home	0 = no
Mat	I have access to *Mathematica* at home	1 = yes

demic year. We have used the data that we collected in each subject as part of our standard monitoring of teaching and learning. For example, to ascertain their reactions to assessment, students in the differential equations class were asked their preferences for assignments. In the statistics class, students were asked about their reactions to the course, including the laboratory component of the course. In the university preparation mathematics course, students were asked to write about their learning during an extended project. In total, the opinions of 175 students were obtained around the issues of teaching and learning mathematics. For the purposes of this chapter, we have concentrated on the sections that relate to the use of technology in teaching and learning mathematics.

Differential Equations Course

In the second-year differential equations course, we investigated students' attitudes using a simple and standard-format questionnaire with a 3-point Likert scale (1 = agree, 2 = neutral, 3 = disagree). Students answered a variety of questions about the type of assignments that they preferred, including whether they were theoretical or practical, how much *Mathematica* was involved, and what amount of choice they wanted in the details and weightings of their assessment. They were also asked to indicate whether or not they had access to a computer and to *Mathematica* at home, and in what group size they preferred to work. The entire cohort of 74 students was surveyed. The questions are to be found in Figure 12.2.

Figure 12.3
Results from Questionnaire for Differential Equations Course

	Women – mean (sd) n = 46	Men – mean (sd) n = 26	p-value for difference
Preferred group size for assignment	2.2 (0.9)	2.0 (0.9)	0.44
"Real" problems in assignments	1.4 (0.6)	1.4 (0.6)	0.81
Use of *Mathematica* in assignments	2.2 (0.7)	2.1 (0.8)	0.67
Other students use *Mathematica*	2.1 (0.8)	2.3 (0.6)	0.32
Theoretical assignments	1.9 (0.6)	2.2 (0.6)	0.04
Access to computer at home	79%	85%	0.53
Access to *Mathematica* at home	19%	8%	0.15

Two-sample t-tests showed that there were no statistically significant differences (or practically significant differences) between women and men, using a p-value of 0.01 (adjusted from 0.05 due to multiple tests). A summary of the results is shown in Figure 12.3. In particular, there were no significant differences in preferred group size for assignments, desire for real problems—those using realistic data or situations—in assignments, use of *Mathematica* in assignments, and having other students in the group do the *Mathematica* component. Nor was there any significant difference between access to a computer or to *Mathematica* at home. The only difference that approached significance was in the desire for theoretical assignments, but this failed to reach significance at the adjusted level of 0.01 and only represented a small difference on the 3-point scale. More complex models, adjusting for home access to a computer and Mathematica, failed to reveal any significant differences, with all p-values > 0.05. The overall picture is that the women and men held similar opinions about their learning of differential equations.

Introductory Statistics Course

The cohort of students in a first-year introductory statistics course was surveyed about their attitudes toward the course during the second-last week of their first semester at university. They were asked general questions about what they had liked and disliked and particularly how they reacted to the technological aspects of the course. The weekly laboratory classes are based on the practical investigations in Petocz (1998) and use the Minitab statistics package. Students were also asked for background information about sex, age, and degree program. The questions used are listed in Figure 12.4.

Figure 12.4
Questionnaire for Statistics Course

Sex: male or female

Age: recent school leaver (within last three years) or mature-age student

Degree: mathematics, maths and finance, maths and computing, other

What have you liked most about the Statistics 1 course?

What would you like to change in the Statistics 1 course?

Do you have any comments about the Minitab labs?

What topic in Statistics 1 would you like more information on? Please be as specific as you can.

There were 30 female and 32 male respondents, reflecting the approximately equal sex balance of our mathematics courses at the University of Technology, Sydney. Most of these (52) were recent school leavers, with the remainder (10) mature-age students. Just over half (34) were enrolled in our mathematics program, with most of the remainder (24) in the mathematics and finance course. A qualitative analysis of the students' comments showed no appreciable differences between women and men in any aspect, and particularly no appreciable difference in their attitudes to the technological components of the course. With respect to the laboratory classes, 6 of the women and 5 of the men noted that they were the best feature of the course. The comments on the laboratories were very similar for women and men, and a summary is given in Figure 12.5. On the positive side, the students said they found the laboratories interesting, useful, and informative, easy to follow, a good way to learn particularly in groups; they were well thought out, had good structure, and were useful to have in advance of the classes; and the tutors were helpful. On the negative side, they said that the laboratories took too much time, that more assistance and explanation were needed, that some of the questions were hard to follow, that the lab times were inconvenient, and that it would be better to do the labs at home or online. This gives 12 positive and 14 negative comments from the women, and 11 positive and 21 negative comments from the men. From a quantitative viewpoint, the men seemed to have a somewhat lower proportion of positive comments than the women (34% as opposed to 46%); however, with the small sample size, this difference is not statistically significant ($p = 0.36$). The majority of comments were negative, so this area of the subject needs some attention, especially the need for more assistance and explanation. These were general written comments that were used as a basis for course evaluation and to identify any problem areas that needed changing: There was no planned formal follow-up with this cohort of students.

Figure 12.5
Frequency of Comments on Laboratories from Survey for Statistics Course

Comments on laboratory classes	Women (n = 30)	Men (n = 32)
Interesting, useful, and informative	4	3
A good way to learn, especially in groups	3	1
Easy to follow	3	0
Well thought out, good structure	0	3
Useful to have in advance	0	1
Tutors helpful	2	3
Took too much time	3	2
More assistance and explanation needed	7	11
Questions hard to follow	2	1
Time for classes inconvenient	2	4
Better to do at home or online	0	3

Preparatory Mathematics Course

The mature-age students (over 20 and many over 30) in the university preparation course in mathematics were asked to choose projects from their textbook (Petocz, Petocz, and Wood 1992). This text contains several precalculus projects in an early chapter (on the topics of Aboriginal counting systems, mortgages, alcohol and driving, women in mathematics, and fractals) and several calculus-based projects in a later chapter (on the topics of carbon dating, greenhouse gasses, elasticity in economics, solving equations, and infinite series). Each project consists of a problem statement and a series of questions starting with quite straightforward and traditional ones and quickly progressing to more complex, open-ended investigations. Students were encouraged to work on these projects in groups, and there were both single- and mixed-sex groupings, as well as some students who preferred to work on their own. The last question in each project (given in full in Figure 12.6) asked students to write reflections about the process of their own investigations and learning, and it is from these reflections that we have taken the quotations below. Some students only wrote a few lines, but many of them wrote much more extensive comments (more than a page in some cases). In contrast to the questions asked of the students in the statistics course, the students in this preparatory mathematics course received very little direction about what specific aspects of their learning they were to write about. For instance, they were not asked specifically about the technological side of their investigations, but several of them included comments on this.

Figure 12.6
Reflective Question in the Project for the Preparatory Mathematics Course

---

Question 10. Write a report on the problem posed at the beginning of this project. Give a brief account of your investigations, describing the problems you faced and the successes you achieved.

We have selected comments that are pertinent to our investigations of the effects of technology on mathematics learning for men and women. Once again, from a large number and variety of reflective comments, it was difficult to see any sex-based thematic differences. Here are some quotations from all-female groups showing the development of positive attitudes toward the use of computer technology including the Internet:

> The experience of working in a team was most valuable and positive, yet challenging at first. Our first obstacle occurred when we began to write our answers. We were unsure of how to share the workload as we did not really know each other. We decided that the method that worked the best was sitting at the computer screen together and composing the answers together. This worked well because we were able to bounce ideas off each other and come up with answers that we were happy with.

> We found this inquiry both challenging and interesting. Coming to the subject with limited mathematical and computer experience we found it difficult to coordinate all efforts and overcome computer problems. These new dimensions in our understanding of mathematics and computer technology have helped us to understand the complexities of group work and to coordinate our efforts into the completed project.

> When we first started working on this project we found it overwhelming as no one had prior knowledge of the subject. We also found it difficult to obtain resources as some books were not accessible and some of the suggested references were not available. The Internet was therefore our best source. Even after we had found relevant information, the topic was still confusing. We were fortunate to have belonged in a team which possessed an equal commitment and enthusiasm for the project. It was pleasing to find that our individual strengths complemented each other.

Solo women had similar positive experiences, but for those of them with less mathematical background the lack of other group members sometimes caused problems:

> The subject was somewhat familiar to me as we took a home loan early this year. However, the technical aspects were not as clear. I never knew the mathematics behind the home loan repayments and how I can use math-

ematics to save on my home loan. When I made all the calculations I was in doubt about their accuracy. Then I found out that there are some loan calculators on the Web which I could use to verify my findings.

I decided to do this project myself, which meant that I could do it in my own time and at my own pace, and I didn't have to travel too far to work on it. It did mean, though, that there was no one to get a second opinion from if I was unsure of something, and I had to do the whole project by myself with no help at all. The worst part of this project for me is putting it together: I am not that great at using Excel, so I am drawing the graphs myself, and my typing is a bit on the slow side!

All-male groups also reported positive experiences, particularly with the use of the Internet and e-mail for communication:

This project has been a huge learning experience for all of us, with many obstacles being crossed along the way. First, getting the relevant books proved to be very difficult. Second, organizational skills were pushed to the limit trying to collate not only relevant information but also human beings into the same time zones—those working 9–5 and those working unsociable hours. Thirdly, trying to communicate effectively, which was solved via the Internet and e-mail.

We obtained our information for this project from two major sources—the Internet and the local library. The main problem that we faced was once again trying to organize a time when both of us were able to get together and compare our results and compile the project. However, with constant communication we managed to find time to spend together to complete the task.

Solo males showed similar appreciation of the available technology:

Doing graphs on a computer was new to me. I had to learn how to use a graphics program so I could print out some graphic representations of the curves and lines mentioned in the questions. These graphs proved very helpful for making predictions and also to verify answers. With the graphs I could ascertain if my answers were not too unrealistic.

These programs were written with Mathematica in a functional language format. The computer allows you to experiment with various series and to compute to large numbers of terms. This would be tedious (even impossible) without the use of a computer.

After reading a small portion of Newton's achievements, I decided that this was an interesting topic. The problems associated with the project were of library access—it simply was not open at the times at which I was able to get there. This led me to other forms of research, in particular the Internet.

These students were not given directions on how to form groups or to work in teams. Part of this extended project is for students to learn to work either solo or in groups with whatever tools that they can use to complete the projects. The quotes above show that the task is difficult and that they took some time to develop a good working relationship with their teammates and many of them learned about computer programs and communication technologies that they had not previously used. One of the aims of the assessment task is for students to develop their own learning strategies when faced with new tasks and new technologies. The above quotes show that this has been successful and that the learning tasks were appropriate and difficult but not impossible.

DISCUSSION

The three sets of data that we have investigated seem to paint a consistent picture of a lack of sex-based differences in the approach of our students to the technology of mathematics education. It seems that there is no significant difference between women and men in the use of computers in mathematics, whether this consists of using Mathematica for finding the solutions of differential equations, a statistics package for analyzing or displaying data, the Internet for finding information for a project, or e-mail for communicating with group members. Despite our earlier finding from a few years ago, we have not found any sex differences in these three quite different sets of data, using quite different questions to investigate the problem.

Of course, our data represent only a small amount of evidence on the question of whether technology in mathematics education is simply "toys for boys." The data come from a relatively wealthy country where many students have easy access to computers and background experience with them. The problems of boys monopolizing scarce computer resources would be unlikely to apply in these contexts. Also, the three authors were the teachers of these three groups, and our joint textbook implies that we have a consistent approach to mathematics learning. Maybe it is not technological tools but rather the traditional solo and competitive models of mathematics education that are less appealing to our female students. The report of Craig (1999) makes the point in the secondary context that the theoretical framework and philosophy of a classroom teacher can have a noticeable effect on students' working methods and study processes. Other research at the tertiary level has reported on the relations between lecturers' experience of their discipline, the way they teach, and consequences for students' learning (Petocz and Reid 2001; Prosser and Trigwell 1999; Reid 2001).

In our particular case, all three of our courses actively encouraged students to work together in groups, and this fact may have been enough to engender more positive female attitudes toward technology (Probert 1999). It is vitally important that women and men have equitable experiences of learning using technology at the tertiary level, since men still seem to be technologically advantaged in the workforce (Butler 1999). The evidence from our "local" experiences shows that it is possible to achieve equity between the sexes in a technological learning environment and indicates a direction that we could be taking to do this "globally."

REFERENCES

Biggs, J. (1999). *Teaching for Quality Learning at University*. Buckingham, UK: Open University Press and Society for Research in Higher Education.

Brown, G., Bull, J., and Pendlebury, M. (1997). *Assessing Student Learning in Higher Education*. London: Routledge.

Burton L. (Ed.). (1990). *Gender and Mathematics: An International Perspective*. London: Cassell Educational Limited.

Burton, L., and Jaworski, B. (Eds.). (1995). *Technology and Mathematics Teaching: A Bridge between Teaching and Learning*. Bromley: Chartwell-Bratt.

Butler, E. (1999). Technologising Equity: The Politics and Practices of Work-Related Learning. In D. Boud and J. Garrick (Eds.), *Understanding Learning at Work* (pp. 132–150). London: Routledge.

Coupland, M.P., and Wood, L.N. (1998). What Happens When the Girls Beat the Boys? In Christine Keitel (Ed.), *Social Justice and Mathematics Education: Gender, Class, Ethnicity and the Politics of Schooling* (pp. 238–245). Berlin: IOWME and Freie Universität.

Craig, D.V. (2000). A League of Their Own: Gender, Practices among Adolescents and Teachers in a Technology-Enhanced Learning Environment. *Journal of Educational Technology Systems*, 28(4), 349–363.

Galbraith, P., and Haines, C. (1998). Disentangling the Nexus: Attitudes to Mathematics and Technology in a Computer-Learning Environment. *Educational Studies in Mathematics*, 36(3), 275–290.

Galbraith, P., and Haines, C. (2000). *Mathematics-Computing Attitude Scales*. Monographs in Continuing Education. London: City University.

Holton, D. (2001). *The Teaching and Learning of Mathematics at University Level—An ICMI Study*. Dordrecht: Kluwer Academic Publishers.

Horgan, J. (1993). The Death of Proof. *Scientific American*, October, 74–82.

Jaques, D. (2000). *Learning in Groups*. London: Kogan Page.

Mangione, M. (1995). Understanding the Critics of Educational Technology: Gender Inequities and Computers 1983–1993. In *Proceedings of the 1995 Annual National Convention of the Association for Educational Communicators and Technology*, Anaheim, CA: AECT.

Mathematical Sciences: Adding to Australia. (1996). Canberra: Australian Academy of Sciences.

Owens, E.W., and Waxman, H.C. (1998). Sex- and Ethnic-Related Differences among High School Students' Technology Use in Science and Mathematics. *International Journal of Instructional Media*, 25(1), 43–54.

Petocz, P. (1996). Higher Degrees and Honours Bachelor Degrees in Mathematics and Statistics Completed in Australia 1993. *Australian Mathematical Society Gazette*, 23(3), 123–133.

Petocz, P. (1998). *Statistical Laboratory Exercises Using Minitab: A Guide to Understanding Data*. Brisbane: Wiley.

Petocz, P., Petocz, D., and Wood, L.N. (1992). *Introductory Mathematics*. Melbourne: Thomas Nelson.

Petocz, P., and Reid, A. (2001). Students' Experience of Learning in Statistics. *Quaestiones Mathematicae*, Suppl. 1, 37–45.

Petocz, P., and Reid, A. (2002). Enhancing the Total Learning Environment for Students of Mathematics. In P. Kahn and J. Kyle (Eds.), *Effective Learning and Teaching in Mathematics and Its Applications* (pp. 106–116). London: Kogan Page.

Probert, B. (1999). Gender Workers and Gendered Work: Implications for Women's Learning. In D. Boud and J. Garrick (Eds.), *Understanding Learning at Work* (pp. 98–116). London: Routledge.

Prosser, M., and Trigwell, K. (1999). *Understanding Learning and Teaching*. Buckingham, UK: Open University Press and Society for Research in Higher Education.

Reeves, M.E. (1992). *Gender, Technology, and Mathematics Education: Working Together to Achieve "Equality."* Paper presented at the annual meeting of the American Educational Research Association, San Francisco, CA. (ERIC Document Reproduction Service No. ED 353 148)

Reid, A. (2001). Variation in the Ways That Instrumental and Vocal Students Experience Learning Music. *Music Education Research*, 3(1), 25–40.

Risvi, F. (2000). Internationalisation of Curriculum. *RMIT Teaching and Learning Strategy*. Available online at http://www.pvci.rmit.edu.au/ioc/.

Sadiki, L. (2001). Internationalising the Curriculum in the 21st Century. Available online at http://www.anu.edu.au/CEDAM/internationalc.html.

Smith, G.H., and Petocz, P. (1994). Proofs: Teaching and Testing—A Tragedy in Three Acts. *International Journal of Mathematical Education in Science and Technology*, 25(1), 139–158.

Smith, G.H., Wood, L.N., Coupland, M., Stephenson, B., Crawford, K., and Ball, G. (1996). Constructing Mathematical Examinations to Assess a Range of Knowledge and Skills. *International Journal of Mathematical Education in Science and Technology*, 27, 65–77.

Tall, D., Blokland, P., and Kok, D. (1985). *A Graphic Approach to the Calculus*. Kenilworth, UK: Rivendell Software.

Chapter 13

Computers in Mathematics:
A Superhighway to Social Justice?

Colleen M. Vale

INTRODUCTION

Mathematics curriculum policy in Australia requires teachers to use information technology as a focus and aid to students' learning and understanding of mathematics (Australian Education Council 1990; Victorian Board of Studies 1995). These policy statements also acknowledge the principle of gender equity and equal opportunity and encourage teachers to use inclusive teaching practices. Research concerning gender equity in mathematics has been extensive and on-going. However, only a few studies have investigated gender in the context of computer-based learning environments, and none of these were conducted in Australia (Forgasz, Leder, and Vale 2000). Researchers have expressed concern that the use of computers and other technologies in mathematics might erode advancements made toward social justice in mathematics (e.g., Barnes 1995; Burton and Jaworski 1995).

In this chapter, I present two case studies of junior secondary mathematics classrooms in which computers were used regularly for learning and doing mathematics. The two classes, from the same school, provided two different computer-based learning environments for students. The year 8 class used desktop computers in a laboratory for two of their five mathematics lessons each week. Students in the year 9 class owned laptop computers and used them when required in their mathematics lessons. I used an ethnographic research design to investigate the sociocultural context of these two learning environments. In the two case studies, I present data about the nature of social interactions in the lessons and the views of the girls and boys in these two classes. As a result of the discussion in the final section of the chapter, I suggest some implications for the teaching of mathematics and social justice in the age of the superhighway.

GENDER EQUITY AND MATHEMATICS

Gender differences in participation and achievement in, and attitudes about, mathematics in Australia are outlined in another chapter in this book (see Chapter 11). The authors present data to show that the gender gap is closing and shifting. They argue that, in any case, the current focus on the poor performance of boys by the media and policymakers in Australia is ill informed, since the poor performance of particular groups of boys and girls is related to low socio-economic status (Teese 2000) as well as gender.

Some studies of technology-based mathematics have reported gender differences in achievement. However, no consistent pattern of results has been revealed; a few studies found that females performed better than males (Boers and Jones 1993; Dunham 1991; Ruthven 1995). Given the male domain associated with computing (Clarke and Chambers 1989; Cobbin 1995), these results appeared to be surprising at the time. The superior performance of girls in tertiary studies seemed to be related to their rejection of the technology. More recently, in a study of the attitudes of tertiary mathematics students, students' attitudes that computers enhanced mathematics learning were more strongly associated with attitudes to computers than to mathematics (Galbraith, Haines, and Pemberton 1999). They did not, however, report findings for males and females.

Recent research into gender equity and social justice has shown that the sociocultural context of mathematics classrooms contributes to the inequitable distribution of mathematical learning (e.g., Barnes 2000; Boaler 1997; Day 1996; Fennema 1995; Forgasz and Leder 1996; Jungwirth 1991). Forgasz and Leder (1996) found evidence of a number of classroom factors that may explain gender differences in attribution. These included teacher and peer behaviors, the nature of the learning activities and associated assessment, and an emphasis on competition. Much earlier, Walden and Walkerdine (1985) claimed that girls were placed in a "no win situation" in mathematics since teachers expected them to be conscientious in order to be successful, yet they actually valued talent and risk-taking behavior. Walkerdine (1990) observed that teachers valued play over conscientiousness as an indicator of real understanding. She argued that teachers therefore had higher expectations and assessment of boys' skills. Jungwirth (1991) analyzed interactions between teachers and students in mathematics classrooms to show that gender differences in these interactions may lead teachers to believe that girls "learn" mathematics while boys "know" mathematics.

Studies of the culture of mathematics have found evidence of the competitive and hierarchical culture of mathematics (e.g., Day 1996) and hegemonic masculinity (Barnes 2000). Boaler (1997) has shown how the different learning goals of girls and boys leave girls at a disadvantage in competitive environments. Her long-term qualitative study of two UK classrooms found that while both boys and girls preferred a mathematics program that enabled them to work at their own pace, their reasoning was different. Girls valued experiences that allowed them to think and develop their own ideas; they were concerned with achieving understanding. Boys, on the other hand, emphasized speed and accuracy and saw these as indicators of success. Boys' preferences enabled them to adapt to the competitive environment of textbook-based mathematics learning environments. In a classroom study by Barnes (2000) two groups of boys exhibiting hegemonic masculinity were identified. The power of one group was physical and intellectual, for the other group, rational and concerned with ideas and knowledge. In both cases the boys' masculine identification with their group was detrimental to their gaining maximum benefit from the collaborative learning environment that she studied. These boys obstructed the learning of others, including girls.

Schofield's (1995) ethnographic study of a secondary mathematics classroom that used a computer-aided instructional tool found that there was an increase in "friendly competition" among the boys and more able students. She identified students' positive and negative attitudes as concerning control over their own learning, an association with playing games, a sense of personal challenge and an increased opportunity to express negative feelings, and a decreased fear of embarrassment. However, she did not include a gender analysis of these attitudes.

Since there have been few studies of secondary mathematics classrooms in which computers were regularly used, I was interested in how the presence and use of computers contribute to the sociocultural context of mathematics learning. It is through social interaction in the classroom that meaning is negotiated, and the culture of a classroom is constituted by what is done by teachers and students in the classroom (Bauersfeld 1995). Bush (1983) argued that technology is accepted or adopted when people see advantage for themselves and that a feminist analysis ought to identify who creates and who accommodates as well as whose opportunities increase and decrease. Furthermore, a culture that is socially just seeks to eliminate exploitation, marginalization, powerlessness, cultural imperialism, and violence (Gerwitz 1998).

In my study of two computer-based mathematics classrooms I wanted to find out what the social interactions would reveal about the learning behaviors and views of girls and boys in these learning environments and whether there were differences for particular groups of girls and boys within these classrooms. Do girls and boys accept or adopt the technology in mathematics? What factors contribute to the learning behaviors and views of boys and girls in these two computer-based mathematics classrooms?

THE CASE STUDIES

Settings

The two case studies are from a study that was conducted in a state urban secondary school in Australia. The students at the school were drawn from a multicultural population of low to middle socioeconomic status. The school was also coeducational with a policy that encouraged the use of computers in core subjects for the compulsory years of schooling, including mathematics. The school was purposefully chosen in order to investigate the sociocultural context of classrooms for students from a low-middle-class background where teachers in a state school were implementing a government and school policy to use computers in their mathematics teaching. Research would suggest, potentially, an interplay of boys' underachievement (because of the socioeconomic setting) with improved motivation (as a result of the technology) and an increase in collaboration and problem solving. I wanted to see if this was borne out.

The school provided at least two different learning environments for students in which computers were regularly used in mathematics lessons within their year 7 to 10 program. Two teachers, who conducted mathematics lessons in different computer-based learning environments, agreed to participate in the study. The first was in a year 8 class with 14 boys and 11 girls. This class used desktop computers in a laboratory setting for two of their five mathematics lessons each week. Some students in this class also owned laptop computers and brought them to school and used them in the computer-based lessons. Higher-achieving students in a range of subjects had been encouraged to join this particular year 8 class, but students with below average mathematics achievement were not excluded from membership of the class. The particular computer-based learning environment for this year 8 class had commenced at the beginning of the year in which the study took place; hence, students had been involved for two terms. The mathematics teacher was male with 16 years' experience. He had used Excel and Logowriter in previous years when teaching mathematics.

Students in the second class, year 9, owned laptop computers and used them for particular tasks when required by the mathematics teacher. The students had elected to be part of the laptop program in the previous year and so had been using laptop computers in their core subjects for six terms when the study commenced. There were 18 boys and 7 girls in this class. The teacher had recorded a broad range of mathematics achievement for students in this class. The year 9 mathematics teacher was also male and had 13 years' teaching experience. He used graphic calculators with year 11 and 12 students but had no previous experience using computers or laptop computers for mathematics with students in the middle years of schooling.

Research Methods

I used an ethnographic research design (Bogdan and Biklen 1992) that involved an analysis of social interactions in the classrooms and the voices of the participants. The settings for the case studies were naturalistic in the sense that the teacher determined all aspects of the mathematics program, and data were collected during mathematics lessons. The researcher negotiated the timing of the study with the school community and the mathematics teachers.

Social interactions in classrooms included teacher-student interactions and student-student interactions; and in computer-based mathematics classrooms, student-computer interactions (Crawford 1996). Data about social interactions were collected by observing and videotaping lessons over a four-week period. I participated in the lessons as an observer, roving the classroom observing students' interactions and work on their computer screens and occasionally providing assistance to students when they requested it. I redirected the freestanding videocamera from time to time to focus on different clusters of boys and girls during the lessons. I wrote field notes and transcribed the videotapes. I also collected documents pertaining to the curriculum and teaching program for each class.

Students' views were collected using individual interviews and a questionnaire. I interviewed four students, two girls and two boys from each class. Specifically, in each class a lower-achieving and a high-achieving boy and girl were selected. I asked the students to describe their experiences in the lessons and to provide their opinions about the use of computers in mathematics. Data were collected from all students through a questionnaire that included both open-ended and closed questions. The open-ended questions asked students whether they thought using computers in mathematics was a good idea or not, and why, and what they liked and disliked about using them in mathematics. Data collected from the closed items on the questionnaire are reported elsewhere (Vale 2001).

I also interviewed the teacher from each class. I asked them about their experiences of teaching mathematics with computers and their objectives and to evaluate the learning environment and the students. The multiple methods of data collection enabled the perspectives of all participants to be included in each case study.

I used qualitative methods to analyze these data (Bogdan and Biklen 1992; Miles and Huberman 1994). I compared the social interactions involving boys and girls according to content, cognitive nature of interaction, degree of collaboration, and socioemotional content. The content of social interactions concerned mathematics, software, computer systems, the learning task, or off-task behavior. The cognitive nature of social interactions that I observed between the teacher and students indicated levels of cognitive interactions and whether these involved the computer (Geiger and Goos 1996). The teachers' interactions with students included instruction, demonstration, takeover, consultation, monitoring, and tutoring. The degree of collaboration that I observed between students also indicated different levels of cognitive interaction: parallel activity, demonstration, takeover, teaming, tutoring, or collaboration (Goos, Galbraith, and Renshaw 1996). The socioemotional content of interactions included positive and negative comments (Lee 1993) about a student's achievement, work, or identity and included verbal and physical harassment. The analysis of the views of students collected from the open-ended questionnaire, the interviews, and social interactions observed in the lessons generated four main themes: pleasure, success, relevance, and power. I compared the views of girls and boys.

In the following two sections I present the data in two case studies, one for each class. Each case study includes a description of the mathematics content and software used as well as the analysis of the social interactions in the classroom and the views of girls and boys. Differences in the social interactions and views of higher- and lower-achieving mathematics girls and boys are identified where they were evident. I have used pseudonyms for the participants when presenting data.

THE YEAR 8 COMPUTER LABORATORY CLASS

Mathematics Content, Software, and Teacher's Methods

The mathematics program for this class included three mathematics lessons in a general classroom and two mathematics lessons in a computer laboratory each week. During the four-week period of the study, the students were learning to solve multistep equations using the balance method and began a topic on straight-line graphs. The six lessons that I observed in the computer laboratory over this time period concerned equations and business arithmetic.

The learning in the computer-based lessons for this class was teacher directed. That is, the teacher set tasks for students to complete with little use of exposition, and the students were expected to work individually. In the first lesson that was observed students were set the task of designing a slide show using Microsoft PowerPoint to present (and explain) the solution of an equation, for example: $5(x - 2)/3 + 1 = 6$. (They had received instruction on PowerPoint in the previous computer-based lesson.) The teacher planned for individual differences by preparing additional tasks for fast workers, and so in subsequent lessons as students completed the equation slide show, they went on to do exercises using Microsoft Excel to calculate percentage increases and investment for fictional businesses. They were familiar with Excel as they had used this software in other mathematical contexts earlier in the school year. While the tasks set by the teacher were closed with respect to mathematics content and skills, they did enable students to incorporate, and thus demonstrate, a range of software skills.

The Teacher's Interactions with Students

During each lesson the teacher initiated interaction with individual students or responded to students' requests for his assistance. During these interactions the teacher monitored student progress; provided instruction on the task, mathematics, or the software; tutored about the mathematics; or demonstrated how to use the software. He provided individual feedback, including praise, or organized individual students to undertake new tasks.

There were more interactions recorded with boys than girls when the teacher monitored progress. On the other hand, there were more interactions recorded with girls when the teacher instructed, and girls made more requests for assistance from the teacher, almost twice as many as the boys. However, care needs to be taken when interpreting these data since two particular girls, Beckie and Jackie, dominated the requests from students for the teacher's assistance. Instructional interactions usually occurred with lower-achieving students and were often for an extended period of time. During such interactions, the teacher provided individual instruction on the mathematical steps, redirected their attention to critical aspects of the mathematical process, corrected their work, and answered or demonstrated their concerns about how to use the software. In the following example the teacher is checking Nadia's slides. Nadia says nothing throughout this interaction, just follows his instructions:

Teacher: Now hold on, hold on. Yeah, right. Click there. Press ah, press enter. Now what? Press space bar . . . [*inaudible*]. Hold on, before you do that, ah, put the cursor in front of the plus, in front of the plus. Okay. . . . Now let's go on and do the underline as well. Keep going. Press space bar. Press space bar. Space bar again. Press ah, yeah space bar again. Again. So that that's fixed that. Let's go on to the next one. All right now, what I suggest you do, get rid of that. Put a "times by 3" up the top there. Now what you should also try to do, all right, just to show the person, make that a different colour.

In these types of interactions the teacher often did the thinking for the student and did not always seek to find out what the student's difficulty was or provide an overview of the task or the way the software worked. While the teacher clearly indicated errors in their work, he did, however, include positive feedback throughout these extended interactions. The teacher believed that he had interacted only with girls in this way:

Teacher: I tend to keep away from the better kids and with her [*Jackie*], I sort of focus all my attention on the kids that are not as good like her and Dani and Beckie and who else? Oh, can't think of anyone else. Yeah it's probably them. (year 8 teacher interview)

However, low-achieving boys, such as Barlo, were also observed receiving this kind of assistance. The teacher's lack of awareness of his own behavior thus indicates that he believed that it was the girls in the class who were the least successful students at using computers for mathematics. He described these girls as *strugglers* who were not confident and needed *to be pushed a lot*.

A higher level of cognitive interaction occurred when the teacher tutored students engaging with them to promote student thinking. There were more recorded episodes of the teacher tutoring boys than girls, and all the tutoring episodes that were recorded involved higher-achieving students. These episodes were usually brief and were few in number. The teacher provided information about the task or the mathematics, made suggestions, asked questions, or interacted with the student to solve a problem.

The teacher consulted boys when he encountered a problem with the software or computers:

Teacher: I'm not sort of afraid to say that, "Hey I'm stuck," and I might even ask a kid like Jason who's pretty good with computers if I have a problem. (year 8 teacher interview)

Through this behavior the teacher indicated that it was the boys whom he believed were the computer experts. In one such episode Jackie was working on her PowerPoint presentation and had the slides in the wrong order. She asked the teacher how to change the order. She had some idea, but the teacher asked Jason anyway. However, he was not able to provide information or solve the software problem. This also occurred on each recorded occasion when the teacher consulted a student.

The teacher personalized his interactions with some boys, calling them *chum* or *mate*. High-achieving year 8 girls like Kirsty were perceived by the teacher to be risk takers—*a goer, not scared*, confident, conscientious, and achieving *a very high standard*—but he did not bestow comments about ability such as the *very intelligent boy* that he used when describing Geoff.

The Learning Behaviors of Girls and Boys

All students worked individually and at their own pace on the tasks set by the teacher. They sought assistance from their peers, especially with respect to the requirements of the task and how to use the software. However, during the computer-based lessons that were observed, the students did not normally collaborate; that is, they did not work together to share ideas or solve problems about the software or the mathematics.

Gendered patterns of behavior were observed. Girls were generally more willing and successful in tutoring their peers than boys. See, for example, the episode below of Kirsty tutoring Angela. She instructs and offers an explanation:

Angela: How do you get the 3 underneath? It just goes there.

Kirsty: You've got it centered. Align it to the right.

Angela: [*Using mouse selects an icon on tool bar*] That one?

Kirsty: Yeah, now you gonna need to do that for here too. [*She points*] So that it's all aligned. [*She places her hand back on her screen*] 'Cos otherwise it'll go funny.

The boys tended to demonstrate or take over the operation of others' computers when trying to assist peers. They made little use of verbal instruction and gave no explanations. For example:

Barlo: Geoff, can you help me insert a line there?

Geoff: Yeh, hang on.

Barlo: Can you help me? [*Geoff takes control of the mouse and does it for him*]

Barlo: [*Makes changes, but he can't delete a line*] Shit!

Boys participated in almost all of the recorded episodes of off-task behavior involving the use of computers, and for the vast majority of these episodes the boys were using laptop computers that they had brought to school to use instead of the desktop computers in the laboratory. Up to five boys brought their laptops to class during the period of observation. These boys loaded and copied games and other files and programs, organized files and memory, troubleshot problems with software, played games, and discussed features of hardware and software. Boys also used the laboratory computers to browse menus of software and galleries of graphics and searched for information on the Internet. It was in the context of off-task activity that boys demonstrated to each other their knowledge of computer systems and software.

Some interactions between students were socioemotive in content and hence conveyed attitudes about other people. For the few that were recorded, most of the episodes were examples of negative attitudes toward others, including the teacher. The behaviors and inferred attitudes of the boys provided examples and evidence of hegemonic masculinity in the class.

The Views of Girls and Boys

The views of students were gathered through observation and analysis of their social interactions in the lessons, their statements made during interview, and their responses to open-ended questions on the questionnaire. The year 8 students were overwhelmingly positive about using computers in mathematics, and this attitude was evident during the lessons that were observed, as there was a buoyant mood in the room and a productive work environment. However, differences in the views of girls and boys did emerge in the social interactions and responses to interview questions and questionnaire items. Only 1 boy, out of 14, and 2 girls, out of 11, did not think it was a good idea to use computers in mathematics.

The social interactions and responses of boys concerned pleasure, relevance, or usefulness as a tool and power of the technology. Boys, especially those with access to laptop computers, displayed pleasure in using computers by engaging in off-task behavior. They also wrote about this: "It is more entertaining. It's not as boring. It is fun." The association with power concerned references to the speed that computers could do things, and one year 8 boy wrote: "POWERPOINT and MICROWORLD. They rule."

The two year 8 boys I interviewed stated that they preferred Excel in mathematics because it was useful: "Help work things out for me" (Vijay) and "It solves problems for you" (Geoff). Vijay elaborated and described Excel as eliminating repetitive tasks, especially calculations. These attitudes indicate a view of computers as a tool for doing mathematics and were supported by responses from boys on the questionnaire such as: "I like using the Excel program because you put in the formula and the computer does the work for you" (year 8 boy). Other responses indicated that using computers in mathematics enabled you to learn valuable computer skills: "You can use Excel and today, computers are taking the world into the next century" (year 8 boy).

Individual boys did comment on computers as learning aids but these were isolated responses: "Because we can learn a lot from computers" (year 8 boy) and "Computers are growing in the world so much . . . it is important that we use them in our learning process" (year 8 boy). The only boy who did not think it was a good idea to use computers in mathematics believed they had a negative effect on learning: "Because a computer can work out all the answers to the questions. Then the student wouldn't have their own ability to solve mathematical problems" (year 8 boy).

Girls' positive responses to using computers in mathematics were not normally associated with pleasure nor with the usefulness of computers. There were exceptions among the high-achieving girls. Kirsty said that mathematics needed its own software because "there's still some things that you can't do [with Excel]." She thought that they could use Graphmatica for their new topic (linear graphs). Girls seemed to be more focused on learning outcomes. They wrote about computers making mathematics "easier" and "learning quicker." One wrote, "Computers can be helpful" (year 8 girl); another, "Computer helps fix up lots of mistakes" (year 8 girl).

The year 8 girls' attitudes toward the computer-based tasks and the software also appeared to be related to aesthetics. This was evident in the classroom behaviors. The girls judged their work and the work of others and, by implication, the value of the software, according to visual presentation criteria. For example, Angela did not like the "look" of the slides that she had created. She described them as "boring" and "crap," and she wanted to be able to use the software to create a more aesthetically appealing product. A few girls wrote that a better presentation could be achieved using computers. The girls in the class may have interpreted the teacher's emphasis on presentation in these lessons as an expectation to conform to gender stereotyped notions of neatness and attractiveness, rather than to communicate mathematical reasoning clearly.

Only the students who were interviewed were asked open-ended questions that may have revealed gender stereotyping of computers. Three of the students, Geoff, Vijay, and Jackie, believed that boys were more interested in computers than girls. Kirsty did not agree with this view. The students were cautious about the effects of the use of computers in mathematics on performance and participation:

Geoff: I think boys are more interested or use computers more often than girls so . . . [that] might motivate them to try to learn more maths. . . . And as for girls, I'm not sure. . . . I think some girls are quite into computers and seeing what they do and some just don't really want them.

Kirsty thought that computers in mathematics would encourage more girls to study mathematics:

Kirsty: I think it would because a lot of girls feel pretty comfortable using computers . . . as long as they've got plenty of support.

A positive attitude toward computers by both boys and girls outweighed instances of negativity in their classroom behavior. The attitudes expressed or displayed about computer-based mathematics concerned pleasure, displeasure, effects on learning, and usefulness as a tool or medium. These attitudes were related to gender. The students' attitudes concerning usefulness reflected the integrated curriculum approach adopted by this teacher in planning the tasks for the computer-based lessons.

Summary

The analysis of social interactions showed that girls and boys accepted the use of computers in mathematics. However, this mathematics classroom advantaged the highest-achieving students. They were comfortable with the competitive environment created by the individualized learning program that enabled students to work at their own pace, and they believed that the computer provided opportunities for learning mathematics. Lower-achieving students did not experience higher-order cognitive interaction with the teacher or their peers. The teacher monitored their progress and provided extended individual instruction, and boys took over their computers to solve the problem for them. Gendered patterns of behavior and views were also observed.

The teacher believed the boys in the classroom to be the computer experts and called on their expertise. He did not use girls as experts even though some girls provided peer tutoring on the software or task and were able to complete the tasks successfully and quickly.

The boys in the classroom adopted the computer. They used it as a tool for doing mathematics and for pleasure. They took control of their own learning, especially through off-task activity to learn about computers. They shared their knowledge as they were observed to tutor and demonstrate. For boys, the computers were also relevant and offered them increased opportunities in computer skills. The nature of the social interactions with other students or the teacher may have contributed to the gender-stereotyped view expressed by some boys and some girls that computers were a male domain.

THE YEAR 9 LAPTOP COMPUTER CLASS

Mathematics Content, Software, and Teacher's Methods

Students in the year 9 class were studying geometry during the four-week period of the study. The students used their laptop computers in five lessons that were observed. For these lessons the teacher used exposition, teacher-directed tasks, as well as an investigation task and a project. In the first computer-based lesson that I observed the students were introduced to the Geometer's Sketchpad software. They completed a teacher-directed oral exercise and were set a homework task to explore the software. In the second lesson, they completed another software familiarization exercise that required students to draw and measure attributes of particular geometric shapes, but the teacher did not check or inquire about their learning from the homework task. A week later, in the third and fourth computer-based lessons, the students completed a guided investigation of exterior angles of a polygon (Rasmussen, Rasmussen, and Bennett 1995, p. 26). This task required the students to draw a pentagon, measure the external angles using Geometer's Sketchpad, formulate a conjecture about external angles, and then test this conjecture by investigating other polygons. While this learning activity theoretically fitted with a constructivist perspective of mathematics learning, the teacher did not introduce the activity or structure the lesson or encourage the students to collaborate in order to facilitate this type of learning.

In the following week the students used their laptop computers and the Geometer's Sketchpad to do a "project." They had to draw seven specified shapes. When interacting with individual students the teacher indicated that he wanted them to provide proof that their drawings included the essential geometric features that defined these shapes. During this lesson the teacher returned to students the pen and paper tests that they had completed in a previous lesson.

The Teacher's Interactions with Students

As with the year 8 class, gendered patterns of interactions between the teacher and students were observed in this year 9 laptop class. The year 9 teacher used demonstration more often in his interactions with girls than boys, and there were more episodes in which the teacher provided instruction or tutoring on mathematics or provided praise to boys than girls. The only recorded episodes of the teacher taking over the students' computer occurred with girls. In the following episode the year 9 teacher takes over Ellen's laptop to show her how to label the vertices on her diagram and ultimately does this task for her so that she can move on to the mathematical component of the task. Ellen is the highest-achieving student in the class.

Teacher: Do you know how to label it?

Ellen: No.

Teacher: All right you, you now press that, click on that arrow . . . [*inaudible*]. Click on a point, any point, now to click on more than one point you've got to use shift, so from now on, while the shift pressed click on OK? [*He watches, points to menu bar*] Go to display. Display and show labels. Now I think what's gonna happen, see how that's got labels, if you want to make that . . . [*inaudible*]. [*He now takes over the mouse and does it for her*] I'll show you.

His reluctance to use demonstration and takeover when assisting boys may have been because he perceived them to be better operators of computers than himself. During the interview the teacher referred to this difference in knowledge and experience:

Teacher: The first time we got 'em [*laptop computers*] out was a daunting experience for me, because they . . . knew a lot more about it than I did. And I was trying to teach them something and they had the experience of being in that situation before that I hadn't. (year 9 interview)

He described the higher-achieving boys as "more inquisitive," "very bright," or showing "initiative." He was more likely to tutor high-achieving boys, that is, argue, explain, or question when interacting with them:

Teacher: [*Referring to worksheet*] Oh, you've done it. Okay, so what do you notice? They add up to 360. [*Lawrie pulls a face as if to say, "Oh yeah" begrudgingly*)

Teacher: [*Reading from the sheet*] Um, move parts of the pentagon to see if the sum changes. Click, go to the first arrow, not that one . . . [*inaudible*]. Okay, the first one. Okay, click on a point, any point. Okay, what happens to those angles?

Lawrie: They dilate, I dunno, they . . .

Teacher: What about the sum? [*Pointing to the screen*]

Lawrie: It doesn't change.

Teacher: Okay.

Lawrie: Oh, it does.

Teacher: No, it doesn't.

Lawrie: Yes, it does. Look, look it's on 370.

Teacher: Ah, but you've got to keep it, you've got to keep it a pentagon though.

The "struggling" boys who "lacked confidence" were given instruction about the software and the task but were not given demonstrations, explanations, or positive feedback. Rather than defining the term *conjecture*, the teacher questioned the low-achieving students as to whether they had reached that step in the investigation.

During the didactic sessions at the beginning of lessons, boys called out answers or were selected to respond in all but one instance. These interactions enabled boys to receive praise from the teacher in a public forum. On the other hand, girls only received praise in the privacy of individual interactions. The public praise of high-achieving male students promoted a competition between them to complete the task first or to score higher on tests. The teacher said in the interview that low-achieving girls "lacked confidence," had "low esteem,"

and displayed a "bad attitude." It is likely that the nature of the teacher's interactions with these students contributed to their low self-efficacy with respect to
computers in mathematics. The following episode shows that they were left to
struggle by themselves:

Brenda: Sir, I have a slight little problem here. [*Teacher turns to look at her screen*]
You should have just taken my first shot. Look at that.

Teacher: Why?

Brenda: You should have just said that my first shot was good.

Teacher: I can't believe this.

Cherie: I can't do it.

Brenda: Now it's half wacked.

Doreen: It's just the computer. It hates you.

Teacher: Beg your pardon?

Doreen: I just thought—[*cut off*]

Teacher: Come on.

Brenda: We've tried it 3 times.

Cherie: We can be with Doreen now.

Teacher: [*Leans over and operates control keys to clear screen*] Do it again.

Brenda: [*Under her breath*] Get nicked.

Teacher: Properly this time. [*He walks away and goes to other students*]

Some students received very little or no individual attention from the teacher.
These students were often absent or did not have a computer or the software.
However, the teacher made no attempt to integrate them into the class, and they
generally remained off task for the entire lesson. These students included 3 of
the 7 girls in the class and 4 of the 18 boys. All of these students (except 1 of
the boys) performed poorly on the pen and paper test for the geometry topic.

The cognitive nature of the individual interactions with students coincided
with the teacher's belief that it was the higher-achieving mathematics students
who gained the most from using the Geometer's Sketchpad:

Teacher: The one thing that is the big advantage with kids and computers is that they're
just not afraid of them at all . . . and that enables them to take a package like that and
work their way through it. And the more inquisitive ones are going to get more out of
it. But the more inquisitive ones are the better students anyway. . . . Students that struggle
with maths through a lack of confidence, often they don't have the confidence to do the
computer work as well, because they think that the two are related and in some ways
they are, but in many other ways they aren't. (year 9 interview)

The nature of his interactions with the higher-achieving students ensured that
these students would succeed with the computer-based tasks. Furthermore, the

skills and knowledge of the computer experts in the class were not passed on through any public discussion of the outcomes of individual explorations of the software or the mathematical investigations.

The Learning Behaviors of Girls and Boys

As in the year 8 class, the students in this year 9 class worked individually and checked their progress with each other. The nature of interactions between students in the year 9 class appeared to depend on interest, knowledge, and experience with laptop computers, the nature of the task, and personal characteristics such as competitiveness or independence. Gender differences in interactions between students were evident and the opposite of those observed for the year 8 class.

Boys were observed successfully to tutor and demonstrate for each other, and they also provided the only examples of peer collaboration:

Che: I done all that. I done all the way to here.

Lawrie: What do you do here, what did you write?

Che: Um, I wrote, um, I found out that all the angles equal up to 360 degrees.

Lawrie: Not matter what shape as long as its perimeter . . . [*inaudible*]

Che: I found it for all pol polygons or something like that equals up to.

Darren: The hexagon equals up to.

Che: It's not a hexagon. Do control later on. No, no, you don't. You go to calculator. Where's your calculator?

Lawrie: I already calculated it . . . [*inaudible*] [*Points to the result on the screen*]

Che: Yeah, well, there you go. You done it all. Now you just write there [*points to the screen*] that all the angles equal up to 360 degrees. That's your conjuncture. [*Waves his hands as if to say "or whatever it is"*]

While girls did work together and assisted each other by tutoring or demonstrating, they were not always successful and often also sought instruction from the teacher.

As with the year 8 class, there were more off-task use of the computer episodes recorded involving boys than girls. In these off-task interactions boys demonstrated their knowledge of computer systems or the Geometer's Sketchpad software and learned about other features, such as animation effects, and potential uses of such software for engineering or architectural drafting in demonstration files. Higher-achieving boys took control of their own learning when they collaborated to install other software on their laptop computers.

Boys were more likely than girls to express a positive sense of their achievements. Boys used interactions with their peers privately and publicly to report their achievement and success to other students. For example, when constructing particular shapes for the project, Ian reveled in his success: "Measure angle.

Yes, it's 105. That was easy. Beautiful. Absolutely beautiful." They received acknowledgment of their success from other boys. There was no evidence of girls acknowledging or praising the computer work of their friends or female peers. On the contrary, there was evidence of lack of interest, and girls had their work devalued by other girls: "That is so boring" (Doreen commenting on Ellen's drawing). Girls were also more likely to make negative comments and gestures about themselves: "I can't do this. I'm so behind" (Ellen).

Hegemonic masculine behavior was observed in the classroom in the way that boys treated their peers. Boys harassed girls, as in the following exchange:

Ian: Ya think ya good, Ellen, but ya not.

Ellen: I know I'm not good.

Boys were verbally harassed by girls, and lower-achieving boys were verbally and physically harassed by other boys. Particular boys perpetrated the most strident examples, one of whom was the highest-achieving mathematics boy in the class. "Ah, that's because—ah, ya dick" (Ian).

The Views of Girls and Boys

The year 9 students were less positive than the year 8 students about the use of computers in mathematics and boys much more positive than girls. Fourteen out of 18 boys (78%) indicated that computers were a good idea compared to 2 out of 6 girls (33%). Three of the girls in the class responded with "sometimes." The boys' interest in the Geometer's Sketchpad, other software, and computer systems was evident during the computer-based lessons that were observed. They smiled, they giggled, and they laughed and were generally happy when using their laptops in mathematics. There were many more episodes recorded of boys discussing computers in off-task conversation or engaging in other computer activity than for girls.

The boys in year 9 held similar views to those in year 8 since they associated the use of computers in mathematics with pleasure. For example: "I don't mind using Sketchpad because it is an interesting program to use" (year 9 boy). "I think it's good because the computer makes the subject more enjoyable, thus causing a greater will to learn" (year 9 boy). Boys created their own pleasurable activities and were excited by the animation and relevance of the software that they were using: "You can actually create your own things" (Howard). There were, however, exceptions, most notably those boys experiencing technical difficulties with the software or their computer or experiencing difficulty using the tools and menu. Ian, a high-achieving mathematics student, appeared to be at odds with other boys. He did not find the tasks sufficiently challenging and was frustrated with the operation of the software.

Girls, on the other hand, and in contrast to the year 8 girls, did not associate the computer-based mathematics lessons with pleasure. They were more likely to be negative about the task, especially the geometrical investigation, and the software. The girls expressed frustration and even dislike and disdain with the software and at least one of the tasks. The failure of two of the girls to bring their computers to school indicates a less-than-enthusiastic attitude about using them in mathematics.

Familiarity with software was an important factor in the girls' views about using computers in mathematics. Ellen, the high-achieving girl, was more comfortable in lessons when she could independently use the software. She preferred Excel:

Ellen: It's the easiest to use. . . . I'm more familiar with it, it's more commonly used, and if you need help you just go to the help menu and, um, it's specifically designed for maths. . . . Like Microworlds isn't, and if you want help with something about maths it won't tell you. (Ellen, interview)

However, she did not think that using computers was a good idea:

Ellen: Computers help maths with the things like calculations in Excel and Sketchpad, but I don't think that they are vitally important, as these calculations can be done in your head. . . . We depend too much on them giving us the answers. (Ellen, questionnaire).

Neither Ellen nor Brenda thought that the Geometer's Sketchpad was relevant to mathematics or real-world applications:

Brenda: I just don't see how someone is gonna ask you how to use Sketchpad. I can in Excel. (Brenda, interview)

The girls wrote comments about the effects on learning such as Ellen's above: "I also feel that by using the laptop it might put us behind" (year 9 girl). Or more negatively, "I don't learn anything. Other kids might, but I don't. . . . All we learn is how to use the program" (year 9 girl). Brenda believed effective instruction about the software was critical for girls' continued participation in computer-based mathematics:

Brenda: If [*girls*] knew how to use the computer and they actually thought that the computer was going to help them, yeah. But if they had no idea about computers it could be more of a hassle than actually helping them. (Brenda, interview)

In contrast to the year 8 boys, the year 9 boys who were interviewed were more circumspect in their responses to questions that may have revealed gender-stereotyped views about computing. The girls who were interviewed supported a view of computing as a male domain: "I don't think girls are genuinely interested in computers" (Ellen, interview). Brenda believed that there were not more girls in the year 9 laptop class because of the domination of the boys:

Brenda: The boys are overpowering. . . . They are very loud and a lot of the girls just, um, 'cos it's scarey to begin with, but when there's so many more boys than the girls, then that's even more nervous and that's why they back off. Even now in the laptop class the girls seem to back off a bit more because you just don't know what they're gonna do." (Brenda, interview)

She believed, therefore, that hegemonic masculine behavior dissuaded and perhaps even threatened girls, so that girls did not want to participate in computer-based learning programs, especially where they thought they may be in the minority and overpowered by boys.

The teacher supported the use of computers in mathematics as a tool and an aid to learning mathematics:

Teacher: [*The Geometer's Sketchpad*] gave students the opportunity to draw some of those shapes and actually learn those properties for themselves. But I find the computer is just a tool really, a fantastic tool. (year 9 interview)

Such a perspective was more likely to accord with girls' views about the use of computers in mathematics, but this was not realized in the classroom during the period of observation. The girls did not generally view the tasks and the Geometer's Sketchpad as aiding their learning of mathematics. However, the teacher also used computers in mathematics to provide a break and alleviate boredom:

Teacher: [*They are learning*] nothing in particular, just more a confidence boost. I thought that getting them to actually construct things might give them better meaning for what they were covering through the textbook. Because it can be pretty boring sometimes. (year 9 interview)

This purpose for the use of computers in mathematics, as a source of pleasure, therefore matched the views and behaviors of boys in the class.

Summary

This classroom also advantaged the high-achieving students, especially the boys. The analysis of the nature of the social interactions with the teacher did reveal differences between particular groups of girls and boys. The teacher contributed directly and indirectly to the exclusion of some students. He monitored and provided intensive instruction or tutoring for the higher-achieving students. He even did the work for the highest-achieving girl in the class. While the teacher did provide instruction to lower-achieving boys, he failed to answer all their questions, especially those concerning mathematical concepts. He belittled the attempts of two girls. As a result, these two girls believed they were incapable of completing the task.

The boys accepted and adopted the computers in this learning environment. As for the year 8 boys, the computers were a source of pleasure and relevance in the mathematics classroom. For the boys the use of computers brought opportunities to be creative and to learn more about the software. They cooperated and collaborated more often than the girls as they shared their knowledge of the software, computers, and the mathematics imbedded in the tasks. The girls viewed the use of computers in mathematics less favorably than boys, and some girls, including the highest-achieving student, rejected the computers. The girls wanted the computer to assist their learning and success in mathematics, but this did not happen for them.

The boys competed over achievement in tests, completion of tasks, and possession of software products. They also dominated the class. There were more of them, they were *rowdy*, and they *overpowered* the girls. Girls were often not visible in the class. They were seated in the periphery of the room, normally quiet and private in their interactions. They were fewer in number. Power was also constituted through exhibitions of hegemonic masculinity in the individual interactions. These elements of the sociocultural context of the classroom further contributed to a masculinized domain.

DISCUSSION

In both these computer-based mathematics classrooms the boys and the girls accepted the use of computers. The analysis of social interactions and views revealed that the high-achieving students, especially boys, were advantaged in these classrooms. Some learning behaviors and views were observed more often for boys or girls, indicating that the culture in the classrooms could be gendered. These findings are supported by the quantitative analysis of the questionnaire data presented elsewhere (Vale 2001).

Masculinized Domains

These two computer-based mathematics learning environments shared similar cultural traits with other mathematics or computing classrooms described as the domain of the boys (Barnes 2000; Boaler 1997; Forgasz and Leder 1996; Schofield 1995). For the most part, students worked individually and used each other to check their work. While boys were comfortable in the individualized and competitive environment with the increased opportunities to hone their skills with computers, the girls sought to use the computers to aid learning and enhance success in mathematics.

Contrary to other research findings (Barnes 2000; Lee 1993; Sutherland and Hoyles 1988), the boys shared their knowledge of software and computers, as they were also observed to tutor, demonstrate, and in a few cases, collaborate on mathematics tasks or computer problems, including those arising in off-task activity. It could be argued that such behavior enhanced the individual and collective knowledge of boys about the software, computers, and related mathematics.

Negative socioemotional interactions showed that some students dominated others, and individuals and groups of students felt *overpowered*. Both girls and boys provided examples of negative socioemotional interactions. Those involving boys provided examples of hegemonic masculinity (Barnes 2000). This occurred when boys competed for attention in the public fora of the classrooms, denigrated girls' and boys' mathematics and computer achievements, took over the students' computers to solve the problem or do it for them, and harassed students verbally and physically.

Contributing Factors

The learning behaviors and views of girls and boys were associated with the teachers' methods and implementation of learning tasks, teachers' attitudes, the nature of the technology, and in one classroom, the gender imbalance in participation. In this final section, I discuss these factors and suggest some implications for computer-based mathematics.

Teachers' Methods and Attitudes. Fennema (1995) argued that gender differences in mathematics varied according to the teacher and that teachers structured their classrooms to favor males and their learning. In these two classrooms the teachers used the computers as a tool and fitted it in with existing curriculum. The teachers' directed and individualized learning approach provided environments where speed and accuracy were values in these classrooms and competition could flourish.

Some of the tasks used by the teachers in the lessons that were observed had the potential to encourage collaborative learning with technology (Geiger and Goos 1996; Goos, Galbraith, and Renshaw 1996). Such an objective would be in accord with the views expressed by girls for the computers to aid their learning and success with mathematics and enable the lower-achieving students to engage in higher-order interactions with their peers. However, the teachers and students interpreted them as individual learning tasks that related to, or replaced, mathematics textbook learning and provided opportunities to learn and practice skills with software and computers. These findings indicate that in order to develop collaboration teachers might need to develop particular strategies and use the technology so that the students can display, discuss, and share their computer-based mathematics work and understandings.

The teachers believed the boys in the classroom to be the computer experts and called on their expertise. The expertise of girls was denied credibility and visibility in the public forum of these classrooms. The computer play of boys displayed through their off-task activity in these two case studies and the preference of girls to seek information about the software from the teacher rather than their peers may have contributed to the teachers' views. The teachers described the boys in terms of their intelligence, perceived ability, and speed, whereas girls were described in terms of their approach or attitude to the tasks and the standard of their work. These findings are similar to those of previous researchers (Jungwirth 1991; Walden and Walkerdine 1985; Walkerdine 1990). If mathematics teachers believe boys "know" about computers and girls "learn" computers, then teachers may have different expectations of boys and girls in computer-based mathematics classrooms (Walkerdine 1990). Furthermore, some girls may be excluded from engaging with the mathematics and some boys may be excluded from developing computer skills (Jungwirth 1991). Teachers therefore need to be aware of the learning behaviors that they value and be more explicit about the computer skills and mathematical understandings to be learned and demonstrated in a computer-based mathematics learning context. Teachers also should be aware of the negative effects of hegemonic masculinity on girls and low-achieving boys and employ specific and deliberate strategies to promote social justice in their classrooms.

The Computers. Did the computers make a difference to gender equity and social justice in these two classrooms? In the two case studies presented the social interactions and views of computer-based mathematics classrooms were related as much to the participants' views of, and behaviors with, computers as mathematics (Galbraith, Haines, and Pemberton 1999). The "control" that students had over the major resource for the computer-based lessons, especially in the case of laptop computers, resulted in gendered patterns of off-task activity. The girls accepted computers in mathematics, while the boys were more likely to create learning opportunities for themselves.

In the two case studies the teachers and the boys held similar views about the role of computers in mathematics. The teachers viewed the computer as a tool in mathematics. One teacher believed that using computers provided an opportunity for students to enjoy mathematics. In so doing, the teachers legitimized the views of boys that computers were a source of pleasure and relevance. Other researchers have found that the positive effects of enjoyment diminished over time and that these positive effects had more to do with novelty than engagement (Ainley et al. 2000; Dix 1999). In this study, it is not clear how an objective of enjoyment in mathematics may actually improve the mathematical outcomes of low-achieving boys and girls, and enjoyment itself appeared to be gendered. One might argue that there appeared to be very little learning of mathematics in these two classrooms.

In the middle years of schooling the use of computers in mathematics is problematic. Are the computers to be used for the learning of mathematics, or do computer-based learning environments provide opportunities for integrating learning across disciplines? These two case studies illustrate the problems and dilemmas of experienced mathematics teachers when adapting their mathematics teaching to computer-based learning environments. The results of this study show that, in promoting a more inclusive learning environment, teachers need to be aware of the views and learning goals and needs of girls and boys. A more student-centered approach, where students are encouraged to generate their own questions and projects, draw on their knowledge of software and mathematics, and work in groups, is more likely to suit the goals of girls and boys (Boaler 1997; Goos et al. 1996).

Gender Imbalance in Enrollment. In one of the case studies presented, there were many more boys in the class. Hence the dominant behavior of the boys determined the dominant behavior of the class. Even though these results may only apply to classrooms with similar participation ratios, they ought not to be dismissed. This was a real, not untypical, class, with real students. The experiences of the students, in such classes, are ones that will shape their future participation, attitudes, and achievement in mathematics. Furthermore, gender differences persist in specialized senior secondary and tertiary mathematics where technology is more widely used. High-achieving girls may be prepared to be "untypical" or persist as "outsiders within" these computer-based mathematics classrooms. However, other girls are likely to "back off" from such masculinized learning environments.

The results of this study reiterate the need for schools aiming for social justice to structure coeducational classrooms for gender balance and to work with parents to realize this objective. For example, a recent study (Ainley et al. 2000) showed parents more positive about their sons' involvement in a secondary school laptop program.

CONCLUSION

Even though there were differences in the culture of these two computer-based mathematics classrooms, the boys in both classrooms were advantaged in these learning environments. The boys were more likely than girls to take control of their learning, share their knowledge of computers, and be perceived as computer experts. Girls viewed computer-based mathematics lessons less favorably than did boys. The expertise of high-achieving girls when using computers in mathematics was denied visibility; they were "outsiders within." Particular high-achieving girls rejected the computers, and other girls "backed off."

Salomon and Perkins (1996) argued that computers in themselves did little to aid learning, and Greenhill, Fletcher, and von Hellens (1999) argued that the use of computers in educational activity may exacerbate cultural inequalities. Hoyles (1998, p. 40) acknowledged that "there is a real danger that 'innovators' focus on the potential of technology for the brightest and ignore the others." The findings from these two case studies support these concerns. Unless the teacher adopts deliberate strategies in computer-based mathematics learning environments to enhance mathematics learning and gender equity, the classroom tends to become a masculinized domain that threatens the principle of achieving social justice.

ACKNOWLEDGMENTS

I would like to thank Gilah Leder for her supervision of this research study and Derek Colquhoun for his helpful advice on an earlier version of this chapter.

REFERENCES

Ainley, M., Bourke, V., Chatfield, R., Hillman, K., and Watkins, I. (2000). *Computers, Laptops and Tools*. ACER Research Monograph No. 56. Melbourne: Australian Council for Educational Research.

Australian Education Council. (1990). *A National Statement on Mathematics for Australian Schools*. Melbourne: Curriculum Corporation.

Barnes, M. (1995). Development and Evaluation of a Gender Inclusive Calculus. In B. Grevholm and G. Hanna (Eds.), *Gender and Mathematics Education, an ICMI Study in Stiftsgarden, Akersberg, Hoor, Sweden, 1993* (pp. 1–13). Lund: Lund University Press.

Barnes, M. (2000). Effects of Dominant and Subordinate Masculinities on Interactions in a Collaborative Learning Classroom. In J. Boaler (Ed.), *Multiple Perspectives on Mathematics Teaching and Learning* (pp. 145–169). London: Ablex Publishing.

Bauersfeld, H. (1995). The Structuring of the Structures: Development and Function of Mathematizing as a Social Practice. In L.P. Steffe and J. Gale (Eds.), *Constructivism in Education* (pp. 137–158). Hillsdale, NJ: Lawrence Erlbaum.

Boaler, J. (1997). Reclaiming School Mathematics: The Girls Fight Back. *Gender and Education*, 9(3), 285–306.

Boers, M., and Jones, P. (1993). Exam Performance and the Graphics Calculator in Calculus. In B. Atweh, C. Kanes, M. Carss, and G. Booker (Eds.), *Contexts in Mathematics Education. Proceedings of the Sixteenth Annual Conference of the Mathematics Education Research Group of Australasia, July 9–13, 1993, Brisbane* (pp. 123–128). Brisbane: Mathematics Education Research Group of Australasia.

Bogdan, R., and Biklen, S. (1992). *Qualitative Research for Education: An Introduction to Theory and Methods*. Boston: Allyn and Bacon.

Burton, L. (1995). Moving Towards a Feminist Epistemology of Mathematics. In P. Rogers and G. Kaiser (Eds.), *Equity in Mathematics Education: Influences of Feminism and Culture* (pp. 209–226). London: Falmer Press.

Burton, L., and Jaworski, B. (1995). Introduction. In L. Burton and B. Jaworski (Eds.), *Technology in Mathematics Teaching: A Bridge between Teaching and Learning* (pp. 1–10). Lund: Chartwell-Bratt Ltd.

Bush, C.G. (1983). Women and the Assessment of Technology: To Think, to Be, to Unthink, to Free. In J. Rothschild (Ed.), *Machina Ex Dea: Feminist Perspectives on Technology* (pp. 151–170). New York: Pergamon Press.

Clarke, V., and Chambers, S. (1989). Gender-Based Factors in Computing Enrollments and Achievement: Evidence from a Study of Tertiary Students. *Journal of Educational Computing Research*, 5(4), 409–429.

Cobbin, D. (1995). *Women's Participation in Nontraditional Fields of Study at the Un-*

dergraduate Level of Higher Education 1989–1993. Canberra: Commonwealth of Australia.

Crawford, K. (1996). Vygotskian Approaches in Human Development in the Information Era. *Educational Studies in Mathematics*, 31, 43–62.

Day, M. (1996). The Experiences of Eight Women Mathematicians. In M. Cresswell (Ed.), *Science—Women and Our Future: Proceedings of the 29–31 May Conference of the New Zealand Association for Women in the Sciences* (pp. 48–50). Wellington: New Zealand Association for Women in the Sciences.

Dix, K. (1999). Enhanced Mathematics Learning: Does Technology Make a Difference? In J. Truran and K. Truran (Eds.), *Making the Difference: Proceedings of the Twenty-second Annual Conference of the Mathematics Education Research Group of Australasia Incorporated, Held at Adelaide, South Australia, 4–7 July, 1999* (pp. 192–199). Adelaide: Mathematics Education Research Group of Australasia.

Dunham, P. (1991). Mathematical Confidence and Performance in Technology Enhanced Precalculus: Gender Related Differences. *Dissertation Abstracts International*, 51, 3353A.

Fennema, E. (1995). Mathematics, Gender and Research. In B. Grevholm and G. Hanna (Eds.), *Gender and Mathematics Education, an ICMI Study in Stiftsgarden, Akersberg, Hoor, Sweden, 1993* (pp. 21–38). Lund: Lund University Press.

Forgasz, H., and Leder, G.C. (1996). Mathematics Classroom, Gender and Affect. *Mathematics Education Research Journal*, 8(2), 153–173.

Forgasz, H., Leder, G.C., and Vale, C. (2000). Gender and Mathematics: Changing Perspectives. In K. Owens and J. Mousley (Eds.), *Mathematics Education Research in Australasia: 1996–1999* (pp. 305–340). Turramurra, New South Wales: Mathematics Education Research Group of Australasia.

Galbraith, P., Haines, C., and Pemberton, M. (1999). A Tale of Two Cities: When Mathematics, Computers and Students Meet. In J. Truran and K. Truran (Eds.), *Making the Difference: Proceedings of the Twenty-second Annual Conference of the Mathematics Education Research Group of Australasia Incorporated, Held at Adelaide, South Australia, 4–7 July, 1999* (pp. 215–222). Adelaide: Mathematics Education Research Group of Australasia.

Geiger, V., and Goos, M. (1996). Number Plugging or Problem Solving? Using Technology to Support Collaborative Learning. In Philip Clarkson (Ed.), *Technology in Mathematics Education: Proceedings of the 19th Annual Conference of the Mathematics Education Research Group of Australasia, June 30–July 3, 1996 at the University of Melbourne* (pp. 229–236). Melbourne: Mathematics Education Research Group of Australasia.

Gewirtz, S. (1998). Conceptualising Social Justice in Education: Mapping the Territory. *Journal of Educational Policy*, 13(4), 469–484.

Goos, M., Galbraith, P., and Renshaw, P. (1996). When Does Student Talk Become Collaborative Mathematical Discussion? In Philip Clarkson (Ed.), *Technology in Mathematics Education: Proceedings of the 19th Annual Conference of the Mathematics Education Research Group of Australasia, June 30–July 3, 1996 at the University of Melbourne* (pp. 237–244). Melbourne: Mathematics Education Research Group of Australasia.

Greenhill, A., Fletcher, G., and von Hellens, L. (1999). Cultural Differences and Information Technology Skills. In D. Meredyth, N. Russell, L. Blackwood, J. Thomas, and P. Wise (Eds.), *Real Time Computers, Change and Schooling: National Sam-*

ple Study of the Information Technology Skills of Australian School Students (pp. 287–292). Canberra: Department of Education, Training and Youth Affairs, Commonwealth of Australia.

Hoyles, C. (1998). Panel Discussion: Looking Through the Technology. In *Pre-proceedings, ICMI Study Conference on the Teaching and Learning of Mathematics at University Level Held in Singapore, 8–12 December, 1998* (pp. 39–40). Singapore: National Institute of Education, Singapore Association of Mathematics Educators, Singapore Mathematical Society.

Jungwirth, H. (1991). Interaction and Gender—Findings of a Microethnographical Approach to Classroom Discourse. *Educational Studies in Mathematics*, 22, 263–284.

Lee, M. (1993). Gender, Group Composition, and Peer Interaction in Computer-Based Cooperative Learning. *Journal of Educational Computing Research*, 9(4), 549–577.

Miles, M., and Huberman, A. (1994). *Qualitative Data Analysis: An Expanded Sourcebook* (2nd ed.). Thousand Oaks, CA: Sage Publications.

Rasmussen, D., Rasmussen, S., and Bennett, D. (Eds.). (1995). *Teaching Geometry with The Geometer's Sketchpad: Teaching Notes and Sample Activities*. Berkeley, CA: Key Curriculum Press.

Ruthven, K. (1995). Pressing On. In L. Burton and B. Jaworski (Eds.), *Technology in Mathematics Teaching—A Bridge between Teaching and Learning* (pp. 231–256). Lund: Chartwell-Bratt.

Salomon, G., and Perkins, D. (1996). Learning in Wonderland: What Do Computers Really Offer Education? In Stephen T. Kerr (Ed.), *Technology and the Future of Schooling: Ninety-fifth Yearbook of the National Society for the Study of Education, Part II* (pp. 111–129). Chicago: University of Chicago Press.

Schofield, J.W. (1995). *Computers and Classroom Culture*. New York: Cambridge University Press.

Sutherland, R., and Hoyles, C. (1988). Gender Perspectives on Logo Programming in the Mathematics Classroom. In C. Hoyles (Ed.), *Girls and Computers: General Issues and Case Studies of Logo in the Mathematics Classroom. Bedford Way Papers 34* (pp. 40–63). London: University of London.

Teese, R. (2000). *Academic Success and Social Power: Examinations and Inequality.* Carlton South: Melbourne University Press.

Vale, C. (2001). *Gender and Computer-Based Mathematics in Selected Secondary Classrooms*. Ph.D. thesis, La Trobe University.

Victorian Board of Studies. (1995). *Mathematics: Curriculum and Standards Framework.* Carlton: Author.

Walden, R., and Walkerdine, V. (1985). *Girls and Mathematics: From Primary to Secondary Schooling. Bedford Way Papers 24*. London: Heinemann.

Walkerdine, V. (1990). *Schoolgirl Fictions*. London: Verso.

Index

About the Contributors

FERNANDO ANDRADE has a bachelor's degree in psychology from the Universidad Católica in Lima, Peru. For four years he has been an assistant researcher at GRADE (Grupode Análisispara el Desarrollo), a Peruvian nongovernmental organization dedicated to doing applied research in social sciences (http://www.grade.org.pe/). Most of the studies in which he has been involved have dealt with student achievement in diverse settings. He has also been a teacher assistant in research methods courses at the Universidad Católica in Lima. He is currently a student in the Ph.D. program in Educational Foundations and Policy Studies at the University of Michigan.

CHRISTINE BREW is a lecturer in primary mathematics and science education at La Trobe University, Bendigo campus, Australia. She regularly presents at national mathematics education research events in Australia and has been a contributor at various international fora including the Psychology of Mathematics Education (PME) and the International Congress of Mathematics Education (ICME), Spain (1996); Adults Learning Mathematics, Boston (2000); Mathematics at Home—Setting a Research Agenda, Washington, DC (2001); and Math and Parent Partnership with the Southwest (MAPPS), University of Arizona, Tuscon (2002). In 2002 she pursued a further research agenda into school improvement initiatives under the auspices of the National Center for School Improvement at Southwest Texas State University.

LEONE BURTON is the editor for the series International Perspectives on Mathematics Education, in which this volume is placed, as well as editor of the present volume. Leone is professor emerita at the University of Birmingham,

United Kingdom, and visiting professor at King's College, London, in mathematics education. Leone's career in mathematics education has spanned teaching and researching in schools and universities, and she has an extensive list of publications including authored books and edited collections, as well as articles and chapters, particularly around enquiry-based learning and social justice. Her most recent book, an edited collection titled *Learning Mathematics: From Hierarchies to Networks*, was published in 1999, and her most recent research has been on the epistemologies of research mathematicians. She is currently working on a book that relates her findings to mathematical pedagogy.

PANJI CATHERINE CHAMDIMBA is a lecturer in mathematics education at Chancellor College, University of Malawi. She has an M.A. (mathematics education) from King's College, University of London, and a Ph.D. in mathematics education from the University of Waikato, New Zealand. The research reported in this chapter was part of her Ph.D. work. Her research interest is in gender and mathematics.

SANTIAGO CUETO has a professional license degree in educational psychology from the Universidad Católica del Perú and a doctorate in educational psychology from Indiana University. He is currently research director at GRADE (Grupo de Análisis para el Desarrollo), a Peruvian nongovernmental organization dedicated to doing applied research in the social sciences, and a part-time professor at the Universidad Católica School of Psychology in Lima, where he teaches courses on research methods and program evaluation. His two main fields of interest are development of national systems for evaluation of teachers and students and factors associated with student achievement in elementary and basic education, especially in rural contexts.

RITA BORROMEO FERRI has a bachelor's degree as a teacher of mathematics, humanities, and German for primary education. She is currently working on her Ph.D. as a researcher at the University of Hamburg, Germany, with Gabriele Kaiser.

HELEN J. FORGASZ is a senior lecturer in mathematics education at Monash University, Australia, Clayton campus. She teaches in the secondary teacher training programs and in postgraduate programs. Her research interests include gender issues, the affective domain, and computers for the learning of mathematics. One of Helen's current research studies involves an examination of equity issues associated with the use of computers in secondary mathematics classrooms. Helen has published widely on a range of mathematics education issues. She recently coedited a book titled *Sociocultural Research on Mathematics Education: An International Perspective* (2001). Helen is the vice president (Research) of the Mathematics Education Research Group of Australasia.

LAURIE E. HART is a professor in the Department of Elementary Education at the University of Georgia. She currently serves as department head and teaches courses about research on teaching and teacher education. Her research focuses on issues of equity and justice in mathematics education and on the preparation of middle school teachers. Her most recent work has examined diverse students' motivation and interest in mathematics and pedagogy for diverse students in mathematics.

HELGA JUNGWIRTH is an Austrian freelance mathematics educator who has worked and published in particular on gender, classroom interaction, adults and mathematics, and methodological questions in mathematical education. She is a staff member of the current project "Innovations in Mathematics, Science and Technology Teaching" of the Austrian Ministry of Education.

GABRIELE KAISER holds a master's degree as a teacher of mathematics and humanities. She completed her doctorate in mathematics education and her habilitation in pedagogy. She is currently a professor in mathematics education at the University of Hamburg, Germany, where her areas of research include modeling and real-world examples, international comparisons, gender, and culture in mathematics education.

GILAH C. LEDER is director of the recently established Institute for Advanced Study at La Trobe University, Australia, Bundoora campus, and a professor in the Institute for Education at the same institution. Her teaching and research interests embrace gender issues, the interaction between teaching, learning, and assessment of mathematics, affect, and exceptionality. She has published widely in each of these areas. Gilah serves on various editorial boards and educational and scientific committees and is past president of the Mathematics Research Group of Australasia and of the International Group for the Psychology of Mathematics Education.

HEATHER MENDICK is a doctoral student at Goldsmiths College, University of London, conducting research in the area of gender, mathematics, and subject choice. Before going back to university, she taught mathematics for seven years, something that she continues to enjoy doing part-time.

PETER PETOCZ is a senior lecturer in statistics at the University of Technology, Sydney, Australia. A refugee from the Hungarian uprising in 1956, Peter obtained a doctorate from the University of New South Wales in stochastic processes. His current work is mainly in the area of applied statistics and mathematics education. Peter has produced several video packages on topics in mathematics and statistics, a CD-ROM on learning ensemble music, and several textbooks. As an applied statistician he works in many areas including health, education, science, and the environment.

HILARY POVEY is a reader based in the Mathematics Education Centre at Sheffield Hallam University, United Kingdom, where she teaches mathematics to intending secondary mathematics teachers and conducts and publishes mathematics education research. She also conducts and publishes research in the general area of education and social inclusion. She is committed in her teaching and in her research to the promotion of social justice.

WALTER G. SECADA is professor of curriculum and instruction at the University of Wisconsin, Madison, where he also directs a Center for Learning and Teaching, focused on Diversity in Mathematics Education (DiME/CLT). Prior to directing the DiME/CLT, he ran a center that helped schools improve the instruction that they provide to "at risk" children; he was associate director of two research centers focused on mathematics education and was a principal investigator in another center on organization and restructuring of schools. Walter has published extensively in many areas of education including Hispanic dropouts. In addition to his collaboration with colleagues from his native Peru on the World Bank–funded study (see Chapter 5), Walter has published widely and presented papers internationally. Among his research interests are school reform, mathematics education reform, equity issues in (mathematics) education, the education of language minority students in the United States, the nature of intellectual engagement by school-age students, and how children negotiate the ages of 6 through 12.

JAN THOMAS is a senior lecturer in mathematics education at Victoria University, Melbourne, Australia. Her research interests include science and technology policy issues, especially as they relate to mathematics and mathematics education; young people's participation in mathematics and science; and linguistic and cultural factors affecting the mathematics learning of students from non-English-speaking backgrounds. In a recent report, Jan documented the brain drain of mathematical scientists from Australia and issues concerned with the supply of appropriately qualified mathematics and science teachers. Jan is vice president of the Federation of Australian Scientific and Technological Societies, part-time executive officer for the Australian Mathematical Society, and a member of the National Committee for Mathematics.

COLLEEN M. VALE is a senior lecturer in mathematics education at Victoria University, Melbourne, Australia. She taught mathematics in secondary schools for a number of years and began researching gender equity as a teacher researcher. She was a cowriter of the new Mathematics Study and writer of the Victorian Certificate of Education that was implemented into secondary schools in 1991 in Victoria before commencing lecturing at Victoria University. In addition to her research activity in gender equity and computer-based mathematics, she is currently working on projects about mathematics in the middle years, primary mathematics classroom discourse, and the professional development of primary and secondary teachers of mathematics.

DUBRAVKA VISKIC teaches mathematics to international students at New South Global, the University of New South Wales, Australia. Having come to Australia from Croatia, she is a particularly successful teacher with students whose first language is not English and with adults returning to mathematics. For many years she has been running an evening preparatory course in mathematics for students who want to return to mathematics and university study and was one of the authors of the textbook for this course. She has also written and published mathematics videos and teaching materials. Involved in mathematics education research, she is a regular presenter at conferences in the area.

DYLAN WILIAM is professor of educational assessment and assistant principal of King's College, London. A former secondary school mathematics teacher, he worked on a number of curriculum development projects including Graded Assessment in Mathematics (GAIM) and on the development of National Curriculum assessment. His main research interests are educational assessment and evaluation (particularly the role of formative assessment) and mathematics education, where his main concern is with issues of social justice, particularly in regard to gender and ability grouping.

LEIGH WOOD is the Director of the Mathematics Study Centre and lectures in mathematics at the University of Technology, Sydney, Australia. Her research interests include the evaluation of curriculum and assessment, particularly for innovative teaching methods using language. Her current work is on the conceptions of mathematics and the relationship between work and learning. She has published two textbooks, 10 mathematics videos, and many articles. She is committed to creating a supportive and equitable learning environment for her students, who come from a wide variety of backgrounds.

ROBYN ZEVENBERGEN is a senior lecturer at Griffith University, Gold Coast campas, Australia. Her work is centered on notions of equity and social justice. She is currently involved in a number of projects including examining classroom practice in terms of the barriers that it creates for learning, particularly in relation to students from socially and culturally diverse backgrounds. She is also part of a large project examining the transition from school to work in relation to the new forms of numeracy needed for the contemporary economy. She has worked across a range of sectors of schooling, with an emphasis on the primary years.